Europeanisation and Renationalisation

Ulrike Liebert
Anne Jenichen (eds.)

Europeanisation and Renationalisation

Learning from Crises for Innovation and Development

Verlag Barbara Budrich
Opladen • Berlin • Toronto 2019

A CIP catalogue record for this book is available from
Die Deutsche Bibliothek (The German Library)

ISBN 978-3-8474-2097-2
eISBN 978-3-8474-1086-7

Die Deutsche Bibliothek – CIP-Einheitsaufnahme
Ein Titeldatensatz für die Publikation ist bei der Deutschen Bibliothek erhältlich.

Verlag Barbara Budrich GmbH
Stauffenbergstr. 7. D-51379 Leverkusen Opladen, Germany

86 Delma Drive. Toronto, ON M8W 4P6 Canada
www.barbara-budrich.net

Jacket illustration by Bettina Lehfeldt, Kleinmachnow –
www.lehfeldtgraphic.de
Picture credits: www.istockphoto.com
Typesetting by Anja Borkam, Jena – kontakt@lektorat-borkam.de
Printed in Europe on acid-free paper by paper&tinta, Warsaw

Table of Contents

Anne Jenichen and Ulrike Liebert
1. The double-edged nature of crises – sources of decline; resources for development 9

I. Europeanisation versus Neo-Nationalism in Times of Crisis

Joachim Schild
2. France's European politics in the face of the polycrisis 21

Ben Crum
3. Living with anti-pluralist populism in Europe: Insights from the Dutch 2017 elections 37

Vratislav Havlík
4. Europeanisation or renationalisation? The Czech Republic facing the euro-, economic and refugee crises 49

Dimitri A. Sotiropoulos
5. In the wake of the economic crisis: the empowerment of (un-)civil society in Greece 65

Stefan Wallaschek
6. The politics of solidarity in Europe's migration crisis: Media discourses in Germany and Ireland 81

Sezin Dereci
7. Civil society as an agent of Europeanisation in EU accession countries: Comparing Turkey and Serbia 95

II. Reexamining the Crisis of European Integration

Anne Jenichen
8. The British EU referendum and ethnic minorities: Lessons for European integration 113

Natascha Zaun
9. EU decision-making in asylum policy: Lessons from the 'refugee crisis' 127

Florian Wittmann
10. State capacity in crisis: EU conditionality and administrative reforms in the post-communist new member states 143

Petra Guasti and David Siroki
11. European Human Rights between transnational order and domestic politics 155

Andreas Heinrich and Heiko Pleines
12. Towards a common European energy policy? Energy security debates in Poland and Germany; the case of the Nord Stream pipeline 169

Gabriele Abels
13. Theorising European integration and Europeanisation through a gendered lens 183

III. European Innovation and Development

Dennis Zagermann
14. The European Central Bank in the euro crisis: The case of the OMT program 199

Tilmann Morata Liebert
15. Global climate change governance from Paris to Montreal: Enabling factors for ambitious EU climate action 215

Anders Hentschel
16. The European governance of economic and monetary crises – lessons for democratic legitimacy 231

Gesche Lange and Ulrike Liebert
17. The European Parliament in hard times: potentials and constraints of governing the Euro crisis 243

Laura Landorff
18. Intergroups as alternative venues to the European Parliament for civil society 265

Adriana Ciancio
19. What democracy for the European Political Union? Lessons for a European party system 281

Conclusion

Ulrike Liebert
20. Europe's unfinished journey: diverging narratives, innovative concepts and political development 297

Authors' notes 317

Index 321

1 The double-edged nature of crises – sources of decline; resources for development

Anne Jenichen and Ulrike Liebert

Introduction

This book contributes to the 'debate on the future of Europe' that the European Commission launched in 2017 and that supposedly will not end when the European elections in 2019 are over. The aim of this debate is to respond to the shocks of 2016 – a year of horrors for the European project, given the unexpected triumph of anti-European forces, first witnessed in the Brexit referendum in the UK in June and then in the US presidential elections in November. The present contributions are written in the vein of hope that it actually might be possible to learn from external and internal shocks and policy failures – and that such lessons will be useful for confronting the future. They are the outcome of individual efforts and collective discussions focusing on the years 2016 and 2017 on the part of European researchers, politicians and policy makers connected to the Jean Monnet Centre for European Studies at the University of Bremen. Their aim is to take stock of responses to the multiple crises the European Union has been struggling with over the past decade. The shared interest is to provide answers to a set of common questions: How can we gain a more nuanced understanding of the different facets of such 'crises', of their double-edged nature as sources of decline and destruction, but also as resources for innovation and development? In this vein, we aim at bringing together analyses of the successes and failures in managing the various crises with innovative ideas and propositions regarding the present and future development of the Union. Each of the chapters draws on state-of-the-art theory, methods and evidence. However, in the present context, the authors are more interested in enhancing the general public understanding and assessment of the EU's responses to the crises, rather than contributing more narrowly to social scientific research.

In the second decade of the 21st century, the post-war European project provides proof of a complex crisis that has fulled pessimistic as well as optimistic narratives concerning the future of the European Union. Following the negative story-lines in response to the crisis, the deepening of European integration has allegedly stalled, and disintegration is looming large. Neo-nationalism has become salient on the European political agenda, with the British decision to leave the EU as its ultimate culmination to date. Member states are more reluctant to 'pool' their sovereignty in sensitive domains of national identity that include control over money, borders, and citizenship identity. National governments are less willing to delegate competences to supranational entities, let alone financial and fiscal powers. By contrast, the more optimistic accounts draw on past experiences of EU crises which have frequently advanced Europeanisation, meaning the progressive harmonisation of shared legal norms and common public policies across the member states. In the present constellation, the Europeanisation agenda suggests that the EU is not in decline but is reinventing itself as a unique engine of change, driving cooperation, coordination and convergence of member states, the structural and cultural diversity of which may have become more pronounced as a result of the crises. In the perspective of Europeanisation, neo-nationalism and the agenda of re-nationalisation cannot provide solutions to the crises. Rather, nationalistic forces appear as a crucial *part* of the problem, as they aggravate the power asymmetries between nationally fragmented democratic governments vis-à-vis the transnational drivers of economic, social and cultural globalisation.

The EU's recent crises and geopolitical conflicts are cases in point concerning the dramatic challenges that global dynamics have posed to European policy makers. These started with the outbreak of the sovereign debt crisis in the euro area at the end of 2009, continued with conflicts with Russia over energy security in 2009 and annexation of the Crimea in 2014, the so-called 'refugee crisis' in 2015 and the Brexit referendum in 2016, followed by a surge of anti-EU populist forces elsewhere, within as well as outside the EU, including Austria, the Netherlands, France, and most recently the U.S. under the Trump presidency. These multiple predicaments have jeopardised the EU's roadmap for an 'ever deeper Union', undermined its commitments to open societies, and weakened solidarity among member states as well as citizens. The EU's era of peoples' permissive consensus in support of European policy makers has given way to falling levels of trust and invigorated nationalist populist Euro-scepticism, hampering common solutions to joint problems, whether in the area of immigration, of economic stagnation, security or global warming. Nevertheless, although rare, crises are not anomalies but normal occurrences in any complex and dynamic system such as the EU.

This introduction starts with clarifying the notion of 'crisis' that informs the present book. It then gives an overview of the twenty chapters contained in the three sections, dealing firstly with the domestic dynamics of Europeanisation versus neo-nationalism, turning secondly to re-examining the EU's crises and, finally, critically reflecting on a selection of cases where European innovation and development have occurred.

Towards a nuanced understanding of 'crisis' in the European context

Drawing on multi-disciplinary approaches to crisis management, crises are generally considered to be normal events in the development of organisations. Irrespective of their size or age, organisations regularly have to adapt to a changing environment. Moreover, they have to correct internal anomalies. Both are challenges to the status quo, which can manifest themselves in either abrupt or cumulative crises (Hwang and Lichtenthal 2000; Roux-Dufort 2009). An organisational crisis is conceived here as 'a low-probability, high-impact event that threatens the viability of the organization [which] is characterized by ambiguity of cause, effect, and means of resolution, as well as by a belief that decisions must be made swiftly' (Pearson and Clair 1998: 60). Consequently, crises should not be interpreted as purely negative incidents because 'these events can also be an opportunity to redesign and restructure a faulty system and turn it into a better one' (Carmeli and Schaubroeck 2008: 192).

Over the EU's sixty years of development, the recent crises have not been the first occurrences to challenge its institutional system. One major example was the 'empty chair crisis' in the mid-1960s, when France, due to its opposition against the planned introduction of majority decisions in the Common Agricultural Policy, stayed away from negotiations in the then European Economic Community's Council of Ministers, thus bringing the whole organisation to a standstill and exposing shortcomings in how the Council was working. The crisis was solved by the 'Luxembourg compromise' in 1966, which reformed decision-making in the Council and allowed for vetoes against resolutions if a member state believed such a resolution to be against its national interest (Palayret, Wallace and Winand 2006). Another crisis occurred when in 2005 the majority of French and Dutch citizens taking part in referenda rejected the ratification of the European Constitutional Treaty, eventually resolved by a compromise leading to the Treaty of Lisbon (2009).

Even though both predicaments have been conceived as major blows against European integration, the most recent difficulties are of a much greater magnitude that puts the whole European project potentially at risk. They feature many attributes of a transboundary crisis: 'These crises have no clear beginning, escalate suddenly, and, in unforeseen directions, exploit linkages between functional and geographical domains' (Boin 2009: 368). In the context of the EU, these kinds of transboundary crises impact all levels of the European multi-layered system of governance, spilling over from one policy sector to another, for instance, from the financial to the fiscal and monetary to the asylum and the border regime. The 'refugee crisis', for example, has divided the EU (Culik 2015), and moreover has put those euro area states hardest hit by the sovereign debt crisis under additional pressure. Consider Italy and Greece, member states already under strain due to the debt crisis, where the largest number of refugees first arrived from Turkey and North Africa. Under the prevailing EU common asylum system, these states were responsible for processing asylum applications and for taking care of the asylum seekers within their territory. Given both countries' scarcity of resources and weak administrative capacity vis-à-vis the scope of the challenge, after unsuccessfully demanding solidarity from European governments, they started to directly forward refugees to other member states (see Zaun's and Wallascheck's chapters in this volume). This practice quickly fuelled dissatisfaction with the Schengen regime and its main pillar: the free movement of people among European member states, creating momentum for populists to fuel a full-blown crisis of legitimacy of the EU.

According to Jürgen Habermas (1973), a legitimacy crisis results from a loss of confidence in the ability of administrative institutions to effectively govern. In fact, trust in European institutions has dramatically decreased since the beginning of the debt crisis, with a further dip occurring during the 'refugee crisis' and slowly recovering since then (Eurobarometer 2018). In the current situation, the EU is at a critical turning point. The crisis, like any other legitimation crisis, 'can be resolved only through recalibration, which necessarily involves the communicative reconciliation of the actor's or institution's social identity, interests, or practices with the normative expectations of other actors within its realm of political action' (Reus-Smit 2007: 172; see also Liebert, ch. 20). As Mlada Bukovansky (2002: 233) already observed more than ten years ago, 'the Concert of Europe shows that legitimacy contests may in the end be managed by political leaders, if those leaders are able to learn the relevant lessons of the day and cobble together an order that takes into account both traditional claims and those of newly empowered (and/or newly dissatisfied) socio-political actors.' Learning from crises, however, is a difficult task, particularly if there are no authoritative and widely accepted explanations of why and how the crisis happened and if the proposed solutions are contested (Boin 2009: 374). This is true regarding the crises that have afflicted the EU since 2010, all of which are at the centre of contention between opposed views. Many of these conflicting views are characterised by the dichotomy of 'Europeanism vs. neo-nationalism'. Though certainly not new, this dichotomy now shapes the EU's politics of crises more strongly than ever before. Highlighting this aspect enables us to capture the major conflict line at the heart of the current political crises. A closer look into the contentions between nationalist and pro-European responses to the crises serves to illustrate the point about this reinforced division.

Europeanisation versus neo-nationalism in times of crises – cases of innovation and development

This book is structured in three parts: The first section 'Europeanisation versus neo-nationalism in times of crises' deals with the new political conflict line that increasingly shapes the domestic politics of the member states. The second part 'Re-examining the crises of European integration' explores some of the most pressing challenges to European unification from different, innovative angles. The final section 'European Innovation and Development' makes the case that the EU's responses to crises, conflict and change were not only marked by policy failures but have also brought about important instances of innovation and development.

The country case studies and comparisons included in section I. 'Europeanisation versus neo-nationalism in times of crises' demonstrate that the emerging battle field between the forces of Europeanisation and those striving for neo-nationalism is neither limited to East-Central European member states nor to the EU-28 but reaches also into candidate and neighbouring states. Moreover, these struggles are not only fuelled by rising right- or left-wing populist political parties: they also have divisive effects within moderate, mainstream and governing political parties, and they can mobilise all sorts of civil as well as non-civil societal movements and organisations. To illustrate these points, each chapter looks more closely into the different national contexts of France, the Netherlands, the Czech Republic, Greece, Germany and Ireland, and Turkey and Serbia.

Here, France is certainly a prominent case in point. It became a most dramatic battle ground for pro- versus anti-European contentions, epitomised by Emmanuel Macron and Marine Le Pen in the French 2017 Presidential elections. As in the UK in 2016 as well as in Italy in 2018, these confrontations have been driven by the EU's 'polycrisis' (Schild, ch. 2). Yet, most importantly, they have fuelled not only despair and anger against the EU but also new hopes for the future of Europe. The winning presidential candidate, Emmanuel Macron, succeeded in communicating his fresh ideas for strengthening the European Union across Europe.

The Netherlands, by comparison, signals less drama and more a normalisation of anti-pluralist populism, even if it does not come out victorious. Exhibiting clear parallels with anti-pluralist movements in other European countries, the Dutch experience raises fundamental questions for the EU as a whole (Crum, ch. 3).

A more peculiar case is the Czech Republic. Despite its close ties to the German economy and while prospering throughout the times of the euro crisis, the economic case for European integration has not contained nationalist populism among the elite and ordinary people, as the domestic politics of the fugee crisis has demonstrated (Havlik, ch. 4).

Greece, although situated at the lowest end of economic prosperity in the Union, and despite conditions of austerity, recession and social hardship, did not avail itself of calls for neo-nationalism (cf. Ellinas 2013). Paradoxically, successive governments have been complying with three euro-area programmes, even including anti-austerity coalitions built by the extreme left and right wing parties. In addition, Greece has witnessed the unexpected growth of civil society engagement in different fields of society severely hit by austerity policies and the influx of refugees fleeing from civil war and terrorism in neighbouring regions (Sotiropoulos, ch. 5).

Finally, two member states that were better capable of fighting off the financial crisis and the rise of Eurosceptic forces, Ireland and Germany; here the contentions about the EU's immigration crisis have revealed deeper political conflicts surrounding the scope and meaning of 'solidarity' (Wallaschek, ch. 6). Within the EU, the pro-active agents working for Europeanisation include many civil society organisations. This is also the case beyond the EU, in candidate countries. Depending on whether they are supported not only by the EU but also on the home front, conditions for NGO's will vary widely, as the comparison of the Western Balkans and Turkey demonstrates (Dereci, ch. 7).

Section II. 'Re-examining the crises of European integration' explores some of the most crucial challenges to European unification, including Brexit and the European 'refugee crisis' as well as the Nord Stream pipeline. It includes contributions that emphasise different angles that have received relatively little attention to date in the prominent crisis narratives but are pivotal to political support for the European project. For instance, the 'remainers' lack of attention to the EU's achievements for minority integration in the UK's Brexit referendum campaign provides a telling angle for understanding its negative outcome. Arguably, the EU could and should have strengthened its already highly acknowledged role in combating racial and ethnic discrimination and expanded its contribution to minority protection. This would help to avoid perceptions of it being a 'white club' and make European identity inclusive of all citizens on its territory (Jenichen, ch. 8). Another impediment is the weak state capacity that helps to explain non-compliance and set-backs to joint intergovernmental decision-making, for instance in the field of the European common asylum system. Here, effective implementation of the EU's asylum policies has been blocked notably by Hungary and Poland, but also Austria and France. Although the EU has sought to draw lessons from these failures of asylum policy in favour of a more realistic concept, real advances are still required (Zaun, ch. 9). The weak administrative systems of several member states are a result of insufficient Europeanisation processes during the accession period that have been further aggravated by the financial and economic crisis. These are critical impediments to the effective implementation of European policies in countries such as Greece, and more generally in the newer member states of East-Central Europe where the rule of law, state administrations and democratic institutions are not yet sufficiently consolidated (Wittmann, ch. 10). Apart from administrative weaknesses, the dynamics of domestic politics can also play out against a common European regime. As critics of the widely-used but misleading term 'refugee crisis' have noted, at its core this is a crisis of humanism, humanitarianism, and human rights. It consists of heated contestations within domestic contexts about whether and to what extent EU member states should commit themselves to the protection of the civil and political rights of refugees and minorities as codified in the European Charter of Human Rights, and how to follow up on them in practice. In this respect, Bulgarian domestic politics is a telling case that illustrates the difficulties of translating European Human Rights norms into effective protection for those who need it most (Guasti and Siroki, ch. 11). Moreover, some promising European projects can be buried under conflicting national interests. In the aftermath of the Crimea conflict and in the context of EU-Russia geo-political tensions, the problem of energy security has gained saliency on the EU's political agenda. In this context, the case of the North Stream pipeline has become a particularly contested issue. Hence, a closer examination of the diverging views of Poland and Germany will shed light on the opportunities and constraints regarding the prospects for a European Energy Union (Heinrich and Pleines, ch. 12).

In sum, with regard to theorising how conflictive European integration has become across a variety of policy domains, a broader conversation between the orthodox theory schools and more heterodox approaches is needed (Abels, ch. 13): For instance, conceiving Europeanisation through a 'gendered lens' offers a promising way for re-interpreting contemporary right-wing populist struggles as a backlash. Arguably, neo-nationalism brings gender-biased interests and identity constructions to the fore vis-à-vis the EU's *acquis comunautaire*, hence its achievements over the past fifty years in building norms, policies and institutions aimed at advancing gender justice, from the principle of non-discrimination and equal rights to the 'mainstreaming' of equal opportunity and equal treatment policies across a variety of policy fields (Abels and Mushaben 2012).

The final section III. 'European Innovation and Development' presents a selection of cases where the EU has been presented with demands for – and arguably did advance, even if not yet fully accomplish – innovative proposals in response to the crises. These European political developments range from the financial and euro crises, climate governance and trade policy to the democratisation of European governance, namely in fields where the member states are divided and the European Parliament has remained weak. These developments can be found in three fields, in particular: First, in the field of Economic and Monetary Union, the pro-active course of action adopted by the

European Central Bank came under critique as a backstop for stabilising EMU against present and future imbalances. Yet, President Mario Draghi's bond-buying programme and monetary policy have proven to be pivotal for the survival of the euro area (Zagermann, ch. 14). Second, the global governance of climate change is probably the field where the EU can be lauded most for its achievements, namely regarding the Paris Agreement of 2015 on an international framework and timetable for emissions reduction. Notwithstanding, in more technical fields, ambitious climate action by the EU is more difficult. This poses the question of what the specific 'enabling factors for ambitious EU climate action' actually are (Morata Liebert, ch. 15). Third, the field of democratising European governance includes several issues where democratic innovations are at stake. Many critics of the EU's crisis management have taken issue with the democratic deficits of the euro area's emergency regime. The ECB, the Eurogroup and the 'Troika' have been criticised as technocratic supranational supervisory agencies with a blind eye towards social justice that reign into the democratic autonomy of national sovereigns in fiscal, economic, labour market and social matters (see Hentschel, ch. 16). By contrast, in these matters, the European Parliament can be qualified as a democratically legitimated agent for European social policy development – one that was partially successful, albeit constrained by the intergovernmental politics of the Employment and Social Affairs Council (Lange and Liebert, ch. 17). Moreover, the European parliamentary practices have developed interesting institutional innovations. In particular, the EP's so-called 'intergroups' build informal, yet institutionalised cross-partisan channels for civil society participation in European parliamentary activities, from legislation to the control of European agencies and the executive (Landorff, ch. 18). Nevertheless, the innovative measures that the MEP's have advanced for strengthening the European political party system remain shelved, and hence wait to live up to the requirements of a democratic European political Union (Ciancio, ch. 19).

Summing up the various efforts to develop the EU politically reveals a number of weaknesses: notably, deficits of harmonizing standards of social security, democratic transparency, control and legitimacy and rule of law. Arguably, the intergovernmental piece-meal approach to managing the euro-crisis has strengthened the technocratic character of EMU at the expense of democratically elected institutions. EU reforms are needed in order to re-build what has been lost due to the crisis: the popular, social and transnational trust that is the necessary foundation for a more resilient EU. At this point in time, it appears doubtful whether its shortcomings can be overcome within the present institutional arrangement of the EU multi-level polity. Therefore, during the next legislative term 2019-24, European leaders and citizens will have to address the difficult choices between alternative scenarios and options for developing the joint problem-solving capacities of the European Union. The European Union's unfinished journey remains uncertain and open ended, depending on the diverging narratives and which properties of crises will prevail: the sources of erosion and neo-nationalism – or the resources for political innovation and the development of more resilient forms of Europeanisation (Liebert, ch. 20).

The starting point of this book was this double-edged nature of crises as sources of decline as well as development. Its chapters contribute to the debate on the future of Europe by discussing lessons learnt and identifying possible innovations arising from different aspects of the crises. Its empirically based reflections address a range of key issues that need to be resolved if the unfinished project of European integration is to cope with its challenges in sustainable ways. Arguably, the key conclusion that can be drawn from these chapters and which is confirmed by the unfolding Brexit tragedy reads as follows: Instead of holding onto 'extreme' solutions such as fully-fledged political federalism with a European central state and a setback to nationalist protectionism, Europeans are capable of seeking for more pragmatic solutions and creative compromises. This requires the Union citizens and the European political leaders to take the lessons from the EU's failures over the past decade to heart. They need to overcome the current tensions between Europeanisation and neo-nationalism for the sake of a political development of Europe that constructively learns from the past. In this case, the crises would not represent sources of decline but rather important resources for Europeans to construct their path forward in the 21st century.

References

Abels, Gabriele and Joyce Mushaben eds. (2012): Gendering the European Union: New Approaches to Old Democratic Deficits (Gender and Politics. Palgrave.

Boin, Arjen (2009): The New World of Crises and Crisis Management: Implications for Policymaking and Research. In: Review of Policy Research, 26(4), 367-377.

Bukovansky, Mlada (2002): Legitimacy and Power Politics, Princeton: Princeton University Press.

Carmeli, Abraham and John Schaubroeck (1998): Organisational Crisis-Preparedness: The Importance of Learning from Failures. In: Long Range Planning, 41, 177-196.

Culik, Jan (2015): Fencing off the east: how the refugee crisis is dividing the European Union. In: The Conversation, September 16, available at: https://theconversation.com/fencing-off-the-east-how-the-refugee-crisis-is-dividing-the-european-union-47586 (last accessed: 10 April 2017).

Ellinas, Antonis A. (2013): The Rise of Golden Dawn: The New Face of the Far Right in Greece. In: South European Society and Politics, 18(4), 543-565.

Eurobarometer (2018): Report: Public opinion in the European Union, Standard Eurobarometer 89, Spring 2018, available at: http://ec.europa.eu/commfrontoffice/publicopinion/index.cfm/Survey/getSurveyDetail/instruments/STANDARD/surveyKy/2180 (last access: 28 January 2019).

Habermas, Jürgen (1973): Legitimationsprobleme im Spätkapitalismus, Frankfurt/M.: Suhrkamp.

Hwang, Peter and J. David Lichtenthal (2000): Anatomy of Organizational Crises. In: Journal of Contingencies and Crisis Management, 8(3), 129-140.

Palayret, Jean-Marie; Helen Wallace and Pascaline Winand, eds. (2006): Visions, Votes and Vetoes: The Empty Chair Crisis and the Luxembourg Compromise Forty Years on, Brussels: P.I.E-Peter Lang.

Pearson, Christine M. and Judith A. Clair (1998): Reframing Crisis Management. In: Academy of Management Review, 23(1), 59-76.

Reus-Smit, Christian (2007): International Crises of Legitimacy. In: International Politics, 44, 157-174.

Roux-Dufort, Christophe (2009): The Devil Lies in Details! How Crises Build up Within Organizations. In: Journal of Contingencies and Crisis Management, 17(1), 4-11.

I.
Europeanisation versus Neo-Nationalism in Times of Crisis

2. France's European politics in the face of the polycrisis

Joachim Schild

Introduction[1]

Polarising debates on European integration are by no means new in France. The country looks back on a rich history of highly divisive debates on Europe, the most important of which were the battle fought in 1954 on the European Defence Community (EDC), the Maastricht referendum in 1992, won by a narrow margin (51 per cent yes against 49 per cent no votes), and the referendum on the 'Treaty establishing a Constitution for Europe' in May 2005, rejected by a clear majority of Frenchmen (55 per cent).

Today, the conditions for the politicisation of European issues and for the spread of Eurosceptic attitudes could hardly be better. For several years, the EU has found itself in a deep crisis mode, a situation referred to as a 'polycrisis' by the president of the European Commission, Jean-Claude Juncker:

> "This European Union has faced its worst economic, financial and social crisis since World War II. And it is still struggling with the consequences. I have often used the Greek word 'polycrisis' to describe the current situation. Our various challenges – from the security threats in our neighbourhood and at home, to the refugee crisis, and to the UK referendum – have not only arrived at the same time. They also feed each other, creating a sense of doubt and uncertainty in the minds of our people" (Juncker 2016).

The European Union's (EU) political and economic performance in dealing with the Eurocrisis and the below average performance of euro area economies compared to the rest of the EU have raised doubts in the minds of many citizens. The traditional narrative of European integration as a project producing more prosperity for all has been questioned. Economic integration in general and the way the euro area crisis was handled in particular have created winners and losers and redistributed wealth and opportunities.

Moreover, citizens could observe in 2015 the collapse of the Dublin regime assigning responsibilities to member states for handling asylum seekers. They

1 The manusript has been finished in February 2017.

also saw the failure of the Schengen regime to avoid external border controls and to uphold internal freedom of movement in 2015. A more or less uncontrolled number of asylum seekers entered the territory of the European Union. This has put a big question mark over one of the core European achievements that had been highly valued by citizens according to all opinion polls: the freedom of movement inside the Schengen area.

This European 'polycrisis' has fed Eurosceptic tendencies both in French public opinion and in French political parties' discourses. Recent developments have to be seen against the backdrop of a longer-term drop in French mass public support for European integration and a rising salience of European issues in inter-party competition. Citizens and parties tend to blame the French economic decline and the persistently high unemployment rates of the last decade at least partly on the European Union and its responsibility for the 'austerity policies' that successive French governments had to adopt.

To what extent does the executive face tighter domestic constraints on its European policy-making since the breakdown of the 'permissive consensus' at the time of the Maastricht Treaty? And how did the current polycrisis affect domestic conflicts on Europe in France? In order to find answers to these questions, we first look at the evolution of public opinion on issues of European integration. In a second step, we assess the politicisation of European issues in French party politics by looking at the salience of 'Europe' for the main French parties, at the evolution of their overall stances towards European integration and at the level of intra-party conflict on Europe. Finally, we will assess in how far European integration constitutes a major issue dimension that will structure domestic political conflict in a more durable way.

Attitudes in mass publics towards the European Union[2]

Already before the start of the financial market crisis, support levels for the European Union among French citizens have dropped compared to earlier decades. Graph 1 displays the long-term evolution of net support[3] measured by the Eurobarometer trend question: "*Generally speaking, do you think that (your country's) membership of the European Community (Common Market) is a) a good thing, b) a bad thing, c) neither good nor bad*". Three observations stand out. Firstly, France follows more or less the European long-term downward trend (see trend line for France). Secondly, the early 1990s marked a turning

2 I would like to thank Lena Helmer for her support in compiling and visualising the data used in this article.

3 Here, the percentage of 'bad thing' is subtracted from the percentage of 'good thing' answers in order to obtain a measure of net support.

point, heralding the end of the 'permissive consensus'. Thereafter, support for European integration never again reached the same level as in the 1970s and 1980s. Thirdly, French support levels were above the European average in the 1970s and 1980s but fell persistently below the European average since the early 1990s (see Graph 1).

Graph 1: Net support for European integration 1973-2011 (in per cent)

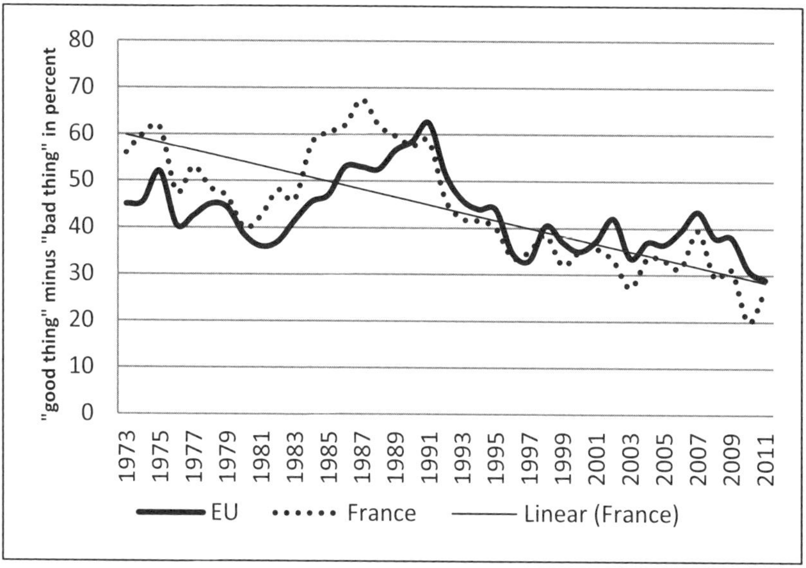

Question: Generally speaking, do you think that (your country's) membership of the European Community (Common Market) is ...? A good thing, a bad thing, neither good nor bad.

Source: Standard Eurobarometer 1-75

Unfortunately, the Eurobarometer surveys do not ask this trend question any longer in EU member states. Hence, we have to make use of other trend questions in order to assess recent trends. We chose two questions repeatedly asked during the last years, one on the image of the EU and the other one on citizens' trust in the EU.

The EU's image clearly deteriorated in France during the last years since the start of the global financial crisis in 2007 (see Graph 2). This trend is by no means specific to France. Positive images nevertheless still prevailed in public opinion until very recently. In the fall 2016 Eurobarometer, negative images turned out to be slightly more widespread than positive ones (31 negative, 29 positive images and 39 per cent of respondents picking the neutral answer category). Immediately before the start of the financial market crisis in 2007, fully 52 per cent still had a positive image of the European Union (see Graph 2).

Graph 2: Positive or negative image of EU (in per cent)

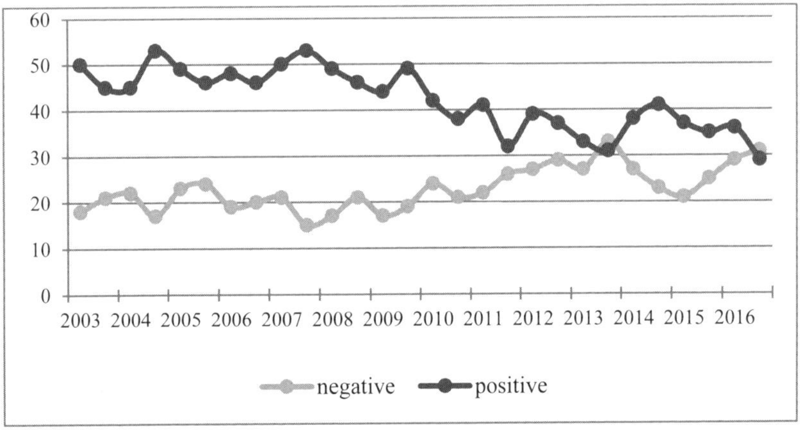

Question: In general, does the EU conjure up for you a positive or a negative image? (in %)

Source: Eurobarometer EB59-EB86

The picture is still darker when we look at trust levels (see Graph 2). Fully two thirds (65 per cent) of the French population did not tend to trust the European Union in fall 2016, up from 34 per cent back in 2007 (Eurobarometer 68).

Graph 2: Trust in the European Union (in per cent)

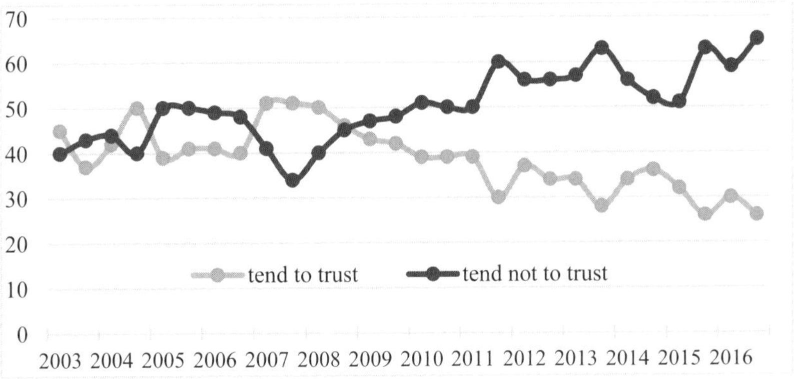

Question: Please tell me if you tend to trust or if you tend not to trust the European Union (in %)

Source: Eurobarometer EB59-EB86.

It seems plausible to assume that the more negative images and lower trust levels derive from more negative evaluations of the EU's performance in times of crises. One of the European Commissions' biannual Eurobarometer survey questions asked respondents to evaluate in a very general way the overall performance of the EU. Do they think "the EU makes the quality of life better in Europe"? According to a recent Eurobarometer survey (Eurobarometer 83, spring 2015), only 40 per cent of the French population (as opposed to 51 per cent in the EU-28) share the idea that the EU makes their lives better whereas as many as 49 per cent explicitly reject this view (versus 39 per cent in the EU-28).

Political actors tend to politicize European issues along the lines of domestic political conflict, shaped in France by the socio-economic and the sociocultural cleavages. So, we might ask in how far we find negative evaluations of the European Union's performance that might be linked to these two cleavage dimensions.

One of the potential reasons for the relatively negative evaluation of the EU's overall performance reported above can be found in the EU's perceived impact on the employment situation in France. Asked whether or not the "EU creates the conditions for more jobs", as many as 58 per cent of the French respondents answered in the negative (EU-28 average: 40 per cent). Only 30 per cent subscribed to this statement (EU-28 average: 49 per cent, data from Eurobarometer 83, spring 2015).

However, these increasingly negative attitudes did not translate into a dwindling support for European Economic and Monetary Union (EMU). 68 per cent of respondents still support the Euro and the EMU, according to the Eurobarometer survey of autumn 2016 (Eurobarometer 86, fall 2016). The right-wing populist National Front (Front national, FN) party, which makes the case for leaving the Eurozone, does not find substantial support in French public opinion on this key issue.

The overall picture we find in France is one of a declining number of citizens seeing the EU as a helpful framework for dealing with their most pressing problems. The IPSOS public opinion research institute asked repeatedly whether the French think that the decision-making power of France or that of the EU should be strengthened in order to "address effectively the major problems of the coming years". In 2015, only 14 per cent of a representative sample of respondents came out in favour of a strengthening the EU's decision-making power (down from 38 per cent back in 2012) whereas no less than 72 per cent considered it more appropriate to strengthen national decision-making power in order to effectively address major problems in the coming years (up from 56 per cent back in 2012, see Graph 4). This is a clear trend towards a 're-nationalisation' of public opinion.

Graph 4: To address effectively the major problems of the coming years... (in %)

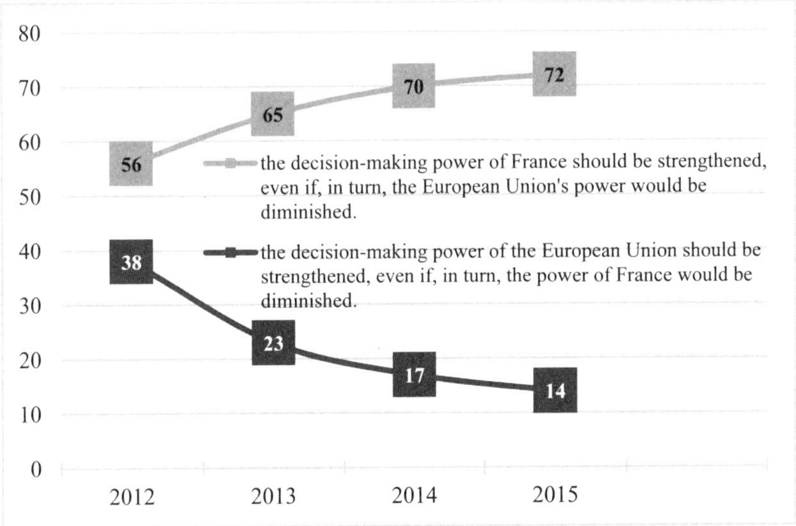

Source: Ipsos/STERIA und Ipsos/Logica Business Consulting.

These critical attitudes regarding the problem-solving capacity and the socio-economic consequences of European integration provide a fertile ground for political strategies of Eurosceptic parties. The same holds true for the sociocultural dimension regarding attitudes towards immigration. According to the Eurobarometer 83 survey from spring 2015, French citizens score slightly above EU average (58 per cent for France, 56 per cent for the EU-28) in expressing negative feelings towards immigrants from outside the EU. In an IPSOS survey, dating from May 2015, no less than 67 per cent of the respondents subscribed to the view that there are "too many immigrants in France". And a majority of 54 per cent think that the "Islamic religion is not compatible with the values of the French society". Surfing on widespread anti-immigration attitudes, the right-wing populist FN could fully exploit the European refugee crisis of 2015 to broaden its support base. This major European crisis in conjunction with the terrorist attacks in Paris in January and November 2015 provided the FN with a formidable window of opportunity which it was able to translate into a strong showing at the polls in 2015. In the regional elections held in December 2015, the FN came out as the most important French political party attracting no less than 28 per cent of the vote in the first round of this election.

Critical attitudes of mass publics towards European integration and EU policy outcomes influence both inter- and intra-party conflict in France, as they can be easily linked to the sociocultural as well as socio-economic issue-dimensions of domestic political debates.

Party stances and party competition on European issues

Party stances and differences between competing parties on Europe can be analysed by using different data sources. Apart from party manifesto data and data gained from newspaper analysis, we dispose of expert surveys. The Chapel Hill expert surveys (Bakker et al. 2015) on party positions towards issues of European integration provide us with data for several French parties since 1999. Hence, we are able to track changes over time.

First, we look at the salience of European issues for different parties. How much variation over time can we observe? In their study of public debates on European issues during national election campaigns in France from 1974-2012, based on newspaper content analysis, Hutter and Kerscher (2014) could show that the salience of European issues followed a clearly upward trend over time. Guinaudeau and Persico (2013) likewise pointed to a rise of European issue salience during the 1990s that started with the Maastricht referendum debate and showed no signs of lasting decline thereafter.

The Chapel Hill expert surveys conducted in 1999, 2002, 2006, 2010 and 2014 provide us with a more nuanced picture. Experts had to evaluate the relative salience of European integration in the parties' public discourse in a given year on an 11-point-scale, ranging from 0 "European Integration is of no importance, never mentioned" to 10 "European Integration is the most important issue". As graph 5 shows, none of the parties for which we have data since 1999 ranked below the neutral middle category of 5. By the end of the 1990s, no established French party could afford to ignore European integration issues. The evolving salience of Europe does not show a clear trend for the two mainstream centre-left and centre right parties, the Socialists (Parti socialiste, PS) and the neo-Gaullist (Le Rassemblement pour la République and L'Union pour un mouvement populaire, RPR/UMP) now Les Républicains. It went somewhat down from 2010 to 2014. The opposite holds true for the populist right and left wing parties, the Front national (FN) and the Left Party (Parti de Gauche, PdG). They both scored above 8 on the 11-point issue salience scale (FN 8.5 PdG 8.1). The Greens (Les Verts), for which we unfortunately have no data for 2014, came close to the FN level in 2010.

Graph 5: Salience of European issues

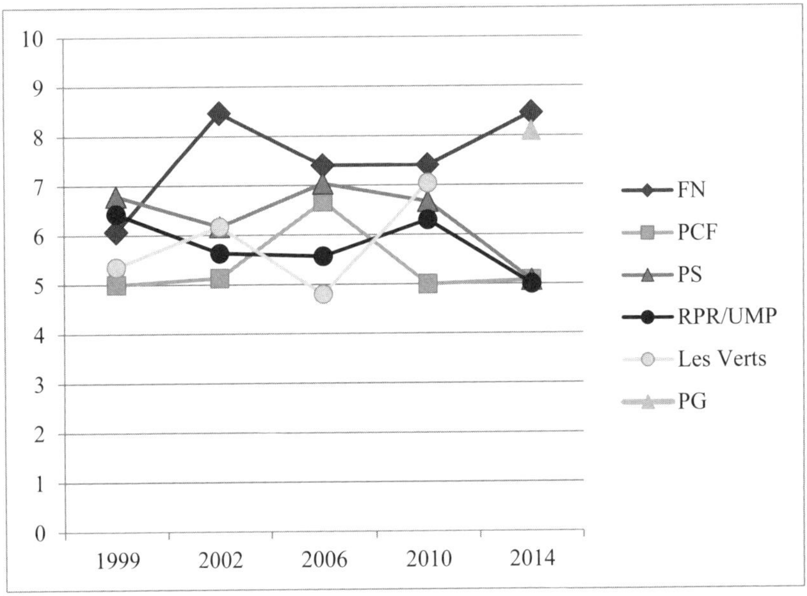

Source: Chapel Hill surveys 1999-2014.

In the 1980s, European integration issues did not have high currency in the FN's discourse. Similar to other fringe parties (Taggart 1998), the FN played with Euroscepticism without making it a core identity marker. Over the past two decades this has changed profoundly. In the 2014 European Parliament Election, the FN "claimed effective 'ownership' over the European issue, winning the bulk of the Eurosceptic vote to top the electoral field" (Goodliffe 2015: 324). Nowadays, this does not only hold true for European Parliament elections. In the national presidential election campaign in 2017, the FN's candidate Marine Le Pen has made widely use of European issues to distinguish herself from her mainstream competitors. It is not by coincidence that the first of her 144 policy proposals presented to the voters deals with France's membership in the EU. She promised to restore the French people's sovereignty – monetary, legislative, territorial, and economic – and to hold a referendum on French membership after negotiations with the EU (Le Pen 2017). The same holds true on the opposite end of the political spectrum. Jean-Luc Mélenchon, the presidenatial candidate of the left-wing populist 'France Unbowed' (La France insoumise) and former president of the Left Party (Parti de Gauche), also campaigned strongly on European issues, trying to make the 2017 presidential election a "referendum on Europe"[4] and playing with the idea of a leave referendum in case the European Union cannot be changed along his preferred lines.

The way the Front National, the Left Party and France Unbowed have made always more use of European issues during the last years testifies to their capacity to react on the 'supply side' to evolutions on the 'demand side' of voter's political-ideological and policy preferences. But we assume the causal arrow to point both ways: The more salient the 'supply' of Eurosceptic discourses by political parties will grow the more they will reinforce Eurosceptic public opinion. With the rising salience of and more polarisation on European issues, we can expect that mass public attitudes towards European political themes will become more structured and less superficial than in the past. If this holds true, Euroscepticism becomes more embedded and institutionalised both in public opinion and in the party system.

For mainstream parties the attempt to make Europe a highly salient issue in public debate comes at a price in case they are internally split on this issue. This was true for the neo-Gaullist party in the 1990s, especially on the occasion of the Maastricht referendum in 1992. And this was also true for the Socialist Party (PS) in the 2000s, especially regarding the 2005 referendum on the European Constitutional Treaty.[5]

The divisive influence of European integration issues on intra-party competition was arguably strongest felt by the French Socialist Party. The PS faced the most dramatic manifestations of an intra-party split, first when it called for a referendum on the European Constitutional Treaty within the party in December 2004 and, five months later, when it campaigned in the French referendum for EU constitutional treaty change (Petithomme 2012; Schild 2005; Wagner 2008).

This pronounced internal split on European integration issues has been made well visible by our expert survey where experts were asked to locate parties on a 11-point-scale ranging from 0 "Party was completely united" to 10 "Party was extremely divided". No other party was ranked higher than the PS in terms of internal divisions on Europe since 2006, a long-term consequence of the 2004-5 referendum experience (see Graph 6).

During the years of the Euro-crisis, the attitudes towards the EU and its management of the euro area crisis have become another sensitive touchstone of intra-party dissent and power struggles. Criticisms of the "austerity-cum-structural-reform-approach" of Germany towards the sovereign debt crisis in the euro area and the policy of fiscal consolidation at the domestic level in

---

4 Le Nouvel Observateur, 24 August 2016: Mélenchon veut faire de 2017 un 'référendum' sur l'Europe (URL: http://tempsreel.nouvelobs.com/topnews/20160824.REU9926/melenchon-veut-faire-de-2017-un-referendum-sur-l-europe.html).

5 For a comparison between these two French referenda on Europe, see Vassallo 2008.

France served as mobilising devices and identity markers for the Socialist Party's left wing. A substantial minority of the Socialist party group in the National Assembly was no longer willing to lend support to its own government and therefore voted, among others, against the French stability program for cutting budget deficits.

Graph 6: Level of intra party dissent on European integration

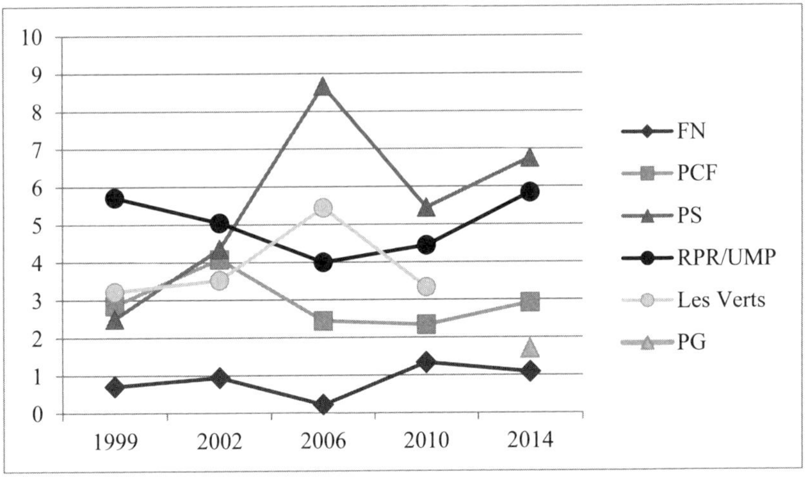

Source: Chapel Hill surveys 1999-2014.

Mainstream parties also contributed to the abovementioned trend of embedding European issues in domestic political debates. Put under pressure from their more extreme competitors, the PS and Les Républicains (LR, the former neo-Gaullist UMP) took up some elements of the extreme-left or –right wing's critical discourses on the EU and "played" with Euroscepticism (Rozenberg 2011). Sure, the centre-left and centre-right mainstream parties are still to be found on the pro-EU side in French debates on European issues. The results of the Chapel Hill expert surveys display, however, a drop of their support for European integration between 2010 and 2014 (see Graph 7).[6] This might reflect the criticisms of both candidates for the presidency in 2012, the then sitting president Nicolas Sarkozy and his challenger François Hollande, as "the two candidates in the second round of the elections went 'EU-negative' to rally additional votes. Sarkozy mentioned, on the one hand, his intention to suspend the Schengen agreements, unless changes in its implementation were made. Hollande, on the other hand, proclaimed his commitment to renegotiate the

6 Experts had to evaluate the "overall orientation of the party leadership towards European integration" in a given year and locate the party on a 7-point scale, ranging from 1 "strongly opposed" to 7 "strongly in favour".

European Budgetary Pact that EU member states had just agreed to in December 2011" (Vassallo 2012: 79).

Graph 7: General party support for European integration

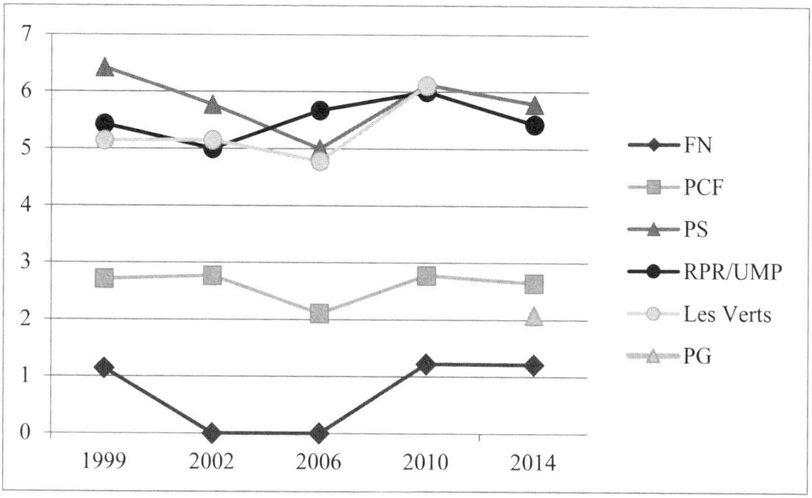

Source: Chapel Hill surveys 1999-2014.

In fact, after his election, François Hollande could not deliver on his (unrealistic) promise to renegotiate the Fiscal Compact. This failure and his efforts to cut back the French public deficit to bring the country back into line with the rules enshrined in the Stability and Growth Pact contributed to a revolt of the "frondeurs" from the Socialist Party's left-wing in the National Assembly. At several occasions, some dozen socialist Members of Parliament voted against their own government and even tabled a motion of censure against it. One of them was Benoît Hamon who won the primary as the left candidate for the French presidency in January 2017. He stands for a clear break with the legacy of the previous Socialist President Hollande in both economic and European policies. Never since the time of François Mitterrand has the Socialist Party base chosen to be represented in the race for the highest political office in France by a contender that was more sceptical about the EU's current trajectory than Benoît Hamon.

A similar kind of critical discourse with Eurosceptic overtones could also be observed inside the French Republican Party (the former UMP). Some of the contenders for the party's primaries to select their presidential candidate took an even more critical stance than the party ever did in the past. This was true for the former president Sarkozy. To a lesser extent, this was also true for François Fillon who made the race in the primaries by developing a public discourse with strong Gaullist accents stressing French sovereignty, independence and the need to redress France.

The reinforcement of these elements of soft Euroscepticism in the discourses of both mainstream parties, PS and Republicans, can be attributed to the institution of primaries for selecting each party's candidate to run for the highest French State office. This type of electoral contest with low participation rates (compared to presidential elections) provides a fertile ground that helps cultivate more radical political positions beyond the party's mainstream. This was especially true for the political left. The winner of the Socialist primary, Benoît Hamon, had always held a marginal position inside the PS and would not have had the slightest chance to be selected as the PS's official candidate by a party convention.

This soft form of Euroscepticism on the part of the mainstream centre-left and centre-right parties created incentives for the challenger parties and candidates to adopt always harder Eurosceptic stances, as the 2017 election campaigns for the presidency and the National Assembly demonstrated. This holds true for both the Front national's candidate Marine Le Pen and candidate of France Unbowed, Jean-Luc Mélenchon.

The former Minister of the Economy during the Hollande Presidency, Emmanuel Macron, was the only candidate to make unambiguously the case for deepening European integration.[7] This liberal, centre-left candidate embraced both European integration and globalisation, standing for a France that is culturally and economically open to the world. This stands in contrast to a trend in French political discourse on Europe that has grown ever more sceptical over time (Rozenberg 2011; Schild 2009). Therefore, both Emmanuel Macron and Marine Le Pen became the most likely candidates for the second and decisive round of the presidential elections. Such a configuration of candidates for the presidential elections would perfectly embody the growing salience and increasing degree of polarisation about issues of European integration in domestic French politics. While Macron appeals to younger, cosmopolitan, urban, highly educated and professionally successful and dynamic parts of the French society, Le Pen finds strong support among the left behind, the 'losers' of globalisation and European integration in the lower, less well educated strata of society, in rural regions and in declining industrial areas. Dubbed 'integration-demarcation cleavage' (Kriesi et al. 2008), this line of conflict is rooted in the social structure and has the potential to restructure domestic politics and the party system in France in a more durable way in the future.

7 See his speech at the Humboldt University in Berlin on 10 January 2017 (URL: https://plone.rewi.hu-berlin.de/de/lf/oe/whi/forum-constitutionis-europas/2017/rede-macron)

Conclusions

Our analysis of trends in public opinion, in party stances and party competition on issues of European integration makes amply clear that the room of manoeuvre for the French president and the French government has shrunk over the past years. France provides a clear example of a trend from a 'permissive consensus' to what Lisbeth Hooghe and Gary Marks called a 'constraining dissensus' on Europe (Hooghe/Marks 2009). When designing its European policy, the French executive has to look more than ever to its societal and political support base. This change can be referred to as a kind of 'domestication' of French European policy, where domestic political considerations gain always more importance (Schild 2008).

At the level of political parties, two conclusions are in order. Firstly, fringe or challenger parties do not use European integration issues only to distinguish themselves tactically from their mainstream competitors. On the contrary, European issues or the Europeanisation of national policies moved towards centre stage in their discourses. This makes Europe much more salient in public debates which thereby become always more polarised. Secondly, a process of clarification among mainstream parties might be underway. As the presidential campaign in 2017 made clear, they can no longer play down European issues in an attempt not to stir up their internal divisions as their challengers attack them precisely on this issue dimension.

So far, the French case has provided evidence for a positive correlation between the level of politicisation – in terms of polarisation and salience of European issues – on the one hand and the spread of Eurosceptic attitudes among mass publics and political parties on the other hand. Front National (renamed 'Rassemblement National' in 2018) gives European issues the highest public visibility and, at the same time, it is the most Eurosceptical among all major parties. Moreover, it has gained a lot of electoral ground since the start of the European 'polycrisis'.

What can we then learn from the French experience? Our tentative conclusion is that the idea to pursue a strategy of politicisation of European issues in order to strengthen the European Union's legitimacy is based on a questionable empirical assumption, namely that higher degrees of politicisation might lead to higher support for European integration.

Political actors with a strong strategic interest in politicising European issues can be found mainly among Eurosceptic challenger parties and also in the Eurosceptic wings of mainstream parties. The more institutionalised opportunities these actors find to publicly express their Euroscepticism – making use of referenda and primaries for candidate selection – the better are the conditions for them to succeed.

It remains to be seen in how far counter strategies to confront Eurosceptics and globalisation sceptics head on, such as developed by Emmanuel Macron, remain successful both in winning elections and in fighting the rampant Euroscepticism in French society. Ultimately, this could lead to a restructuring of the party system as the European cleavage might further gain importance for inter-party competition.

References

Bakker, Ryan/Edwards, Erica/Hooghe, Liesbet/Jolly, Seth/Koedam, Jelle/Kostelka, Filip/Marks, Gary/Polk, Jonathan/Rovny, Jan/Schumacher, Gijs/Steenbergen, Marco/Vachudova, Milada/Zilovic, Marko (2015): 1999–2014 Chapel Hill Expert Survey Trend File. Version 1.13 Available on chesdata.eu. Chapel Hill, NC: University of North Carolina, Chapel Hill.

Goodliffe, Gabriel (2015): Europe's salience and 'owning' Euroscepticism: Explaining the Front National's victory in the 2014 European elections in France. In: French Politics, 13, 4, pp. 324–345.

Guinaudeau, Isabelle/Persico, Simon (2013): EU politicization through the lens of salience: How the EU enters the French, British and German electoral agenda (1986-2009). In: French Politics, 11, 2, pp. 143-168.

Hooghe, Lisbeth/Marks, Gary (2008): A postfunctionalist theory of European integration: From permissive consensus to constraining dissensus. In: British Journal of Political Science, 39, 1, pp. 1-23.

Hutter, Swen/Kerscher, Alena (2014): Politicizing Europe in hard times: Conflicts over Europe in France in a long-term perspective, 1974–2012. In: Journal of European Integration 36, 3, pp. 267-282.

Kriesi Hanspeter/Grande, Edgar/Lachat, Romain/Dolezal, Martin/Bornschier, Simon/Frey, Timotheos (2008): West European Politics in the Age of Globalization, Cambridge: Cambridge University Press.

Le Pen, Marine (2017): 144 engagements présidentiels, URL: https://www.marine2017.fr/programme/

Juncker, Jean-Claude (2016): Speech by President Jean-Claude Juncker at the Annual General Meeting of the Hellenic Federation of Enterprises. Athens, 21 June 2016 (http://europa.eu/rapid/press-release_SPEECH-16-2293_en.htm).

Petithomme, Mathieu (2012): Containing the sleeping giant in EU referendums? A comparison of the strategies of confinement of EU issues of the RPR (1992) and the PS (2005). In: French Politics 10, 2, pp. 105–133.

Rozenberg, Olivier. (2011): Playing softly with Euroscepticism: The 2009 European Elections in France, in: Robert Harmsen/Joachim Schild (eds.): Debating Europe: The European Parliament Elections 2009 and Beyond, Baden-Baden: Nomos Verlag, pp. 51-68.

Schild, Joachim (2005): Ein Sieg der Angst – das gescheiterte französische Verfassungsreferendum. In: Integration 28, 3, pp. 187-200.
Schild, Joachim (2008): Die „Domestizierung" französischer Europapolitik. In: Frankreich-Jahrbuch 2008, hrsg. vom Deutsch-Französischen Institut, Wiesbaden: VS Verlag für Sozialwissenschaften, pp. 29-49.
Schild, Joachim (2009): Europapolitik in einer verunsicherten Gesellschaft. In: Joachim Schild/Henrik Uterwedde (eds.): Die verunsicherte Französische Republik. Wandel der Strukturen, der Politik – und der Leitbilder? Baden-Baden: Nomos Verlag 2009, pp. 193-218.
Taggart, Paul (1998): A touchstone of dissent: Euroscepticism in contemporary western European party systems. In: European Journal of Political Research, 33, 3, pp. 363-388.
Vassallo, Francesca (2008): The failed EU constitution referendum. The French case in perspective, 1992 and 2005, in: Finn Laursen (ed.): The rise and fall of the EU's Constitutional Treaty, Leiden: Nijhoff, pp. 411-429.
Vassallo, Francesca (2012): The EU discourse in the 2012 French presidential election. In: French Politics, Culture & Society 30, 3, pp. 79-95.
Wagner, Markus (2008): Debating Europe in the French Socialist Party: The 2004 internal referendum on the EU constitution. In: French Politics, 6, 3, pp. 257–279.

Abbreviations

Title	Abbreviaton
European Defence Community	EDC
European Monetary Union	EMU
European Union	EU
Les Républicains	LR
L'Union pour un mouvement populaire	UMP
Front National	FN
Parti Socialiste	PS
Parti de Gauche	PdG
Rassemblement pour la République	RPR

3. Living with anti-pluralist populism in Europe: Insights from the Dutch 2017 elections[1]

Ben Crum

1. Introduction

Never before did a Dutch election attract as much attention from foreign media as the one on 15 March 2017. Journalists swarmed to the Netherlands, driven by one big question: Will Geert Wilders win? Wilders became a topic of particular interest thanks to the dramatic votes of 2016: the Brexit referendum in the United Kingdom and the election of Donald Trump as President of the United States. The prospect thus lured that the Netherlands would see a similar dramatic turn-around, one that would be indicative of a transnational 'rise of populism'. Dutch Prime Minister Mark Rutte qualified – and dismissed – such expectations as a 'domino theory' which suggests that with one or two countries falling prey to populist movements, the rest will follow automatically (Jonker 2017).

Eventually, Wilders was not the big victor of 15 March. He got 13.3 percent of the vote-share, corresponding to 20 of the 150 seats in the Dutch Lower House, which is five seats more than he got at the previous elections in 2012 but four less than his best result to date in 2010. What is more, the Freedom Party certainly did not become the biggest party, and it was effectively sidelined from the government to be formed. Ironically, soon, commentators started to float a reverse domino theory, in which the relative loss of Wilders was prefigured by the win of Alexander Van der Bellen of the presidential elections in Austria and followed in May 2017 by the victory of Emanuel Macron over Marine Le Pen in the French presidential elections.

However, if anything, the experience of the Dutch elections signals *the normalization of anti-pluralist populism*, even if they do not come out victorious. While for a long time, anti-pluralist populist parties could still be treated as an aberration and a rather marginal phenomenon, recent elections indicate that

1 The main argument of this paper was first presented as a talk at the Danish Institute for International Studies. I thank Cecilie Stokholm Banke and Marlene Wind for hosting me and for their feedback on that occasion.

they are there to stay as a significant political force in many political systems. Considerable attention has been devoted to those EU member states, Hungary and Poland, in which we witness actual backsliding in terms of political pluralism and the rule of law (Bánkuti/Halmai/Scheppele, 2012; Müller 2015a; Closa/Kochenov 2016; Schipplak/Treib 2017). However, the normalization of anti-pluralist populism and the potential threat it poses to democratic pluralism in Europe is a phenomenon that applies to a much wider range of European countries, including for instance France, Germany, Austria, Finland, and Denmark.

In this paper, I use the Dutch case to discuss this development and its broader implications for Europe at large. After characterising anti-pluralist populism, I turn to the Dutch 2017 elections and analyse their outcome as well as their historical context. While the Dutch case obviously has some particular features of its own, there are clear parallels with anti-pluralist movements in other European countries and it certainly raises fundamental question for Europe as a whole.

2. What is anti-pluralist populism?

Too often the term populism remains rather intuitive and fuzzy. It is used in a pejorative way to refer to political movements that are considered as distorting the way 'democratic politics as we know it' works. Calling politicians 'populists' is often a way to disqualify them. Hence it is important to be precise. For that, I propose to depart from two basic understandings of populism.

In the first way, it is only natural for politicians to be populists: they should listen to the people at large and appeal to them. That is exactly what we expect politicians to do in a democracy. In this sense, all politicians should be populists; the only respect in which they are likely to vary is that some have less ideological spine and thus cater more openly for the popular vote compared to politicians who more insist on particular ideological principles. This is probably what the Dutch prime minister Mark Rutte (Jonker 2017) referred to on election night when he distinguished "the wrong kind of populism" from, what is supposedly, the "the right kind".

However, when we today talk about populist politicians, we are often not just referring to opportunist politicians but to something more specific. Importantly, populism is not inherently related to a particular ideological view. In general, we recognize that there can be both left-wing and right-wing populists. Drawing on the work of Margarat Canovan (1999) and Jan-Werner Müller (2015b; 2016), we can say that populism is rather about a certain style of politics and the underlying understanding of the nature of democratic politics in pluralist societies. Populists distinguish themselves because they rely on a moral notion of a homogenous and pure people that is united by a single common identity and interest, and it is them – the populist politicians – who represent, articulate or even embody, this single united interest.

By implication, populists challenge a pluralist understanding of modern societies in which it is natural that multiple competing interests and identities coexist. Instead, you are either with or against the people. As Jan-Werner Müller (2015b: 86) puts it: "populists consistently and continuously deny the very legitimacy of their opponents (as opposed to just saying that some of their policies are misguided)". What is more, and indeed fundamental, is that Müller adds that in their denial of the legitimacy of political alternatives, populists are ultimately "willing to risk a crisis of liberal democracy [i.e. the basic political structure/constitution] itself".

Thus, to complete the argument, why do we care so much about the rise of populism in the UK, the US and the Netherlands? It is basically because of the threat that if they would take effective control, liberal democracy itself may be at risk.

The anti-pluralism that characterizes populism in this interpretation also logically positions it against European integration or indeed any internationalist political engagement, as their inter-national character inherently brandishes these arrangements as pluralist. Populists perceive such international pluralism as an encroachment on the 'pure' national identity they claim to represent, and hence are bound to oppose international political arrangements. Thus, it is no coincidence that all national political parties that we can characterize as anti-pluralist populists tend to oppose European integration.

Now, as said, the anti-pluralist populists have not taken control in the Netherlands. Importantly, however, they have not gone away either and it does not look like they will. Instead, they seem to become a permanent force in the Dutch parliament with a vote share of, depending on how you count, between 20 per cent to up to one third of the parliament. What is more, the presence, and continuous political competition, of this sizable minority is felt throughout the party landscape. Many mainstream parties have felt the need to pick up on the kind of issues – like migration, nationalism, Euroscepticism – that these parties highlight and to adjust their positions in their direction. These circumstances reflect what I characterize as "the normalisation of populism".

3. The 2017 Dutch elections

Even if the Freedom Party had to leave the position of the biggest party in the Dutch Lower House to the Liberal-Conservatives of the VVD, the outcome of the 2017 Dutch elections was quite spectacular in several respects. 38 of the 150 seats in parliament (i.e. more than 25%) changed party. Notably, 29 of the seats that changed party came from the biggest loser of the elections, the Labour Party (PvdA) which, after having served a difficult 4-year terms as junior partner in the government, saw its seat share crumble from 38 to a mere 9 seats. Notably, the other major loser was its senior partner, Mark Rutte's VVD, which lost 8 seats but nevertheless remained the biggest party with 33 seats in parliament – indeed, the smallest biggest party the Netherlands has ever seen.

As said, Geert Wilders' Freedom Party was among the winners and ended second with 20 seats coming from 15. The Christian-Democrats even won one seat more, which got them to 19 seats, the same number that the progressive liberals of D66 secured coming from 12 seats in 2012. The biggest gains were however secured by the Greens of GroenLinks who revenged their pitiful 4 seats result in 2012 by moving up to a, for them, unprecedented number of 14 seats, the same number as their more left-wing brethren from the Socialist Party who got to 14 seats by losing one. While the Christian-conservative parties, Christian-Union and the Calvinists of the SGP remained stable at 5 and, respectively, 3 seats, there was more turmoil among the other smaller parties. Notably, the Party for the Animals and the Party for the Pensioners (50+) both went up from the two seats they held previously, the Animal Party to 5 and 50+ to 4 seats. Finally, two parties succeeded in entering parliament for the first time: the migrants-oriented party DenK with three seats and the conservative anti-establishment and anti-Europe party, Forum for Democracy with two.

Table 1: After election seat share of parties in Dutch Lower House

Parties	**2010**	**2012**	**2017**
VVD (Conservative Liberals)	31	41	33
PvdA (Labour Party)	30	38	9
CDA (Christian-Democrats)	21	13	19
PVV (Freedom Party)	24	15	20
D66 (Progressive Liberals)	10	12	19
SP (Socialist Party)	15	15	14
GroenLinks (Greens)	10	4	14
ChristenUnie (Christian-Union)	5	5	5
SGP (Calvinist Party)	2	3	3
PvdD (Party for the Animals)	2	2	5
50PLUS (pensioners party)		2	4
DenK (Diversity Movement)			3
Forum voor Democratie (Forum for Democracy)			2
Total seats	**150**	**150**	**150**
Number of parties	**10**	**11**	**13**

With this outcome, the formation of the new Dutch government was bound to take considerable time. By all indications, the core of the government coalition would need to be formed by the VVD, the CDA and D66. Geert Wilders' Freedom Party was ruled out as a credible coalition partners by all parties, including Wilders' former party, the VVD. In turn, its major losses also ruled the PvdA out as a credible partner.

Still, the combination VVD-CDA-D66 falls 5 seats short of the absolute majority of 76 seats that is usually needed for a stable government in the Netherlands. Hence, a fourth partner was needed. While attempts to involve GroenLinks, as the major election winner, into the coalition failed, negotiations turned to the Christian-Union. Negotiations lasted over the summer of 2017, but on 26 October a new majority government was inaugurated with the support of the four parties: VVD, CDA, D66 and the Christian-Union.

4. The evolving structure of Dutch politics

If we position the 2017 elections in the Netherlands in its broader historical context, it underlines the overarching trend of the demise of the big parties. This is a trend that of course has its parallels elsewhere; the absence of the classical big parties in the latest presidential run-off in France is a major example. Still, the trend in Dutch politics is particularly pronounced and steady. If we look at the three big parties that have been central to Dutch politics – CDA, PvdA and VVD – we see that they would take well over 80% or even over 90% of the parliamentary seats in the 1950s. Since then, their share has gone down, even if one or the other of them would sometimes bounce back at the cost of the others. Actually, until the mid-1970s there were three mainstream Christian-Democratic parties, with the Catholic KVP the most prominent one. As they saw their vote share decline, they merged into the CDA.

The party landscape that emerged from the mid-1970s onwards basically had the newly merged CDA in a pivotal positon in the middle. Depending on the election outcome, it would either form a coalition on its left-hand side with the Labour Party or on its right-hand side with the liberal-conservative VVD.

Figure 1: Evolution of the seat share of the three main parties in the Dutch parliament

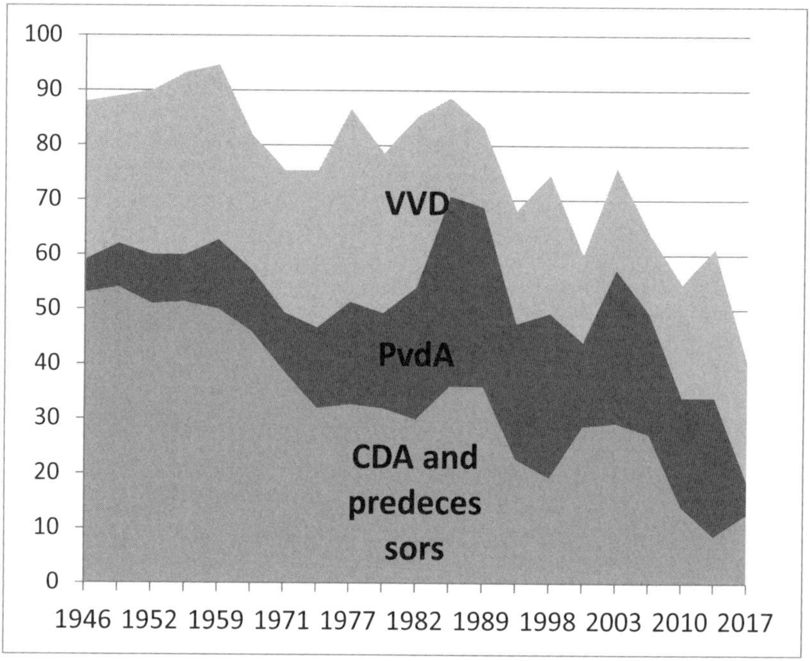

This straightforward left-right logic was however brutally disturbed when in 1994 the CDA had a disastrous election result dropping from 54 seats to 34. For the first time since 1917 no Christian parties were involved in the government coalition. Instead, Prime Minister Wim Kok formed a so-called "purple" coalition that joined his Labour Party with the liberal conservative VVD and the progressive liberals of D66.

While the purple coalition thus broke the hegemony of the Christian-Democrats, it also indicated that the ideological differences between the main Dutch parties had become very small, leaving little to choose for the average voter.

It is on this sense of a lack of electoral choice and a sense of closed-up elite politics that Pim Fortuijn successfully mobilized in the 2002 election campaign. As is well-known, Pim Fortuijn was shot by an animal activist in the week before the 2002 elections. But it is on the same kind of sentiments that Geert Wilders has been campaigning ever since he left the VVD-party in 2004: a disgust of the establishment and resentment against migrants (especially Muslim migrants) and against internationalism (especially European integration).

While the governing parties thus demonstrated that all combinations were possible and thus that all party differences were surmountable, voters – like in most Western countries – became ever less loyal to them. In the Netherlands, such loss of loyalty becomes easily visible as there is no threshold for new parties to enter the parliament and there is hence a considerable number of parties competing for the vote. Figure 2 demonstrates how voter volatility has shot up ever since the mid-1990s, with the 2017 elections coming second with 38 of the 150 seats transferred after 2002 (the Fortuijn election) when this was 46.

Figure 2: Seat transfers between parties per elections

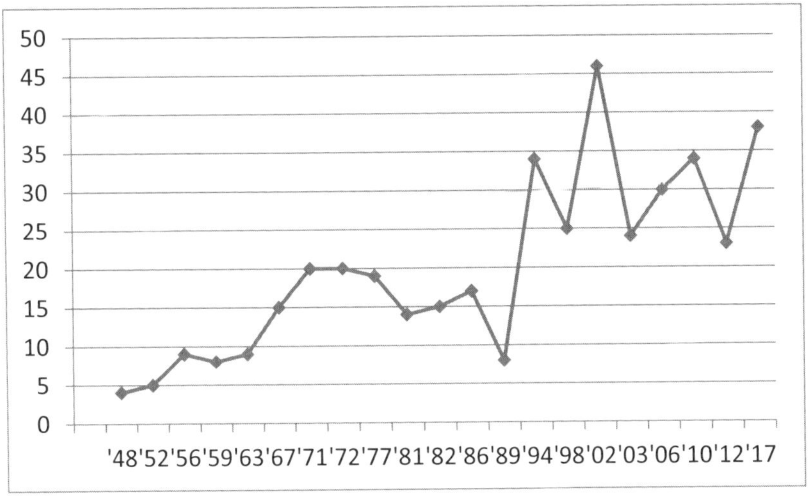

Presumably the increase of voter volatility also reflects a trend of ideological preferences becoming more diverse and less coherent (cf. Blumenstiel 2014). Voters vary on ever more dimensions. Ideological preferences in terms of left and right have become detached from preferences on ethical issues, on international cooperation, on the environment and on migration. In other words, we find a greater number of ideological combinations and, hence, voters inevitably have to compromise on some issues once they cast their vote for one party rather than another.

5. Populism and identity politics in the 2017 election campaign

The fragmentation of the ideological space in Dutch politics was also clearly apparent in the terms on which parties waged the election campaign towards the 2017 elections. While socio-economic (left-right) differences certainly played a role, parties invoked a wide range of themes to distinguish themselves from the others. Notably, for instance the Socialist Party put the issue of health care in the spotlight and campaigned for rolling back the previous privatization policies in the sector. Similarly, the Greens highlighted climate change-related issues.

Nevertheless, the key issue that overshadowed all others in the 2017 election campaign was the issue of Dutch identity, what it involves and how to demarcate 'good' Dutch citizens from the others. Obviously, this is an issue that reflects above all Geert Wilders' agenda, in which the Dutch identity is systematically opposed to the 'others' of Muslim immigrants and European integration. Wilders' prominence on the Dutch political scene and his high standing in the polls forced most of the other parties to clearly position themselves on the identity issue as well. Most notably, Prime Minister Mark Rutte decided early in the campaign to put out an advertisement in the main Dutch newspapers with a letter to all Dutchmen. Key message of this letter was a call to behave "normally". Notably, this call was not directed against any one misbehaving, but particularly pointed the finger at migrants. Thus, Rutte wrote: "We feel a growing unease when people abuse our freedom to mess things up around here, while they have actually come to our country because of that freedom. People who do not want to adjust, and who reject our habits and values. [...] Behave normally or go away" (Rutte 2017). Clearly, with this message, Rutte sought to appeal directly to voters who potentially would be attracted by Wilders' rhetoric.

But Rutte was not alone in adopting the identity issue. Christian-Democrat leader Sybrand Buma also adopted a harsh tone on migration and went public arguing that Dutch school children should learn the national anthem and sing it while standing. In turn, newly elected Labour leader Lodewijk Asscher gave his own spin to the identity focus by claiming his own kind of "progressive patriotism". Thus, Wilders was extremely successful in ensuring that identity politics, and the question who belongs to the 'right' Dutch people and who does not, became centre stage in the campaign.

The identity focus of the campaign was reinforced when in the week before the elections the Turkish government decided to send Turkish ministers to the Netherlands to hold campaign meetings for the upcoming constitutional referendum in Turkey. While there have been some candidates of Dutch parties who have made a particular effort to get the vote of Dutch expats, the public campaigning of Turkish AK politicians on Dutch soil came as direct provocation in the midst of the Dutch election campaign. The government and Prime Minister Rutte in particular were clear that this could not be tolerated and when the Turkish ministers did not withdraw voluntarily, they were eventually physically prevented from meeting in the Netherlands.

In the light of the general evolution of Dutch politics, it is important to observe that the identity issue is not just another issue but that it has the potential to become deeply divisive. The reason for this is that the emphasis on particular identities undermines the recognition that modern democratic societies are inherently plural and that politics under those conditions is exactly about creating conditions under which people with competing interests and competing values can nevertheless live peacefully together. In that sense, the identity issue fits perfectly the populist agenda, but it risks undermining the essential ability of political parties to reach out across societal differences.

In one of the first academic reflections of the Dutch 2017 elections, Catherine de Vries (2017) demonstrates that identity-related concerns about European integration, migration and national control in international affairs have indeed come to play a prominent role in Dutch voter decisions. Notably, however, De Vries adds that these new concerns "should not necessarily be understood as a cultural backlash, but rather seem a reflection of increased economic insecurity". The people who are more likely to adopt, what de Vries calls, "parochial" positions tend to be those with lower levels of education and with structural concerns about making ends meet. While these findings underline that cultural and economic concerns are often difficult to unravel empirically, I would even add disillusionment with the established political order as a third, logically related, feature.

6. Conclusion

In the end, the Dutch elections of 15 March 2017 underline that Dutch politics tends to become ever more fragmented, with the traditional big parties becoming medium-sized, and the need for no less than four parties to form any majority coalition. This tendency is reinforced by the way in which Wilders has led many of the mainstream parties to define themselves in identity terms, and to disassociate themselves from specific groups in Dutch society. One implication of this combination of political fragmentation and the prominence of identity politics is that building a stable government coalition becomes an ever-greater challenge. This is certainly underlined by the rather drawn out process of government formation that followed the 2017 elections in the Netherlands.

The second implication of the mix of political fragmentation and identity politics, which is of broader significance for European politics at large, is that even if anti-pluralist populist parties do not prevail, this does not mean they go away. On the contrary, anti-pluralist voices remain prominent in Dutch politics and are essentially waiting in the wings for the established parties to fail. This concerns of course above all Geert Wilders' PVV whose ideal prospect towards the next election might well be a broad-based coalition that leaves him as the main voice of the opposition. However, Wilders is not alone. The Forum voor Democratie is now the second party in parliament that consistently exploits the disillusionment with democratic politics as we know it.

Even if the case of the Netherlands is rather typical and distinct, it thus also raises fundamental questions about the place of anti-pluralist populism across the European continent. The first question is how European democracies can live with the continued presence of anti-pluralist populism in its midst. Although the support for anti-pluralist populists varies from country to country, this is also an urgent question in Italy, France, Germany, Austria, Finland, Hungary, Poland and Denmark. Here it is an open question whether populist parties can effectively be socialized into the pluralistic democratic process or whether, once they are handed the power, they are destined to undermine political pluralism. The only viable strategy here seems to be an empirical one that continuously monitors these parties on their words and actions: those parties that stand strong for pluralist democracy cannot leave unexposed any move to undermine the essentials of pluralist democracy: basic rights for all, a free and open press, the inviolability of the constitution and the rule of law, and no use of physical intimidation. Anti-pluralist parties often enough play by the game, and at times they may even be accommodated within pluralist institutions. However, their continuous presence should not make it possible for them to move the boundaries on the democratic essentials over time.

Continuous vigilance is no guarantee that anti-pluralist parties will not, sometimes, in some countries, get the upper hand, as they already have in Hungary and Poland. That raises the fundamental question what other European states can and should do when this happens (cf. Closa and Kochenov 2016). We cannot claim the right to interfere directly in domestic democratic process. However, it is hard to escape the impression that individual EU states, as well as the EU as a whole, have so far been rather unsuccessful in responding to the developments in Hungary and Poland. In any case, if countries are sliding into anti-pluralism, any turn-around eventually will have to come from within these countries themselves. Hence, an approach that focusses on compliance and insistence on the normative correctness of the European majority is likely to be unproductive. Instead, European responses are best guided by the question what is likely to be most helpful for pluralist movements in the countries concerned to facilitate their return to ascendancy.

In any case, events over the last few years have removed any illusions that the future of Europe will be decided in Brussels. Instead the fate of Europe will be decided in the member states. That is why national elections, and referendums, are of key importance. Europe cannot save individual states – that is something that they can only do themselves. Still, the Europe that is built on societal pluralism and international diversity should not become hostage to the courses adopted by individual member states. Hence, rather than responding to anti-pluralist movements in this or the other country, governments committed to pluralism and diversity are well-advised to form a European core that gathers around a positive agenda in which the basic values of pluralism, freedom and diversity are underlined and actively strengthened.

References

Bánkuti, Miklós/Halmai, Gábor/Scheppele, Kim Lane (2012): Hungary's Illiberal Turn: Disabling the Constitution. In: Journal of Democracy 23, 3, pp. 138-146.

Blumenstiel, Jan Eric (2014): Voter Fragmentation and the Differentiation of Vote Functions. In: Weßels, Bernard/Rattinger, Hans/Roßteutscher, Sigrid/Schmitt-Beck, Rüdiger (eds.): Voters on the Move or on the Run? Oxford: Oxford University Press, pp. 17-39.

Canovan, Margarat (1999): Trust the People! Populism and the Two Faces of Democracy. In: Political Studies 47, 1, pp. 2-16.

Closa, Carlos/Kochenov, Dimitry (eds.) (2016): Reinforcing Rule of Law Oversight in the European Union. Cambridge: Cambridge University Press.

De Vries, Catherine (2017): The cosmopolitan-parochial divide: changing patterns of party and electoral competition in the Netherlands and beyond. In: Journal of European Public Policy. Electronic pre-publication at http://dx.doi.org.vu-nl.idm.oclc.org/10.1080/13501763.2017.1339730

Jonker, Ulko (2017): Hoe de goede populist won van de verkeerde. In: Het Financieele Dagblad, 18 March 2017.

Müller, Jan-Werner (2015a): Should the EU protect democracy and the rule of law inside member states? In: European Law Journal 21, 2, pp. 141-60.

Müller, Jan-Werner (2015b): Parsing populism: Who is and who is not a populist these days? In: Juncture 22, pp. 80-89.

Müller, Jan-Werner (2016): What is Populism? Philadelphia: University of Pennsylvania Press.

Rutte, Mark (2017): Aan alle Nederlanders. In: NRC Handelsblad, 22 January 2017.

Schlipphak, Bernd/Treib, Oliver (2017): Playing the blame game on Brussels: the domestic political effects of EU interventions against democratic backsliding. In: Journal of European Public Policy 24, 3, pp. 352-365.

4. Europeanisation or renationalisation? The Czech Republic facing the euro-, economic and refugee crises

Vratislav Havlík

1. Introduction

Since its accession to the European Union (EU) more than a decade ago, foreign observers have described the Czech Republic (CR) as a country holding (sometimes more, sometimes less) Eurosceptic positions. Even by 2016, the country, in contrast to some other European states, had not adopted the common European currency, the euro, and due to the positions of the Eurosceptic former President Václav Klaus, the CR was the last of all Member States to ratify the Lisbon Treaty. The right-conservative government of Petr Nečas also refused to support the "Fiscal Pact", the EU instrument for resolving future economic crises. In connection with the so-called "Refugee Crisis", Czech politicians in 2016 actively joined in the formation of a Central European anti-immigration coalition, raising their voices against European Union proposals for a quota system for the distribution of refugees.

These Eurosceptic phenomena are even more interesting if we compare the CR to the situation in other Member States. The country was not hit particularly hard by the economic crisis relative to other European states. This is particularly true if the economic (as opposed to political) impacts of the crisis are considered. The duration of economic decline and the following stagnation was relatively short and was soon compensated for by significant growth. Not only did industrial growth foster economic growth, also money from the EU's Structural Funds did. Despite initial scepticism, the country received the good news that after the lucrative years of 2006-2013, it would still gain substantial amounts in the future. The CR is and, at least until 2020, will be a net recipient EU Member State, and the drop in funds for EU Regional Policy for 2014-2020 has been rather small. Considering these points, it would not be reasonable to expect a massive expansion in Eurosceptic discourse in the CR. Yet, Euroscepticism has nonetheless developed also in the CR. As this phenomenon is interesting for international comparative studies of Europeanisation and accompanying trends of Eurosceptic populism, the Czech case must therefore be further analysed. At first glance, the Czech case might seem paradoxical: in macroeconomic terms, the economic crisis was relatively moderate and short; yet it had significant consequences for the party system. These consequences were not necessarily direct; for instance, no single-issue anti-European party has established itself. The main trigger of change in the Czech party system was not so much the economic crisis itself as a broad dissatisfaction with how leaders sought to resolve it and other issues (cf. Hloušek/Kaniok 2014: 12). The electorate did not primarily call for parties that would solve EU issues differently; rather they called for new, non-traditional parties with fresh leadership. Indeed, the period since 2010 has been characterised by the Czechs' turning away from traditional parties and their embracing of emerging political parties and movements.

The aim of this chapter is twofold. First, to describe the influence of the economic crisis on the Czech party system, and second, to describe the growth of party and public Euroscepticism as one of the consequences of the economic crisis. The analysis consists of six parts. The second part briefly presents some key economic and labour market data. The third part analyses the role of former President Václav Klaus in the context of the debate around the economic crisis. As a known Eurosceptic, Klaus emerged as an agenda setter in the debates surrounding the crisis, warned about the disadvantages of future adoption of the euro in CR, and emphatically contributed to the Czech government's opposition to the steps taken by the European Commission to prevent future crises. Klaus therefore took advantage of the Eurozone's economic crisis to criticise the EU. In the fourth part, the reactions of political parties will be analysed. In this respect, attention will focus primarily on voters' dramatic shift away from the party which up to that point had been dominant, the ODS (Civic Democratic Party); to a certain extent this is also an indirect fallout from the economic crisis. Therefore, the topics of the stability of cleavages and the possible Europeanisation of patterns of party competition will also be discussed. The fifth part will focus on the Czech discussion concerned with the adoption of the euro; unlike the party system, this discussion was directly affected by the economic crisis. The sixth part will shed light on the position of the Czech public. The last part will examine the impacts of the ongoing migration crisis and compare them with the impacts of the economic crisis.

The argument developed in this chapter is based on (1) Eurobarometer and Czech Statistical Office data, (2) primary sources (newspaper articles and interviews, to map the public discourse) and (3) academic literature tracing the development of Czech Euroscepticism.

2. The European economic crisis and the debate in the CR

While the CR experienced a noticeable increase in unemployment after 2008 (see Graph 1), in absolute numbers this was in no way a massive increase. The same situation was observable in the case of the national budget deficit. While in 2008 the government spent over 86 billion CZK (2.2% of GDP) more than it took in, in 2009 this rose to 218 billion, and in 2010, 179 billion CZK. The situation calmed down by 2013, when the Czech national deficit returned to pre-crisis levels. However, these numbers are no cause for alarm considering the overall debt of the country. Government debt amounted to about 29% of GDP in 2008, 46% in 2013 and 43% in 2014. The country is thus still a long way away from approaching the 60% threshold that EU fiscal regulations consider the warning zone.

Graph 1: Unemployment in the CR, 2008-2014

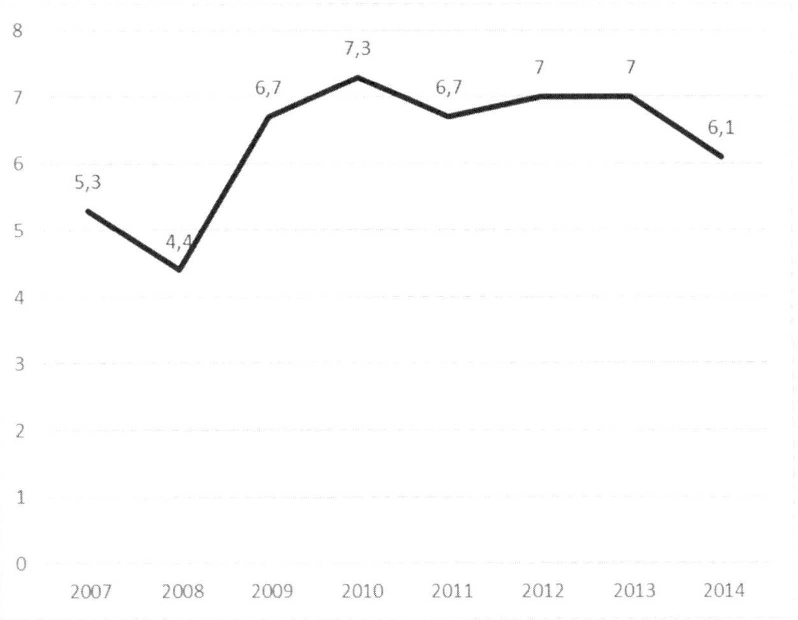

Source: Czech Statistical Office

In sum, it can be said that while a noted rise in unemployment and a visible (though not devastating) fall in economic performance occurred, the CR emerged from the crisis relatively unscathed if we compare it to countries in Western – and certainly Southern – Europe. Despite the low impact of the crisis on the CR, which, at least when looking at economic data, cannot be seen as catastrophic, significant changes in Czechs' identification with the EU, as well as in the party system, have occurred, driven by the Eurosceptic discourse of the Czech President.

3. Václav Klaus as a "driver" of Czech Euroscepticism

A key role in the debate on Europeanisation in the CR was played by Václav Klaus (Prime Minister 1992-1997, and later President 2003-2013) and with him his conservative-right party, the ODS (Civic Democratic Party). It was Václav Klaus, ODS chairman at the time, who in the mid-1990s had added the EU as one of his favourite topics of contention. While Klaus has been relatively consistent in his positions on the EU, during the late 90's, a change from a relatively moderate Eurosceptic view into a rather vocal critic of EU developments cannot be denied. During his presidential term (2003-2013), he made European integration one of his main issues. As President, he took advantage of key political duties of his office, and for ten years served as the agenda setter for European issues. As a famous critic of the current form of the EU Klaus paradoxically contributed to the Europeanisation of public discourse in the CR. This was not because key political parties agreed with him, but the opposite. In addition to "his" ODS (which did not always agree with him), he was often criticised for his "too anti-Europe" and "too pro-Russia" stances. His strategy of negative positions on the EU had a serious effect on the political debate in the CR. Practically all key political actors were dragged into the discussion and thus had to address the topic. Kopeček describes Klaus' politics in the following way.

> The skilled debater cleverly took advantage of the aura of the Presidency and successfully turned interviews toward topics that he wanted to discuss, or that he felt were a priority. He developed a full thematic repertoire, with specific modifications, additions, and emphases, which he maintained to the end of his Presidency. Its most visible aspect was the criticism of the direction of the EU (Kopeček 2012: 157).

Over the course of his term, he initiated heated debates over many major (in addition to a few minor) European issues, particularly about the Lisbon Treaty, the crisis of Greece, and the crisis of the Eurozone; more recently, after his term, the debate on the migrant crisis can be added to this list. In addition to well-known publications from that time (numerous essays, columns, and press interviews), he also critiqued the Union and addressed the economic crisis in multiple books, which gained a great deal of media attention. While it is not possible to model the past, the course of the discussion on various select topics associated with the EU (including the economic crisis) could have possibly been completely different had Václav Klaus not been in a key position at that time.

4. The influence of the economic crisis on the party system

Since 2004, Europeanisation has had no serious impact on the content and logic of Czech party politics. Although we can find some (relatively few) reactions to European issues in party manifestoes, the format of partisan competition has remained intact (Hloušek/Pšeja 2009: 534; Hloušek/Kopeček 2008; Hloušek/Kaniok 2014).

Ongoing research (Havlík/Havlík 2014) on the Europeanisation of Czech political parties indicates that the salience of European issues in party platforms has been relatively low for a long time – only 5.28% of all sentences concern the EU. The 2013 elections experienced no notable growth in the Europeanisation of party platforms (salience 6.61%). If the issue of economic crisis was mentioned, it occurred in a national, rather than European context. In the following analysis of the effects of the economic crisis, it is thus necessary to differentiate between the changes caused directly by European issues (Greek crisis, euro instability), and those that were merely secondary effects of the crisis that influenced Czech macroeconomic indicators (inflation, unemployment, economic growth).

The economic crisis had a visible effect on the party system of the CR, however indirect. It cannot be said that the weakening of established parties and the formation of new ones which took place between 2010 and 2013 was a direct effect of European issues as such. In other words, this was not the result of the emergence of a European issues cleavage – i.e. a nationalism-universalism cleavage. TOP 09 and Public Affairs, new parties that sprang up out of the protracted crisis of established parties, are rather interesting phenomena, but their formation cannot be seen as a result of the economic crisis. To a very limited extent, the case of TOP 09 relates to the topic of European integration vis-à-vis the Eurosceptic ODS. The issue of Europe was nevertheless a secondary element for the rise of TOP 09 and otherwise was in no way associated with the economic crisis.

After the crisis had mostly passed, the CR had a government under the leadership of the conservative Prime Minister Petr Nečas (ODS), resulting from the 2010 elections. The government was composed of three parties – ODS (conservative, Eurosceptic), TOP 09 (conservative, euro-optimistic) and Public Affairs (protest). The first major chance for conflict arose over the Fiscal Pact, which Prime Minister Nečas, together with British Prime Minister David Cameron, refused to sign. This step by Nečas somewhat divided his governmental coalition, as the other parties in the government were rather supportive. However, Nečas had the support of President Klaus, who thanked Nečas for refusing and who acted as a clever opinion maker during the whole affair (Lidovky.cz 2012). "For us it is totally unacceptable. The idea of shifting it to the Brussels technocrats, bureaucrats" (Česká televize 2012). The government weathered this crisis, but it demonstrated that the topic of Europe could act as a divisive factor on the Czech political scene. This was not the first time. While the issue of Europe in the context of Czech partisan competition has not been a cleavage for a long time, there exist particular situations in which the issue played an important role. The debate on Lisbon Treaty accession was certainly one of the reasons for the fall of the Mirek Topolánek (ODS) government in 2009. Europeanizing efforts were interpreted as "following Brussels' orders" and the entire debate was presented in an "us and them" tone. The Fiscal Pact was judged as unacceptable in the CR from the very start, as it was understood and explained as an attempt by Brussels to limit Czech sovereignty in deciding on its own budget.

The right-wing government of Petr Nečas reacted to the economic downturn with budget cuts and austerity. The problem, however, was the method selected for cutting back. The government, whose strongest party (ODS) was known for its sympathy for low taxes and its resistance to tax hikes, introduced a tax increase on high-income segments of the population in 2012 (Deník Referendum 2012). The deep cuts and the raising of taxes, for which the coalition parties (especially ODS) had to pay a steep political price, can be understood as one of the effects of the economic crisis, as Vít Hloušek and Petr Kaniok note:

> However, during a period of economic crisis, the government's austerity policy proved to be a double-edged sword. (…) The right-wing coalition not only made some unpopular restrictions in many policy areas, including welfare expenditure, but also increased indirect taxes (including VAT), contrary to both parties' pre-electoral declarations (Hloušek/Kaniok 2014).

The elections in 2013 thus only confirmed the trend that had started some years before. The party that gave the CR three Prime Ministers and had always won at least 20% of the votes (even exceeding 35% in 2006) received less than 8% in 2013, and thereby just barely surpassed the electoral threshold of 5%. The economic crisis was not the only factor contributing to the collapse of ODS, but the clumsy reaction of the governing elites to the crisis undoubtedly added to the party's marginalisation. For a party that instituted a 'flat tax' during its 2006-2009 term for all income segments of the population, even moderately progressive taxation was seen as a departure from right-wing policy, and as a strange and thoroughly 'leftist' step. The economic crisis and the fall of the main conservative party, however, did not imply the strengthening of its long-time rivals. Support for the opposition Social Democrats (ČSSD) also dropped in 2013, though they managed to limp to victory with a total of 20.45% of the vote. This was the worst result for ČSSD since 1992. Both 'main' parties competing for power (ODS and ČSSD), who combined won over two-thirds of the overall vote in 2006 (80% of the seats in the Chamber of Deputies), saw their combined support drop significantly in 2010 to only 42% and, in 2013, to paltry 28%.

Voters in the 2013 election turned to "new" solutions, among which were the newly formed parties ANO 2011 and the Dawn of Direct Democracy (Úsvit přímé demokracie). Both were the products of processes that had been unfolding for some years in the CR. These include a long-term lack of trust in the established elites and the issue of unsuccessful campaigns against corruption, as well as a climate of economic crisis and recession (Havlík 2015). Regarding the vote count, ANO is particularly interesting: it is led by multi-billionaire Andrej Babiš, who identified himself as a non-politician that wanted to run the country like a business. This is outlined by Kopeček (2016a: 744), who explains the origin of ANO and its specificity:

> The leader's appeal aimed at the removal of politicians and in fact the elimination of politics as such. The effect of this appeal was to significantly strengthen the repercussions of the centre-right government's scandalous fall in the summer of 2013, pushing the established party system towards collapse.

It is pointless to address the rise of this populist party in the context of Europeanisation, as the party itself never discusses Europe. ANO has never substantively addressed the topic of Europe, nor does it have a deeply developed program. The rise of this party, however, is one of the many by-products of the economic crisis and as such is interesting in the debate on transformations in the Czech party system. As Vlastimil Havlík (2015: 212) points out, "the worsening economic situation in the Czech Republic served as another opportunity for criticism of the established political parties and governments." In other words, the emergence of ANO 2011 occurred as a response to the established elite, while the ongoing crisis served as a convenient cudgel for criticizing the economic steps of the government. ANO 2011 and ODS did not compete over European issues in the 2013 elections. The economic crisis and austerity, however, greatly influenced voters' attitudes, determining the course of the campaign as well as the election results. The Czech system after the 2013 elections thus has seen extensive reshaping of the party landscape and growing fragmentation of the party system overall (Havlík et al. 2014). The system currently is not in a condition in which the current socio-economic, i.e. left-right, cleavage should be discounted, but experts should continue to give extra attention to current unfolding changes (Hloušek/Kaniok 2014: 11-12).

5. The partisan debate about joining the European common currency

In the CR, the economic crisis nevertheless had one fundamental effect, this time directly. The ailing debate on adopting the common European currency taking place before the crisis was essentially finished. This can be seen in the opinion of Miroslav Kalousek, the conservative (though pro-European) Finance Minister, who already had doubts about Euro adoption in October 2008.

> I have always been convinced that an early adoption date for the euro is the correct path. But at a moment when many Eurozone countries say that the Stability and Growth Pact must not be essential and important, we must carefully think about a Eurozone entry date (Idnes.cz 2008).

This was the same minister who in May 2007 had explicitly proposed an adoption date of January 1, 2012 (Novinky.cz 2007). The Prime Minister and head of the Eurosceptic ODS eventually shelved euro adoption indefinitely in 2010, de facto arguing that it would be a poor fit for the CR in the long term. For them, adoption of the common currency would only be possible when "the costs of keeping the crown outweigh the costs of joining the euro" (Idnes.cz 2010). After that point, Czech parties practically began to compete over who least wanted to deal with euro adoption. The Euro-optimistic Social Democrats, led by Bohuslav Sobotka, proposed a date of around 2020 shortly after taking power in 2014 (Česká televize 2014). However, under pressure not from economic forces, but clearly political ones, the PM had to backtrack on quick euro adoption. Not only did he announce that his government would not set a date for euro adoption, he approached euro adoption in general rather sceptically. "If we do not achieve balanced budgets and continue with convergence, then we cannot propose a date for euro adoption" (České noviny 2016).

For an analysis of the reasons why Czech political parties have for all practical purposes ruled out timely adoption of the euro, it is necessary to look at changing public discourse over time, and hand in hand with it the course of the economic crisis. From the point of view of agenda setting, the coalition party ANO has presented itself very pragmatically since 2014; at every step, the party keeps an eye on public opinion, which has not been favourable. Babiš thus began to explore the idea of a referendum, but after a long time explained that while he was an opponent of the euro, he also saw its advantages. In the media, however, he more often focused on disadvantages. "Everybody knows that Greece doesn't pay its debts" (Česká televize 2015). He increasingly hinted at his stance against adoption of the common currency.

> As long as I am Minister of Finance and Greece is a member of the Eurozone, I will be against entry. The Eurozone has rules for new members to enter, but it doesn't know how to deal with those who should leave, with those who don't belong there (Ministry of Finance of the CR 2015).

In this situation, when a key coalition partner refuses to discuss the adoption of the European currency, and the Social Democrats led by the Prime Minister announce that euro adoption is not domestically suitable, then the euro issue in the CR is virtually dead, or at least dormant for the next several years. It is thus not necessary to dwell on the fact that the current refusal to debate about euro adoption has not been about the lack of fulfilment of the convergence criteria, as the CR in recent years has fulfilled all the adoption conditions (inflation, national budget deficit, overall national debt, and interest rates of the central bank) except for participation in the European Exchange Rate Mechanism (which was a conscious decision). As pointed out above, the stifling of debate on setting a date for euro adoption can be seen in the very low level of public support for such a step. While there was clear support for euro adoption by the Czech population in 2001-2005 (always over 50%, see CVVM 2015), in 2006-2009, the opposition camp started to balance out supporters, and by the peak of the crisis, in 2010, the number of opponents to euro adoption dramatically rose to around three-quarters of the respondents. Resistance to the euro began to fall slightly after 2014, but public opinion polls still indicate that Czechs are solidly opposed to adopting the euro. Thus, party-political resistance to euro adoption largely became established during the economic crisis. New obligations that would be placed on the CR in connection with euro adoption – in particular the risk of having to contribute to emergency bailouts of other eurozone members – are being highlighted. Therefore, the delay in euro adoption can be seen as one of the few direct impacts on the CR of the economic crisis in the eurozone.

6. The influence of the economic crisis on society

The Czech population clearly felt the economic crisis and issues related to it, such as loans for a bankrupt Greece and other southern states, the formation of a European mechanism for solving the crisis, etc. It is only possible to speculate about direct reasons for increasing Czech dissatisfaction with the EU, whether the reason was the loans to Greece, or instead news about growing unemployment in the CR. However, the fact is that affection for the EU among Czechs fell sharply during the crisis. On the basis of Eurobarometer, in the period shortly after the accession of CR to the EU, between slightly less than half and half of those polled supported Czech membership in the Union, while only about 10% regarded membership as a "bad thing." The number of EU opponents began to increase after 2008; more interestingly, however, there is a clear decline in the number of those who regarded the EU as a "good thing," which originally hovered around 50% in 2008, but fell to around 30% in 2010.[1]

Graph 2: Generally speaking, do you think that (your country's) membership of the EU is...?

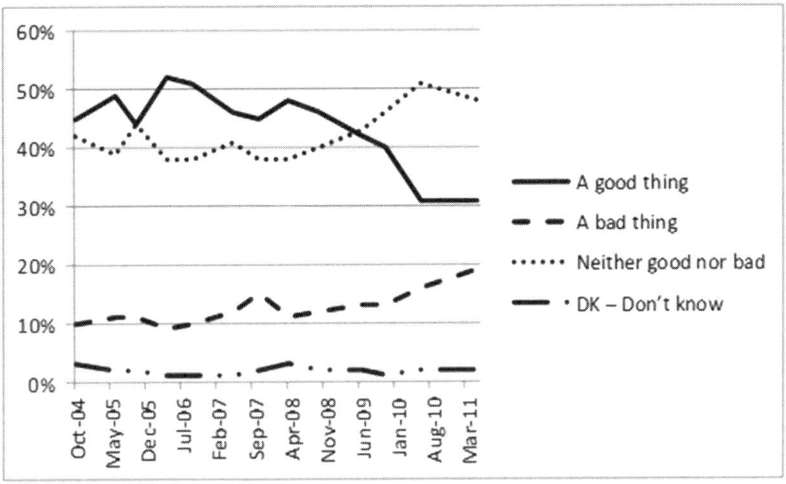

Source: Eurobarometer Surveys

These and similar statistics illustrate that while in 2006 the EU had a "very positive" or "fairly positive" image for about half of Czechs, by 2009 this number began to steeply slide; in 2013, only a fifth shared this feeling, with opponents of the EU over 35%. Slight growth in the positive image of the EU among Czechs occurred after 2012, incidentally correlating with the marked upturn in the Czech economy and the fall in unemployment. The relatively negative relationship of the Czech population to the Union is reflected in the context of election results (especially in the founding of the populist Dawn party) as well as in the context of the debate on euro adoption in the CR, which parties

1 This type of statistic was used by Eurobarometer until 2011; from that time on there is no available data from Eurobarometer on this question.

avoided (see above) because they were conscious of the fact that it had little support among Czechs.

Graph 3: In general, does the European Union conjure up for you a very positive, fairly positive, neutral, fairly negative, or very negative image?

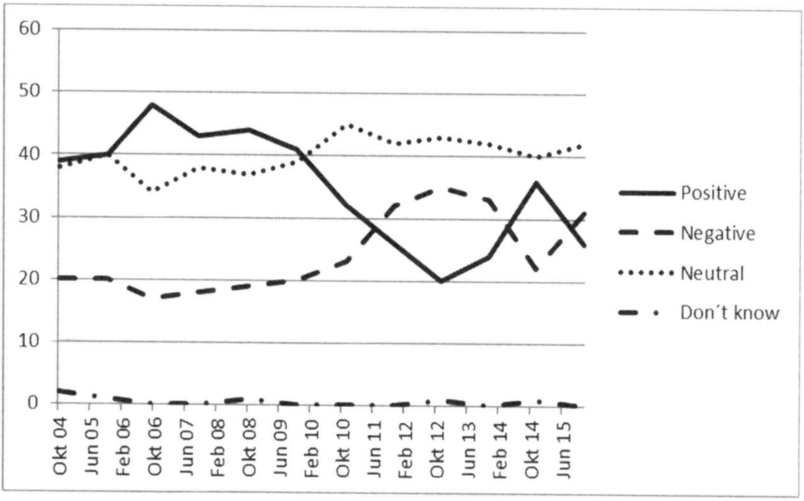

Source: Eurobarometer Surveys

7. The migration crisis: a new wave of Euroscepticism?

Shortly after the return of economic stability and strong growth, the CR was faced with another "crisis," this time of immigration. Its course is particularly interesting in the CR, as the migration wave skipped the country and the number of "new" migrants located in the CR in 2015 and 2016 was only in the dozens; however, "history" repeated itself and Eurosceptic groups as well as coalition parties inveighed against EU immigration policy. As Graph 3 shows, the image of the EU, which began to quickly improve in 2013, reached its peak in 2014 and followed a steep downward course in 2015 correlating with the migration crisis.

The reaction of Czech politicians to the migration crisis was similar to the "debate" on the adoption of the common currency. The clearly oppositional position of the Czech public had a likely effect on the position of the political elite. Just as with the case of the common currency, the degree of consensus among the political elite regarding their opposition to the "German solution" has been remarkable. Parties of the right as well as the left have come out against a quota system on the distribution of refugees. Indeed, party elites have generally called for reinforcing the internal borders of the Schengen area (Idnes.cz 2016). The relative agreement across the political spectrum, irrespective of whether from a traditionally pro-Europe or from a Eurosceptic party, is a key factor here. Even the strongly pro-Europe TOP 09 issued a press release outlining a change in their platform, calling for a *de facto* cap on immigration. This can be seen in phrases such as "The establishment of more rigorous asylum regulations and their strict maintenance" or "The creation of asylum centres outside of Europe under international protection" (TOP 09 2016). The traditionally pro-Europe Christian Democrats also reacted similarly, speaking of "the rejection of any obligatory distribution quotas, which does not address the situation as such, but merely its effects" (see the KDU-ČSL website). In other words, the admission of refugees is outside politically acceptable boundaries in the CR and rejection of this step forms the basis of discussion, with various levels of severity. Other parties have opposed the allocation quotas as well; ODS and ANO 2011 (as well as the Communists, indirectly, see Týden.cz 2015) have even called for filing a complaint at the European Commission, similarly to what Slovakia and Hungary have done.

Generally speaking, Czech politicians are largely sceptical about taking in refugees, with widely varying degrees of radicalism regarding this "unified" scepticism. Another important aspect of the formation of the parties' final positions is the fact that these rather sceptical positions regarding migrants were obstructed by their own members. Indeed, this may be why they did not adopt more radical positions: The elites of various parties (particularly TOP 09 and ČSSD) have sometimes been incapable of deciding on even basic positions regarding the crisis, and individual opinions of party elites have ranged from clearly anti-immigrant to enthusiastically pro-immigration (though these are rather unusual). Up to this point, the immigration issue has not become permanently entrenched in the Czech political debate, and instead has manifested itself in waves whenever the CR was forced to take a position on distribution quotas. Lubomír Kopeček (2016b: 3) sees crisis potential lurking behind this relatively quiet situation:

> The migrant crisis will continue to have a significant impact on Czech politics and society and may disrupt government unity. The gap between a well-educated urban population advocating for tolerance and the majority of the society that rejects refugees will provide an opportunity for political mobilisation, which could be exploited by President Zeman and others.

The dissatisfaction of the general population may indeed be too tempting for political parties, as it could be converted into votes. Other than small organisations like the Bloc against Islam, SPD (Freedom and Direct Democracy) and

The Dawn of Direct Democracy, parties have resisted the temptation to exploit the migration crisis as a wedge issue up to this point, but that could change with the approach of elections to the Chamber of Deputies (which take place in 2017) and the presidential election at the beginning of 2018.

8. Renationalisation or Europeanisation? The Czech Republic after the crises

The economic crisis has left clear marks on the CR. While in 2017 it is a prospering country, with very low unemployment and strong economic growth, some changes that the crisis brought have revealed themselves to be more permanent. Among these was the significant fall in support for parties which we would describe in the entire 20-year post-Velvet-Revolution era (1989-2009) as "traditional" (ODS in particular, but also ČSSD). Parties with a completely different style of doing politics than the established parties were familiar with anchored themselves in the party system. The transformation of the style of "how to do politics" to a large extent coincided with the aforementioned growth of the protest character of parties and also with the general growth in populism. The drop in support of "traditional" parties, however, cannot be explained through the Europeanisation of patterns of party competition. Even after 2010, the presence of the topic of "Europe" in partisan competition remained barely noticeable and generally very low. If any instability shook the Czech party system, it was at most an indirect effect of the crisis. The changes in the Czech party system were therefore not primarily initiated by an economic shock, but rather by an ill-advised response on the part of the government party, the ODS, which pushed through increased taxation of the rich. In terms of its financial effect, the latter was largely symbolic and failed to bring much into the state coffers, but it was seen by the party's electorate as a betrayal of its programme.

The economic crisis left marks not only on the party system. The long-discussed adoption of the Euro has been put off indefinitely. All efforts of parties to discuss an adoption date have evaporated, first for the reason that ANO, a key government party, is disinclined to adopt the common currency, and also because the public is against it (both reasons are likely interrelated). In society overall, Eurosceptic stances have proliferated, which is demonstrated by statistics concerning citizen support for the European Union and Czech EU membership.

From a long-term perspective, it appears that Europeanisation is a very volatile phenomenon and fails to show any clear trends. From the perspective of the salience of European issues in party platforms, we see a relatively low degree of Europeanisation, as debate on the content of individual policies often collapses into mentioning EU financial advantages, which for the country means receiving money from the EU structural funds. The exceptions to this have only been the running discussion (or public hysteria) regarding the ratification of the Lisbon Treaty and currently the migration crisis. Creeping renationalisation, which is offered as a name for the phenomena occurring in the CR during the crisis, may be a possible expression to describe current politics as well, though it is too early to evaluate it with equal confidence. As the chapter shows, since around 2014, a slight but definite correction of trends caused by the crisis (dissatisfaction with the Union, number of opponents of euro adoption) has occurred. It is therefore an open question of how Czechs' relationship with the EU will unfold in the following years in light of the unforeseeable development of the migration crisis.

References

All online sources accessed January 2, 2017.

Česká televize (2012): Klaus. Euro je katastrofa. Česká televize, April 5 (http://www.ceskatelevize.cz/ct24/ekonomika/1180130-klaus-euro-je-katastrofa).

Česká televize (2014): Sobotka plánuje přijetí Eura vroce 2020. Pro je prezident i část opozice. Česká televize, April 4 (http://www.ceskatelevize.cz/ct24/ekonomika/1038935-sobotka-planuje-prijeti-eura-v-roce-2020-pro-je-prezident-i-cast-opozice).

Česká televize (2015): Babiš. K přijetí Eura by se Češi měli vyjádřit v referendu. Česká televize, May 31 (http://www.ceskatelevize.cz/ct24/domaci/1532640-babis-k-prijeti-eura-se-cesi-meli-vyjadrit-v-referendu).

České noviny (2016): Sobotka. Při přijetí Eura potřebuje ČR zlepšit veřejné finance. České noviny, January 29 (http://www.ceskenoviny.cz/zpravy/sobotka-pro-prijeti-eura-potrebuje-cr-zlepsit-verejne-finance/1308829).

CVVM (2015): Občané o přijetí eura a dopadech vstupu ČR do EU – duben 2015 (http://cvvm.soc.cas.cz/media/com_form2content/documents/c1/a7382/f3/pm150512.pdf).

Czech Statistical Office (www.czso.cz).

Deník Referendum (2012): Klub ODS se drolí. Proti zvyšování daní jsou nejméně dva poslanci.

Deník Referendum, September 4 (http://denikreferendum.cz/clanek/13878-klub-ods-se-droli-proti-zvysovani-dani-jsou-nejmene-dva-poslanci.

Eurobarometer Surveys (http://ec.europa.eu/public_opinion/index_en.htm).

Hanley, Seán (2012): Dynamics of new party formation in the Czech Republic 1996–2010. Looking for the origins of a 'political earthquake'. In: East European Politics 28, 2, pp. 119-143.

Havlík, Vlastimil (2015): The Economic Crisis in the Shadow of Political Crisis. The Rise of Party Populism in the Czech Republic. In: Kriesi, Hanspeter/Pappas, Takis S. (eds.): Populism in the Shadow of the Great Recession. Colchester: ECPR Press, pp. 199-216.

Havlík, Vlastimil et al. (2014): Volby do Poslanecké sněmovny 2013. Brno: munipress.

Havlík, Vratislav/Havlík, Vlastimil (2014): From the Return to Europe to Easy Money. Europeanization of Party Manifestoes in the Czech Republic. In: Liberal or other democracy? 25 years after the "Annus mirabilis" in Central Europe. 19th Annual Conference of Central European Political Science Association.

Hloušek, Vít/Kaniok, Petr (2014): Europe and the 2013 Czech Parliamentary Election, October 25-26 2013. In: EPERN Election Briefing 74.

Hloušek, Vít/Kopeček, Lubomír (2008): Cleavages in Contemporary Czech and Slovak Politics. Between Persistence and Change. In: East European Politics and Societies 22, 3, pp. 518-552.

Hloušek, Vít/Pšeja, Pavel (2009): Europeanization of Political Parties and the Party System in the Czech Republic. In: Journal of Communist Studies and Transition Politics 25, 4, pp. 513-539.

Idnes.cz (2008): Kalousek si rozmýšlí rychlé zavedení Eura. Nesouhlasí sreakcí eurozóny na krizi. Idnes.cz, October 11 (http://ekonomika.idnes.cz/kalousek-si-rozmysli-rychle-zavedeni-eura-nesouhlasi-s-reakci-eurozony-na-krizi-gpb-/ekonomika.aspx?c=A081011_091456_ekonomika_vem).

Idnes.cz (2010): Nečas. termín zavedení Eura současná vláda řešit nebude. Idnes.cz, December 5 (http://ekonomika.idnes.cz/necas-termin-zavedeni-eura-soucasna-vlada-resit-nebude-p1n-/ekonomika.aspx?c=A101205_132258_ekonomika_spi).

Idnes.cz (2016): Postoj Bavorska k migraci je nám blízký, pochválil Sobotka kritika Merkelové. Idnes.cz, January 13 (http://zpravy.idnes.cz/sobotkovi-se-libi-bavorsky-postoj-k-migraci-fzk-/domaci.aspx?c=A160113_210102_domaci_pku).

KDU-ČSL (www.kdu.cz).

Klaus, Václav (2011): Evropská unie bez iluzí. Praha: Knižní klub.

Kopeček, Lubomír (2012): Fenomén Václav Klaus. Brno: Barrister & Principal.

Kopeček, Lubomír (2016a): "I'm Paying, So I Decide": Czech ANO as an Extreme Form of a Business-Firm Party. In: East European Politics and Societies 30, 4, pp. 725-749.

Kopeček, Lubomír (2016b): Czech Republic. In: Nations in Transit. Freedom House (https://freedomhouse.org/sites/default/files/NiT2016%20Czech%20Republic.pdf).

Lidovky.cz (2012): Klaus pochválil Nečase. Jednal jako zodpovědný politik. Lidovky.cz, January 31 (http://www.lidovky.cz/klaus-pochvalil-necase-jednal-jako-zodpovedny-politik-pps-/zpravy-domov.aspx?c=A120131_164855_ln_domov_ogo).

Ministry of Finance of the Czech Republic (2015): Andrej Babiš. dokud budu ministrem financí a Řecko veurozóně, budu proti přijetí Eura (http://www.mfcr.cz/

cs/aktualne/v-mediich/2015/andrej-babis-dokud-budu-ministrem-financ-22112).
Novinky.cz (2007): Kalousek chce přijetí Eura vroce 2012. Novinky.cz, May 10 (https://www.novinky.cz/ekonomika/114800-kalousek-chce-prijeti-eura-v-roce-2012.html).
Pravec, Josef (2015): Babiš hledá šafáře a ideologii. Ano se mění vpravicovou stranu. Ihned.cz, February 27 (http://ekonom.ihned.cz/c1-63599780-babis-hleda-safare-a-ideologii-ano-se-meni-v-pravicovou-stranu).
TOP 09 (2016): Devět priorit TOP09 pro řešení migrační krize (http://www.top09.cz/proc-nas-volit/fakta-a-argumenty/devet-priorit-top-09-pro-reseni-migracni-krize-19646.html).
Týden.cz (2015): ODS: Buď lhal o kvótách Sobotka, nebo tajemník Prouza. Týden.cz, September 29 (http://www.tyden.cz/rubriky/domaci/politika/ods-bud-lhal-o-kvotach-sobotka-nebo-tajemnik-prouza_357322.html).

Abbreviations

Title	**Abbreviaton**
Central and East Europe	CEE
Civic Democratic Party (Občanská demokratická strana)	ODS
Czech Republic	CR
Czech Social Democratic Party (*Česká strana sociálně demokratická*)	ČSSD
European Union	EU
Freedom and Direct Democracy (Svoboda a přímá demokracie)	SPD

5. In the wake of the economic crisis: The empowerment of (un-)civil society in Greece

Dimitri A. Sotiropoulos

1. Introduction

Civil society has long been associated with the consolidation and maintenance of young democracies (Diamond 1994) as well as with the higher or lower performance of institutions in advanced democracies (Putnam 1993). Civil society is understood here as a pluralist socio-political arena, which includes Non-Governmental Organisations (NGOs), professional associations, charities, labour unions, grass-roots movements, and informal, local and national networks of citizens, expressing their concerns and delivering services to people in need, all of which play a fundamental role in legitimizing democratic governance. Civil society plays such a role by continuously trying to approximate representative, participatory and deliberative norms (Liebert/Trenz 2011: 27). This function is put at risk in the context of an economic crisis.

After the onset of an economic crisis, civil society associations, in addition to contributing to representativeness, responsiveness and accountability of democratic institutions, may become vehicles of social protest. Social solidarity networks may step in, to help people who have fallen in poverty or social exclusion and have limited or no access to welfare institutions. In such instances, civil society becomes a protagonist of political developments and social innovation. It is in such moments that civil society can best develop its potential to overcome the regulatory deficits and the democratic shortfalls of modern democracies (Liebert/Trenz 2011: 7). These twin deficits are created by the increasing complexity of the problems which national governments and supra-national entities, such as the European Union (EU), are called upon to solve in a rapidly changing international environment.

The type of impact of a strong civil society depends on its organisation and values. Associational life may be vibrant not only because citizens pursue political liberties, but also because of the mobilisation of organisations and groups pursuing illiberal causes or motivated by exclusionist (e.g. racist) values. Groups which constitute an "uncivil society" (Kopecky/Mudde 2003) may even violate human rights in order to implement what they believe is a higher-order cause (e.g. an ethnically homogeneous society, a stateless egalitarian society, etc.). In such cases, the strengthening of civil society may lead to the undermining of democracy (Berman 1997). The examples of extremely radical, anti-parliamentary leftist groups or of neo-Nazi, racist, anti-migrant groups which have resorted to political violence in Greece after the economic crisis had erupted, illustrate this point.

In what follows, I will first present some basic information on the social effects of the economic crisis in Greece, discuss civil society before the economic crisis and then analyse how civil society has evolved in the wake of the crisis. I focus on social protest and social solidarity activities and also instances of uncivil society. I will conclude arguing that civil society has been empowered since the onset of the economic crisis, but it has followed varying trajectories, some of which do not necessarily lead to positive political developments and social innovation.

2. The economic crisis

In May 2010, Greece faced the prospect of a chaotic default, owing to its inability to service its soaring public debt (129 per cent of the GDP in 2009). The first Memorandum of Understanding (MoU), signed between the Greek government and the "Troika" of International Monetary Fund (IMF), European Commission and European Central Bank (ECB) in May 2010 was accompanied by a set of austerity measures in return for necessary loans. However, Greece's public debt kept increasing. As the aims of the first Memorandum were only partly achieved, a similar, second Memorandum was signed between Greece and its creditors in February 2012. Austerity measures produced economic recession and dramatic social consequences (Giannitsis/Zografakis 2015). Compared to the period before the crisis, unemployment and social exclusion soared (Table 1).

Since 2010, successive governments have cut salaries and pensions, raised income and property taxes and rolled back the Greek welfare state. These were the socialist party "Panellinio Sosialistiko Kinima" (PASOK) government in 2009-2011; the coalition government of PASOK and the conservative New Democracy party (ND) which, supported by smaller parties on their right or on their left, stayed in power in 2011-2014; and the Coalition of the Radical Left (Syriza) which won two consecutive elections in January and September 2015 and twice formed a government coalition with the far-right party "Independent Greeks" (Anel). After a short-lived attempt to reverse the Memorandum policies on its own in 2015, the Syriza-Anel coalition government signed another

Memorandum with Greece's creditors and continued the austerity policies of its predecessors. How did civil society react to the welfare retrenchment and economic austerity?

Table 1. The social consequences of the economic crisis in Greece

		2008	2013	2015
Unemployment rate	8%	28%	24%	
Youth unemployment		22%	59%	50%
Share of people at risk of poverty or social exclusion	28%	35%	36%	

Source: Eurostat, http://ec.europa.eu/eurostat/data/database

3. Civil society in post-1974 Greece

After Greece's transition from authoritarian rule in 1974, only a few segments of civil society grew, consisting of well-organised liberal professions and public sector workers, while the majority of NGOs, informal networks and social movements remained underdeveloped (Mouzelis/Pagoulatos 2005, Clarke/Huliaras/Sotiropoulos 2015). Civic activism was noticeable only in very few policy sectors, such as in environmental policy, yet environmental NGOs were rarely consulted by policy-makers. Voluntarism did not develop either, except for a brief period before the Athens Olympic Games of 2004.

The reason for civil society's underdevelopment was the early emergence of strong party organisations, such as the organisations of the socialist (PASOK) and communist parties (KKE, KKE Interior) and later that of the conservative party (ND), which created their front organisations or factions after the democratic transition of 1974. Examples were party-led factions within the labour movement, the civil service, the personnel of state-owned enterprises (SOEs), the local government, the student movement and even the women's movement. For instance, the nationwide Confederation of Workers of Greece (GSEE), which was completely dominated by unionists of the banks and the SOEs, and the corresponding confederation of civil servants (ADEDY), reacted or refrained from reacting to government policy measures, depending on whether the governing party controlled the majority in the leading organs of the confederations or not.

As a result, parties were present in every single sector of civil society, stifling any autonomous collective action. At the same time, the central government also intervened by subsidizing the functioning of particular civic associations, as ministers had a free hand in distributing funds to associations of their electoral district in a typical patronage fashion (Mavrogordatos 1993).

4. Civil society after the onset of the economic crisis: social protest

After having signed the first Memorandum of Understanding (MoU) with the Troika in May 2010, the government faced strong opposition from various social groups against the austerity policies it had decided to adopt. Opposition activities included frequent strikes, demonstrations and sit-ins by labour unions (Tsakatika/Eleftheriou 2013). Social protest was not spearheaded by the most negatively affected groups, such as the unemployed and the private sector employees, but by the self-employed, including professionals, and the relatively highly paid SOE employees. For example, in 2010-2014 owners of trucks and taxis frequently blocked traffic circulation in order to resist the government's decision to provide new licences for trucks and taxis, thus opening what was a 'closed shop' occupation. Similarly, pharmacists closed their businesses to resist the government's plan to grant licences for new pharmacies. Public sector unions frequently went on strike resisting any sort of change, not only salary decreases. For instance, in the winter of 2010-2011 public bus drivers went on repeated strikes, resisting the government's decision to transfer excess personnel from the public bus company to other SOEs.

The Indignant People's Movement

The most visible social movement after the crisis broke out was the movement of the 'indignant people' gathering in the square in front of the Greek Parliament for three months between May and July 2011. Participants of the 'indignant' movement believed that all other channels of political expression and political participation were closed off to them and that the government had stopped listening to the people.

Demonstrators gathered daily on the square to protest the austerity measures of the government and to experiment with direct democracy (general assembly of all those present, local referenda). They disputed parliamentarianism, condemned the political class in its entirety, and tolerated some violence against politicians, when politicians and journalists, passing by the square, were physically attacked (Kollia 2012, reporting field research by Vassiliki Georgiadou).

The "Won't Pay" Movement

The "Won't Pay" movement emerged after the state-owned public transportation companies in Athens and Thessaloniki announced increases in the price of bus tickets in 2010. The movement also fought against price hikes on toll fees imposed by the privately-owned companies building and maintaining Greece's national highways. The reasons behind the emergence of this movement lay in the widespread perception that while the government was cutting wages and salaries, in the context of Greece's economic adjustment, it was reluctant to control the cost of utilities (such as public transportation or electricity) in a commensurate manner.

A different kind of "Won't Pay" movement emerged in 2011. When the government saw that the tax collecting authorities were unable to meet their tax revenue targets as the year was coming to close, it imposed a new tax on home ownership. The government announced that this tax would be proportional to the size of property owned by tax payers and would be included in the electricity bills of the Public Power Corporation (DEI), the single provider of electricity in the country. In reaction, there were public calls, including a call by Syriza's leader, Alexis Tsipras, not to pay the electricity bills.

Sit-ins and occupation movements

Although the occupying of state-owned buildings by protesters was not a new phenomenon in Greece, it acquired new proportions during the crisis. Between 2005-2009 there had been frequent occupations of university buildings, during left-wing protests against the passage of university reforms. Starting in mid-2010, public sector employees began protesting salary cuts by occupying the headquarters of the Ministries of Finance, Development, Health and Labour, while Syriza and other left-wing party factions of students captured university buildings. In parallel, the communist-led labour union "All-Workers Militant Front" (PAME), which already before the crisis had split from the GSEE, periodically attained international publicity by occupying the Acropolis and the port of Piraeus.

Explaining social protest after the onset of the crisis

The post-crisis social protest can be explained on various grounds. First, the adoption of harsh austerity policies in 2010 by a government, i.e. the PASOK government, just half a year after it had come to power on the promise to adopt expansionist policies, naturally sparked protest. The adopted policies were class biased, distributing the burden of Greece's economic adaptation in an unequal manner, which disproportionately affected the salaried strata.

Secondly, long-term cultural patterns of Greek politics are conducive to radical social protest. There is widespread belief that governments cannot be trusted and that the only possible logic of political interaction is a zero-sum logic, which renders a consensual outcome of policy making improbable. Moreover, the long-term political party polarisation between ND and PASOK in 1981-2011 had also diffused an understanding of politics which does not aim at negotiation and compromise, but only at the complete victory of one side over the other.

Thirdly, after the elections of 2012, when a new bipolar party system emerged, a new pattern of polarisation crystallised. The old, acute feud between ND – PASOK was replaced by a new fiercer rivalry between the government coalition of ND and PASOK, on the one hand, and Syriza, on the other. Depending on the policy issue, the communist KKE and extra-parliamentary left would side with Syriza or pursue their own opposition tactics. Therefore, one cannot characterize all protests as signs of revitalisation of civil society during the crisis in Greece. For instance, while part of the occupation movement emerged as a result of civic action against the austerity policies, another part was the result of short-term political calculations by Syriza, KKE or the extra-parliamentary Left.

To sum up this section, it is debatable to what extent social protests in 2010-2014, particularly the mobilisation of civil servants and students, are a manifestation of a rising civil society in the context of a severe economic crisis, or whether it is an outgrowth of political party competition. Left-wing party organisations were heavily involved in all the aforementioned social movements. However, the size of the extremely unpopular austerity measures implemented after Greece's first bailout (May 2010), and replicated with new measures of the second bailout (February 2012), was so large, that even pro-government voters protested against austerity. Still, the large-scale grassroots mobilisation of civil society gave its way to more strategic modes of party political mobilisation. Opposition parties, such as Anel, Syriza and smaller parties to the left of Syriza, eventually rode on the protest waves noted above.

5. Political parties and civil society in the wake of the crisis

The economic crisis brought about a gradual entanglement of non-partisan protest movements with parties of the opposition, as party militants were able to imbue the protests with an anti-capitalist and anti-European rhetoric. A typical example was the long-term strike of workers in the private, steel producing factory "Halyvourgia" in Western Athens. The strike, which lasted for nine months in 2011-2012, started when workers refused to accept salary cuts. However, the largest faction of the factory-based union wanted to reach a compromise, while a smaller but radicalised faction did not agree. The communist-led smaller faction physically blocked the opening of the factory's gates and periodically occupied part of the national highway passing by the factory. Meanwhile, the neo-Nazi Golden Dawn party also sent in its own party cadres to show support and distribute food and other goods to striking workers. Eventually, the strike was called off in July 2012, after the courts had decided that the strike was illegal, most union members left the site of the strike, and the Riot Police forced the gates of the factory open.

A similar entanglement between civic society and political parties can be traced in the evolving mass rallies in Athens in 2010-2012. Research has shown that at least 31 consecutive protest events took place in the span of 24 months (Kousis 2015). Participation in the protest events was comparatively small in the early period of the crisis. However, it reached a peak at three points in time, namely in May 2011 (when the government put forward the so-called 'medium-term fiscal strategy program 2013-2016'), in September – October 2011 (when the government was drafting an austerity budget for two consecutive years, 2013-2014) and in January 2012 (when the government passed additional austerity measures).

Moreover, these three peak moments of social protest, when masses of people flooded the streets of Athens, coincided with the apex of mobilisation of the parties opposing the government. At that point, civil society took a back seat in social protest. Participation in demonstrations, organised by party organisations, grew significantly. This pattern was probably owed to several reasons: first, after the spontaneous protest movements which sprang up in the wake of the first Memorandum, a certain fatigue overtook movement participants who were not card-carrying party members and realised that their reaction did not alter government policy. Second, earlier protesters may have changed their priorities, by focusing on personal strategies necessary for survival in a situation of declining income and dwindling welfare services. And third, spontaneous social movements, such as the 'indignant people's movement', could not last long, because they lacked resources, discipline and leadership.

Protest movements which initially gained a lot of publicity and momentum, rallying together citizens of variable political beliefs, such as the 'Won't Pay' movement, gradually lost steam, as opposition parties transformed specific protest events into larger anti-government and anti-EU mobilisations.

6. Social solidarity organisations and networks

Since the spring of 2010 civil society has emerged not only as an array of social protests, but also as a series of collective initiatives for providing social solidarity. This development occurred while state funds, on which NGOs relied before 2010, were almost completely depleted. Further on, in August 2012, the government froze all state funds earmarked for NGOs, through a letter sent by the Deputy Minister of Finance to all Ministries. And in February 2014 it was revealed that a criminal investigation was under way for the misuse of funds dispensed by the Ministry of Foreign Affairs to Greek humanitarian NGOs throughout the 2000s.

Yet, despite such negative publicity, after 2010 some not-for-profit foundations, Greek annexes of international NGOs and local parishes of the Greek Orthodox Church mobilised to help people hit by the crisis. They used donations by individuals and sponsors and embarked on the provision of basic staples, medical and social services to people in need. In contrast to the past, when only formal associations used to engage in charity work, informal groups were also active in the field. Large not-for-profit foundations, such as the Niarchos Foundation, coexisted with small informal social networks which neither had a formal organisational structure nor were they registered with any official authority.

Provision of food and shelter

For example, both formal and informal civic associations started providing food to poor people. The Church ran soup kitchens every day in the centre of Athens, while in the western and southwestern neighbourhoods of Athens volunteers cooked several hundred meals a day (The Financial Times 2012).

Further on, a few NGOs, linked with municipal authorities, monitored the living conditions of the homeless, making rounds in the city centres to offer them blankets, food and medical help.

Moreover, informal networks of volunteers served as intermediaries between restaurants, hotels and bakeries with food to spare, and homeless charities and food banks, by putting the former in touch with the latter (Henley 2012a). The more politicised volunteers identified with a country-wide left-wing social solidarity movement rather than with any charity network, implying that they rejected traditional, philanthropic encounters between the well-to-do and the rest.

Cultural and educational services

After 2010, low-income families could not afford private cramming school lessons, deemed necessary for pupils preparing to take university entrance examinations. Volunteering high school teachers founded 'social cramming schools' where pupils took lessons for free. Another informal group focusing on culture and community work was the "Atenistas". It first appeared in Athens in 2010 and then spread to another 11 cities. The "Atenistas" engaged in cultural events and recycling, combined with maintenance work in run-down streets and squares of Athens.

Solidarity markets and distribution networks

After 2010, informal groups organised bartering networks, in the context of which they exchanged goods and services for vouchers or online credits. In 2012, there were at least 22 such social solidarity groups in 17 cities. In some cases, participants exchanged vouchers or on line credit for other goods, creating thus what is termed a "Local Exchange Trading System", which existed for a while in a few cities. The most well-known was in Volos, where the local currency was known as the "TEM" and a specific bartering street market existed.

Another celebrated case is the "potato movement" (Henley 2012b). Typically, farmers sell their products to middlemen who then transfer the agricultural produce to cities and sell it to supermarkets and grocery stores, inflating thus the original price of the product. In the wake of the crisis potato producers in the Northern Greek town of Katerini decided to sell directly to consumers, leaving out the middlemen. Producers travelled to city centres to sell their products or planned to receive orders directly from consumers.

Healthcare

After 2010, a rising number of the unemployed and the self-employed, who had stopped paying health insurance to their occupation-based social security funds, lost access to public health care. They resorted to the Greek branches of international health care NGOs, such as the "Doctors without Borders" and the "Doctors of the World" which in the wake of the crisis expanded their services to Greece. In addition, informal networks of health care provision emerged. They consisted of doctors, nurses and social workers, who created make-shift clinics usually in spaces provided by the municipal authorities in various cities. These clinics were called 'Social Medical Centres'. In 2012, there were 33 such clinics in 29 cities. In parallel, pharmacists volunteered to set up 'Social Pharmacies'.

In brief, as the state started rolling back its welfare functions, citizens stepped in to occupy the newly available public space. Activists who were not interested in the foundation of typical NGOs and in fact distrusted NGOs because of their earlier patronage-based relations with the state, grouped together in order to create small social safety nets at various locations all over Greece. The crisis inspired and necessitated social innovation 'from below' that was targeted towards welfare provision.

7. Uncivil society in the wake of the crisis

In parallel with the emergence of civil society after 2010, there was a rise of uncivil society. For instance, racist and fascist groups, spearheaded by the neo-Nazi Golden Dawn party, mobilised against foreign migrants as well as against Greek political elites. In the neighbourhood of Aghios Panteleimonas Acharnon, in Athens, Greek residents formed small 'vigilante groups'. Carrying sticks and knives, they effectively prevented migrants from using public spaces, such as a square or a children's playground. Claiming that they reacted to crimes committed by foreign migrants, vigilante groups supported by Golden Dawn harmed or even killed foreign migrants and whomever supported them. For instance, in January 2013 two Golden Dawn members stubbed to death a Pakistani migrant in Athens, and in September 2013 another

Golden Dawn member, called in by his fellow party members, stubbed to death Pavlos Fyssas, a Greek left-wing hip hop singer. Undoubtedly, these were the gravest examples of uncivil society mobilisation.

Democratic life was also harmed by extreme leftist groups which used to join demonstrations to pursue their own anti-system ends. In May 2010, during the first in a series of general strikes, three bank employees lost their lives in Athens, when demonstrators from an anarchist group torched a bank branch. On another occasion, on 28 July 2011 in the port of Piraeus, angry taxi drivers succeeded in preventing coach buses from carrying tourists from cruise liners to the city, by throwing oil on the streets and turning asphalt into a gliding mirror. This created a life-threatening situation for coach bus drivers and passengers wishing to leave the port.

Another frequent occurrence was the long-term occupation of various abandoned buildings by groups of squatters and the extra-parliamentary Left. The latter used to prepare and keep petrol bombs in the occupied buildings in order to attack policemen - even when no demonstration was taking place - and to wage battles against the Riot Police whenever the latter attempted to recapture such government owned buildings. The most dramatic episode was the eviction of anarchists from the former high school building known as "Villa Amalia" in the centre of Athens. The building had been occupied since 1990, the police evicted the anarchists in December 2012, the latter recaptured the building a few weeks later and were finally evicted in January 2013.

Other instances of social protest which could be classified as manifestations of uncivil society were local enclaves of violent resistance against the implementation of legislation and court decisions. An extreme example was the movement of residents of the Keratea village (south-east of Athens), who in 2010-2012 resisted the installation of a waste management plant in their area, a project that had been approved by the parliament and the courts. Yet, some villagers dag in a deep ditch at the major thoroughfare passing outside their village, and thus temporarily barred circulation between Athens and the south-eastern part of the Attica region, and even erected barricades to block access to their village. A similar example was the movement of the residents of Skouries village in the Halkidiki prefecture of Northern Greece in 2012-2016. Part of the village community opposed the installation of a new gold-mining operation by a private company in their area, a project that had also passed the tests of parliamentary vote and court approval. Yet, some villagers erected barricades, blocked access to their village for extended periods of time and even supported a group which invaded the company's property and torched trucks and machinery.

In view of the above, one cannot interpret either the harassment of migrants by right-wing militants or the collective damage of state and private property by left-wing militants as signs of the revitalisation of the civil society during the crisis in Greece.

8. Conclusions

Before the crisis in Greece, voluntary associations were unable to function as vehicles of democratic participation. With the exception of well-organised unions of SOEs and professional associations, they were weak vis-à-vis political parties and the state. For a long time, labour unions, the student movement and other associations were internally divided along the lines of political party competition. Confederations of employees and also NGOs used to be financially dependent on funds obtained from the central government. Acute antagonisms among the major political parties and a polarised political culture prevented the emergence of an autonomous sphere of civil society. In other words, civil society hardly played a political role, as political representation was mostly confined to participation through political parties. Moreover, civil society's deliberation potential was never materialised.

Yet, the class-biased and harsh austerity measures taken by the government since 2010 under conditions imposed by Greece's creditors, provoked a wave of social protests that initially were not led by political parties opposing the government. Grass roots movements rallied against income and pension policies, against rises in the cost of public services and cuts in social spending. Civil society was empowered in the sense that large numbers of participants joined such movements and participated in strikes and demonstrations. The poor and the socially excluded who, metaphorically speaking, normally did not have a 'voice', probably spoke through such movements.

Moreover, in the wake of the economic crisis NGOs spontaneously mobilised to support people in need and a plethora of informal groups and networks emerged in the social solidarity sector. Informal networks consisting of loose circles of like-minded citizens or neighbours, engaged in community work and helped provide food, clothes, shelter, health care and educational services to the most vulnerable people.

In brief, the economic crisis has opened a window of opportunity for Greek civil society which has experienced the chance to further develop in the future and strengthen its role vis-à-vis the political institutions. This opportunity has been seized less by NGOs and more by inchoate groups and networks which in the future might (or might not) develop more permanent organisational structures. This will depend on the duration of the crisis, on the fluctuation of demand for the services of informal groups and networks and on the supply of funds, time, skills and other resources by citizens and private sponsors to those informal collective actors.

In parallel to the above solidarity efforts, atypical, often violent, forms of uncivil society activism have also emerged. Since 2010, there have been occupations of government buildings, organised efforts to storm the parliament as well as physical attacks against politicians. These were instances where protesters put the limits of liberal democracy to test. Attacks by small racist groups against migrants, which for a long time were tolerated by the Greek police, and violent acts of destruction of state and private property by radical left-wing groups also tested the limits of parliamentary democracy. Yet, in Greece, democratic institutions continue to function, while large numbers of citizens have exercised their collective rights through social protest and social solidarity. These mixed and contradictory trends show how complicated the nature of political developments and social innovation in times of economic crisis is.

Acknowledgements

The author thanks Ulrike Liebert for encouragement and Dimitris Bourikos, Alexander Fraser, Georgia Gleoudi, Akis Sakellariou and Myrtia Vellianiti for research assistance. Research for this chapter has been supported by the Athens-based ELIAMEP research foundation, the "Thales" Project of the University of the Peloponnese and the Athens Office of the Konrad Adenauer Stiftung.

References

Berman, Sheri (1997): Civil Society and the Collapse of the Weimar Republic. In: World Politics 49, 3, pp. 401-429.

Clarke, Jennifer/Huliaras, Asteris/Sotiropoulos, Dimitri A., eds. (2015): Austerity and the Third Sector in Greece. Surrey: Ashgate.

Diamond, Larry (1994): Toward Democratic Consolidation. In: Journal of Democracy 5, 2, pp. 4-17.

(The) Financial Times (2012): Volunteers Step In As Poverty Soars, 16 April 2012.

Giannitsis, Tassos/Zografakis, Stavros (2015): Greece: Solidarity and Adjustment in Times of Crisis. In: Hans Boeckler Stiftung, Macroeconomic Policy Institut, Study no. 38 (http://www.boeckler.de/pdf/p_imk_study_38_2015.pdf, last access 1 September 2016).

Henley, John (2012a): Greece on the Breadline: How Left-overs Became a Meal. In: The Guardian, 14 March 2012 (https://www.theguardian.com/world/blog/2012/mar/14/greece-breadline-leftovers-dinner, last access 3 January 2017).

Henley, John (2012b): Greece's Cut-Price Potato Movement Shows Greeks Chipping In. In: The Guardian, 27 March 2012 (https://www.theguardian.com/

world/2012/mar/27/greece-breadline-potato-movement-eurozone-crisis, last access 3 January 2017).
Kollia, Eleftheria (2012): The Square was Full of Indignant People. In: To Vima, 22 July 2012 (http://www.tovima.gr/society/article/?aid=467898, last access 3 January 2017).
Kousis, Maria (2015): The Spatial Dimensions of the Greek Protest Campaign against the Troika's Memoranda and Austerity, 2010-2013. In: Ancelovici, Marcos/Dufour, Pascale/Nez, Héloïse (eds.): Street Politics in the Age of Austerity. Amsterdam: Amsterdam University Press, pp. 147-173.
Kopecky, Peter Mudde, Cass, eds. (2003): Uncivil Society? Contentious Politics in Post-Communist Europe. London: Routledge.
Liebert, Ulrike/Trenz, Hans-Joerg (2011): The "New Politics of European Civil Society": Conceptual, Normative and Empirical Issues. In: Liebert, Ulrike/Trenz, Hans-Joerg (eds.): The New Politics of European Civil Society. London: Routledge.
Mavrogordatos, George (1993): Civil society under populism. In: Clogg, Richard (ed.): Greece, 1981-89: The Populist Decade. London: St.Martin's Press, pp. 47-63.
Mouzelis, Nicos/Pagoulatos, George (2005): Civil society and citizenship in post-war Greece. In: Birtek, Faruk/Diamandouros, Nikiforos/Dragona, Thaleia/Frangoudaki, Anna/Caglar Keyder (eds.): Citizenship and Nation State in Greece and Turkey. London: Frank Cass, pp. 87-103.
Putnam, Robert (1993): Making Democracy Work: Civic Traditions in Modern Italy. Princeton: Princeton University Press.
Tsakatika, Myrto/Eleftheriou, Costas (2013): The Radical Left's Turn towards Civil Society in Greece: One Strategy, Two Paths. In: South European Society and Politics 18, 1, pp. 81-99.

Abbreviations

Title	Abbreviaton
All-Workers Militant Front	PAME
Coalition of the Radical Left	Syriza
Communist Party of Greece	KKE
Confederation of civil servants	ADEDY
Confederation of Workers of Greece	GSEE
European Central Bank	ECB
European Union	EU
Independent Greeks	Anel

Title	Abbreviaton
International Monetary Fund	IMF
Memorandum of Understanding	MoU
New Democracy party	ND
Non-Governmental Organisation	NGO
Panellinio Sosialistiko Kinima	PASOK
Public Power Corporation	DEI
State-owned enterprise	SOE

6. The politics of solidarity in Europe's migration crisis: Media discourses in Germany and Ireland[1]

Stefan Wallaschek

1. Introduction

More than one million refugees and migrants came to Europe in 2015. This situation triggered a public debate about the role of solidarity in refugee issues. The former UN Secretary General Ban Ki-moon spoke about Europe's migration crisis as a "crisis of solidarity" (Ban 2016). Solidarity has been one of the most often invoked concepts in this crisis and the related media debate. How can we make sense of these public references to solidarity?

Even though part of the answer might be that the naming of solidarity is *window dressing*, this might underestimate the relevance of ideas in political and societal debates. Instead of dismissing a closer examination of solidarity or focusing on *traditional* analyses of solidarity[2], I will take a closer look at the *discursive construction of solidarity* in the media (Wallaschek 2019).

I argue that solidarity has multiple meanings and by reconstructing these from the discourses, I demonstrate the conceptual plurality of solidarity. I assume that solidarity is a "contested concept" (Gallie 1956). Various concepts are raised by actors to argue for or against solidarity. These discursive struggles about solidarity have been barely considered in recent studies (Stjernø 2009; Wallaschek 2016a). I will show that political, cultural and social solidarity are the most salient types of solidarity while security and demarcation are the strongest counter-concepts to solidarity in the media debate in 2015. Focusing on this year gives a crucial insight into the climax of media coverage of migration and refugee issues during the crisis.

The chapter proceeds as following: First, the theoretical framework of my ideational research is briefly outlined and concepts of solidarity are described.

1 I would like to thank Anne Jenichen, Ulrike Liebert, Sandra Reinecke and the reviewer for their valuable comments on earlier drafts of this text.

2 *Traditional* studies on solidarity either investigate social policy and welfare state issues or examine opinions and attitudes of individuals on solidarity (e. g. Boräng 2015; Ciornei/Reechi 2017; Oorschot 2000).

After that, the method, case selection and data are presented, before the results of my analysis are shown. The final section reflects on the findings and future research perspectives.

2. An ideational-discursive approach to solidarity

An ideational-discursive framework focuses on the ideational foundations of politics and locates ideas in a broader discursive-institutional framework (Béland/Cox 2011; Schmidt 2012). In general, "interpretive approaches to political science focus on the meanings that shape actions and institutions, and the ways in which they do so" (Bevir/Rhodes 2003: 17). Depending on certain beliefs and ideas, arguments can change. Politicians adjust their reasoning or propose new ideas. Different interpretations of a political problem are reconstructed by analysing the claims and justifications of actors. Investigating the different rationales helps understand what actors perceive as a problem and how they deal with it (Hajer 1995: 42–45).

While previous studies have shown the relevance of ideas and frames in political decision making processes (e. g. Blyth 2015; Wonka 2016), solidarity as specific concept is less investigated. Closa and Maatsch (2014) have demonstrated that solidarity is used as justification in parliamentary debates about the Euro crisis. Based on this, it is assumed that solidarity is also a relevant concept in Europe's migration crisis. However, solidarity might have different meanings and actors deploy their own understanding of solidarity. Based on this and according to the theoretical work on solidarity, solidarity is distinguished into different concepts of solidarity.[3] In the following, political, cultural and social solidarity are briefly described due to their high salience in the German and Irish media discourse (see below).

Political solidarity is based on claiming that a certain *we* should work together in a political context to deal with an issue. This could include new legislative actions, creating new political instruments or changing politics in general. Many actors reflect about the political context and conclude that in order to create solidary relations, political institutions and policies have to be changed (Kneuer/Masala 2015).

Cultural solidarity emphasises shared norms or traditions between the giver(s) and taker(s) of solidarity, such as the European enlightenment, religious roots or speaking the same language. To share a common cultural background or to belong to the same cultural group is a crucial aspect for acting in

3 On the theoretical foundations of solidarity, see Bayertz (1998), Brunkhorst (2002) and recently Wallaschek (2016b).

solidarity within this justification (Walzer 2006). This cultural framing is used to highlight the values on which the EU is built upon, or it is used to criticise others who seem to ignore these.

Social solidarity refers to welfare and social policy issues as well as to helping in the neighbourhood, supporting integration of refugees and migrants by local communities and organisations (Ferrara 2014; Hamann/Karakayali 2016). Social solidarity can be seen as the ideational base of volunteers and citizens. This justification is related to helping migrants and refugees who are settled in the local context.

It has to be noted that each concept of solidarity can have a different geographical scope. Solidarity can refer, as Ciornei and Recchi (2017) have shown, to the international or transnational level, but also to the national or even sub-national level. This differentiation is taken into account for the following analysis to encounter solidarity in its plurality.

3. Case selection, method and data

This chapter investigates notions of solidarity in the German and Irish media arena in 2015. The media arena is the location where political actors such as national governments present their politics to the general public. By articulating their positions to a broader audience, they legitimise their political actions (Koopmans/Statham 2010). Despite the existence of unequal power structures and resource disparities (Kriesi et al. 2007; Van Dalen 2012), the media arena is a place where numerous actors with different political positions appear. Although readership is declining, printed newspapers are crucial, because "thresholds for audience members are particularly low and societal reach is exceptionally large" (Wessler et al. 2008: 5). By focusing on newspapers, I identify and reconstruct concepts of solidarity in the debate on the migration crisis. I examine the media coverage in 2015 in the Irish Times (IT) and Irish Independent (IInd) for Ireland as well as the Süddeutsche Zeitung (SZ) and Die Welt (DWe) for Germany. These selected quality daily newspapers are among the most important ones in their respective country, have a large circulation and represent the political cleavage of centre-left and centre-right positions.

It can be expected that the German debate was more politicised due to the high influx of refugees, and that German actors might more often refer to the idea of solidarity. Ireland was – at least partly due to its geographical location - not in the centre of taking in refugees and thus the Irish debate might have been less intense. I will illustrate these expected differences by examples from the newspaper material.

The selection of newspaper articles is based on a keyword search in the database *Factiva*. I selected 767 articles from four quality newspapers and coded 551 claims with the RQDA package in R (Huang 2016). The coding is based on the *Political Claims Analysis*, developed by Ruud Koopmans and Paul Statham (1999, 2010) and further elaborated by Pieter de Wilde (2013). A claim contains four elements: Actors (claimants) speak (action) about something (issue) and express an opinion (position) about it. Additionally, I emphasise the category of justification, because I am interested in the reasons of why actors argue for or against solidarity and in the geographical scope actors refer to in their justification. Regarding the manual coding of the claims, I applied a nominalistic approach. This means that I have only coded claims with the term solidarity or close synonyms in it (see table 1). This strengthens the validity and the reliability of the coding procedure of such a contested term like solidarity, but decreases the number of identifiable claims in newspapers. The following table presents an overview of the amount of claims and articles in the four selected newspapers.

Table 1: Amount of claims and articles in four newspapers

source/time period	**2015 claims**	**2015 articles**
Süddeutsche Zeitung	218 (39 %)	394 (51 %)
Die Welt	198 (36 %)	223 (29 %)
Irish Times	86 (16 %)	95 (13 %)
Irish Independent	49 (9 %)	55 (7 %)
Total	551 (100 %)	767 (100 %)

Note: The results are based on a keyword search. For Germany: "(Flüchtling* or Flucht* or Migrant* or Einwander* or Zuwander* or Asyl*) and Solidar* and (EU or Europ*)". For Ireland: "(Refugee or escape or Migrant* or Migration* or Immigrant or Immigration* or Asyl*) and (solidar* or mutual w/1 support* or cooperat*) and (EU or Europ*)". An Asterisk controls for multiple word endings. Duplicates of articles were excluded.

In comparison, the German discourse is more dense and includes more articles and claims than the Irish discourse. Furthermore, the centre-left newspapers SZ and IT contain more articles and claims than the centre-right newspapers.

The next section gives a brief overview about Europe's migraton crisis in 2015 and after that the most frequently used concepts of solidarity –political, cultural and social solidarity –will be analysed. Then, the anti-solidarity justifications demarcation and security are examined.

4. Solidarity in Europe´s migration crisis

2015 was a turbulent year in terms of immigration and asylum seeking. Migrants and refugees[4], coming from conflict zones in the Middle East, Sub-Saharan Africa and Central Asia, challenged the EU border regime, the Dublin agreements and revealed the "asymmetric way", in which the EU migration and asylum policy was developed (Monar 2014: 620).

The public attention on migration issues and solidarity was very high in the *long summer of migration*, starting from August until the beginning of October 2015.[5] Especially three distinct events created much media coverage. On August 28th, a lorry with several dozen dead migrants was found at a highway in Austria inducing a public outburst. Shortly after, on August 31st, and as a reaction to the increasing amount of refugees, German Chancellor Angela Merkel said what later became a key slogan: "We will manage it and where something hinders us, it must be overcome" (2015).[6] Lastly, on September 3rd, a picture of the drowned three-year-old boy Alan Kurdi, lying dead on a beach at the Turkish coast, received a lot of media attention and produced public reactions about the deadly journey of migrants and refugees crossing the Mediterranean.

The following analysis includes the whole year 2015 demonstrating that even before these incidents, solidarity was discussed in the media and among the main political stakeholders. Looking at the specific justifications for pro- or contra solidarity claims helps to understand how solidarity is framed.

4.1 Three notions of solidarity

The most prevalent concepts of solidarity in 2015 are *political*, *cultural* and *social solidarity*. From a total number of 551 claims, 112 claims (20 per cent) contained the justifiation political solidarity while in 52 claims (10 per cent)

---

4 Migrants, refugees, asylum-seekers and displaced persons have different legal statuses and rights. I describe these people as "refugee and migrants" if both groups could be meant in a statement, following a suggestion by the UNHCR (2015).

5 The *long summer of migration* is a depiction of the events in 2015 from pro-movement activists (Kasparek/Speer 2015).

6 The translations of all German statements in the text are my own.

cultural solidarity was used as justification for political actions in times of crisis. Social solidarity was deployed 30 times (5 per cent) in 2015.[7]

Political solidarity refers mainly to the scope of the EU, for example improving the European asylum policies. For instance, the journalist Martin Wolf argues for active solidarity with border states such as Greece, and the German politician Michael Roth demands a European solidarity mechanism.

> Solidarity is also needed to help overstretched countries on the frontiers, notably Greece and Italy. It is hard to see how the border-free Europe of today will be maintained without a well-resourced border protection and immigration service (IT, September 23rd).

> "We need more solidarity. We need more humanity", claimed Michael Roth, the German Minister of State for Europe, in Luxembourg on Tuesday. "We are very, very open to develop mechanism of solidarity which commits all member states to do more than before", he emphasised (SZ, June 24th).

By focusing on solidarity among EU member states, the statements create a new dimension of exclusion, because migrants and refugees are not an active part in this claim and justification. European solidarity is addressed and frames migrants either as passive or even as a threat to the EU (member states), as Wolf states when he is arguing for more border protection. Solidarity here strengthens the social bonds among the member states and marks the exclusion of refugees.

These examples underline the relevance of political solidarity as a crucial frame of how to engage politically in the migration crisis. Across the newspapers and among the actors, establishing solidary mechanisms seems to be perceived as the most important way to deal with the crisis and create co-operation among the EU member states.

The *cultural framing of solidarity* is used to highlight the values on which the EU is built upon, or criticism is raised why other actors disregard this fundamental principle. The following example shows not only the cultural framing of solidarity, but also the exchange of ideas and opinions via national newspapers. In this case, Frank-Walter Steinmeier and Sigmar Gabriel, both German social democrats (SPD), wrote an opinion piece together in which they emphasised solidarity as common ground for cooperation among EU member states, which was published in several European newspapers, including the Irish Times:

> Europe is facing a great challenge for our generation. Never before have so many people fled political persecution and war as today, many seeking refuge

7 The rest of the claims either contained no justification which is the case in 19 per cent of all claims or refered to other justifications. The salience of the solidarity justifications, first political then cultural and third social solidarity holds true for the German and Irish case.

> with us in Europe. [...] As Europeans, we owe it to ourselves and to the world to rise to the great challenge posed by these people looking for help. The response so far does not meet the standards that Europe must set for itself. [...] We need a European asylum, refugee and migration policy founded on the principle of solidarity and our shared values of humanity. (IT, August 27th).

This sort of claim can be found among different actors. The president of the German Employers' Association, Ingo Kramer, argued similarly in the discussion on a common solidarity mechanism among EU member states that the EU foremost is a community of solidary values:

> Ingo Kramer said, the EU is ,"a community of solidary values, not a community of benefits". And whoever does not receive refugees could not demand solidarity from other countries [in other circumstances] [...] (SZ, November 25th).

Referring to cultural solidarity emphasises the ideational foundations of the EU and demands a value-driven account of politics in the migration crisis. In 2015, it is especially used to criticise others who oppose solidarity actions and to demand more solidarity.

Lastly, social solidarity refers to welfare and social policy issues as well as to helping in the neighbourhood, supporting integration of refugees by volunteers in a social manner. Social solidarity is related to the transnational level by working as the base of voluntary actions for refugees. It is also related to local contexts in which migrants and refugees settled in.

> Many Irish people want to help directly. [...] I suggest that a website based on the likes of Daft.ie or Airbnb could be set up through funding from the Department of the Environment. [...] We could call it RAFT.ie (Refugee Accommodation, Food and Transport), where families with spare rooms could offer a safe 'life-raft' to bring refugees closer to safety. Householders can upload photos of the rooms, the numbers they can take and the period of time they can host one refugee, a family or a couple. You might be able to give English lessons, help with form-filling, introduce people into the community, help children with school integration - or just provide warmth, clothing and food, and help them find work. Simply make them feel safe (IInd, October 31st).

Citizens are also quite visible in the debate on social solidarity due to their letters to the editor or reports about their local activities.

> The [...] solidarity is needed for another task: helping refugees integrate successfully. This is going to be difficult and costly. They will need assistance with learning the language and housing. Richer countries will have to assist the less-well-off ones. A revitalised European economy would also help (IT, September 23rd).

This demonstrates that solidarity is not only an elitist concept or is not just used in headlines for newspaper articles. The coverage of concrete solidarity actions by ordinary citizens or the public demand to act in solidarity with refugees shows the variety of solidarity in the discourse. Not only political actions on the European level are discussed, but also the social activities that have happened in 2015 (see also Hamann/Karakayali 2016).

The use of one of these justifications in the media debate is not exclusionary. For instance, actors refer to political as well as cultural solidarity depending on the actual debate or event. Thus, the identification of different notions of solidarity underlines the need to carefully investigate public debates on solidarity in Europe's migration crisis. There is not necessarily a fixed actor preference towards one notion of solidarity over another type of solidarity. Moreover, there are also justifications that are opposite to solidarity and I will present two of them – demarcation and security – in the following section.

4.2 Unmaking solidarity: demarcation and security

The most dominant justifications for opposing solidarity are *demarcation* and *security*. In 551 claims in 2015, demarcation and security were each used 43 times (taken together 16 per cent of all claims) and most often in the German discourse. *Demarcation* is the strongest reason for non-solidarity and is against the border crossing of migrants. As the following report in the Irish Times shows, setting up fences and creating special police forces shall demonstrate the sovereign national power.

> An additional steel border fence is now being erected [at the Hungarian border], and more than 2,100 police officers and cadets will form fast-reaction "hunting" units, equipped with four-wheel-drives, helicopters and dogs, to respond to incidents. Hungary's parliament is expected to debate the deployment of soldiers to the border (IT, August 31st).

Demarcation frames in their extremist versions are the physical attacks and hate speeches against incoming refugees and are linked to racist and nationalist arguments (see also Jäckle/König 2017). The next media report on a radical right-wing protest in Italy shows that such anti-refugee protests were already happening before the *long summer of migration*.

> Members of Casa Pound, a neo-fascist organisation, appeared in Rome. As soon as the bus with 19 African refugees arrived who were to be accommodated at the Casale San Nicola, right-wing extremists waved the Italian flag, shouted hate slogans, raised their right arm for the fascist salute and blocked the entrance (SZ, July 22nd).

The demarcation justification can be seen in protest and demonstrations against a so called abuse of asylum or in claims for the deportation of irregular refugees. Claims for demarcation fundamentally contest the need for solidarity.

The justification for security shifts the statement from solidary actions to issues of border control and safety. Instead of helping boat people, border control and surveillance of the Mediterranean by Frontex should be enhanced to stop irregular migration and prosecute human traffickers. The refugee disappears in this justification. This re-shaping of the migration crisis by focusing on smugglers and human trafficking can be observed at the European level as well. In April 2015, a 10-points action plan to deal with the increasing numbers of refugees was presented at a European Council meeting which focuses on security issues.

> A 10-point action plan on migration was outlined at a joint foreign and home affairs European Council meeting on April 20th. The action plan focuses primarily on military action against smugglers and refers, for example, to "systematic efforts to capture and destroy vessels used by the smugglers" (IT, April 23rd).

Besides setting up national fences and border control, migration processes are seen as threats to national societies as well as the European community. Instead of showing solidarity with refugees who come to Europe, the claim for solidarity is reversed and used to justify security measures at the national and European borders.

> Warsaw wants to prevent a revision of asylum law based on the population of the EU member states. Until now Poland receives only few refugees in relation to its population size – in 2014 only 114 Syrians have applied for asylum. It is not surprising that the head of government Ewa Kopacz primarily insists on better border security in the Mediterranean at the EU summit in Brussels. "Our solidarity primarily rests upon strongly supporting Frontex. We will send our border police officers" (DWe, April 25th).

The *security* justification is mostly facilitated by far right and conservative politicians, but also by politicians from the so called Visegrád Group (Poland, Slovakia, Czech Republic and Hungary) as the claim by the former Polish Prime Minister Ewa Kopacz illustrates. The justification is used to either prevent further European cooperation or to focus on smuggling and human trafficking; instead of helping refugees or establishing legal routes for them.

The contrasting justifications to solidarity demonstrate that even though claims for solidarity are the most frequent ones, the contestation of solidarity is an essential part of the discourse as well. Proposing political solidarity as European mechanisms to take in refugees or relocate refugees among EU member states is one side. The other side is giving up the Schengen Agreement and renationalising border control and refugee policies.

5. Conclusion

Solidarity became a crucial concept in the public debate on Europe in 2015. This chapter aimed at revealing the different meanings of solidarity and the discursive counterparts to solidarity. Solidarity is not a concept with one uncontested meaning, but has a variety of understandings. The three most salient meanings – political, social and cultural solidarity – in the debate on Europe's migration crisis were examined. The reconstructed notions of solidarity in the discourses emphasise the careful assessment of solidarity claims. Solidarity can contain different notions which refer to various perceptions of the migration crisis. Looking more precisely at these constructions helps us to understand how actors, by referring to solidarity, understand and make sense of crisis situations.

The use of political solidarity in both national discourses demonstrates that the media debate goes beyond the framing of renationalisation *or* Europeanisation. Both processes are captured in the discussion on solidarity which underlines the relevance of both national solidarity and European solidarity in the debate on the migration crisis.

The framing of cultural solidarity in 2015 was almost always related to common European values and norms, respectively the lack of these by the criticised actors. This cultural Europeanisation of solidarity is a hint towards the high importance of solidarity as fundamental idea in European societies and the European treaties.

Social solidarity is used as justification in the debate in regard to voluntary work and support for refugees. It has an explicit transnational dimension in the German and Irish context by showing solidarity with foreigners in need.

The demarcation and security justifications in the debate were often put forward as a renationalisation of politics and sovereignty. If European cooperation and co-ordination were addressed, then as the demand to strengthen border control and surveillance measures in the Mediterranean. Extreme forms of these claims were expressed as physical attacks and right-wing radical speeches against refugees and volunteers in the migration sector. Even though pro-solidarity claims were far more frequent than anti-solidarity claims, the discourse has shifted in 2015 from more pro-solidarity at the climax of the *long summer of migration* to more anti-solidarity discourses in the winter. This underlines the contestation of solidarity in the discourse and that the call for solidary actions is not a given consensus.

The debate about the refugee situation in Europe is *about* refugees, not *with* refugees. I have identified some claims made by migrants, but in general these voices have been invisible and silenced (see also Khosravinik et al. 2012; Lünenborg et al. 2011). Talking about migration and refugee issues without listening to migrants and refugees is like talking about the economy without economists or legal issues without consulting lawyers and judges. If public discourses included more migrants and refugees voices in the future, they would be less paternalistic and contain more accounts on what refugees need and say about how a solidary relationship in Europe should look like.

Europe's migration crisis is seen as a European issue in German and Irish newspapers. The used geographical scopes in the justification corroborate this finding. Political solidarity mostly refers to the international level within the EU and suggests that solidary actions should happen among the EU member states. Social and cultural solidarity bear a strong transnational dimension by claiming the need of voluntary actions with refugees and migrants. Security claims contain either a more national or a more international dimension. Border control and surveillance are proposed as measures in the nation-state but also as joint actions at the Southern European borders. Only demarcation contains this explicit national(istic) framing in Germany and Ireland.

This discourse similarity in the geographical scope of concepts can be seen as a first hint towards a shared understanding of solidary problem solving. National solidarity is neither in Germany nor in Ireland the dominant notion while claims for types of international and transnational solidarity are made in Europe's migration crisis. Even if security measures are often not in line with international solidarity obligations, the claims for joint security actions still demonstrate the political will to cooperate within the EU. In times of renationalisation and Euroscepticism, European cooperation is more than ever necessary. Robert Schuman declared in 1950 that Europe "will be built through concrete achievements which first create a de facto solidarity" (Schuman 1950). Nowadays, the concrete achievements as well as solidarity are at stake. It should be in the interest of the political elites and national populations to strengthen the idea of solidarity as crucial value and guiding principle for political actions in the European Union.

Future research should investigate the (changing) actor constellation in Europe more concretely to account for different party positions on migration and asylum policies. Analyzing public discourses in Central and Eastern European countries might also reveal different actor constellations due to their skeptical view on European solidarity in the migration crisis. Moreover, future studies could examine the influence of different media systems on the coverage of such an European issue and the role of social media for the discussion on solidarity in Europe's migration crisis.

References

Ban, Ki-Moon (2016): Refugee Crisis about Solidarity, Not Just Numbers. http://www.un.org/press/en/2016/sgsm17670.doc.htm [accessed 31.05.2017].

Bayertz, Kurt (1998): Begriff und Problem der Solidarität. In: Bayertz, Klaus (Hrsg.): Solidarität: Begriff und Problem. Frankfurt a. M.: Suhrkamp, S. 11–53.

Béland, Daniel/Cox, Robert Henry (Hrsg.) (2011): Ideas and Politics in Social Science Research. Oxford: Oxford Univ. Press.

Bevir, Mark/Rhodes, R. A. W. (2003): Interpreting British Governance. London: Routledge.

Blyth, Mark (2015): Austerity: The History of a Dangerous Idea. Oxford: Oxford Univ. Press.

Boräng, Frida (2015): Large-Scale Solidarity? Effects of Welfare State Institutions on the Admission of Forced Migrants. In: European Journal of Political Research 54, 2, S. 216–231.

Brunkhorst, Hauke (2002): Solidarität: Von der Bürgerfreundschaft zur globalen Rechtsgenossenschaft. Frankfurt a. M.: Suhrkamp.

Ciornei, Irina/Recchi, Ettore (2017): At the Source of European Solidarity: Assessing the Effects of Cross-border Practices and Political Attitudes. In: Journal of Common Market Studies, 55, 3, S. 468–485.

Closa, Carlos/Maatsch, Aleksandra (2014): In a Spirit of Solidarity? Justifying the European Financial Stability Facility (EFSF) in National Parliamentary Debates. In: Journal of Common Market Studies 52, 4, S. 826-842.

Ferrera, Maurizio (2014): Solidarity in Europe after the Crisis. In: Constellations 21, 2, S. 222–238.

Gallie, Walter B. (1956): Essentially Contested Concepts. In: Proceedings of the Aristotelian Society 56, S. 167-198.

Hajer, Maarten A. (1995): The Politics of Environmental Discourse: Ecological Modernization and the Policy Process. Oxford: Clarendon Press.

Hamann, Ulrike/Karakayali, Serhat (2016): Practicing Willkommenskultur: Migration and Solidarity in Germany. In: Intersections. East European Journal of Society and Politics 2, 4, S. 69–86.

Huang, Ronggui (2016): RQDA: R-based Qualitative Data Analysis. Version 0.2-8. http://rqda.r-forge.r-project.org/[accessed 31.05.2017].

Jäckle, Sebastian/König, Pascal D. (2017): The Dark Side of the German 'Welcome Culture': Investigating the Causes behind Attacks on Refugees in 2015. In: West European Politics 40, 2, S. 223-251.

Kasparek, Bernd/Speer, Marc (2015): Of Hope. Hungary and the long summer of migration. http://bordermonitoring.eu/ungarn/2015/09/of-hope-en/[accessed 31.05.2017].

Khosravinik, Majid/Krzyzanowski, Michal/Wodak, Ruth (2012): Dynamics of Representation in Discourse: Immigrants in the British Press. In: Messer, Michi/Schroeder, Renee/Wodak, Ruth (Hrsg.): Migrations: Interdisciplinary Perspectives. Vienna: Springer, S. 283–295.

Kneuer, Marianne/Masala, Carlo (2015): Politische Solidarität. Vermessung eines weiten und unerschlossenen Feldes. In: Kneuer, Marianne/Masala, Carlo (Hrsg.): Solidarität: Politikwissenschaftliche Zugänge zu einem vielschichtigen Begriff. Baden-Baden: Nomos.

Koopmans, Ruud/Statham, Paul (1999): Political Claims Analysis: Integrating Protest Event And Political Discourse Approaches. In: Mobilization. An International Journal 4, 1, S. 203–221.

Koopmans, Ruud/Statham, Paul (2010): The Making of a European Public Sphere. Media Discourse and Political Contention. New York: Cambridge Univ. Press.

Kriesi, Hanspeter/Tresch, Anke/Jochum, Margit (2007): Going Public in the European Union: Action Repertoires of Western European Collective Political Actors. In: Comparative Political Studies 40, 1, S. 48–73.

Lünenborg, Margreth/Fritsche, Katharina/Bach, Annika (2011): Migrantinnen in den Medien: Darstellungen in der Presse und ihre Rezeption. Bielefeld: transcript.

Merkel, Angela (2015): Sommerpressekonferenz von Bundeskanzlerin Merkel. Thema: Aktuelle Themen der Innen- und Außenpolitik. https://www.bundesregierung.de/Content/DE/Mitschrift/Pressekonferenzen/2015/08/2015-08-31-pk-merkel.html [accessed 31.05.2017].

Monar, Jörg (2014): Justice and Home Affairs. In: Jones, Erik/Menon, Anand/Weatherill, Stephen (Hrsg.): The Oxford Handbook of the European Union. Oxford: Oxford Univ. Press, 613–626.

Oorschot, Wim van (2000): Who Should Get What, and Why? On Deservingness Criteria and the Conditionality of Solidarity Among the Public. In: Policy & Politics 28, 1, S. 33–48.

Schmidt, Vivien A. (2012): Discursive Institutionalism. Scope, Dynamics, and Philosophical Underpinnings. In: Fischer, Frank/Gottweis, Herbert (Hrsg.): The Argumentative Turn Revisited. Public Policy as Communicative Practice. Durham: Duke Univ. Press, S. 85–113.

Schuman, Robert (1950): The Schuman Declaration – 9 May 1950. https://europa.eu/european-union/about-eu/symbols/europe-day/schuman-declaration_en [accessed 31.05.2017].

Stjernø, Steinar (2009): Solidarity in Europe: The History of an Idea. Cambridge: Cambridge Univ. Press

UNHCR (2015): UNHCR Viewpoint: 'Refugee' or 'migrant' - Which Is Right? http://www.unhcr.org/news/latest/2015/8/55df0e556/unhcr-viewpoint-refugee-migrant-right.html [accessed 31.05.2017].

Van Dalen, Arjen (2012): Structural Bias in Cross-National Perspective: How Political Systems and Journalism Cultures Influence Government Dominance in the News. In: The International Journal of Press/Politics 17, 1, S. 32–55.

Wallaschek, Stefan (2016a): Sammelbesprechung: Krise der Solidarität - Solidarität in der Krise. In: Zeitschrift für Vergleichende Politikwissenschaft 10, 1, S. 93–102.

Wallaschek, Stefan (2016b): Solidarität in der Europäischen Union. Anmerkungen zur aktuellen Debatte. In: Widerspruch: Münchner Zeitschrift für Philosophie 35, 62, S. 97–114.
Walzer, Michael (2006): Sphären der Gerechtigkeit: Ein Plädoyer für Pluralität und Gleichheit. Frankfurt a. M.: Campus.
Wessler, Hartmut/Peters, Bernhard/Brüggemann, Michael/Kleinen-von Königslöw, Katharina/Sifft, Stefanie (Hrsg.) (2008): Transnationalization of Public Spheres. Basingstoke: Palgrave Macmillan.
Wonka, Arndt (2016): The Party Politics of the Euro crisis in the German Bundestag: Frames, Positions and Salience. In: West European Politics 39, 1, S. 125-144.
de Wilde, Pieter (2013): Representative Claims Analysis: Theory Meets Method. In: Journal of European Public Policy 20, 2, S. 278–294.

Abbreviations

CDU	Christlich Demokratische Union
DWe	Die Welt
EU	Europäische Union
IInd	Irish Independent
IT	Irish Times
SPD	Sozialdemokratische Partei Deutschland
SZ	Süddeutsche Zeitung

7. Civil society as an agent of Europeanisation in EU accession countries: Comparing Turkey and Serbia

Sezin Dereci

1. The question of civil society as an agent of Europeanisation

The concept of civil society has received an important place in European political and normative debate (Liebert/Trenz 2011). The European Commission (EC) is committed to ensuring civil society participation in every phase of EU policy-making, from policy design to implementation (Kohler-Koch/Finke 2007; Finke 2007). The EC's initiatives to boost the participation of European civil society organisations (CSO) in decision-making is replicated in its relations with civil societies beyond the EU's borders in EU enlargement countries. The central aim of this chapter is to draw on evidence from Turkey and Serbia to determine under which conditions civil society actors from accession states can push decision makers for further reforms that facilitate the Europeanisation process.

In the Europeanisation literature, assessments of the impact of European Union (EU) enlargement processes mainly focus on changes in national contexts, highlighting the ways and conditions under which enlargement changes the identity, interests and behaviour of governmental and societal actors (Schimmelfennig/Sedelmeier 2005: 9). During the accession process, the EU deploys legal, political and material resources and establishes new institutions (ideas, meanings, rules, norms) (Börzel/Risse 2007: 493). EU accession results from the adjustment of national politics and policies to European standards: By decreasing their initial misfit over time, accession states qualify for EU membership. Yet, the EU's effectiveness to transform the Central and Eastern European countries' government and administrative capacities have been rather limited or at least indefinite (Parau/Bains 2008: 110; see Wittmann in this volume). No causal link between the implementation of EU conditionality and successful rule transfer in particular policy areas has been found (Schimmelfennig/Sedelmeier 2004: 670). Moreover, having explored the accession of Central and Eastern European Countries, Kutter and Trappmann (2010: 53) argue that the EU accession process harms the accountability of public policy making, since central governments should reach consensus on all provisions set by the EU for becoming a full EU member regardless domestic veto players. Consequently, the accession process tends to strengthen the position of the executive branches of the applicant country since they control the accession process and direct the pace of transformation. Under their dominance, input-based forms of legitimation of the accession process can be harmed, if political choices do not reflect the 'will of the people' and if the state and the political transformation are not backed by cohesive societal support (Scharpf 1999).

Due to the intensification and diversification of scholarly discussions over the role of civil society in European governance, the roles attributed to CSOs in accession countries have changed and extended over time. A major reason is that the EU's relation to accession states is hierarchical by nature. The EU imposes its rules by means of conditionality, in other words, it sets the rules of the game. In this context, the participation of civil society in governing the accession process is embraced as a counter-balance to the over-powerful and somehow reform-resistant executives of accession countries. In return, this new political opportunity structure offers CSO's potential empowerment, expanding possibilities to raise their claims at the domestic level or in multilevel arenas (Börzel 2010: 1-2; Knodt 2002: 182). EU policy towards civil society in accession states is composed of different elements with complementary goals, whereby the EC imposes conditionality (political instruments) and provides EU funding (financial instruments) to promote civil society development. The EU aims to develop CSOs of accession countries into "agents of Europeanisation". Hence, it seeks to strengthen societal support by building the capacities of civil society, by initiating their access to policymaking, and by disseminating ideas and expertise through transnational and regional networks. By intervening into the political opportunity structure of the non-member state, the EU eventually empowers non-state actors to participate in the accession process. Thus, the EU's 'acquis conditionality' enables state and civil society relations to transform. It establishes governance mechanisms that provide new access channels to CSOs. The multilevel nature of the EU polity extends the political realm in ways that allow for the mutual transfer of expertise between state actors and their non-state counterparts. To explore the question under which conditions civil society actors of accession states can effectively make a difference regarding processes of Europeanisation, the next section will take a closer look at the cases of Turkey and the Western Balkans.

2. A closer look at Turkey and the Western Balkans

Having extensively analysed the Europeanisation process of Turkey myself (Dereci 2013), I have found that the EU's top-down transformative impact has been quite limited. Despite the significance generally attributed to conditionality, Turkey's adoption of the EU's acquis has been so selective and has followed so different trajectories across different policy areas and issues that other factors must be scrutinised, as well. To explain the drawbacks of Turkish accession, the literature tends to focus on the credibility of the acquis conditionality. Müftüler-Bac (2002: 93) argues that EU level variables such as institutional set-up of the EU and public attitudes towards Turkish membership within the member states can explain the direction of the accession process rather than Turkey's performance in aligning to the *acquis communautaire*. Noutcheva and Aydin-Düzgit (2012) conclude from their assessment of the EU's impact on the rule of law in the Western Balkans and Turkey, that the reversals in rule-of-law performance in these countries can be explained by both EU level and domestic factors (elite preferences). According to Schimmelfennig (2008) the credible accession conditionality is only a necessary condition but not a sufficient one to explain success of EU impact upon Croatia, Serbia and Turkey. His comparative study has shown that high political compliance costs for the national governments explain drawbacks in accession. In their comprehensive volume covering a wide range of issues concerning Turkey and European integration, editors Ugur and Canefe (2004) map different ways in which researchers make sense of Europeanisation, proposing that Turkey's internal dynamics relate to the debates on Europeanisation and convergence, rather than framing them in the terms of EU-Turkey relations purely as a "foreign" or "external" policy issue. Wunsch (2015) argues that the EU's efforts to foster an enabling environment in the Western Balkans are perceived by CSOs as insufficient to secure their inclusion in policy making. She stresses the hostile political culture that precludes any engagement of CSOs, even if the EU pushes for their formal involvement. Similarly, İçduygu (2011) argues that the EU's impact on civil society in Turkey is highly ambivalent, and the contribution of CSOs to the EU accession process frequently indecisive. His explanation of this outcome points to three factors, the "ill-functioning mechanisms of the EU's enlargement regime, particular problems inherited from the state–society relations and socio-political culture in Turkey" (İçduygu 2011: 381).

3. My argument

For determining under which conditions CSOs from an accession country can push the state towards Europeanisation, I will assume that the credibility of the accession process is a key condition to be taken for granted. The key issue here is, whether or not EU leverage is salient for political elite preferences to favour ongoing reforms towards EU accession. Furthermore, I argue that the salience of EU leverage for elite preferences is a necessary condition for boosting EU accession processes, but not a sufficient one, as it depends on how the "ground level" (mass public attitudes) is shaped by political cultural contestations in the national setting. In this framework, I claim that civil society will act as a set of "norm-entrepreneurs" of the Europeanisation process which can mediate among interests, provided that there is participatory engineering at the national level that develops *a) durable institutional mechanisms for sustainable civil society participation in policy-making; and b) public policies as an enabling environment for civil society development.*

The subsequent comparative empirical analysis will compare Turkey and Serbia to trace the impact of changing opportunity structures on civil society participation in EU accession processes. Turkey is clearly a very specific case considering the long and disrupted accession timeline (see below). Moreover, Turkey's membership in the near future has become less likely. By contrast, despite some challenges, Serbia is expected to become a member of the EU eventually. The following parts examine these two cases consecutively, looking at the credibility of the EU incentives as a main mechanism of influencing democratic institutional change, and tracing the changes in their respective institutional frameworks and public policies regarding participatory mechanisms and enabling environments for civil society development. While specifically engaging with the Turkish and Serbian accession processes, the analysis aims to identify general trends in the interaction between the EU and civil society in the accession states.

4. Turkey

4.1 The declining salience of EU leverage

The declaration of Turkey's candidacy in 1999 has boosted reforms regarding the democratic political environment for civil society. EU- Turkey relations were upgraded when the December 2004 Brussels Council decided to open up accession negotiations with Turkey the following year. Between 2000 and 2005, when the reform process was at its peak, substantial changes were realised, including a series of reforms to establish the legal foundations regulating state and society relations, and the law of associations updated and liberalised substantially in 2004 (Göksel/Güneş 2005; Kubicek 2011). Despite strong salience of EU leverage for Turkey at that time, opposition to Turkey's entry into the EU became visible. For example, the European Commission highlighted that the accession process of Turkey was particularly challenging for both, for the country itself and the EU, given that Turkey was different from previous cases due to "Turkey's population, size, geographical location, economic, security and military potential, as well as cultural and religious characteristics" (European Commission, Turkey 2004 Progress Report: 4-6). In this phase, the credibility of the acquis conditionality deteriorated, since some core EU countries questioned the "absorption capacity" of the Union for further enlargements and therefore proposed "privileged partnership" as an alternative to full membership for Turkey (Noutcheva/Aydin-Düzgit 2012; Yılmaz 2012). Discourse analyses of French and Dutch rejections of EU Constitutional Treaty reforms in the 2005 referendums highlight that the mass publics of two founding members of the Union refused further enlargements of the EU in general and the accession of Turkey in particular (Startin/Krouwel 2013: 67). On the other hand, Turkey's position in the Cyprus conflict has been one of the major challenges that slowed down the reform process. In December 2006, the Council decided to suspend negotiations on eight chapters of the acquis and not to close any of the remaining chapters until Turkey opened up its seaports and airspace to Greek Cyprus as required by Turkey's customs union with the EU. In addition to slowed down accession negotiations, and taking into consideration the uncertainty of the EU's institutional make-up and the halted enlargement process until 2020, the external leverage of EU political conditionality has become almost insignificant for Turkish elites. By that time, Turkey's strategic orientation towards EU membership weakened as a response to the EU's reluctance to facilitate Turkey's accession process, no major improvements have been made since the 2004 and 2008 reform packages. Moreover, the EU anchor was especially undermined in the eyes of the Turkish political elite after 2013, as the EU's position towards the Arab uprisings and shifts in Middle Eastern politics was perceived as inconsistent and in conflict with Turkey's foreign policy at that time. A final significant turning point was when the EU member states were hesitant to accept refugees when they flocked into Europe. Considering Turkey's hosting of over 2.5 million refugees under the "open-door" policy of the *Justice and Development Party* towards refugees, the EU's position was considered in direct contradiction to European norms and values.

4.2 Unsustainable participatory mechanisms

Despite some improvements, the EU process has not led to significant changes in the institutional set-up of policy making by introducing new channels that would allow stakeholders to participate in the political accession processes. When EU-Turkey relations were at their peak, namely when Turkey was granted candidacy status and accession negotiations started, both state and civil society were enthusiastic to work together. State authorities were also particularly willing to include all relevant stakeholders by offering them voice in dialogue meetings, thereby fulfilling the EU criteria that called for the inclusion of civil society in the process. The Turkish Economic and Social Council was set up in 2001, enabling consultations among economic and societal actors. However, CSOs could only be invited to attend the meetings at the discretion of the Prime minister. The Human Rights Consultation Board of Turkey was established as a venue allowing for the exchange of views between the government and CSOs. However, this trend has proven unsustainable: As the pace of EU-Turkey relations has slowed down, and the relative significance of the process has diminished for all actors, both state and civil society have increasingly failed to show extra effort in working together towards the accession process.

Besides the slowing down of the pace of accession, a triple deficit has also handicapped the institutionalisation of participatory mechanisms to the benefit of CSOs: the lack of institutional capacities, of codes of conduct and of cooperation culture. Different from the positive trend of adopting strategic documents or developing models for civil society-public sector cooperation in the Western Balkan, in Turkey an overreaching national strategic document supporting mechanisms for CSO-Government cooperation is not existent. At the central level, the most important piece of legislation on this issue is the *Regulation on the Procedures and Principles of Drafting Legislation* (19/12/2005, 9986) that stipulates that Ministries may consult CSOs on draft laws, but does not make consultation mandatory. Furthermore, according to Clause 7 of the Regulation, if and when consulted, CSOs should provide their comments on the draft laws within thirty days. If they do not provide their comments within this time frame, they are considered to have issued an affirmative opinion on the draft law. Last, but not least, following the consultation stage, draft legislation is sent to the Prime Minister's office for amendments, with no further procedures available for CSOs to provide their comments. CSOs cannot review drafts until they are put on the agenda of the General Assembly of Turkey.

The conditions of the state of emergency introduced in July 2015 after the failed military coup attempt brought the risk of undermining democratic standards due to bypassing consultative mechanisms and parliament in the law-making process. Mechanisms of checks and balances have not been put in place as safeguards against disproportionate measures and to preserve the separation of powers as well as the rule of law. The state of emergency permits the Council of Ministers, chaired by the President, to issue statutory decrees that carry the force of law. Furthermore, according to Law no. 2935, the Council of Ministers is granted the power to issue regulations suspending or restricting fundamental rights and freedoms including the freedom of association. The statutory decrees passed under the three-month state of emergency cannot be appealed.

4.3 Changing environment for civil society development

There is no doubt that by adopting a series of reforms under the national program to align with the EU acquis, in relative terms, Turkey was better able to provide political space to and enable the mobilisation of civil society throughout the 2000s. When the reform process was at its peak, Turkey had implemented a series of reforms that promoted the democratisation process, including reforms of its basic legal framework that affected civil society. Turkey continued to operate, however, under the 1982 Constitution, which was written immediately following a military coup. Although there are basic guarantees for rights and freedoms, the Constitution is not up to the standards of developed democracies. Up until 2004, when the new Association Law was enacted in Turkey, the autonomy of the Turkish CSOs was fairly restricted. The new Law was viewed positively by both civil society and the EU. It lifted some of the constraints from civil society. Between 2004 and 2008, within the scope of the EU accession process, the regulatory environment of civil society has been improved and various laws and regulations pertaining to civil society were reviewed and amended to enhance freedom of association in Turkey. Finally, Turkey adopted the 2008 Foundations Law which further improved the legal environment for CSOs.

In 2015, the Gezi protests rapidly spread throughout Turkey, arguably becoming the largest wave of protests in recent Turkish history. They brought a momentum for the growth of civil society activism in search of more democratic rights. Yet, in response, the government enacted restrictive laws that paved the way for a state of constant readiness to curb basic freedoms for the sake of preserving "national security" or "public order". The state administration took severe measures to restrict the right to freedom of assembly in Turkey, especially when assemblies would turn into anti-government demonstrations. Furthermore, the state of emergency regime significantly violated and undermined the right of Turkish civil society to freely choose among media of mass communication to receive and share information or to express critical views of public policies and actions. According to the 2016 Freedom of Press Report, the Turkish system of 'non-free media' ranked last in the European regional ranking and was included among the countries that suffered the largest declines since 2015. Internet censorship and blocking or slowing access to social media networks by the authorities has increased in the last couple of years, posing challenges to exercise freedom of expression (Freedom House, Turkey Report 2016).

In 2015-2016, Turkey experienced several destabilising pressures. Issues pertaining to realpolitik (e.g. instability spill over from Syria, a series of terrorist attacks, the flow of refugees) dominated the political agenda. There was neither societal discussion nor concrete steps taken towards political reforms to sustain an enabling environment for civil society development. On top of this, the attempted 2016 coup was an unforeseen incident and caused a severe interruption in policy making routines. Following the failed army coup, on 21 July 2016 the Turkish authorities informed the Secretary General of the Council of Europe that Turkey would notify derogation from the European Convention on Human Rights under Article 15 of the Convention. The State of Emergency approved by the National Parliament on July 21th for three months allowed authorities to effectively react, investigating and punishing those responsible for the attempted coup. The statutory decrees passed under the State of Emergency included measures that restricted the civil society sector in general and suspended more than 1500 CSOs in particular.

5. Serbia[1]

5.1 Salience of EU leverage

In 2008, the signing of the Stabilisation and Association Agreement (SAA) between Serbia and the EU indicated the choice of the Serbian Government in favour of EU accession, launching a new impetus to reforms. After the May 2012 parliamentary elections, when Serbia's new coalition government came into power, there was clear evidence that the EU pre-accession process became top policy priority. The central executive of Serbia associated Europeanisation with modernisation and acknowledged the possibility that EU membership can be a solution to evident problems. The coalition government led by the strong leader Vučić demonstrated its commitments to EU accession and far-reaching economic reforms as the key policy outlook. In April 2013, Serbia signed the

1 This section draws on empirical findings from a study visit of Turkish key government and CSO stakeholders to Serbia to Review Participatory Programming of EU Funds and "Sectoral Civil Society Organisations" (SECO) Mechanism, organised by Technical Assistance to Civil Society Organisations (TACSO) funded by European Union, during 24-28 October 2016.

Brussels Agreement that normalised relations with Kosovo. After overcoming this longstanding obstacle to EU accession, in December 2013, the European Council approved negotiations on Serbia's accession to start in January 2014. Following the accession negotiations, the EU's leverage to transform the domestic political setting in Serbia became stronger. The more the prospects for EU membership became evident, the more the domestic reform agenda was oriented towards strengthening the rule of law and public administration reform. The Serbian European Integration Office (SEIO) led and coordinated preparations for the "National Priorities for International Assistance 2014-2017, with projections for 2020" (NAD 2014). Acknowledging the strategic objective of the Serbian economy to accelerate EU accession, this strategic planning document aims at implementing the systematic reforms needed to meet the Copenhagen criteria. More specifically, NAD reflects the objectives set out in other donor planning documents, predominantly the European Commission's "Indicative Strategy Paper for Serbia" (2014-2020).[2]

5.2 Institutionalisation of CSO participation: The "National Convention on the European Union"

The EU accession process of Serbia has facilitated the improvement of participatory mechanisms accompanied by changes in the perception of civil society and state collaboration in governing the accession to the EU. In the preparation of the NAD strategic planning, SEIO established "Sectoral Civil Society Organisations" (SECO), a structured mechanism for civil society- public sector cooperation in planning and implementing international development assistance funds. According to CSO representatives, the SECO consultation mechanism is empowering the whole sector because it serves as a platform that enables exchange of information among CSOs and their engagement with developing assistance planning, and, in particular, with the programming and monitoring of the Instrument for Pre-Accession Assistance (IPA).

The adoption of a number of legal amendments and regulations has enhanced the position of the Serbian Parliament in the process. The resolution adopted in December 2013, aims at its close involvement in the EU accession negotiations and also introduces consultation procedures with stakeholders, including CSOs, for developing draft propositions. The "National Convention on the European Union" (NCEU) was set up as a platform for civil society in the accession negotiation process in June 2014, with the aim to facilitate cooperation between the Serbian parliament and civil society during the process of

2 http://ec.europa.eu/neighbourhood-enlargement/sites/near/files/pdf/key_documents/2014/20140919-csp-serbia.pdf

EU accession negotiations. NCEU allows for thematically structured debates on issues of Serbia's accession to the European Union, involving representatives of governmental bodies, political parties, NGOs, experts, syndicates, private sector and representatives of professional organisations. The Convention was initiated by the European Movement in Serbia and currently gathers more than 700 organizations including CSOs as well as 19 faculties, 12 research institutes, 24 professional associations, 11 unions and 3 business associations. Their cooperation with the Government was formalised after a consultation process which was led since May 2015 by the "Chief of Negotiations" team and the cabinet of the Ministry of EU integration. Regulations include modalities of communication with NCEU, level of transparency and level of availability of information and documents related to the EU accession process.

By a decision adopted in August 2015, the Government of Serbia recognised NCEU as the key channel for informing citizens about the EU accession process. The parliament holds regular committee meetings and consultations with NCEU that bring together civil society organisations under thematic groups with the purpose of involving them in the accession negotiations process (European Commission, Serbia 2015 Progress Report: 6). Since its establishment, NCEU has held 93 meetings that were attended by more than 1,500 participants, publishing nine publications, and reaching with its working groups a membership of more than 700 civil society organisations.

5.3 Enabling environment for civil society development

Serbia has taken a series of efforts to improve the legal framework of associations and foundations, including the Law on Associations (October 2009), the Law on Endowment and Foundations (November 2010), and the Law on Volunteering (May 2010). The Government Office for Cooperation with Civil Society ("The Office" thereafter) became operational in 2011 and serves as the main institutional mechanisms to support the development of a dialogue between the Government and CSOs. It also assists in planning and mainstreaming the general policy to facilitate an enabling environment for civil society development in Serbia. The Office has been supported by the technical assistance within the EU's Instrument for Pre-Accession Assistance (IPA) program of support to civil society 2011-2013; it also benefits from the three-year project "EU support to the Office for Cooperation with Civil Society", funded by 1.2 million €.

Already in the first three years of its operations, the Office was successful in facilitating policy change in two areas: The Ministry of Finance and Economy amended 'The Law on Accounting Implementation' following a policy proposal prepared by the Office that recommended different rules of accounting to be adopted for non-profit entities. The Office has initiated also a change of Article 41 of the Government's Rules and Procedures on public hearings regulating public debates in law making. Amendments to Article 41 established mandatory public hearings, making them the rule rather than an exception, and providing reasonable timeframes for their duration.[3]

These improvements by Serbia notwithstanding, the EU has repeatedly stressed CSO cooperation as a condition for the proper implementation of available mechanisms. In 2013, The European Economic and Social Committee recommended that "(…) Priority should be given to raising awareness among public authorities as to the benefits of cooperation with CSOs, both in the early stages of designing public policies and later, when they are implemented (…)."[4] The Office actively promotes the recognition of the role of civil society within public administration, advocates for reform, prepares policy proposals, and provides trainings, capacity building activities and information sharing, not only to the public administration, but also to CSOs, at different levels and in varying thematic areas. The Office became a focal point with regard to development of an enabling regulatory environment to sustain civil society participation in public policy making and to strengthen the financial sustainability of CSOs. The Office drafted the first national "Strategy for enabling environment for development of CSOs in Serbia 2015 – 2019" and had widely consulted and finalised the document by mid-2015. This document is a stepping stone for creating better national legal and financial frameworks for the sustainable development of civil society and its effective cooperation with state institutions. Nevertheless, the "National strategy for an enabling environment for development of CSOs 2015-2019" still has not been adopted.

6. Conclusion

In summary, on the way to EU accession, the emergence of a vibrant civil society and its empowerment is not just an end in itself but also a means. Civil society is expected to perform differing roles to correct the legitimation deficiencies of accession processes controlled exclusively by the EU and national executives. By its very nature, an accession process leads to a hierarchical fund/norm giver and a taker relation. The objective of supporting

3 http://civilnodrustvo.gov.rs/office/office-annual-reports/office-annual-reports.206.html
4 http://www.eesc.europa.eu/?i=portal.en.rex-opinions.28355

civil society within accession states is to increase the efficiency and effectiveness of accession processes, since the implementation phase would produce best results if the beneficiary country had a strong ownership of the plan with the full consent of its people. Over time, the EU has aimed to overcome this asymmetrical relation in the favour of the beneficiaries, trying to determine ways in which the popular will can be incorporated into the design of the proposed programs. At this point, the Union has focused on the involvement of civil society and other relevant stakeholders at the national level, supporting participatory mechanisms that can bring national representatives and civil society together. Having a say in the accession process is perceived as a means for enhancing the recipient state's willingness to cooperate. On the other hand, the EU intrinsically values civil society participation as a control mechanism to ensure checks and balances at the national level. Given that the accession process is all about injecting new policies and instruments into the system of governance, civil society can be a counter-weight to oppressive governments that reject the progressive reforms that the Union designates. Moreover, the EU perceives civil society organisations as alternative sources of information and interpretation that contribute to a healthier, less biased account of the situation in recipient countries.

As an external anchor, potential EU membership constituted a powerful driving force and primary impetus for change both in Serbia and Turkey. My analysis of the Turkish accession process indicated that within this framework several reform oriented steps were taken to improve the legal framework in the period 2004-2008 when the prospect of EU membership was most vivid. However, contrary to the Serbian case, when the prospects for EU membership became more irrelevant and distant, the EU conditionality did neither help improve CSO-public sector relations nor the creation of new institutions, thus the adoption of strategic documents and policies to improve civil society participation came to a halt. Under such circumstances, CSOs could not any more act as a "norm entrepreneur". Civil society lost its role as a participant in governance and cooperative partner of state and political institutions that might have provided substantive inputs for legitimate policy making and reforms.

References

Börzel, Tanja A./Risse, Thomas (2007): Europeanization. The Domestic Impact of European Politics. In: Jørgensen, Knud Erik/Pollack, Mark A./Rosamond, Ben (eds.): Handbook of European Politics. London: Sage Publications, pp. 483-504.

Börzel, Tanja A. (2010): Why don't you always get what you want. EU Enlargement and Civil Society in Central and Eastern Europe. In: Acta Politica 45, 1, pp. 1-10.

Dereci, Sezin (2013): The changing roles of NGOs and economic interest groups in Turkey's Europeanization process. Diss. Bremen: University of Bremen/Bremen International Graduate School of Social Sciences.

European Commission (2004): 2004 Regular Report on Turkey's progress towards accession, COM(2004) 656 final, retrieved April 10, 2017 (http://www.ab.gov.tr/files/AB_Iliskileri/Tur_En_Realitons/Progress/Turkey_Progress_Report_2004.pdf).

European Commission (2015): Serbia 2015 Report. Accompanying the document communication from the Commission to the European Parliament, the Council, the European Economic and Social Committee and the Committee of the Regions, COM(2015) 611 final, retrieved April 10, 2017 (https://ec.europa.eu/neighbourhoodenlargement/sites/near/files/pdf/key_documents/2015/20151110_report_serbia.pdf).

Finke, Barbara (2007): Civil Society Participation in EU Governance. In: Living Reviews in European Governance 2, 2, retrieved February 15, 2017 (http://europeangovernance.livingreviews.org/Articles/lreg-2007-2/).

Freedom House (2016): Turkey Report, retrieved April 10, 2017 (https://freedomhouse.org/report/freedom-press/2016/turkey).

Göksel, Diba Nigar/Güneş, Rana Birden (2005): The Role of NGOs in the European Integration Process. The Turkish Experience. In: South European Society and Politics 10, 1, pp. 57-72.

İçduygu, Ahmet (2011): Interacting Actors. The EU and Civil Society in Turkey. In: South European Society and Politics 16, 3, pp. 381-394.

Knodt, Michele (2002): Regions in Multilevel Governance Arrangements. Leadership Versus Partnership. In: Grote, R. Jürgen/Gbikpi, Bernard (eds.): Participatory Governance. Political and Societal Implications. Wiesbaden: VS Verlag für Sozialwissenschaften, pp. 177-196.

Kohler-Koch, Beate/Finke, Barbara (2007): The Institutional Shaping of EU-Society Relations. A Contribution to Democracy via Participation? In: Journal of Civil Society 3, 3, pp. 205-221.

Kubicek, Paul (2011): Political Conditionality and European Union's Cultivation of Democracy in Turkey. In: Democratization 18, 4, pp. 910-931.

Kutter, Amelie/Trappmann, Vera (2010): Civil society in Central and Eastern Europe. The ambivalent legacy of accession. In: Acta Politica 45, 1, pp. 41-69.

Liebert, Ulrike/Trenz, Hans-Jörg (eds.) (2011): The New Politics of European Civil Society. London, New York: Routledge.

Müftüler-Bac, Meltem (2002): Turkey in the EU's Enlargement Process. Obstacles and Challenges. In: Mediterranean Politics 7, 2, pp. 79-95.

Noutcheva, Gergana/Aydin-Düzgit, Senem (2012): Lost in Europeanisation. The Western Balkans and Turkey. In: West European Politics 35, 1, pp. 59-78.

Parau, Cristina/Bains, Jerry W (2008): Europeanization as empowerment of civil society. all smoke and mirrors? In: Maloney, W.A./van Deth, Jan W. (eds.):

From National Toward International Linkages. Civil Society and Multi-Level Governance. Cheltenham: Edward Elgar Publishing, pp. 109-126.
Scharpf, Fritz. W. (1999): Governing in Europe. Effective and Democratic? Oxford: Oxford University Press.
Schimmelfennig, Frank (2008): EU Political Accession Conditionality after the 2004 Enlargement. Consistency and Effectiveness. In: Journal of European Public Policy 15, 6, pp. 918-937.
Schimmelfennig, Frank/Sedelmeier, Ulrich (2005): The Europeanization of Central and Eastern Europe. Ithaca, NY: Cornell University Press.
Schimmelfennig, Frank/Sedelmeier, Ulrich (2004): Governance by Conditionality: EU Rule Transfer to the Candidate Countries of Central and Eastern Europe. In: Journal of European Public Policy 11, 4, pp. 661-679.
Startin, Nicholas/Krouwel, Andre (2013): Euroscepticism re-galvanized: the consequences of the 2005 French and Dutch rejections of the EU constitution. In: Journal of Common Market Studies 57, 1, pp. 65-84.
Ugur, Mehmet/Canefe, Nergis (2004): Turkey and the European Integration. Introduction. In: Ugur, Mehmet/Canefe, Nergis (eds.): Turkey and the European Integration. Accession, Prospects and Issues. London: Routledge, pp. 1-17.
Wunsch, Natascha (2015): Beyond instrumentalisation. NGO monitoring coalitions in Croatia, Montenegro, and Serbia. In: East European Politics 31, 4, pp. 452-467.
Yilmaz, Gözde (2012): Exploring the Implementation of Minority Protection Rules in the "Worlds of Compliance". The Case of Turkey. In: Perspectives on European Politics and Society 13, 4, pp. 408-424.

Abbreviations

Title	Abbreviation
European civil society organisations	CSOs
European Commission	EC
European Union	EU
Instrument for Pre-Accession Assistance	IPA
National Convention on the European Union	NCEU
National Priorities for International Assistance	NAD
Sectoral Civil Society Organisations	SECO
Serbian European Integration Office	SEIO
Stabilisation and Association Agreement	SAA
Technical Assistance to Civil Society Organisations	TACSO

II.
Reexamining the Crisis of European Integration

8. The British EU referendum and ethnic minorities: Lessons for European integration

Anne Jenichen

1. Introduction

On 23 June 2016, a slim majority of the British population voted for leaving the European Union.[1] Since not only British but also Commonwealth citizens over 18 residing in the United Kingdom (UK) were eligible to vote in the EU referendum, it was expected that about ten to sixteen percent of voters would be from an ethnic minority (Alibhai-Brown 2016; The Guardian 2016).[2] The referendum in the United Kingdom therefore was not only about the integration ability of the European Union (EU) with respect to the British population, it also represented a critical test case for the EU's minority and integration policy: Has the EU been able to convince ethnic minorities of its attractiveness? Has it been able to offer benefits to minorities, whether material or immaterial ones, or advantages compared to national policies to generate support for the EU among minority communities?

The results of ethnic minority voters in the referendum suggest an affirmative answer to these questions. Unlike the British white population, ethnic minorities predominantly voted for remaining in the EU: Two thirds of those describing themselves as Asian (67 percent), almost three quarters of black voters (73 percent), and seven in ten Muslims (70 percent) voted to remain (Lord Ashcroft Polls 2016).[3]

1 51.9 percent at a voter turnout of 72.2 percent (The Electoral Commission 2016).

2 'Ethnic minority' here, according to the common usage of the term in the British context, refers to group distinctions based on differences from the majority population on grounds of skin colour, nationality, ethnic or national origin, or religion. They include non-Western and non-white groups, such as naturalised immigrants from non-European countries and second- or more-generation citizens whose ancestors had come to the UK from outside of Europe. In the British political context, the abbreviations BME (Black and Minority Ethnic) or BAME (Black, Asian and Minority Ethnic) are usually used to describe this group; on its composition see below.

3 These numbers are based on a survey of 12,369 people after they had voted. Other polling agencies unfortunately did not include the category of voters from ethnic minorities into their surveys.

In order to better understand the difference in the ethnic minority voting results as compared to the overall results, I analyse the arguments brought forward by representatives of the British BME community during the referendum campaigns. The analysis is based on a qualitative analysis of their depiction of the EU in UK national newspapers (using Nexis), in blog entries on newspaper websites, as well as on websites of minority organisations and representatives prior to the referendum (1 January-23 June 2016). Since the main objective of the chapter is to draw lessons for the EU's minority policy, I primarily focus on arguments related to issues of immigration and integration.

As one would expect from the voting result, the portrayal of the EU was primarily positive, acknowledging the EU's efforts to fight discrimination against minorities. The analysis, however, also reveals the widespread view of the EU as a 'white club', rendering further strengthening of minority rights protection by the EU and the serious tackling of xenophobia and racism in Europe crucial if the EU wants to maintain and enhance support among ethnic minorities in its member-states.

The chapter is structured as follows: I first provide some information on the EU's minority and integration policy and the situation of ethnic minorities in the EU, and particularly in the UK. I then present the main arguments used by ethnic minority representatives for or against 'Brexit'. The last part of the chapter discusses their lessons for the EU's minority and integration regime.

2. What has the EU done for ethnic minorities?

The EU itself has never really developed an explicit minority protection regime. It primarily relies on norms and mechanisms of, as well as cooperation with, the Council of Europe and the Organization for Security and Cooperation in Europe (OSCE) (Galbreath/McEvoy 2012). The first time that minority issues had found their way into EU policy was at the beginning of the 1990s. The Copenhagen criteria stipulated the membership requirements for candidate countries seeking accession to the EU and made membership for Central and Eastern European countries conditional on the respect for the rights of minorities. Internally, however, the EU did not introduce any corresponding measures before 2009. With the Treaty of Lisbon, amending the Treaty on European Union (TEU), article 2 TEU now asserts that the EU is founded on respect for human rights, including the rights of persons belonging to minorities. In addition, the EU Charter of Fundamental Rights (CFR), proclaimed in 2000 but legally effective only since the Treaty of Lisbon, provides for equality and non-discrimination based, among other things, on the membership of a national minority (art. 21). However, despite their symbolic significance, TEU and CFR alone are unlikely to offer minorities any meaningful protection. There are no explicit EU competences and policies to support special rights of minorities. Moreover, there is no common definition of 'minority' in the EU context (Guliyeva 2014). Therefore, there is no agreement on whether ethnic minorities also fall into the category of national minority, only then they would get special protection. As Galbreath and McEvoy argue: "Without a common position on what constitutes a national minority, it remains unlikely that EU member-states would agree on prescriptions for minority rights protection" (2012: 177).

However, there has been a range of activities in the areas of non-discrimination, cultural diversity, integration of migrants, and social exclusion that also enhance minority protection (De Witte/Horváth 2008). The Treaty of Amsterdam, in effect since 1999, introduced the principle of non-discrimination. Most important for minorities certainly have been the two Equality Directives, adopted in 2000, the Race Equality Directive and the Employment Directive. They require member-states to protect individuals against direct and indirect discrimination and harassment on the grounds of religion, belief, racial or ethnic origin, primarily in employment. The Race Directive, in addition, also relates more broadly to education, housing and social protection. It was modelled on the 1976 UK Race Relations Act, which was amended in 2003 to give effect to the Directive in the UK and was later replaced by the UK Equality Act (2010). In 2003, furthermore, the EU Long-Term Residents Directive was adopted. It establishes a set of rights for legally residing third-country nationals that is close to the set of rights enjoyed by EU citizens themselves, including rights to residence, education, employment, and non-discrimination vis-à-vis citizens of the host state. In addition, there have been several initiatives by both the European Commission and the European Parliament since the 1990s, such as action programmes and the exchange of best practices, to promote dissemination and adoption of organisational good practice in the field of racial and ethnic non-discrimination in employment, and to raise awareness and stimulate debate on diversity issues also in other fields, such as education (De Witte/Horváth 2008; Wrench 2007).

Overall, "EU minority policy is extremely multi-faceted, but also scattered and indirect, based as it is on a series of commitments to advance cultural diversity, or combat ethnic discrimination, rather than on minority protection per se" (De Witte/Horváth 2008: 382). Protection comes from different sources, including case law, secondary legislation, such as the Race Directive, funding policies, and policies relying on principles enshrined in international instruments like those of the Council of Europe. Even though there has been pressure from the Commission to combat discrimination against Europe's immigrants and ethnic minorities, the lack of coherence of the approach and also a lack of clear commitment to minority questions is a criticism frequently expressed (De Witte/Horváth 2008; Guliyeva 2014).

The situation of ethnic minorities in the EU and the UK

There are good reasons for a minority protection regime in Europe. "Discrimination on the grounds of ethnic origin continues to be regarded as the most widespread form of discrimination in the EU" (Special Eurobarometer 2015: 7; also, European Union Agency for Fundamental Rights 2016). Ethnic minorities in Europe, therefore, are often economically, socially and politically disadvantaged compared to the majority populations in their countries. This includes less integration in the labour market, higher unemployment rates, lower average incomes, and less job security (Kahanec/Zaiceva/Zimmermann 2010); less access to adequate housing (Fonseca/McGarrigle/Esteves 2010); as well as stark under-representation in political institutions (Bloemraad 2013).

The situation of ethnic minorities in the UK does not really differ from that story. In the 2011 census, 12.9 percent of citizens considered themselves as belonging to an ethnic minority, with Asian and Asian British (6.9 percent, primarily with Indian and Pakistani origin), as well as Black and Black British (3.0 percent)[4] constituting the largest minority groups (Office for National Statistics 2011).[5] Even though protected from discrimination on grounds of race, religion or belief under the UK Equality Act, these ethnic minorities face disadvantages in terms of remuneration, employment and other labour market outcomes, with individuals with Bangladeshi and Pakistani background the most disadvantaged, followed by black groups of African origin (Kahanec/Zaiceva/Zimmermann 2010). Even though the share of BME members of the House of Commons increased in the last two elections (from 2.3 percent in 2005 to 4.2 percent in 2010 and 6.3 percent in 2015), it still is considerably below the almost 13 percent share of ethnic minorities in the overall population (Audickas 2016: 5). Similar under-representation is visible with respect to ministerial appointments and in other public sector organisations, such as the police, the judiciary, the armed forces, and the national fire and rescue services, as well as among teaching staff in publicly funded schools. The only exception is the National Health Service in which, at least in England, ethnic minority background staff is over-represented

4 The categories 'Asian British' and 'Black British' are self-designation entries used in official UK ethnic classifications which mainly refer to people from the former British colonies in Asia and Africa, who have been residents of the UK for a long time and consider themselves as British.

5 In addition to that, though with some overlap, there is a large share of foreign-born population in the UK. In England and Wales, for instance, 13 percent of all residents in 2011 were born outside of the UK, primarily in India, Poland, Pakistan, Ireland and Germany (Office for National Statistics 2013). However, this number includes a large share of non-citizens who are not eligible to vote in the UK, and therefore did not participate in the EU referendum.

(Audickas 2016). Even though awareness for ethnic discrimination and inequality has risen both in the British population and in political parties (Sobolewska 2013), ethnic minorities are yet far away from being equally represented. Racist and xenophobic sentiments, moreover, are a serious problem in the UK. The increase in hate crimes during the Leave campaign and in its immediate aftermath (Joseph/Duell 2016; National Police Chief's Council 2016; Versi 2016b) is a clear sign of that, fueled by stereotypical (mis)perceptions and misrepresentations of immigration (Cooper 2016; Ipsos MORI 2014; Ipsos MORI, The UK in a Changing Europe and Full Fact 2016: 23-28).

The discrimination of minorities does not only affect their socio-economic standing. It also affects their political behaviour. An important difference throughout Europe between minority and majority populations is that the voter turnout of minorities tends to be lower than that of majority populations (Sandovici/Listhaug 2010). This is similar in the UK, where, despite many similarities in democratic engagement between minority and majority population, ethnic minority citizens participate less in elections than their white counterparts. Particularly telling is the observation that second-generation black citizens and those of Pakistani and Bangladeshi background, who have grown up in Britain, are less engaged than first-generation immigrants from the respective regions (Sanders et al. 2014).[6] An explanation provides the "paradox of social integration": as groups integrate socially, they become more aware of and sensitive to inequality of treatment, which is particularly challenging for black, Pakistani and Bangladeshi minorities often confronted with institutional racism and Islamophobia (Sanders et al. 2014: 136).

Personal experiences of discrimination also affect the identity processes of minorities. It, for instance, can lead minorities to turn away from national identity. Muslims who perceived more personal discrimination, for example, were, in a study by Fleischmann and Phalet (2015), more committed to their ethnic and religious identities while simultaneously distancing themselves from their country and city. In the UK, however, even though perceived hostility and discrimination in a study by Platt (2014) did reduce identification with the national majority, minorities on average nevertheless did not pass into a strengthened ethnic identity.

We do not have any knowledge yet on whether Europe could, and does, serve as an alternative, or additional, dimension of identification for minorities feeling alienated from their host country. The referendum results might point to that direction. The only study on European identity of minorities I am aware of is Cinnirella and Hamilton's (2007) qualitative study on members of the South Asian population in the UK. In this study, minorities display more positive feelings of identification with Europe than their white counterparts, as

6 It is important to note, though, that Asian minorities display more institutional trust and support of democracy than the white majority, whereas the institutional trust displayed by black minorities is considerably lower (Sanders et al. 2014).

well as a positive correlation of European identification with British identity. The results on white Britons, by contrast, confirm previous findings of a much stronger sense of national identity negatively correlated with European identity.

In the UK, ethnic minorities have been more likely to vote for Labour than white Britons (Sanders et al. 2014)[7]; and in the EU referendum Labour voters leaned more, though not exclusively, towards 'Remain'. This, in addition to the previously described, already contributes to an explanation of the voting behaviour of ethnic minorities in the referendum.[8] In order to approach the question further, the next section will look into the arguments put forward by representatives of minority communities during the campaigns.

3. The EU from the perspective of ethnic minorities in the referendum campaigns

The voting behaviour of ethnic minorities, of course, is not only informed by their minority status. Both supporters and opponents of a potential Brexit from BME communities shared many arguments with their white fellow campaigners. Since I am particularly interested in the lessons that one could draw from the referendum for the EU's minority policy, I focus in the following primarily on those arguments that clearly related to issues of immigration and integration (what most of the debate did anyway).

Before turning to the images of the EU used in these arguments, it must be noted that the role of ethnic minorities in the referendum was a relatively marginal issue. Up to the referendum, Nexis found in almost six months only 22 British newspaper articles (mainly in The Guardian) that gave a voice to members of ethnic minority communities. Consequently, not many ethnic minority representatives and organisations got a public voice in the EU referendum campaigns. My cursory survey of more than 30 websites of organisations representing ethnic minorities in the UK revealed that only a few focused on the referendum at all, indicating a lack of interest of many BME citizens in the EU question. Those considering the referendum all encouraged their members and viewers to register and vote. Concerned about the traditionally lower voter turnout among minorities, organisations such as Operation Black Vote (OBV), the QED Foundation and a voter turnout campaign by the think tank British

7 Since the last couple of elections, however, increasing numbers of Asian voters have moved to the Conservatives and the Liberal Democrats (Heath 2015).

8 Unfortunately, there have been no numbers available on the voter turnout of minorities in the referendum.

Future called on BME voters to participate in the referendum in order to make their distinct voices heard and to contribute to shaping the UK's future (Asian Express 2016; Morris 2015; Operation Black Vote 2016). Whereas these organisations did not give any voting recommendations, others, such as the Muslim Association of Britain and the organisation Muslim Engagement and Development (MEND), openly supported the Remain campaign. The same applied to the Sikh Federation, which campaigned for 'Remain' after a survey had shown that 66 percent of its members wanted to stay in the EU (O'Neill 2016). Only one of the surveyed organisations asked their members to vote for Leave, Muslims for Britain, a network formed during the referendum campaign period. Moreover, there were prominent ethnic minority individuals supporting the Leave campaign, such as the Tory employment minister Priti Patel, the Labour MP for Birmingham Perry Bar, Khalid Mahmood (who later left the campaign due to its racist undertones), and UK Independence Party's (UKIP) spokesman on immigration and Member of the European Parliament (MEP) Steven Woolfe.

The lack of presence of BME voices in the debate, however, resulted not only from a reluctance to speak out but also from a lack of attention of both campaigns. Race equality activists, such as OBV's Simon Woolley, criticised both the Leave and the Remain campaign for not targeting minority communities: "For months we've been excluded from this debate, but it's clear our votes are up for grabs and could make a difference" (in O'Neill 2016). The only campaign organisation that targeted the BME community was actually UKIP, which, in a move to mobilise BME voters for the Leave campaign, tried to pit established black and Asian minorities in the UK against immigrants from the EU. Prominent statements by UKIP spokesman Steven Woolfe, for instance, referred to competition with regards to entry requirements: "If granny wants to come over from Pakistan or India for a wedding, they have got more difficulties in terms of visas and getting visas than would a granny from either Spain or France". He also referred to the alleged competition on the job market: "If you look at the black community, they are more likely to be struggling on low wages in the low skilled and unskilled areas, and that's the area that has been affected by large-scale migration". According to him a "fairer immigration system which favours arrivals from the Commonwealth over Europeans should be at the heart of the Leave campaign's pitch" (in Sculthorpe 2016). His arguments, however, were quickly countered by other members of the BME community criticizing, for instance, the allegedly immigration-friendly stance of UKIP as "poisonous lies" (Alibhai-Brown 2016). Besides issues of immigration, the most frequently discussed issues in the public debate analysed here were the xenophobic undertones of the Leave campaign, criticised, for example, in an open letter of 20 Labour Members of Parliament (MPs) from different ethnic minority backgrounds as coming "right from the UKIP playbook" (Labour 2016).

Two images of the EU dominated the debate among ethnic minorities in the UK. Supporters of the Leave campaign focused primarily on the EU as a system which consistently discriminated against its non-white populations. This image resonated well with the frequent view that the European immigration system is unfair because it favours European internal migration over immigration from countries outside of Europe. However, it also resonated with the widespread concern about the rise of the far-right within Europe. Race equality activists, for instance, argued during the campaign that a feeling had developed within the black community that the EU is "anti-black" and that "(m)ainland Europe is far and away more racist … than the people of this island" (in O'Neill 2016). As a report from the race equality think tank Runnymede Trust had pointed out already in 2015, "(s)ome [BME people] view Europe in explicitly ethnic or racial terms, identifying 'Fortress Europe' as a way of keeping out non-white immigrants while allowing significant levels of European migration" (Khan/Weekes-Bernard 2015: 3). They "are ambivalent about the benefits of the European Union" as they are "less likely to take advantage of free movement; i.e. very few move about for work and (arguably) feel less 'solidarity' or 'shared identity' with others in Europe" (ibid.). However, the voting result in the EU referendum confirmed what the report also had found, namely that ethnic minorities have nevertheless been latently pro-EU due to concerns about nativism.

The opposing image of the EU, often invoked in the Remain campaign and apparently more convincing for a majority of BME voters in the UK, given their voting behaviour in the referendum, referred to the EU as an active supporter of non-discrimination and rights, including those of workers and of the poor. Arguments in this vein highlighted the funding of efforts against racism and xenophobia by the EU, and EU anti-discrimination measures such as the Race Directive: "staying in the EU will strengthen the cause of racial equality" (in O'Neill 2016). In the face of growing racism, xenophobia, Islamophobia and hate crimes, leaving the EU would, by contrast, pose a risk for ethnic minorities in the UK. The Muslim Labour MEP and former Lord Mayor of Manchester, Afzal Khan, for instance, argued in his campaign leaflet: "EU fundamental rights help ensure that Muslims have the freedom to practice their religion, while EU anti-discrimination measures are vital in tackling hate speech and hate crimes across Europe. (…) By leaving the EU the UK would lose (…) the protections that EU law gives to Muslims in Britain" (Khan 2016). These risks could even be aggravated by the economic risks of leaving the EU: "What we do know is that when the economy suffers a shock – as a wide range of experts predict if we leave – it will be the youth unemployment rate that rises the most and a disproportionate number of young ethnic minority Britons are already out of work" (Labour 2016).

The relationship with the Commonwealth, origin of most of Britain's ethnic minorities, figured prominently in the arguments of BME supporters of both campaigns, relating not only to immigration but also to trade relations. Whereas many Leave supporters hoped that, when leaving the EU, "our links with the Commonwealth countries will get stronger" (in O'Neill 2016), Remain supporters argued that both were important (Labour 2016). The latter, for example, underlined what Baroness Patricia Scotland, Secretary-General of the Commonwealth, had also made clear: Commonwealth countries themselves worried about the effects on their influence in the EU if Britain left (Umunna 2016). They stressed the deals of the EU with many of these countries, such as Pakistan and Jamaica, easing restrictions on trade, and the development aid to these countries boosted by the EU beyond the UK's contributions and presence. Muslim campaigners, in addition, stressed the EU's role in promoting peace, stability and human rights worldwide (Khan 2016; Versi 2016a), implicitly framing it as counterweight to American military force in many Muslim countries.

4. Which lessons for EU minority policy?

Despite the only limited competences in the area of minority protection and some member-states' reluctance to expand the EU's role in that area, the EU's efforts to combat racial and ethnic discrimination is acknowledged by British minorities, as the preceding analysis has illustrated. On the other hand, however, one should not forget about the criticisms of the EU by a large number of BME voters voiced prior to the referendum. There is a perceived inequality between – white – minorities from other EU countries and – non-white – minorities from outside of the EU, both in terms of immigration and labour market competition. Fueled by UKIP's propaganda, much of this is based on misperceptions and misrepresentations and could therefore be tackled by enhanced efforts of informing European citizens in an unbiased way about scale and function of immigration in Europe. But that the EU is often regarded in ethnic or racial terms indicates a serious problem that can only be addressed through the further strengthening of minority rights protection by the EU and the serious tackling of xenophobia and racism in Europe.

The EU already does a lot to protect minorities against discrimination. However, it would be possible to make European minority protection more coherent. One possibility would be to make the European minority protection regime, developed by the Council of Europe and the OSCE, which in the past has focused primarily on 'old', i.e. historically established, minorities in Eastern Europe (e.g. the Roma), effective also for 'new' minorities in Western Europe. This would mean putting pressure not only on new but also on old member-states to recognise migrants and their descendants as national minorities, which do not only merit equal opportunities through non-discrimination but also special protections and promotion to finally achieve equal access to resources and representation (Galbreath/McEvoy 2012: 186ff).

In addition, the EU as a legal entity (which it is since the Treaty of Lisbon) could ratify the Council of Europe's Framework Convention for the Protection of National Minorities, which – as legally-binding – has been the strongest international legal instrument for the protection of minorities in Europe so far (ibid.). Even though most EU member-states have ratified the convention, the ratification by the EU itself would have legal consequences for all EU member-states and furthermore be a strong signal of the EU's commitment to minority protection.

References

Alibhai-Brown, Yasmin (2016): Ethnic minorities are being sold poisonous lies on the benefits of Brexit: If we leave, Britain will become less hostile to those from the East and South? Dream on. In: Independent, 8 February 2016, p. 26.

Asian Express (2016): EU referendum: Debate affects 8 million of BME people in the UK: Ethnic minority vote is key to EU referendum, 18 February 2016 (https://www.asianexpress.co.uk/2016/02/debate-affects-8-million-of-bme-people-in-the-uk/, last access: 13 Dec 2016).

Audickas, Lukas (2016): Ethnic Minorities in Politics and Public Life. House of Commons: Briefing Paper No. SN01156 (http://www.parliament.uk/briefing-papers/sn01156.pdf, last access: 26 June 2016).

Bloemraad, Irene (2013): Accessing the Corridors of Power: Puzzles and Pathways to Understanding Minority Representation. In: West European Politics 36, 3, pp. 652-670.

Cinnirella, Marco/Hamilton, Saira (2007): Are all Britons reluctant Europeans? Exploring European identity and attitudes to Europe among citizens of South Asian ethnicity. In: Ethnic and Racial Studies 30, 3, pp. 481-501.

Cooper, Charlie (2016): EU referendum: Immigration and Brexit – what lies have been spread? In: The Independent, 21 June 2016.

De Witte, Bruno/Horváth, Enikö (2008): The many faces of minority policy in the European Union. In: Henrard, Kristin/Dunbar, Robert (eds.): Synergies in minority protection: European and International law perspectives. Cambridge: Cambridge University Press, pp. 365-384.

European Union Agency for Fundamental Rights (2016): Fundamental Rights Report 2016 (http://fra.europa.eu/en/publication/2016/fundamental-rights-report-2016, last access: 25 June 2016).

Fleischmann, Fenella/Phalet, Karen (2015): Identity Conflict or Compatibility: A Comparison of Muslim Minorities in Five European Cities. In: Political Psychology 37, 4, pp. 447-463.

Fonseca, Maria Lucinda/McGarrigle, Jennifer/Esteves, Alina (2010): Possibilities and Limitations of Comparative Quantitative Research on Immigrant's Housing Conditions. PROMINSTAT Working Paper No. 06 (https://ec.europa.eu/migrant-integration/index.cfm?action=media.download&uuid=29E22B3F-ACF6-F151-07039CA8D076E9AC, last access: 26 June 2016).

Galbreath, David J./McEvoy, Joanne (2012): The European minority rights regime: towards a theory of regime effectiveness. Basingstoke: Palgrave Macmillan.

Guliyeva, Gulara (2014): Defining the Indefinable: A Definition of 'Minority' in EU Law. In: Malloy, Tove H./Marko, Joseph (eds.), Minority governance in and beyond Europe: celebrating 10 years of the European yearbook of minority issues. Leiden: Brill Nijhoff, pp. 165-198.

Heath, Anthony (2015): Ethnic Minorities at the Ballot Box. In: Khan, Omar/Sveinsoon, Kjartan (eds.): Race and Elections. London: Runnymede Perspectives, 6-7 (available at: http://www.runnymedetrust.org, last access: 2 Dec 2016).

Ipsos MORI (2014): Perceptions and Reality: Public Attitudes to Immigration (download at: https://www.ipsos-mori.com/researchpublications/publications/1634/Perceptions-and-Reality-Public-attitudes-to-immigration.aspx, last access: 26 June 2016).

Ipsos MORI/The UK in a Changing Europe/Full Fact (2016): European Union: The Perils of Perception (download at: http://ukandeu.ac.uk/research-papers/the-perils-of-perception-and-the-eu/, last access: 26 June 2016).

Joseph, Anthony/Duell, Mark (2016): BBC presenter is called 'P***' on the streets as police probe racist attacks and calls to hate-crime hotline soar 60% in the wake of vote to leave the EU. In: Mail Online, 27 June 2016.

Kahanec, Martin/Zaiceva, Anzelika/Zimmermann, Klaus F. (2010): Ethnic Minorities in the European Union: An Overview. Bonn: IZA Discussion Paper, 5397.

Khan, Afzal (2016): Five reasons for Muslims to vote for Britain to remain in the EU, campaign leaflet (unpubl.).

Khan, Omar/Weekes-Bernard, Debbie (2015): This is Still About Us: Why Ethnic Minorities See Immigration Differently. Runnymede Report on Race and Immigration (http://www.runnymedetrust.org/uploads/Race%20and%20Immigration%20Report%20v2.pdf, last access: 13 Dec 2016).

Labour (2016): There is no doubt: ethnic minority Britons benefit from Britain's EU membership (open letter by 20 BME Labour MPs) (http://www.rushanaraali.org/there-is-no-doubt-ethnic-minority-britons-benefit-from-britains-eu-membership/, last access: 13 Dec 2016).

Lord Ashcroft Polls (2016): How the United Kingdom voted on Thursday… and why (http://lordashcroftpolls.com/2016/06/how-the-united-kingdom-voted-and-why/, last access: 25 June 2016).
Morris, Nigel (2015): EU Referendum: 'Third campaign' launched to encourage disaffected Britons to vote. In: The Independent, 31 December 2015.
National Police Chief's Council (2016): NPCC submission to the Home Affairs Select Committee Hate Crime Inquiry (http://www.npcc.police.uk/NPCC%20letter%20HASC%20Hate%20Crime%20Inquiry%20submitted.pdf, last access: 13 Dec 2016).
Office for National Statistics (2011): 2011 Census (http://www.ons.gov.uk/census/2011census, last access: 26 June 2016).
Office for National Statistics (2013): Immigration Patterns of Non-UK Born Populations in England and Wales in 2011 (www.ons.gov.uk/ons/dcp171776_346219.pdf, last access: 26 June 2016).
O'Neill, Sean (2016): Hostility towards 'anti-black' EU may bolster Brexit. In: The Times, 16 March 2016.
Operation Black Vote (2016): The EU-Referendum – Why You Should Vote, campaign leaflet (unpubl.).
Platt, Lucinda (2014): Is there assimilation in minority groups' national, ethnic and religious identity? In: Ethnic and Racial Studies 37, 1, pp. 46-70.
Sanders, David/Fisher, Stephen D./Heath, Anthony/Sobolewska, Maria (2014): The democratic engagement of Britain's ethnic minorities. In: Ethnic and Racial Studies 37, 1, pp. 120-139.
Sandovici, Maria Elena/Listhaug, Ola (2010): Ethnic and Linguistic Minorities and Political Participation in Europe. In: International Journal of Comparative Sociology 51, 1-2, pp. 111-136.
Sculthorpe, Tim (2016): Ethnic minorities want Britain to leave the EU because they are 'feeling the strain' of unlimited immigration, UKIP claims. In: Mail Online, 26 January 2016.
Sobolewska, Maria (2013): Party Strategies and the Descriptive Representation of Ethnic Minorities: The 2010 British General Election. In: West European Politics 36, 3, pp. 615-633.
Special Eurobarometer (2015): Discrimination in the EU in 2015: Report (http://ec.europa.eu/COMMFrontOffice/PublicOpinion/index.cfm/Survey/getSurveyDetail/instruments/SPECIAL/surveyKy/2077, last access: 25 June 2016).
The Electoral Commission (2016): EU referendum results (http://www.electoralcommission.org.uk/find-information-by-subject/elections-and-referendums/upcoming-elections-and-referendums/eu-referendum/electorate-and-count-information, last access: 17 March 2017).
The Guardian (2016): For women of colour, the EU equals hope (open letter by almost 140 BME women), 22 June 2016.
Umunna, Chuka (2016): Amplifying the 'Great' in Great Britain: Ethnic Minority Britons Benefit From Our EU Membership. In: Huffington Post UK: The Blog, 9 May 2016 (http://www.huffingtonpost.co.uk/chuka-umunna/eu-referendum-chuka-umunna_b_9865830.html, last access: 13 Dec 2016).

Versi, Miqdaad (2016a): For British Muslims, there's only one choice on Europe: vote remain. In: The Guardian, 29 March 2016.
Versi, Miqdaad (2016b): Brexit has given voice to racism – and too many are complicit; Since the EU referendum I have collated more than 100 racist incidents. Politicians and the media are fuelling this fire. In: The Guardian, 28 June 2016.
Wrench, John (2007): Diversity Management and Discrimination: Immigrants and Ethnic Minorities in the EU, Aldershot: Ashgate.

Abbreviations

Title	**Abbreviaton**
Black and Minority Ethnic	BME
Black, Asian and Minority Ethnic	BAME
European Union	EU
EU Charter of Fundamental Rights	CFR
Member of the European Parliament	MEP
Member of Parliament	MP
Muslim Engagement and Development	MEND
Operation Black Vote	OBV
Organization for Security and Cooperation in Europe	OSCE
Treaty on European Union	TEU
United Kingdom	UK
UK Independence Party	UKIP

9. EU decision-making in asylum policy: Lessons from the "refugee crisis"

Natascha Zaun

1. Introduction

In 2015 and 2016, the European Union (EU) experienced the largest inflow of asylum-seekers in its history, with around 1.2 million people applying for asylum in each of these two years (Eurostat 2017). This inflow highlighted the persistent and profound deficiencies of the Common European Asylum System (CEAS) to achieve its key aims: first, to provide harmonised ('common') asylum standards across the EU and, second, to establish a distribution scheme determining which Member State is responsible for the assessment of individual asylum claims.

The obvious failure of the CEAS is sobering and puzzling at the same time, as the EU had developed a multitude of policy instruments since the Europeanisation of this policy area with the Treaty of Amsterdam in 1999. The 2001 Temporary Protection Directive, for instance, provides rules on how to act in situations of mass inflow. Yet, this provision has not been applied in the crisis, due to, among others, the absence of a clearly defined distribution mechanism for asylum-seekers (Gluns/Wessels 2017).

In sum, the absence of a functioning EU policy and not the – albeit unprecedented – inflow of asylum-seekers has led to a real situation of crisis. On the one hand, this is a humanitarian crisis in which refugees who come to Europe in search of protection are confronted with inhumane border protection practices resulting in the death of many of those trying to cross the Mediterranean. On the other hand, the EU has witnessed a real confidence crisis in which freedom of movement, a cornerstone of European integration, has been repeatedly questioned through unilateral border closures of several Member States, including Germany, Austria, Sweden and Denmark.

The crisis has also seen a new mode of decision-making at the EU level, which questions previous steps of integration. Despite the fact that decisions were supposed to be made under qualified majority in the Council, they were mainly taken at the level of the heads of state and government in a rather intergovernmental setting during the "refugee crisis". This illustrates a process of retrenchment (renationalisation) of decision-making, which seems to be part of a wider phenomenon and could also be observed in the Eurozone crisis (see Jachtenfuchs and Genschel 2018).

This contribution aims to explain why EU asylum policy largely failed to achieve its two key aims, namely policy harmonisation and a "fair" distribution of asylum-seekers among Member States, and to discuss lessons that could be drawn from both failures regarding the future development of EU asylum policy.

My argument is that due to collective action problems, Member States have no incentives to provide protection to refugees and asylum-seekers themselves. Instead, they have a preference for shifting responsibilities on to other Member States. Top recipient countries are therefore particularly interested in cooperation at the EU level, as they perceive this to be the only way to make other states commit to taking a share of their refugees. Hence, they promote two types of cooperation, namely 1) physical relocation of applicants (shifting people) and 2) policy harmonisation (shifting policy). While the former has an obvious redistributive function, the latter has an implicit one: a strong divergence of asylum systems can explain why some Member States receive larger numbers of asylum applications than others. For instance, if states do not provide any rigorous asylum procedure or apply restrictive policies that render recognition almost impossible for certain groups, they are likely to deter potential applicants and force them to seek protection elsewhere.[1]

In the following section I briefly analyse the policy dynamics which underlie EU asylum policy-making. In a second step, I discuss why the EU failed to come about with a working distribution scheme during the 'refugee crisis'. After that, I analyse the failure of asylum policy harmonisation in the EU. In the concluding section I assess what these findings suggest for the reform of the CEAS.

2. Overcoming collective action problems through European integration

European cooperation in the area of asylum policies is designed to overcome collective action problems that are common in non-coordinated forms of co-

1 The impact of restrictive policies on the number of asylum applications is contested (Brücker et al. 2002: 89, Menz 2008: 401, Holzer/Schneider 2002: 75-102, Thielemann 2006).Yet, the assumption of this causal link being active has influenced asylum policy-making significantly (Barbou des Places 2003: 3, Zaun 2017: 62).

operation on refugee protection. I will first briefly describe the collective action problems present in the area before I assess how the EU tried to overcome these problems.

All states benefit from the security and stability that is provided through refugee protection, because refugees are an anomaly in the post-Westphalian system of nation states: when they flee their country of origin, they are no longer related to a state that provides them with protection (Betts 2003: 276-277). If no other state takes responsibility for refugees, they have no access to basic rights and societal life, which may cause conflict and instability. Having an international normative framework on refugees, a refugee regime, is thus beneficial to all states, as it provides structure and rules. Yet, states have few incentives to actively provide protection themselves. In fact, it is much more attractive for states to wait for other states to assume responsibility for refugees and free-ride on them (Suhrke 1998; Betts, 2003; Thielemann/El-Enany 2010; Noll, 2003; Roper/Barria 2010). This is related to the fact that the public good of 'stability ensured through refugee protection' is largely non-excludable (i.e. no one can be excluded from it) and non-rival (i.e. usage by one actor does not diminish the good).[2] A state that does not actively protect refugees, e.g. by hosting them, still benefits from the stability and security provided through the existence of the system and the commitment of others. As refugees are associated with material and even electoral costs, governments try to avoid these costs through deterring refugees and asylum-seekers, using policies that make immigration impossible or highly unattractive for them (Thielemann 2006).

In the EU context, this led to a situation of 'downward' regulatory competition (race to the bottom) in protection standards for asylum-seekers and refugees in the 1990s. Top recipient countries, which could be termed 'strong regulators' as they tended to have elaborate and densely regulated asylum systems, introduced restrictive policies with the aim of reducing their application numbers (Zaun 2017b: 61-71). When one country introduced restrictive policies, others would do the same in order not to stand out as being 'soft touch' (Vink 2005: 106). This approach, however, was becoming increasingly unsustainable, as Member States could not endlessly downgrade domestic rights, which were protected through courts. A point in case is that of the United Kingdom (UK), which tried to transfer asylum-seekers persecuted by non-state actors back to France and Germany in line with the Dublin Convention. The asylum-seekers in question had entered the UK through these two countries. However, the UK's attempt failed due to court rulings stating that returning these asylum-seekers violated the norm of *non-refoulement*, a fundamental principle of international law forbidding to return someone to a country where they would face persecution. In contrast to the UK, Germany

2 Betts (2003), however, sees also excludable benefits, which makes it an *impure* public good.

and France at the time did not recognise asylum-seekers which were persecuted by non-state actors such as rebel groups but only those persecuted by state authorities (UK Court of Appeal 1999). Divergence of asylum-standards were hence clearly becoming a problem in the eyes of governments which felt that they received a bigger share due to their more generous policies. In addition to negative regulatory competition (race to the bottom) between strong regulators, strong regulators were also highly concerned about the absence of any effective asylum legislation in weak regulator countries, including Italy and Greece as well as those states that were to accede the EU in 2004 or soon thereafter. Strong regulators feared that the absence of functioning asylum systems in these countries would motivate further secondary movements towards strong regulating countries which already received comparatively large numbers of asylum-seekers anyways (Zaun 2017: 16).

North-Western European strong regulators, such as Germany, the UK, France, the Netherlands, Sweden and Austria (Zaun 2016: 139, Zaun 2017b: 32) had been critical of secondary movements already since the opening of internal borders with the Schengen Agreement in 1985. With internal freedom of movement being introduced through the Schengen Agreement, North-Western strong regulators were no longer in the position to control their external borders so that potential asylum-seekers reaching any of the border states could travel further North. This fear was nurtured by the fact that many of the Southern (and the acceding Central-Eastern) Member States had comparatively 'porous' borders, which were not as strongly enforced as those in the North (Niemann 2006: 196-198). In exchange for becoming part of Schengen, Italy and Greece had to sign the Dublin Convention (Thielemann/Armstrong 2013). The Dublin Convention contained a catalogue of criteria according to which responsibility for an applicant should be determined. In essence, these criteria suggested that the state responsible for an asylum-seeker's entering of the Schengen area, e.g. through issuing a visa or through lax border control, should be held responsible and assess the asylum-seeker's claim. This approach placed most of the responsibility on the border countries.

Yet, with large refugee inflows entering the EU subsequent to the disintegration of the Soviet Union and Yugoslavia in the 1990s, it became clear that the Dublin Convention was poorly enforced and that countries such as Germany, Sweden and Austria were receiving a particularly large share of asylum-seekers (Niemann 2006: 196-198). Germany, which was a top recipient at that point therefore proposed the introduction of a refugee distribution mechanism. Like its national distribution scheme, the *Königsteiner Schlüssel*, this distribution key should consider three capacity variables, namely population, territory and gross domestic product of the state in question when redistributing asylum-seekers. Yet, given the lack of interest of those states receiving lower numbers of asylum applications, this quota system was never adopted (Thielemann 2003: 259-260).

As to policy harmonisation, Member States had not been able to agree on anything other than general principles throughout the 1990s (Zaun 2017: 64-68). Hence, strong regulators promoted further European integration of the policy area to ensure a more credible and better enforceable commitment of their weak regulating counterparts (Stetter 2000, Barbou des Places 2003). European asylum cooperation had the clear aim to ensure a more even refugee distribution through effective policy harmonisation and the introduction of an instrument to enforce the redistribution towards border countries.

After the (partial) communitarisation of asylum policies with the Treaty of Amsterdam, the EU therefore passed the Dublin II Regulation (Council 2003a). It takes up most policy ideas of the Dublin Convention, but as part of the European legislative framework it can be more easily enforced. For example, the Dublin II Regulation was also accompanied by the Eurodac Regulation (Council 2000) which suggested the collection of asylum-seekers' finger-prints to detect applicants who had already applied in one of the border countries. Additionally, the EU adopted several directives of which the Qualification Directive (harmonising grounds of recognition and content of status), the Procedures Directive (harmonising asylum procedures), and the Reception Conditions Directive (harmonising rights for those who are not yet recognised refugees but undergo an asylum procedure) were the most important ones (Council 2003b, Council 2004, Council 2005). These directives were introduced to develop common minimum standards for the protection of asylum-seekers and refugees. Of course, Member States were free to adopt more generous standards, but they were not allowed to fall below the threshold of these standards.

Several Member States, however, were unhappy with the limited degree of harmonisation and attributed this to the fact that asylum policies were only partly communitarised. For instance, the European Parliament (EP) was only consulted and not a co-legislator, the Council decided under unanimity instead of qualified majority vote and the competences of the Court of Justice of the European Union (CJEU) were clearly limited. The Treaty of Amsterdam had suggested a revision and potential full harmonisation of asylum policies after a period of five years. Germany, receiving lower numbers of asylum applications towards the finalisation of the Amsterdam Treaty, had blocked any full communitarisation of the area at the time (Hellmann et al. 2005: 151-153). Yet, around 2005, when full harmonisation was to be discussed again, the UK, otherwise an unlikely supporter of enhanced European integration, was receiving high numbers of applications and became a strong supporter of full communitarisation. In a package deal with Germany the UK received full communitarisation of the area, accepting that labour migration, an issue that had become important for the German chancellor, would not be fully communitarised yet (Ibid.: 154).

After the full communitarisation of asylum policies, a second round of legislative instruments including the so-called "recast directives" and the Dublin III Regulation were adopted. This time, the directives aimed at a full harmonisation of asylum policies in EU Member States. This was undoubtedly an ambitious aim, as even the first phase instruments proved to be poorly implemented, with some Member States still having only inchoate asylum systems. The European Court of Human Rights (ECtHR) judgments of *MSS vs Belgium and Greece* (ECtHR 2011) and *Tarakhel vs. Switzerland* (ECtHR 2014) as well as the CJEU judgment *NS vs. Secretary of State for the Home Department* (CJEU 2011) provide evidence for the poor asylum systems to be found in Greece and Italy, for instance, which eventually led to the suspension of Dublin transfers to these countries.

On paper, however, full harmonisation of asylum policies officially had been achieved by 2015, the year of the 'refugee crisis'. In the following two sections I will explain why responses were poor, both as regards the solidarity with states that received large numbers of applications as well as concerning the comparability of asylum standards across the EU. This will allow me to draw conclusions on the viability and potential effectiveness of future reform.

3. Shifting people

In this section I provide an explanation for the absence of an effective mechanism for responsibility-sharing with top recipients in the EU. On 22 September 2015, the Council, backed by the EP, agreed to the relocation of 120,000 asylum-seekers from 'frontline' states. These countries had been key entry points for asylum-seekers and were overwhelmed by the recently increasing inflow. Part of this process was the proposal of a temporary quota system distributing refugees based on the size of the population of the new host country (40% weighting), the total GDP (40% weighting) and two corrective factors, namely the average number of asylum applications per one million inhabitants over the previous five years (10% weighting with a 30% cap of the population and the GDP effect) and the unemployment rate (also 10% with the same 30% cap) (European Commission 2015). In addition, the proposal also recommended discussions on a permanent quota system relying on the same parameters. However, these were aborted already in early 2016. Instead, a revised version of the Dublin Regulation (Dublin IV) according to which refugees could be distributed in times of crisis to take pressures off 'frontline' states has been under discussion since May 2016. This is quite striking, as the Dublin system has obviously been inapplicable since transfers to Greece and Italy under certain conditions were ruled unlawful. Although not fully dismissed by the time this chapter is written, the proposal for a any kind of quota system was declared 'finished' by then Council President Fico in September 2016 (Zalan 2016). Since September 2016, negotiations revolve around an even less binding system of 'flexible solidarity', proposed by the Visegrad states. According to this proposal, states that do not want to receive any refugees can provide financial support and expertise instead.

Drawing on Betts (2009), I argue that the Suasion Game can explain the stability of the Dublin regime and the absence of a real and fair distribution scheme. The game envisages two states, the host-state and the non-host state. Of course, these categories should be understood as two points on a continuum rather than clearly separable categories, as in practice most states receive some refugees. Yet, some countries are clearly top recipients, whereas others receive comparatively few asylum-seekers. The non-host state has two options: to offer responsibility-sharing (cooperation) or not to offer it (defection). Since all Member States have incentives to minimise their intake of refugees, however, non-hosts that do not want to receive (additional) refugees prefer unilateral action or the *status quo* to cooperation. Top host states also want to minimise their intake of refugees; responsibility-sharing would be a viable option for them to achieve this aim. However, host states have nothing to offer in return and are hence in a less favourable bargaining position. The host state therefore faces two different options: to offer asylum (cooperation) or not to offer it (defection). In line with the Suasion Game host states have no alternative to cooperation, both because it is their obligation under international law to process asylum claims made on their territory and because of an inherent threat to security and stability if there are large numbers of people present on its territory deprived of access to any civil or social rights (see above). The non-host state's commitment to responsibility-sharing, on the other hand, is purely discretionary. Given this power asymmetry, the equilibrium is Cooperate-Defect, which means that the host-state opts for protection whereas the non-host state defects from cooperation and refrains from offering responsibility-sharing.

This behaviour could also be observed during the "refugee crisis". While top recipient countries had a clear interest in lowering their numbers through engaging other Member States in responsibility-sharing, those Member States on the low receiving end had no incentives at all to raise their numbers through a permanent quota system. In both cases this can be explained through restrictive voter preferences, fuelled by populist parties that have increasingly gained ground in EU Member States in recent years (Zaun 2018).

Thus, low recipient Member States such as Poland, the Czech Republic, Slovakia, Romania and Hungary[3] were also rather critical towards the (temporary) crisis relocation of 120,000 asylum-seekers. Except for Poland, these

3 At the beginning of the "refugee crisis", Hungary was in fact one of the top recipient countries in the EU. However, with its inhumane and highly restrictive practices and

Member States eventually voted against the agreement. Yet, as they were not able to build a blocking minority, the agreement was nevertheless adopted.

While several Member States, including France, Spain, Bulgaria, the Baltic states and the Visegrad countries were rather cautious with their support for the temporary scheme and would only position themselves rather late in the negotiations, they were clear opponents of a permanent quota system. Permanent quotas would have implied a continuous redistribution of refugees from the top hosts of asylum-seekers, Germany and Sweden, and the transit countries Italy and Greece. Top hosts had thus no alternative but to offer access to asylum procedure to those present on their territory. Non-hosts did not opt for responsibility-sharing as keeping the *status quo* of unilateral action was much more beneficial to them. Rising populism, fuelled by media discourse around terrorist attacks in some of the more culturally mixed Western European top hosts, is an additional factor explaining the particularly critical attitude of some of the Central and Eastern European Member States towards asylum-seekers. Additionally, many states are not willing to support the main recipient countries Germany and Sweden, which are not only two of the wealthiest European Member States, but which were also criticised by their fellow Member States for having invited large numbers of asylum-seekers to Europe through their open-door policies (see Zaun 2018).

Top hosting countries therefore needed to reduce rising electoral pressures through minimising their numbers of asylum applications using other means. German chancellor Merkel received a lot of criticism domestically for her temporary open border policy. Not only the populist party *Alternative für Deutschland,* but also members of her own party, particularly Bavarian Prime Minister Horst Seehofer, were very vocal in voicing their criticism. Merkel's chancellery thus brokered the EU-Turkey deal, which aimed at minimising the inflow of asylum-seekers into Europe by 'illegalising' any asylum applicant who entered Greece and did not wait for resettlement to Europe in Turkey. As the deal suggested an exchange of those irregularly entering Europe and those waiting for being relocated from Turkey, this was expected to disincentivise refugees from crossing the Greek border without permission and thus, in the long run, minimise numbers of asylum applicants in Europe altogether. Through this deal and other policy restrictions, Merkel was successful in regaining electoral support (Infratest Dimap 2016, Zaun 2018).

Issue linkage is usually considered an instrument to overcome the Suasion Game dynamics (Betts 2009: 37). If hosts are able to propose a package deal, either giving non-hosts something they need or threatening with non-agreement on another policy proposal that is important to the non-hosts, they can create leverage. Only Italy and Greece made an attempt into this direction, suggesting that the Visegrad states should no longer receive Structural Funds

---

the subsequent invitation by German chancellor Merkel, asylum-seekers moved on to Germany and Sweden, in particular, from late August 2015 on (see Zaun 2018).

if they continued denying any solidarity towards transit and host countries. Eventually, some of the EU budget was re-allocated to migration related purposes (Euractive 2016). However, it was not an option to completely deny the Visegrad states any access to Structural Funds, because the EU budget is spent according to specific criteria and as long as states can fulfill these criteria they have access to this funding.

In a nutshell, refugee distribution in line with a capacity-based quota system failed due to the lack of will of those states that currently receive few applications. These states are not ready to trade the current *status quo* for a cooperation that would force them to host additional asylum-seekers on a regular basis. Thus, the *unfair status quo* of the Dublin system remains, placing the responsibility completely on the border countries and shaming them for their porous borders. As Member States are unable to agree on refugee distribution internally, the issue is externalised through strengthened border control (e.g. with the help of the newly introduced European Border and Coast Guards) and by shifting the responsibility to countries outside of the EU (e.g. through the EU-Turkey Deal).

4. Shifting policy

After having explained the absence of a fair and functioning distribution scheme for asylum-seekers, I will now provide an explanation for the low degree of harmonisation in EU asylum policy. One might indeed wonder how it is possible that after two legislative rounds aiming at the establishment of a *Common* European Asylum System refugee policies still differ to an extent that some countries still do not even have a clearly defined asylum procedure with standardised procedural rules. Both the strong regulatory (mainly Northern European) and the weak regulatory (mainly Southern European) approach towards asylum and immigration have advantages for refugees (see Finotelli 2009 arguing for the weak regulatory approach and Zaun 2017: 33-36 for the strong regulatory approach). Yet, it is striking that these two approaches still co-exist in the EU after various attempts of harmonisation.

As mentioned above, initiatives for harmonisation came particularly from the side of the strong regulators, which hoped that the introduction of an asylum system with sound procedures and substantial rights for applicants would make it easier for asylum-seekers to apply for protection already in the low regulating border countries. Clearly, the strong regulators’ focus was on the distributional implications of policy harmonisation rather than the strengthening of refugee protection. Interestingly, most strong regulators expected their own regulatory system to be among the most generous of the

Member States (Zaun 2017: 67). Strong regulation and high protection standards, however, do not necessarily coincide. In fact, each strong regulator has a specific mix of both restrictive and liberal (i.e. "rights protecting") policies in place. When negotiating at the EU level, strong regulators became aware of this and tried to avoid any changes of their asylum law through EU directives (Ibid.: 172-176). Particularly, they tried to avoid standards higher than their national ones being adopted as – under minimum standards and common standards – this would force them to change (more specifically: raise) their national standards. While a strong regulator with a particularly liberal approach on access to the labour market for asylum-seekers wanted standards to be raised in those Member States that provided it late or not at all, the same Member States was quite reluctant to change its policies on other issues on which it had a more restrictive policy in place. Thus, EU asylum policies did not result in upward regulatory competition and EU asylum policies on the highest protection level (race to the top), but rather centred around the lowest common denominator of the strong regulators (Ibid.: 176). However, in various instances the standards agreed on exceeded those previously applied in the weak regulating Member States, particularly Italy and Greece. Having no credible experience and expertise in the area of asylum policies, these countries were less vocal in the negotiations and more prone to compromise than strong regulators with their long-standing experience and their high stakes in the topic. Additionally, weak regulators' positions were regularly not taken seriously. Even during the high inflow of refugees into Greece and Italy after the so-called "Arab Spring" in Northern Africa and the Middle East, both countries received little support, as other Member States underlined that their problems were purely home-made and a result of their poorly working asylum systems (Ibid.: 176-206).

In sum, EU asylum harmonisation tried to impose the regulatory model(s) present in strong regulating Northern European Member States onto the weak regulating Member States in the South of Europe. This unidirectional approach resulted in a transfer of norms from the North to the South without these norms resonating at all with national norms and practices. Given the poor administrative capacity in the weak regulating states, these norms were not openly contested during the negotiations and they were actually implemented on paper (with some directives even being literally transposed into national law). However, they were not implemented in practice. This explains why to date asylum procedures in Greece lack formalisation and reception centres in Italy do not provide remotely sufficient places for the number of applications received (Zaun 2017: 235-239).

5. Sharing responsibility based on capacity: How EU asylum policies could make a difference

The previous sections have discussed the assumption that since the early beginnings of EU cooperation in this area the aim of EU asylum policies has been the redistribution of asylum-seekers. Top recipient countries in North-Western Europe, which had strongly regulated asylum systems, tried to shift the asylum-seekers they received towards other North-Western strong regulators or towards the South-Eastern weak regulators. They employed two means to achieve this aim: First, they would initiate a physical redistribution towards the border countries by making them, as first entry points for asylum-seekers, responsible for the processing of the application. They achieved this through a package deal which, in exchange for agreeing to Dublin, granted the border countries access to the Schengen Area. Dublin, however, failed, given the highly disparate conditions that asylum-seekers found in EU Member States. Court rulings clearly stated that transferring an applicant to Italy and Greece could entail *refoulement* and degrading treatment, given the poor asylum systems of these countries. Second, they initiated policy harmonisation to establish the same standards in all Member States in order to make all Member States equally attractive. Of course, none of the strong regulators was ready to change their own system which resulted in policy harmonisation being barely ambitious in the first place. And in the cases where upgrades of protection standards had been achieved on paper (in the weak regulating states) they did not translate into practice.

The combination of these two policy failures, i.e. 1) the failure to develop a fair capacity-based distribution system and 2) the obvious capacity gap to process asylum applications and to host asylum-seekers that still exists between strong and weak regulators, fuelled the management crisis that we witnessed after the high inflow of asylum-seekers in 2015.

We can therefore draw several lessions for the reform process. First, forcing the border countries to take the biggest share of refugees at the same time as trying to build effective asylum systems in these countries was doomed to fail right from the beginning. Any attempt to reform European asylum policies will need to take the variable capacities of the hosting states into account. The distribution key adopted in the emergency relocation process, which accounted for the diverse capacity of Member States, was therefore a step into the right direction. From this perspective, an permanent quota system would be a much better approach than the perpetuation of the Dublin system or a system of 'flexible solidarity'.

The section on policy harmonisation has stressed that the lack of such harmonisation is mainly based on a lack of administrative capacity in the weak regulating border countries. Therefore, adopting a new round of EU Directives (or even Regulations) will not ensure more and better compliance. Instead, further capacity building and exchange between those countries that have long-standing experience in receiving refugees and those countries that do not, are necessary. Extending the competences of the European Asylum Support Office (EASO), as is currently discussed and partly already done, could help to bridge this capacity gap.

Externalising refugee flows through measures such as the EU-Turkey deal or the deal with Libya in 2008, is not a sustainable solution, because it makes the EU dependent on undemocratic and instable regimes with a questionable human rights party record. With rising numbers of forcibly displaced people worldwide, the issue of refugee protection is here to stay and the EU will need to do better in its response. After all, only a minority of refugees ever reaches Europe, while the majority is hosted by much poorer countries and regions in the immediate neighbourhood of the refugee sending countries.

References

Barbou des Places, Ségolène (2003): Evolution of Asylum Legislation in the EU. Insights from Regulatory Competition Theory. EU Working Paper RSC 2003/16: San Domenico di Fiesole.

Betts, Alexander (2003): Public Goods Theory and the Provision of Refugee Protection. The Role of the Joint Product Model in Burden-Sharing Theory. In: Journal of Refugee Studies 16, 3, pp. 274-296.

Betts, Alexander (2009): Protection by Persuasion. International Cooperation in the Refugee Regime. Ithaca: Cornell University Press.

Brücker, Herbert/Epstein, Gil S./McCormick, Barry/Saint-Paul, Gilles, Venturini, Alessandra/Zimmermann, Klaus (2002): Managing Migration in the European Welfare State. In: Boeri, Tito/Hanson, Gordon H./McCormick, Barry (eds.): Immigration Policy and the Welfare System. A Report for the Fondazione Rudolfo Debenedetti. Oxford: Oxford University Press, pp. 1-167.

CJEU (2011): Joined cases of N.S. v. United Kingdom and M.E. v. Ireland. C-411-10 and C-493-10. Luxembourg. Available at: http://www.asylumlawdatabase.eu/en/content/cjeu-c-411-10-and-c-493-10-joined-cases-ns-v-united-kingdom-and-me-v-ireland (accessed 19 January 2017).

Council (2000): Council Regulation (EC) No 2725/2000 of 11 December 2000 concerning the establishment of 'Eurodac' for the comparison of fingerprints for the effective application of the Dublin Convention. OJ L 316/15. 11 December. Available at: http://eur-lex.europa.eu/LexUriServ/LexUriServ.do?uri=CELEX: 32000R2725:EN:HTML (accessed 19 January 2017).

Council (2003a): Council Regulation (EC) No 343/2003 of 18 February 2003 establishing the criteria and mechanisms for determining the Member State responsible for examining an asylum application lodged in one of the Member States by a third-country national. 18 February. Available at http://eur-lex.europa.eu/legal-content/EN/TXT/HTML/?uri=URISERV:l33153&from=EN (accessed 19 January 2017).

Council (2003b): Council Directive 2003/9/EC of 27 January laying down minimum standards for the reception of asylum-seekers. OJ L 31/18.6 February. Available at http://eur-lex.europa.eu/(accessed 19 January 2017).

Council (2004): Council Directive 2004/83/EC of 29 April 2004 on minimum standards for qualification and status of third country nationals or stateless persons as refugees or persons who otherwise need international protection and the content of the protection granted. OJ L 304/12. 30 September. Available at http://www.refworld.org/pdfid/4157e75e4.pdf (accessed 16 May 2015).

Council (2005): Council Directive 2005/85/EC of 1 December 2005 on minimum standards on procedures in Member States for granting and withdrawing refugee status. OJ L 326/13. Available at http://eur-lex.europa.eu/LexUriServ/LexUriServ.do?uri=OJ:L:2005:326:0013:0034:EN:PDF (accessed 19 May 2015).

ECtHR (2011): M.S.S. v. Belgium and Greece. Application Number 30696/09. Strasbourg. Available at: http://hudoc.echr.coe.int/sites/eng/pages/search.aspx?i=001-103050 (accessed 18 January 2017).

ECtHR (2014): Tarakhel v. Switzerland. Application No. 29217/12. Strasbourg. Available at: http://hudoc.echr.coe.int/sites/eng/pages/search.aspx?i=001-148070 (accessed 18 January 2017).

Euractive (2016): EU to slash funds to Eastern Europe to step up migration budget. 13 September. Available at: https://www.euractiv.com/section/eu-priorities-2020/news/eu-to-slash-funds-to-eastern-europe-to-step-up-migration-budget/(accessed 7 August 2017).

Eurostat (2017): 1.2 million first time asylum-seekers registered in 2016, 16 March. Available at: http://ec.europa.eu/eurostat/documents/2995521/7921609/3-16032017-BP-EN.pdf/e5fa98bb-5d9d-4297-9168-d07c67d1c9e1 (accessed 8 August 2017).

European Commission (2015): Proposal for a Regulation of the European Parliament and of the Council establishing a crisis relocation mechanism and amending Regulation (EU) No 604/2013 of the European Parliament and of the Council of 26 June 2013 establishing the criteria and mechanisms for determining the Member State responsible for examining an application for international protection lodged in one of the Member States by a third country national or a stateless person. 9 September. Available at «http://eur-lex.europa.eu/resource.html?uri=cellar:92b8154b-56cd-11e5-afbf-01aa75ed71a1.0007.02/DOC_1&format=PDF» (accessed 2 May 2016).

Finotelli, Claudia (2009): The North-South Myth Revisited. A Comparison of the Italian and German Migration Regimes. In: West European Politics 32, 5, pp. 886-903.

Gluns, Danielle/Wessels, Janna (2017): Waste of Paper or Useful Tool? The Potential of the Temporary Protection Directive in the Current 'Refugee Crisis'. In: Refugee Survey Quarterly 23, 2, pp. 57-83.

Hellmann, Gunther/Baumann, Rainer/Bösche, Monika/Herborth, Benjamin/Wagner, Wolfgang (2005): De-Europeanization by default? Germany's EU policy in defence and asylum. In: Foreign Policy Analysis 1, 1, pp. 143-164.

Holzer, Thomas/Schneider, Gerald (2002): Asylpolitik auf Abwegen. Nationalstaatliche und Europäische Reaktionen auf die Globalisierung der Flüchtlingsströme. Opladen: Leske + Budrich.

Infratest Dimap (2016): Politikerzufriedenheit Angela Merkel/Horst Seehofer. Available at http://www.infratest-dimap.de/umfragen-analysen/bundesweit/ard-deutschlandtrend/2016/maerz/(accessed 19 December 2016).

Genschel, Philipp/Markus Jachtenfuchs (2018): From market integration to core state powers. The Eurozone crisis, the refugee crisis, and integration theory. In: Journal of Common Market Studies, 56, 1, pp. 178-196.

Menz, Georg (2008): "Useful" Gastarbeiter, Burdensome Asylum-Seekers, and the Second Wave of Welfare Retrenchment. Exploring the Nexus Between Migration and the Welfare State. In: Parsons, Craig A./Smeeding, Timothy M. (eds.): Immigration and transformation of Europe. Cambridge: Cambridge University Press, pp. 393-418.

Niemann, Arne (2006): Explaining Decisions in the European Union. Cambridge: Cambridge University Press.

Noll, Gregor (2003): Risky Games? A Theoretical Approach to Burden-Sharing in the Asylum Field. In: Journal of Refugee Studies 16, 3, pp. 236-252.

Roper, Steven D./Barria, Lilian A. (2010): Burden-Sharing in the Funding of UNHCR. Refugee Protection as an Impure Public Good. In: Journal of Conflict Resolution 54, 4, pp. 616-637.

Stetter, Stephan (2000): Regulating Migration. Authority Delegation in Justice and Home Affairs. In: Journal of European Public Policy 7, 1, pp. 80-103.

Suhrke, Astri (1998): Burden-Sharing During Refugee Emergencies. The Logic of Collective versus National Action. In: Journal of Refugee Studies 11, 4, pp. 396-415.

Thielemann, Eiko/Armstrong, Carolyn (2013): Understanding European Asylum Cooperation under the Schengen/Dublin System. A Public Goods Framework. In: European Security 22, 2, pp. 148-164.

Thielemann, Eiko/El-Enany, Nadine (2010): Refugee Protection as a Collective Action Problem. Is the EU Shirking its Responsibilities? In: European Security 19, 2, pp. 209-229.

Thielemann, Eiko (2003): Between Interests and Norms. Explaining Responsibility-Sharing in the European Union. In: Journal of Refugee Studies 16, 3, pp. 253-273.

Thielemann, Eiko (2006): The effectiveness of governments' attempts to control unwanted migration. In In: Parsons, Craig A./Smeeding, Timothy M. (eds.): Immigration and transformation of Europe. Cambridge: Cambridge University Press, pp. 442-472.
UK Court of Appeal (1999): R v. Secretary of State for the Home Department, Ex parte Adan and Others, 23 July. Available at http://www.refworld.org/docid/3ae6b6ad14.html (accessed 19 January 2017).
Vink, Maarten P. (2005): Limits of European Citizenship. European Integration and Domestic Immigration Policies. Basingstoke: Palgrave.
Zalan, Eszter (2016): EU Migrant Quota Idea is Finished, Ficos Says. In: Euobserver, 27 September. Available at: https://euobserver.com/migration/135245 (accessed 18 January 2017).
Zaun, Natascha (2016): Why EU Asylum Standards Exceed the Lowest Common Denominator. The Role of Regulatory Expertise in EU Decision-Making. In: Journal of European Public Policy 23, 1, pp. 136-154.
Zaun, Natascha (2017): EU Asylum Policies: The Power of Strong Regulating States. Basingstoke: Palgrave.
Zaun, Natascha (2018): States as Gatekeepers in EU Asylum Politics. Explaining the Non-Adoption of a Refugee Quota System. In: Journal of Common Market Studies, 56, 1, pp. 44-62.

Abbreviations

Title	Abbreviaton
Common European Asylum System	CEAS
Court of Justice of the European Union	CJEU
European Asylum Support Office	EASO
European Court of Human Rights	ECtHR
European Parliament	EP
European Union	EU

10. State capacity in crisis: EU conditionality and administrative reform in the post-communist new member states

Florian Wittmann

1. Introduction

The current illiberal tendencies in Poland and Hungary were accompanied by massive changes in the state apparatus. Fluctuation of personnel after elections is nothing new for the postcommunist Central and Eastern European Countries (CEECs) – however, the unprecedented scale has triggered debates about the ability of the European Union to secure the rule of law in these countries. While the long-term effects of such changes remain to be seen, it is not for the first time that state capacity in these countries becomes an issue of debate. Already the accession of the post-communist CEECs was accompanied by fears about the emergence of an "Eastern problem" (cf. Sedelmeier 2008), as it remained an open question whether these countries would be able to fulfil their duties as EU member states.

This chapter takes a closer look at the state capacity of the post-communist CEECs and the power and constraints of the EU to promote administrative reform. Unravelling the constraints and pitfalls of EU conditionality are key for understanding the role the EU can play for ensuring sufficient administrative capacity. Poor administrative capacity in its member states does not only undermine the inner working of the EU, but also renders it vulnerable against current challenges and crises. The absence of a capable administration is a major obstacle for fulfilling the membership obligations, such as transposing EU rules into national legislation (cf. Haverland/Romeijn 2007). Moreover, the absence of sufficient administrative capacity can undermine the working of EU policies, such as Cohesion Policy. The ability to absorb EU funds hinges on sufficient administrative capacity to cope with the complex procedures of managing and distributing EU resources (Bachtler/Gorzelak 2007).

This chapter shows that while on average state capacity is still lower than in many of the old member states, differences are not as pronounced as expected. Furthermore, it is highlighted that the main problem arises from the inability of the EU to ensure sufficient reform progress during the short accession period. Consequently, a re-consideration of existing strategies is necessary in order to maximize the efficiency of EU conditionality and prepare national administrations better for their working in the EU.

2. Administrative capacity in the CEECs

In contrast to the optimistic accounts after the downfall of communism, the hope for a quick adjustment of CEECs to a Western European style administration did not materialise. Instead, the reform process was rather slow-paced and characterised by incomprehensive reforms and limited progress, lagging behind the accomplishments in other areas (cf. Verheijen 2007: 311). Administrative reforms were particularly complicated due to two factors: Firstly, governments faced the challenge that while being key actors in the necessary economic and political reforms, administrations were subject to reform demands (cf. Buzogány/Stuchlík 2010). Secondly, the demand for reform was far more comprehensive than in the case of the new democracies of Southern Europe (Verheijen 2007: 312). The "'real socialist' administrative system" (König 1992) was characterised by the system of nomenclature and the subordination to the implementation of the communist party's decisions. Therefore, the bureaucracy in the CEECs suffered from high levels of politicisation and low levels of professionalism (Goetz/Wollmann 2001: 883f.).

Relying on the widely-used indicator of government effectiveness of the World Bank (Kaufman/Kraay 2016), figure 1 maps the differences of the overall quality of the administration and the working of the state apparatus in the 28 EU member states. This yields several insights. Firstly, on average, post-communist new member states rank below their Western counterparts. However, there are noteworthy differences between countries. Whereas Romania and Bulgaria are at the bottom of EU member states, the Baltic republics rank similar to Spain and Portugal and ahead of Italy and Greece. Moreover, when taking the 90% confidence intervals into consideration for cross-country comparison (as suggested by Kaufman et al. 2010: 13f.), the differences between old and new member states are even less pronounced. Except for the top performers (Netherlands, Finland, Denmark) and worst-performers (Romania, Bulgaria, Hungary, Croatia) the differences among other member states hardly come out as significant. Within a confidence interval of 90%, e.g. no significantly different levels of government effectiveness can be assumed between Poland and Portugal.

Figure 1: Government Effectiveness of EU member states (Own presentation based on Kaufman/Kraay (2016), percentile ranks including 90% confidence intervals)

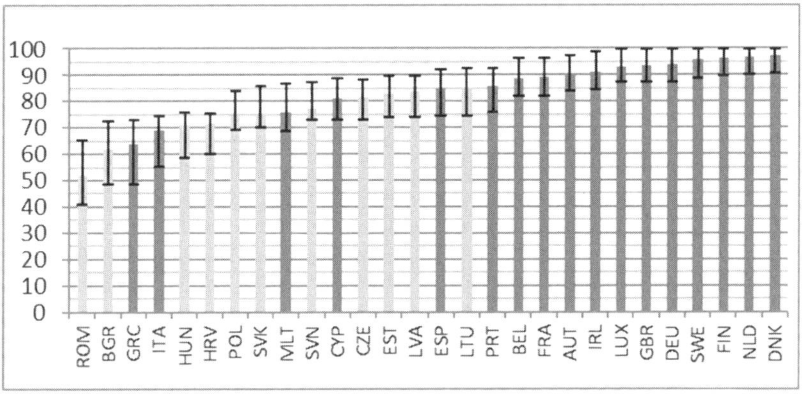

This perspective is also confirmed when taking into consideration several studies that research the consequences of fund absorption and compliance with EU demands. Sedelmeier (2008) finds that in the first years after EU accession, formal compliance rates with EU law in new member states were not worse than in old member states, with some of the post-communist countries ranking even among the top performers. In a similar vein, Tosun (2014) reports absorption rates for the new member states, which joined the EU in 2004, being even above the average of old member states. However, as Baun/Marek (2014: 140) report, some countries (especially Romania, but also Bulgaria, Hungary, the Czech Republic, and Slovakia) face difficulties in spending money from EU regional policy.

Thus, the emerging image is more complex than a general "Eastern problem" due to low administrative capacity. Rather there is a remarkable heterogeneity among countries, raising the question where these differences stem from. Whereas some countries, such as Lithuania, rank similar to many old member states, other countries like Romania or Bulgaria are substantially lagging behind in their administrate capacity. Why did some of the post-communist new EU member states achieve levels of administrative capacity similar to those of the older member states, whereas others did not? Did the "transformative power" (Grabbe 2006) of the EU fail to promote administrative reform in the pre-accession.

3. The EU and administrative reforms

3.1 Administrative reform and the EU accession process

Given the concerns about the insufficient progress in the field of civil service reform in post-communist countries in the 1990s, the EU undertook measures to promote the development of administrative capacity in these countries. For the first time during an EU enlargement, administrative capacity was linked to the membership perspective, making civil service reform a precondition for EU accession (Dimitrova 2002: 171). Reform progress was evaluated by the annual SIGMA reports (a joint initiative of EU and Organisation for Economic Co-operation and Development, OECD) whose findings were incorporated into the progress reports of the European Commission. While the linkage of reform progress to the accession perspective created strong incentives for reforms, applicants could benefit from technical and financial support from the PHARE and *twinning* programme.

To which extent did these efforts, however, result in an increase of state capacity? A closer look at the World Bank indicators and their development over time reveals a rather sobering picture. Since 1998, the year when official accession talks started with the first CEECs (Estonia, Poland, Slovenia, Hungary, and Czech Republic), there was only a modest improvement in most countries compared to 2004 (1st Eastern enlargement) and 2015 (the most current data available). In fact, only Latvia's pathway can be interpreted as a significant increase in administrative capacity, while Lithuania is a borderline case. Whereas Bulgaria and Romania improved their position over time, the changes yet cannot be interpreted as significant. Other countries showed either insignificant increases (Czech Republic, Estonia) or revealed even stagnating or deteriorating trends of government effectiveness (Hungary, Slovenia, Slovakia, Poland).

To sum up, the overall picture is one of only limited progress and indicates the absence of substantial improvement of administrative capacity in most CEE countries. These findings suggest that the problems with administrative capacity in the post-accession period mainly stem from insufficient reform progress prior to EU accession. Why did, despite efforts, EU pressure for administrative reform did not result in more tangible results? In the following I highlight several aspects that undermined the ability of the EU to successfully promote the development of institutional capacity.

Figure 2: Government Effectiveness 1998-2015 in CEECs (Own presentation based on Kaufman/Kraay (2016), percentile ranks including 90% confidence intervals)

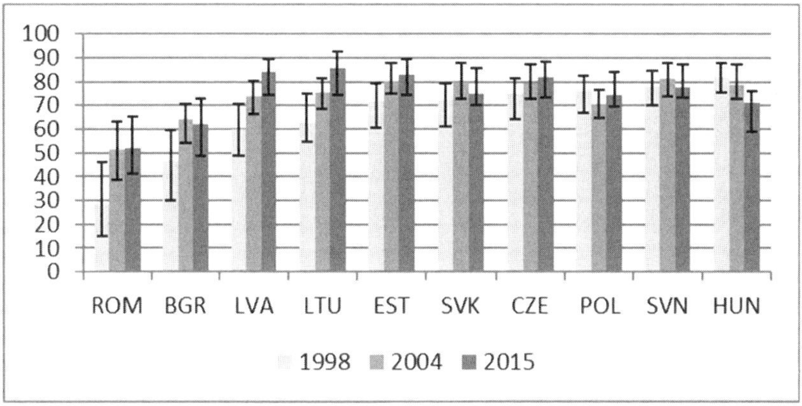

3.2 The limits of EU conditionality

First, EU conditionality, i.e. making EU accession conditional on the fulfilment of certain reform measures, was less effective than anticipated. This is in line with the findings that the effects of conditionality should not be overestimated (Haughton 2007). Above all, the effectiveness of conditionality was undermined by the limited means of the European Commission to thoroughly monitor reform achievements in the field of civil service. On the one hand, the EU lacked a blueprint for administrative reform, only providing a set of shared principles, the so called *European Administrative space* (cf. Cardona Péreto/Freibert 2007: 52). That gave candidate countries substantial leeway when undertaking reform steps. On the other hand, the ability to monitor was undermined by the fact that civil service reforms did not constitute a separate point in accession negotiations, but instead were dispersed across several chapters (cf. Meyer-Sahling 2009: 79).

Consequently, not all reforms were in line with EU demands, but partly even ran counter to it. The reform in Slovakia was designed in a way that allowed the incumbent government to secure posts of loyal employees against a dismissal in case of the anticipated loss of the upcoming elections (cf. O'Dwyer 2002: 31). In a similar vein, in Hungary an exceptionally well paid Senior Public Servant staff was created whose approximately 300 members were hand-picked by the Prime Minister and did not require other qualification than a university diploma (Gajduschek 2007: 350). Many of these positions were filled prior to the 2002 elections and triggered concerns about lacking qualifications and politicisation.

Secondly, the ability of the EU to exert pressure on countries varied according to applicants' membership perspectives (Dimitrova 2005: 86ff.). Countries enjoying a relatively secure negotiation position due to their size and overall progress, such as Poland, Hungary, or the Czech Republic, faced substantially less constraints than countries with more precarious perspectives. This is well illustrated by the extreme case of the Czech Republic which was the only country to join the EU without an implemented civil service act. Sigma's (2003: 1) early warnings "that the Czech Republic has passed a law on civil service only to comply with the formal requirements" turned out to be true as the implementation of the law was postponed several times and finally abandoned in 2007.

Besides this outstanding case of non-reform, the existing variance is well illustrated by a comparison between Latvia, which was one of the countries with an endangered membership perspective, and Hungary, which enjoyed a relatively safe membership perspective. An assessment of the pre-accession reforms along the benchmarks used by Meyer-Sahling (2009) allows mapping the differences between these two countries. Latvia, one of the laggards in the area of civil service reform adopted civil service reforms only under massive pressure from the EU (Dimitrova 2005: 88). However, these rules were relatively comprehensive and mostly in line with EU demands (cf. Figure 3).

Figure 3: Pre-accession level of reforms (Own assessment based on Sigma country reports and Meyer-Sahling 2009; +: fulfillment of EU criteria, o: partial fulfillment; - : no fulfillment).

	LVA	**HUN**
implemented *Civil Service Law*	+	+
job protection of civil servants	+	o
training programmes	+	o
administrative independence (merit-based promotions)	+	-
compulsory advertisement of job vacancies	+	-
central coordination of civil service	o	o
performance evaluation system	o	o
regulations for rights and duties of civil servants	o	o
recruitment process	o	-
transparent and predictable salary system	o	-

Hungary, by contrast, one of the vanguards of civil service reform in the 1990s, did not invest major efforts in its civil service reforms during the EU accession process. Consequently, civil service legislation in Hungary was considered as a "legal façade" that allowed governments to exercise substantial influence on the administration (Gajduschek 2007: 351). Contrary to Latvia, there was no obligation to advertise job vacancies publicly and also the procedure for merit-based promotions was seen as far less developed and more prone to political influence.

3.3 The small window of opportunity for reform

As administrative reforms require sufficiently long time periods (Politt 2011), an additional problem arose from the short "window of opportunity" in which reforms took place. The ability of the EU to push for substantial civil service reforms was severely limited. As civil service legislation is not part of the *acquis communautaire*, the influence of the EU decreases after accession as even permanent deviations cannot be sanctioned by EU institutions (cf. Epstein/Sedelmeier 2008). Consequently, national governments enjoy substantial leeway once they became members of the EU. However, the influence of the EU did not start vanishing with EU accession. It had already declined from the moment when accession talks had successfully been finished (cf. Steunenberg/Dimitrova 2007; Haughton 2007), so in case of the CEECs as early as from the end of 2002. However, Bulgaria and Romania, which joined the EU in 2007, were subjected to the newly created *Mechanism for Cooperation and Verification*. This allows the EU to retain some leverage towards these states even after accession, as the overall institutional quality and the level of corruption in these countries raised serious concerns.

A closer look at the timing of reforms in the candidate countries suggests an often-problematic constellation. Virtually all countries undertook substantial parts of their reforms only shortly prior to accession (cf. Dimitrova 2005: 85). Slovakia, Slovenia, Estonia, the Czech Republic and Latvia adopted new laws regulating the civil service or civil servants in 2001 or 2002. Hungary passed amendments to its Civil Service Law from 1992 in 2001, whereas similar processes took place in Lithuania and Bulgaria in 2002 and 2003, respectively. As the formal adoption of civil service legislation is only a first step and the implementation and materialisation of effects require a longer time perspective (Pollitt 2011), this left only a short window of opportunity for reform under the auspices of EU conditionality.

Moreover, reform sustainability was undermined by the fact that in most countries reforms were primarily undertaken due to EU conditionality pressure and hence could not rely on domestic support (Dimitrova 2002: 186). Moreover, Cardona/Dannequin (2010: 11) highlight that reform demands towards CEEC implied double-standards which undermined their legitimacy towards accession candidates. In particular, the demand to depoliticize national administrations by completely refraining from political appointments would also be an obstacle for many old member states.

Given the aforementioned constraints, it comes as no surprise that civil service reforms came under pressure even prior to formal accession, starting with the Slovakian government to dismantle its reforms at the end of 2002. Most other countries similarly showed some sign of reform backsliding and (partially) revoked pre-accession reforms. Reform efforts in line with EU guidelines, therefore, were strongly limited (Meyer-Sahling 2009).

4. Lessons learned: conclusions

So, what are the lessons learned? As argued above, administrative capacity plays a crucial role for the working of the European Union. However, in the case of CEECs, the attempts of the EU to promote administrative reform produced only limited effects. Whereas some countries such as Lithuania caught up with older member states and rank above some of the old member states, other countries are still substantially lagging behind. The EU's instruments to boost overall development of administrative capacity via conditionality turned out to be limited and mainly restricted to those countries which did not possess a safe membership perspective such as Latvia. Therefore, in many countries no substantial increase of state capacity could be observed during the accession process.

These insights also suggest several lessons for the future role of the EU seeking to ensure a well-working state apparatus in its member states. Firstly, once countries become member states of the EU, the possibilities of the EU to ensure administrative capacity are severely limited. Consequently, there should be a stronger focus on the pre-accession period which – despite the limitations of EU conditionality – still allows exerting some pressure on applicants' countries. This should be accompanied with attempts to increase the effectiveness of EU conditionality.

To promote the civil service reforms in accession states effectively the EU should abandon the practice of dispersing the issue across several negotiations chapters. In combination with more realistic and clear guidelines for reform this could help to increase the European Commission's surveillance over the reform process and boost legitimacy for civil service reforms within candidate countries. However, the ability to set standards for candidate countries remains a challenge, given the wide variety of institutional solutions within current member states, resulting so far in rather broad principles of the *European Adminstrative Space*.

Secondly, the EU should push for a long-term approach which encourages candidate countries to start with civil service reforms at the very beginning of the accession process. This can help to overcome the problem of the short time period available for civil service reforms and the subsequent risk of adopting laws only for the sake of fulfilling EU demands. Therefore, it is also necessary to shift the focus away from the formal adoption of laws towards the actual implementation of civil service legislation.

While emphasizing the need for a stronger focus on pre-accession reforms, this chapter also highlighted the varying institutional quality across all member states. Finding ways to ensure sufficient administrative capacity also within the older and newer member states, despite the limited means the EU has in areas beyond the acquis communitaire, will be crucial for better preparing the European Union for current and future challenges. However, national administrative capacity is only one component for dealing with crises. In a similar vein, adequate capacities are also necessary at the European level to timely react on upcoming challenges and to provide effective policy solutions.

References

Bachtler, John/Gorzelak, Grzegorz (2007): Reforming EU cohesion policy. In: Policy Studies 28, 4, pp. 309-326.

Baun, Michael J./Marek, Dan (2014): Cohesion policy in the European Union. London: Palgrave Macmillan.

Buzogány, Aron/Stuchlík, Andrej (2010): Wandlungen in Kafkas Schloß? Verwaltungsreform und -Modernisierung in Mittel- und Osteuropa. In: Hill, H. (ed.): Verwaltungsmodernisierung 2010. Verwaltungsressourcen und Verwaltungsstrukturen, Band 17. Baden-Baden: Nomos, pp. 287-314.

Cardona, Francisco/Dannequin, Thomas (2010): Can Civil Service Reforms Last? The European Union's 5th Enlargement and Future Policy Orientations. SIGMA Working Paper.

Cardona, Francisco Péreto/Freibert, Anke (2007): The European Administrative Space and Sigma Assessments of EU Candidate Countries. In: Croatian Public Administration 7, 1, pp. 51-59.

Dimitrova, Antoaneta (2002): Enlargement, Institution-Building and the EU's Administrative Capacity Requirement. In: West European Politics 25, 4, pp. 171-190.

Dimitrova, Antoaneta (2005): Europeanization and Civil Service Reform in Central and Eastern Europe. In: Schimmelfennig, F./Sedelmeier, U. (eds.): The Europeanization of Central and Eastern Europe. Ithaca, NY: Cornell University Press, pp. 71-90.

Epstein, Rachel/Sedelmeier, Ulrich (2008): Beyond conditionality: International institutions in postcommunist Europe after enlargement. In: Journal of European Public Policy 15, 6, pp. 795-805.

Gajduschek, György (2007): Politicisation, professionalisation, or both? Hungary's civil service system. In: Communist and Post-Communist Studies 40, 3, pp. 343-362.

Goetz, Klaus H./Wollmann, Hellmut (2001): Governmentalizing central executives in post-communist Europe: A four-country comparison. In: Journal of European Public Policy 8, 6, pp. 864-887.

Grabbe, Heather (2006): The EU's transformative power: Europeanization through conditionality in Central and Eastern Europe. Basingstoke: Palgrave Macmillan.

Haughton, Tim (2007): When Does the EU Make a Difference? Conditionality and the Accession Process in Central and Eastern Europe. In: Political Studies Review 5, 2, pp. 233-246.

Haverland, Markus/Romeijn, Marleen (2007): Do member states make European policies work? Analysing the EU transposition deficit. In: Public Administration 85, 3, pp. 757-778.

Kaufmann, Daniel/Kraay, Aart (2016): The Worldwide Governance Indicators (WGI) project (http://info.worldbank.org/governance/wgi/index.aspx#home, last access 20 November 2016).

Kaufmann, Daniel/Kraay, Aart/Mastruzzi, Massimo (2010): The Worldwide Governance Indicators. Methodology and Analytical Issues. Policy Research Working Paper, 5430 (http://elibrary.worldbank.org/doi/pdf/10.1596/1813-9450-5430, last access 20 November 2016).

König, Klaus (1992): The Transformation of a 'Real-Socialist' Administrative System into a Conventional Western European System. In: International Review of Administrative Sciences 58, 2, pp. 147-161.

Meyer-Sahling, Jan-Hinrik (2009). Sustainability of Civil Service Reforms in Central and Eastern Europe: Five Years After EU Accession. SIGMA Papers, No. 44.

O'Dwyer, Conor (2002): Civilizing the State Bureaucracy: The Unfulfilled Promise of Public Administration Reform in Poland, Slovakia, and the Czech Republic (1990-2000) (http://escholarship.org/uc/item/23m654p8, last access 30 May 2016).

Pollitt, Christopher (2011): 30 years of public management reforms: Has there been a pattern? (http://blogs.worldbank.org/governance/30-years-of-public-management-reforms-has-there-been-a-pattern, last access 14 April 2016).

Sedelmeier, Ulrich (2008): After conditionality: Post-accession compliance with EU law in East Central Europe. In: Journal of European Public Policy 15, 6, pp. 806-825.

SIGMA (2003): Czech Republic: Public Service and the administrative framework assessment. Paris.

Steunenberg, Bernard/Dimitrova, Antoaneta (2007): Compliance in the EU enlargement process: The limits of conditionality. In: European Integration online Papers 11, 5.

Tosun, Jale (2014): Absorption of Regional Funds: A Comparative Analysis. In: Journal of Common Market Studies 52, 2, pp. 371-387.
Verheijen, Tony (2007): Public Administration in Post-Communist States. In: Peters, G. B./Pierre, J. (eds.): Handbook of public administration. London: SAGE, pp. 311-320.

Abbreviations

Title	Abbreviaton
Central and Eastern European Countries	CEEC
European Union	EU
Organisation for Economic Co-operation and Development	OECD
Poland and Hungary: Assistance for Restructuring their Economies	PHARE
Support for Improvement in Governance and Management	SIGMA

11. European Human Rights between transnational order and domestic politics

Petra Guasti and David Siroky

1. Introduction

The European Court of Human Rights (ECtHR) is often regarded as the most important human rights court worldwide. In recent years, the established pan-European human rights regime has experienced significant pushback – not only from member states but also from transnational actors, such us the European Court of Justice. In April 2013, the EU's accession to the European Charter of Human Rights (ECHR, the Court) became official. It was a further step towards a pan-European human rights regime and recognition of ECHR's pivotal role in this process. However, in December 2014, the EU's accession to ECHR was effectively halted by a decision (ECJ Opinion 2/13)[1] of the European Court of Justice (ECJ) regarding competencies between the ECJ and the European Court of Human rights (ECtHR).

Historically, the cooperation between the European Union and the Council of Europe was limited by existing legal provisions of the EU. In 1996 the ECJ ruled in Opinion 2/94 that (EU) Community law prevented accession to the ECHR before "substantial change in the existing Community system for the protection of human rights" and due to the lack of compatibility among the two legal systems (Community law and international human rights law). A significant shift in EU law occurred in December 2000 with the enactment of the Charter of Fundamental Rights of the European Union in Nice (OJ 2000 C 364). For the first time, international human rights treaties, as well as ECJ and ECtHR case law, were recognised as fundamental to the European human rights regime, and the both hurdles identified in the 1996 ECJ judgement were removed.

The Treaty of Lisbon (which entered into force in December 2009) further reiterated this and opened up the possibility of the EU's accession to the ECHR, giving the European Council the task to draft the accession agreement. The drafting process culminated in April 2013, when legal documents for the EU's

1 http://curia.europa.eu/juris/document/document.jsf?docid=160882&doclang=en

accession to the European Convention on Human Rights (ECHR) were submitted for review to the ECJ (and were subsequently to be reviewed by the EU member states). Unfortunately, in December 2014, the ECJ issued an adverse opinion on the EU's accession to the ECHR effectively bringing the process to a halt (Opinion 2/13). The ECJ reiterated the centrality of fundamental rights as an integral part of the general principles of EU law and recognised the "special significance" of the ECHR for EU law. Its decision was based on refuting the potential of an external body – the European Court of Human Rights – to review the application of EU law, the exclusive domain of the ECJ (Guasti 2017, cf. Lazowski and Wessels 2015).

Several proposals have been put forward, to resolve this gridlock - including a (partial) merger of the ECtHR and ECJ. And although EU's accession to the ECHR will be a more long-term process, and the European human rights regime remains fragmentary, the growing linkages and epistemic convergence between the two institutions hint at the emergence of a European normative system. The primary obstruction to more integration is institutional competition (especially as perceived by the ECJ), lack of consensus among EU institutions and growing criticism of the ECtHR by the member states (cf. Scheeck 2005, Provost 2015).

Simultaneously, considerable dissatisfaction is mounting against the ECtHR from different angles of Europe. In the UK, compliance with the ECHR is a politically salient issue. British politicians, legal scholars and legal practitioners substantial dissatisfaction with the Court has been voiced, some even suggesting that the UK might pull out of the ECHR altogether. One of the UK's most vocal opponents of the ECtHR is Theresa May, who regards the ECHR as limiting the powers of the British Parliament, and as ineffective and overall detrimental to human rights, as it allegedly binds the hands of governments in favour of citizens (Guardian 2016). In April 2016, as the UK's then-Home Secretary (and as of August 2016 Prime Minister) Theresa May raised the issue again in relationship to a possible rejection of the changes to the British Bill of Rights proposed by then-Prime Minister David Cameron in 2015 (one of the more contentious issues was prisoner voting). However, the UK never undertook any formal steps incompatible with its membership in the ECHR and continued to adhere to the Court's rulings.

Also, Russian politicians have been highly critical of the judgments of the ECtHR on human rights violations in Chechnya. In both countries, voices repeatedly surfaced regarding the UK's and Russia's possible exit from the ECHR. Whereas these were mostly rhetorical exercises in the UK, Russia has acted. In July 2015, the Russian Constitutional Court took an unprecedented step and ruled in the highly salient Yukos case that national laws should take precedence over decisions of the ECtHR. In 2014 the ECtHR Yukos ruling awarded shareholders of the now-defunct oil company Yukos €1.9 billion euros in compensation by the Russian government. This ruling was the first of its kind among all ECHR member states and is openly in breach with the ECHR.

As Guasti (2017) has demonstrated the case of Russia is the most extreme – over the past two years, Russia has moved from 'partial compliance' to full rejection of the ECtHR's authority. In December 2015, for example, the Russian Duma adopted an Amendment to the Federal Constitution (Federal Law No.7-FKZ) allowing the Russian Constitutional Court to decide whether to implement rulings of international human rights courts. In April 2016, the Russian Constitutional Court amendment was applied for the first time in ruling that a decision of the ECtHR (*Anchugov and Gladkov v. Russia*) cannot be implemented in Russia because measures aimed at its implementation would contradict the Russian Constitution.

Next to Russia also Bulgaria is among the countries that continue to defy the ECtHR judgments. Both countries exhibit a similar pattern of 'partial compliance' with the ECtHR's judgments – mostly in the form of monetary compliance (i.e. compensation of damages awarded to victims in judgments finding violations of human rights) rather than legal compliance (implementing legal changes to prevent the occurrence of similar violations). The case of Bulgaria is less extreme than Russia but telling. Bulgaria is selected here as a country which has the highest number of judgments per capita and year issued against it (at this stage judgements are always against the country – which failed to protect the human rights of individuals within its legal system). The Bulgarian Government continues to respect the Court's judgment in monetary terms – paying damages to the victims – but defies the legal implications of the ECtHR's judgments. We argue that the reasons for this behaviour that undermines the efficacy of the European human rights regime are rooted in domestic politics and in the interests of actors who are vested with judicial authority. Our analysis shows that the effective protection of human rights of minorities (in particular, the Roma) is a politicised and unpopular issue in Bulgaria, and the establishment of an independent judiciary remains a politically divisive bone of contention.

2. The European Court of Human Rights: Judgment without justice?[2]

Since the European Court of Human Rights (Court) came into force in 1953, it has aimed to define and protect a set of civil and political rights for all persons within the Council of Europe member-states, regardless of whether those persons are refugees, immigrants, stateless persons, or citizens (ECHR 2013a, Moravcsik 2000).

The Court hears applications concerning member-state violations of one or more of the human rights outlined in the Convention and its protocols. Individuals, companies, NGOs (i.e., private applicants) or other member-states (i.e., interstate applicants) can lodge a complaint against a state and file an application to the Court (for more on the admissibility of cases to the ECHR see Guasti et al. 2016, and Guasti 2017). The European Court of Human Rights can deliver judgments and issue advisory opinions (ECHR 2013a, 2013b). The judgments of the Court are binding on the states concerned and have been effective in causing governments to revise their legislation and administrative practices. Although the Court exercises some clout in the domestic affairs of contracting states, there is a provision that gives states the ability to infringe on human rights. States can circumvent their human rights obligations by invoking 'the margin of appreciation doctrine,' which allows countries to impose limitations on the human rights and freedoms of their citizens in cases of public emergency (Nigro 2010).

The Court is embedded in the legal framework of its member states. Over the past two decades, the court has also increased in prominence as the number of cases skyrocketed. More countries acceded the European Convention on Human Rights in the 1990s, which contributed to an increase in applications filed with the Court. Between 1959 and 1998, for instance, the ECtHR ruled on a total of 837 applications. However, the number increased to 177 judgments in 1999 alone, 695 judgments in 2000, and 888 judgments in 2001. From 2005 to 2012, the number of judgments delivered by the ECtHR was consistently over 1,000 per year (ECHR 2013).

The literature surrounding the European Court of Human Rights casts it in a very positive light, and there is a broad consensus among scholars that the court is effective. As Moravcsik (2010) notes, state compliance with the Court's judgments is nearly as consistent as that of domestic courts. Many empirical examples substantiate this statement. For instance, in a recent case,

---

2 Based on Guasti, P., Siroky, D. S., & Stockemer, D. (2016). Judgment without justice: on the efficacy of the European human rights regime. *Democratization*, 1-21.

Amos (2012) cites the Court's decision that asylum applicants who suffered illnesses could resist deportation from the UK based on Article 3. The British government accepted this judgment. Moravcsik (2010) refers to a case in which the Court found the United Kingdom's exclusion of homosexuals in the armed forces a violation of the ECHR, and the UK government complied with the judgment. Van der Vet (2012) lists cases of the disappearances of Chechens presented to the Court by human rights lawyers and NGOs to highlight how international organisations or groups can successfully litigate on behalf of individuals. Although it is not always possible to determine what has happened to the victim, Van der Vet showed that the Court was able to obtain financial compensation from the Russian authorities (ibid.). By March 2011, Russia had paid a total of 1.3 million Euros for material damages and 12.7 million Euros for moral damages to Chechen applicants.

The literature also concurs that the ECtHR's influence extends beyond single cases. For example, Scribner and Slaughter (2009) highlight how domestic courts use the ECtHR as a reference for their judgments to go beyond (and even against) existing domestic norms. Moreover, as Moravcsik (2010) suggests, ECtHR judgments affect domestic agenda-setting by providing crucial incentives for avoiding future disputes. Helfer and Voeten (2011) substantiated this in their study of the LGBT issue, and demonstrate that the influence of the ECtHR judgments "increase the likelihood that all European nations—even those whose laws the court has not explicitly found to violate the Convention—will adopt progressive LGBT policies." In short, the literature agrees that the Court has made significant contributions to the enhancement of human rights in Europe by establishing new opportunities for individuals to reach redress at both the domestic and supranational level (Cichowski 2010).

Although the Court has made significant judgments and shaped the behaviour of states towards greater respect for human rights, it has been empirically demonstrated (Guasti et al. 2016) that in the current setting the Court is unable to protect the most vulnerable by issuing judgments against those countries with the worst human rights records. Studies have demonstrated that compliance with the Court's rulings can be politically unpopular and divisive domestically (Hillbrecht 2010) and that countries are more prone to compensate victims and cover the costs of litigation than to amend legislation or change institutional practices (Guasti 2017).

In a well-functioning human rights regime, judgments delivered against any given state should reflect micro-level demand for arbitration on human rights issues, and thus be negatively related to the ability of domestic institutions to provide adequate redress for alleged human rights violations and grievances (Hafner-Burton 2011). As the Court has no mandate to prosecute independently, it depends on individuals, national or international organisations, and on states to consider a case (Anagostou 2013). Submitting a claim to the court involves overcoming two hurdles by demonstrating in a legally compelling manner that (1) the domestic court options have been exhausted and (2) the case falls within the existing mandate of the ECHR. For many countries with less developed human and institutional capacity, which is also where one would expect worse human rights records, these hurdles are sufficiently large to prevent citizens from successfully reaching judicial redress at the Court (Guasti et al. 2016).

And while one might expect fewer judgments to be lodged against more democratic and wealthier countries, recent comparative analyses found the opposite (ibid.). In countries with more judicial independence, cases are more likely to be resolved at the domestic level, and citizens do not need to seek redress at the European Court of Human Rights. Where redress is required in more democratic countries with judicial independence, the higher human capacity of citizens in wealthier countries leads to more referrals and more judgments (ibid.). Under human capacity, we sum social and economic capital of citizens, their ability to navigate complex rules and seek support – i.e. from human rights NGOs (ibid.).

3. Bulgaria between domestic politics and transnational justice

To illustrate our argument on the interaction between transnational justice and domestic politics, we examine the case of Bulgaria, which has the most judgments per year issued against it. Between 1992 and 2016 the Court issued 614 judgments against Bulgaria; of those, 557 (90%) found at least one violation. In 2014 alone, there were 3329 applications, of which 928 (28%) were deemed admissible. Judgments were issued in 18 cases, and a violation was found in every case (Table 1).

Although both the economic and political situation in Bulgaria improved over time, as reflected in Table 1, Bulgaria's transition to democracy (which began in February 1990) was not smooth. Bulgaria joined the Council of Europe (and adopted the ECHR) in 1992; it joined NATO in 2004 and became a member of the EU in 2007. It continues to grapple with the communist legacy of anti-legalism, and there is a protracted struggle for the independence of the judiciary (Guasti 2014). Civil liberties, such as freedom of speech, religion, and assembly have improved; but accountability, corruption, and regulatory enforcement remain a challenge (BTI 2006-2016).

Table 1. Overview of all variables in Bulgaria 1995-2015

	1995	1997	2002	2005	2007	2009	2012	2014
Judgments	0	1	23	45	60	61	64	18
CIRI HR index	.66	.66	1.3	1	1.7	1	1	n/a
Independent judiciary	1	1	1	1	1	1	0	n/a
GDP per cap.	1603	1292	2025	3734	5512	6439	7198	7299
Population	8.3	8.1	7.7	7.5	7.3	7.2	7.3	7.3

Source: authors' compilation

By law, Bulgarian courts are independent, but poor pay leaves the judiciary vulnerable to political and economic manipulation, and inadequate funding undermines the institutional capacity of courts. On numerous occasions over the last 15 years, the government and the parliament have been in more or less open conflict with the judiciary over its independence. The World Justice Project (WJP) has continuously evaluated Bulgaria as the weakest regional performer concerning the rule of law.

The lack of judicial reform was a major challenge for Bulgaria's entry into the EU. In 2003, judicial and constitutional reforms aimed to improve the system of checks and balances and with it the country's chances of joining the EU. A recent survey points to significant and substantial progress in judicial independence (Judicial Reform Index (JRI) for Bulgaria by American Bar Association; 'Bertelsmann Transformation Index), but also shows that corruption is endemic in the Bulgarian judiciary. Not surprisingly, distrust in the courts is very high in Bulgaria with over 74% of Bulgarians saying that the courts do not function properly. Political interference in the judiciary is rampant—in a letter addressed to PM Saksokoburggotski, 266 judges accused the Minister of Interior of intentionally undermining the judiciary.

In 2006 and 2007, the EU used its leverage before Bulgaria's accession to ensure that significant judicial and anti-corruption reforms were passed (Vachudova 2005, 2009). The Bulgarian judiciary continued to have limited accountability and transparency during this period (BTI Bulgaria Country Reports 2006-2016). Regarding human rights, Bulgaria struggled with the implementation of human rights and fundamental freedoms embedded in the European Charter of Human Rights and other international human right treaties. Both the ECtHR and international human rights NGOs, such as Bulgarian Helsinki Watch and Amnesty International, reported some instances in which the rights of minorities were restricted, police violence ensued, and detainees and people with disabilities were ill-treated.

For some years, the Bulgarian judiciary was under permanent reform – procedural changes, institutional revamping, all with modest results. The EU conditioned Bulgarian accession by the introduction of the special Cooperation and Verification Mechanism to track Bulgaria's (and Romania's) post-accession progress on the judiciary and anti-corruption reform efforts. Still, the struggles between politics and judiciary continued – the former accusing the judiciary of incompetence, the latter accusing the political elite of interference (Spendzharova and Vachudova 2012). The political and economic elite had no genuine interest in establishing a functioning and impartial, independent judiciary (Guasti 2014). In 2007, an independent judicial inspectorate was established as an institution to investigate delays in pending cases, but this inspectorate has thus far failed to come up with any serious findings.

In 2008, after Bulgaria had lost 52 further cases at the ECtHR the previous year (2007), and the costs of violations between 1992 and 2007 reached 1.3 billion USD, the Ministry of Justice established a special group of observers to the Court. The number of verdicts continued to grow (61 in 2009 and 69 in 2010). To avoid ECtHR litigation, the Minister announced her intention to establish a Bulgarian Human Rights Court which would strictly adhere to deadlines for issuing rulings and compensate substantiated violations. As of 2016, this body has not come into existence yet.

In 2012, one of the key pro-reform figures – Judge Miroslava Todorova (Chairperson of the Association of Bulgarian Judges) was dismissed for poor performance. Her demise was perceived as an effort to curb the growing influence of a reform-minded group within the judiciary. This group of judges and prosecutors is unpopular with the government and with the proponents of the status-quo within the judiciary. For many, including ten human rights NGOs and the EU, the dismissal of Judge Miroslava Todorova represented a tipping point in the assault on judicial independence in Bulgaria. In its 2012 Report, the EU highlighted the "failure to respect the separation of powers" and a continuous effort on behalf of the political elite to undermine public trust in the judiciary (BTI 2016: 9). In June 2012, for the first time, judges took to the streets and openly protested against political interference in the judiciary.

According to some, the main hurdle for the effective protection of human rights in Bulgaria is not the institutional setup, the laws, and regulations or lack thereof, but "with the unwritten norms and values of the actors vested with judicial authority" (BTI 2016.). In the meantime, the marginalisation of minorities, long delays in trials, and discrimination against LGBT individuals and those who have HIV/AIDS continues.

In March 2015, the Court highlighted Bulgaria's inability "to adequately investigate" cases as a systemic problem. In over 45 judgments against Bulgaria, the Court found that the Bulgarian authorities had failed to comply with its ECHR obligation to carry out effective investigations into cases (ECHR 2015). In the latest case, the Court awarded 15,000 Euro in punitive damages and 2,500 Euro in expenses and costs. These findings are in line with Hawkins and Jacoby's (2010) argument that countries are willing to pay punitive damages and expenses upon the Court's order, but are less willing to amend existing laws to prevent future violation of fundamental rights and freedoms (similar on Russia, Guasti 2017).

In March 2015, the Court found that the Bulgarian authorities had failed to investigate the 2004 police killing of a young Roma, Boris Mihaylov. Citing a breach of Article 2 (the right to live) and the excessive use of force, the Court awarded the Mihaylov family 16,000 Euro in punitive damages and 6,000 Euro in court expenses (ECHR 2015). This case lends some support to an assumption that the general reasons for Bulgarian non-compliance are rooted in domestic politics. It is not that the Bulgarian state authorities are unable to address the issues, but that they are unwilling to do so, as it would be interpreted domestically as a further concession to the unpopular Roma minority.

4. Conclusions

The ECtHR has been successful on several fronts. It has strengthened the legal protection of human rights in Europe. Its decisions are predominantly recognised by national governments and have contributed to limiting discrimination against minorities both within the continent and beyond. However, human rights violations do not seem to translate into human rights violation judgments from the ECtHR. Hence those most in need of ECtHR protection – citizens of smaller, less democratic and less affluent states – are *less* likely to be protected under the ECHR (Guasti et al. 2016).

The in-depth analysis of the Bulgarian case shows that the reasons for (Bulgarian) non-compliance are rooted in domestic politics. The effective protection of human rights of minorities (in particular, Roma and Macedonians) is a politicised and unpopular issue, and the establishment of an independent judiciary remains politically divisive in many Council of Europe states which underwent democratisation in the last two decades. Strong political actors that favour the status quo act as veto players against judicial reforms, and thus violations of human rights continue (Hillbrecht 2010, Grzymala-Busse 2007).

Democratization and Europeanization are regarded as a significant contribution to the empowerment of minorities and as a key contributing factor to politicising the protection of human rights (Bustikova 2017). The domestic political actors understood that diversity and inclusiveness are essential Western values, and implemented necessary changes to the newly established democratic order. Some of these changes turned out to be 'political mimetism', and after the EU accession, some of the liberal facades in CEE fell (Levitz and Pop-Eleches 2010, Spendzharova and Vachudova 2012). The external actors, such as transnational advocacy groups, empowered and assisted ethnic and religious minorities, in becoming more assertive in pursuing their demands – domestically and at the ECtHR level (Dimitrova and Pridham 2004, Gorzev 2013, Bustikova 2014). As the number of judgments finding violations and awarding monetary remedies grew, so did the mobilisation of actors hostile to minorities (Giddens and Case 2014).

What follows and extends beyond the case of Bulgaria is that political radicalism is not primarily associated with racism, but ought to be understood as a backlash against the politicisation of minority accommodation (for more on this see Bustikova 2014). Thus, the radical right support originates from the opposition to the externally induced policy changes, such as enhancement of minority rights – perceived as disrupting the existing ethnic relations (Bustikova 2014). Hence, adherence to international human rights norms incurs a significant domestic political cost – further concession to unpopular ethnic and religious minorities by the governments are interpreted as weakness by the rising radical right. Governing elites in Bulgaria, as in Russia, attempt to offset this perceived weakness by resorting to partial compliance – complying with financial demands, but resisting domestic political change (see Guasti 2017, Bustikova 2017).

From a more practical standpoint, the analysis highlights that the European human rights regime does not offer the same protection to all citizens of the 47 member states of the ECHR. There is still no mechanism in place that stops human rights abuses that occur on a daily basis in some Council of Europe countries. This reminds us that the struggle for the universal respect of human rights, despite all its progress, still has some way to go. In future research, scholars and the Court itself would benefit from paying more attention to the role of the institutional and human capacity of citizens and organisations to bring cases to Strasbourg in the first instance. There is much more to be learned from unpacking the black box of capacity, and its effect on human rights and democratisation.

References

Amos, Merris (2012): The dialogue between United Kingdom courts and the European Court of Human Rights. In: International & Comparative Law Quarterly 61.3 (2012): 557-584.

Anagnostou, Dia (Ed.) (2013): The European Court of Human Rights: Implementing Strasbourg's Judgements on Domestic Policy. Edinburgh: Edinburgh University Press.

Asthana, Anushka. Mason, Rowena (2016): 'UK must leave European convention on human rights, says Theresa May'. In: The Guardian 25.4.2016 https://www.theguardian.com/politics/2016/apr/25/uk-must-leave-european-convention-on-human-rights-theresa-may-eu-referendum (last visited 29.3.2017)

BTI – Bertelsmann Transformation Index 2003, 206, 2008, 2010, 2012, 2014, 2016.

Bustikova, Lenka (2014): Revenge of the radical right. In: Comparative Political Studies 47(12): 1738-1765.

Bustikova, Lenka (2015): The Democratization of hostility: Minorities and radical right actors after the fall of communism. In: Minkenberg, M. ed. Transforming the Transformation. New York: Routledge, pp. 58-79.

Bustikova, Lenka (2018): Chapter 33: The Radical Right in Eastern Europe. In: Oxford Handbook of the Radical Right. Oxford University Press.

Cichowski, Rachel A. (2006): Courts, Rights, and Democratic Participation. In: Comparative Political Studies 39(1): 50–75.

Cichowski, Rachel A. (2010): International Courts and Democracy. Paper prepared for delivery at the RIGS Research Seminar, University of California, Irvine, CA.

Dimitrova, Antoaneta, Pridham, Geoffrey Pridham (2004): International actors and democracy promotion in Central and Eastern Europe: The integration model and its limits. In: Democratization, 11(5), 91-112.

ECHR (2013a): Overview 1959-2013, 'European Court of Human Rights (Strasbourg). Accessed on February, 14, 2014 from www.echr.coe.int/Documents/

ECHR (2013b): The Court in Brief. Strasbourg: Council of Europe, 2013e. Accessed February 21, 2014. www.echr.coe.int/Documents/Court_in_brief_ENG.pdf.

ECHR (2015): Systemic problem of ineffectiveness of investigation in Bulgaria. ECHR 070.

Elster, Jon, Offe, Carl, Preuss, Ulrich K. (1998): Institutional Design in Post-Communist Societies: Rebuilding the Ship at Sea. Cambridge: Cambridge University Press.

Givens, Terri E., and Case, Rhonda E. (2014): Legislating Equality: The Politics of Antidiscriminatory Policy in Europe. Oxford: Oxford University Press.

Gorzev, Yonko (2013): Political Opposition and Judicial Resistance to Strasbourg Case Law Regarding Minorities in Bulgaria. In: The European Court of Human Rights: Implementing Strasbourg's Judgements on Domestic Policy, edited by Dia Anagnostou, 122–142. Edinburgh: Edinburgh University Press.

Grzymala-Busse, Anna (2007): Rebuilding Leviathan: Party Competition and state exploitation in post-communist democracies. Cambridge: Cambridge University Press.

Guasti, Petra (2014): Beyond EU Conditionality: Analysing the Key Factors Affecting Rule of Law in Central and Eastern Europe after the EU Accession. In: Kostova, D. et al. Institutional Trust. (pp. 215-248). Sofia: MD Academic Publishing.
Guasti, Petra, Siroky, David S., and Stockemer, Daniel (2016): Judgement without justice: on the efficacy of the European human rights regime. In: Democratization, 1-21.
Guasti, Petra (2017): The EU and Russia in the Pan-European Human Rights Regime. In: EU-Russia relations in crisis: understanding diverging perceptions eds. Casier, Tom & Joan DeBardeleben. London: Routledge.
Hafner-Burton, Emilie M. (2011): International Regimes for Human Rights. ILAR Working Paper 2011(11).
Hawkins, Darren and Jacoby Wade. (2010): Partial compliance: A comparison of the European and Inter-American Court of Human Rights. Journal of International Law and International Relations, 6, 1, 35-85.
Helfer, Laurence R. and Voeten, Erik (2011): Do European Court of Human Rights Judgments Promote Legal and Policy Changes? Working Paper Available online http://www.law.uchicago.edu/files/files/HelferVoeten.Chicago.IL.Workshop.14April.2011.pdf
Helfer, Laurence R. (2008): Redesigning the European Court of Human Rights: Embeddedness as a Deep Structural Principle of the European Human Rights Regime. In: European Journal of International Law 19(1): 125–159.
Hillebrecht Courtney (2010): The European Court of Human Rights, Domestic Politics and the Ties that Bind: Explaining Compliance with international human rights tribunals. Presented at Annual Meeting of International Studies Association, New Orleans, LA.
Janis, Mark W., Richard, S. Kay, and Anthony W. Bradley (2008): European Human Rights Law: Text and Materials. Oxford: Oxford University Press.
JRI (2004): Judicial Reform Index for Bulgaria (2004). American Bar Association.
Levitz, Philip, and Grigore Pop-Eleches, G. (2010): Why no backsliding? The European Union's impact on democracy and governance before and after accession. In: Comparative Political Studies, 43(4), 457-485.
Meehan, Nathan (2009): Human Rights Imprisoned: Institutional Human Rights Non-Compliance in Council of Europe Member States. In: International Journal of Comparative and Applied Criminal Justice 33(1): 119–142.
Moravcsik, Andrew (2000): The Origins of Human Rights Regimes: Democratic Delegation in Postwar Europe. In: International Organization 54(2): 217-252.
Nigro. Raffaella (2010): The Margin of Appreciation Doctrine and the Case-Law of the European Court of Human Rights on the Islamic Veil. In: Human Rights Review 11(4): 532.
Polakiewicz, Jörg (2013). EU law and the ECHR: Will EU accession to the European Convention on Human Rights square the circle? Available at SSRN 2331497.
Scheeck, Laurent (2005): Solving Europe's Binary Human Rights Puzzle. The Interaction between Supranational Courts as a Parameter of European

Governance. Questions de Recherche/Research questions (15). Available from http://www.ceri-sciences-po.org/publica/qdr.htm.
Scribner, Druscilla L., and Tracy H. Slagter (2009): Domestic Institutions and Supranational Human Rights Adjudication: The ECtHR and the IACtHR Compared. APSA 2009 Toronto Meeting Paper.
Spendzharova, Aneta B., Vachudova, Milada A. (2012): Catching Up? Consolidating Liberal Democracy in Bulgaria and Romania after EU Accession. In: West European Politics, 35(1): 39-58.
Vachudova, Milada A. (2005): Europe Undivided: Democracy, Leverage, and Integration after Communism. Oxford: Oxford University Press.
Vachudova, Milada A. (2009): Corruption and Compliance in the EU's Post-Communist Members and Candidates. In: Journal of Common Market Studies 47(AR): 43-62.
Van der Vet, Freek (2012): Seeking Life, Finding Justice: Russian NGO litigation and Chechen Disappearances before the European Court of Human Rights. In: Human Rights Review 13(3): 303-325.
Voeten Erik (2007): The politics of international judicial appointments: Evidence from the European Court of Human Rights. In: International Organisations. 61: 669–701

12. Towards a common European energy policy? Energy security debates in Poland and Germany, the case of the Nord Stream pipeline[1]

Andreas Heinrich and Heiko Pleines

1. Introduction

The European Union (EU) has experienced several crises related to gas imports from Russia, first in 2005/06 and then most prominently in January 2009 when deliveries through Ukraine were halted for 13 days, leaving several Central Eastern and South Eastern EU member states without any gas supplies during the winter heating season. The expectation at the time was that the crises would promote a common EU response to energy imports. The call was for a joint approach to external energy security challenges which would reconcile conflicting national interests slowly but surely, similarly to the reforms of the EU's internal energy market.

Using the example of Germany and Poland, this chapter examines how discrepancies between EU member states' understanding and articulation of energy security impact the development of a common European energy policy. Germany and Poland are both prominent in the EU's energy debates and although they face similar energy security challenges on many occasions, they often opt for diverging interpretations and policy solutions. The most controversial energy issue in German-Polish relations is clearly the construction of the Nord Stream pipeline, which allows for direct natural gas deliveries from Russia to Germany bypassing the traditional transit countries, among them Poland. That is why in Poland Nord Stream is seen as politically motivated and as a threat to the country's energy security. When the project started in 2006 then defence minister of Poland, Radosław Sikorski, linked the German-Russian pipeline agreement to the Ribbentrop-Molotov (Hitler-Stalin)

1 This publication has been prepared as part of the research project 'Towards a common European energy policy? Energy security debates in Poland and Germany', which has been financially supported by the German-Polish Science Foundation.

pact.[2] This chapter will trace the related debates in Poland and Germany from 2004 to 2016.

2. The Nord Stream pipeline

The Nord Stream pipeline was added to an extensive pipeline network for westward gas exports from Russia. Already in the second half of the 1960s the construction of a wide gas pipeline network had enabled the Soviet Union to become the world's largest exporter of natural gas. The centre pieces of this pipeline grid were the pipelines 'Brotherhood' and 'Northern Lights' which, running through Ukraine and Belarus, connect Russia with Central Eastern Europe. These export pipelines were complemented by the Yamal-Europe pipeline which was inaugurated in the late 1990s and built through Belarus and Poland to Germany. Plans for a second line of the Yamal pipeline (Yamal II) to double its capacity never materialised (Heinrich 2014).

In reaction to repeated and protracted conflicts with transit countries on the territory of the former Soviet Union, especially with Ukraine in 2005/06, 2009 and 2014/15, which resulted in disruptions of Russian gas supplies to European customers, the diversification of export routes became an important part of Russia's natural gas export strategy.

The Nord Stream pipeline became the first Russian export pipeline to Western Europe avoiding transit countries. This 1200-kilometre-long pipeline, consisting of two lines, runs from the Russian town of Vyborg beneath the Baltic Sea to Ludmin near Greifswald in Germany. The construction agreement between Gazprom, which holds a legal monopoly on Russian gas exports since 2006, and its German partners E.ON Ruhrgas and BASF was signed in September 2005 with the explicit support of the German and Russian governments. Fierce criticism of the Nord Stream project was voiced primarily by Poland and the Baltic States which saw their energy security threatened by a pipeline that would bypass them; Sweden cited concerns for the ecology of the Baltic

2 Cf. e.g., 'Poland recalls Hitler-Stalin pact amid fears over pipeline', *The Guardian*, 1 May 2006, available online at https://www.theguardian.com/world/2006/may/01/eu.poland. For a clarification by the Polish Ministry of Defense see: 'Minister Sikorski o współpracy w dziedzinie energetyki', *Ministerstwo Obrony Narodowej*, 30 April 2006, available online at http://www.mon.gov.pl/artykul_wiecej.php?idartykul=1696. Speaking of a misinterpretation, the press release states: 'The minister did not place the Ribbentrop-Molotov pact and the pipeline agreement on the same level. He referred to painful historical events to explain Poles' sensitivity to agreements made without their knowledge. He used the Ribbentrop-Molotov pact to picture emotions raised by the construction of the pipeline' [authors' own translation].

Sea as major reason for its opposition (Bouzarovski/Konieczny 2010; Larsson 2007; Lidskog/Elander 2012).

The pipeline was inaugurated at the end of 2011. However, due to the EU's legal requirements Nord Stream has so far not been able to use its full capacity. This is because the connecting pipelines in Germany are subject to the EU's third-party access regulations. According to these regulations, which apply to telecommunication, electricity and natural gas, production and transport have to be separated. For gas pipelines this means that 50 per cent of the pipelines' capacities have to be made available to competitors. As a result, only half of Nord Stream's capacity could be used in its first year of operation. After a second connecting pipeline was inaugurated in November 2013, Nord Stream was able to increase its utilization to 36 billion cubic metres per year, i.e. two thirds of its capacity.

3. Analysing pipeline debates

Our analysis focuses on the perception of the Nord Stream project in German and Polish debates about energy security. For the period from 2004 to 2014, German and Polish press reporting and parliamentary debates regarding the perceived risks and threats related to the Nord Stream gas pipeline were examined using a software-based but non-automated quantitative and qualitative content analysis. As the focus is on national public debates only mass media with nation-wide coverage that address a national audience in the respective country were included. Because of a regular and more substantiated coverage, the analysis was restricted to quality print media. For both countries, the selection includes the most popular print media and the most important media for the major political camps. The general text corpus (concrete corpus) of mass media reporting for the analysis was generated from all media listed in Table 1. All articles with any meaningful reference to the topic and with a reference to energy security were included, based on multiple searches in electronic databases.[3]

3 German media reports were selected and coded at the Research Centre for East European Studies at the University of Bremen (coder: Thomas Sattich, coordinator: Andreas Heinrich). Polish media reports were selected and coded at the University of Poznań (coders: Agata Stasik and Aleksandra Lis, coordinator: Aleksandra Lis). A detailed description of the methodological approach, including the creation of the text corpus and the coding scheme for content analysis, is available online at http://www.forschungsstelle.uni-bremen.de/UserFiles/file/04-Forschung/documentation_data-collection.pdf. All quotes were translated by the authors.

Table 1: List of mass media included in the analysis

Poland	Dziennik/Dziennik Gazeta Prawna
	Gazeta Wyborcza
	Polityka
	Rzeczpospolita
Germany	Der Spiegel
	Süddeutsche Zeitung
	Taz
	Die Welt
	Die Zeit

In order to identify the positions of important political actors, debates and inquiries in the German and Polish parliaments related to the Nord Stream pipeline were analysed in the same way as media reporting based on searches in the online archives of both parliaments.[4]

4. The Polish debate about Nord Stream

In Poland, the discussion of the Nord Stream pipeline – in the media as well as in parliament and across all party lines – has been overwhelmingly negative. Nord Stream is seen as politically motivated and as a threat to Poland's energy security; it has been argued that Russia would be able to interrupt gas deliveries to Poland without harming Germany and other West European consumer countries as soon as the pipeline construction is finished. Additionally, the construction of Nord Stream would result in environmental damage, in a loss of transit fees for Russian gas presently transported through Poland via the Yamal-Europe pipeline and in a blockage of the harbour entrance in Świnoujście for larger vessels (which in turn would hamper the diversification of energy supplies).

There has been a remarkably large debate in the Polish parliament (resulting in 118 documents included in this analysis). The key arguments made can be illustrated by the following quotes from the plenary debate on the issue in the Polish parliament which took place in 2005 and 2008. Soon after the 2005 debate parliamentary elections brought a government coalition to power which was led by the Law and Justice Party (PiS). The Civic Platform

4 Plenary debates were selected and coded at the Research Centre for East European Studies at the University of Bremen by Andreas Heinrich with support from Barbara Holli. All quotes were translated by the authors.

(PO) under Donald Tusk was the strongest opposition party at the time and the governing party in 2008.

> 'The realization of these plans means for Poland the omission of the construction of the Yamal II pipeline [through Poland], the loss of transit fees and, therefore, the deterioration of its economic position. Additionally, it would block the construction of a gas pipeline between Poland and Norway and, thereby, hinder a diversification of gas supplies. Experts point to serious obstacles with underwater pipeline crossings' (Deputy Adam Stanisław Szejnfeld, PO, 2005).

> 'The majority of public opinion in our country considers this investment an attempt by Russia to increase its influence in Central Eastern Europe. This opinion is shared by our current Foreign Minister Radosław Sikorski, who compared the construction with the Ribbentrop-Molotov pact. [...] In my opinion, there is a real danger that after the Baltic Sea pipeline is finished Poland will be pressured by Russia. The gas conflicts between Ukraine and Russia are evidence that such blackmail is possible' (Deputy Jarosław Jagiełło, PiS, 2008).

In Polish media reporting (in total 106 documents) the perception of the Nord Stream pipeline is similar. The following excerpts from the opinion leading newspapers Rzeczpospolita (conservative) and Gazeta Wyborcza (liberal-left) illustrate this.

> 'Today, Russia and Germany will sign an agreement to build a pipeline through the Baltic Sea. Poland and other Central European countries are concerned that the investment will disturb solidarity within the European Union. [...] We are concerned that the Baltic pipeline is a landmine set to destroy solidarity within the EU. "From the perspective of the European Union, the Russian-German project is not a positive undertaking, because it is excluded from the concept of common EU policy" stated [Polish President Alexander] Kwasniewski in an interview with Radio ZET' (Gazeta Wyborcza: Kublik 2005).

> 'Compared with a chess match Russia's aim in Europe is not check but the permanent check mate to enforce Europe's subordination. [...] Some observers [...] call Russia's energy policy a new Cold War. [...] The gas pipelines Nord Stream and South Stream will not only be a symbolic "new Iron Curtain" but a real "gas curtain" separating the continent into a German-dominated Europe and a Central Eastern Europe that returns into the lap of mother Russia. [...] For centuries Russia and Germany have consistently increased their sphere of influence. To believe that Germany, after its re-unification again a European great power, and Russia, experiencing a renaissance fuelled by high prices for energy resources, would omit their century-old ambitions is naive' (Rzeczpospolita 2008).

Overall, historical references are very common in the Polish debate about the Nord Stream pipeline in the press as well as in parliamentary debates (Heinrich 2007). These references convey Poland's negative images of Russia – and to a lesser extent of Germany – which is very much influenced and shaped by the contemporary Polish national identity discourse. These negative images have become institutionalised in the formal discourse of textbooks and media (Zarycki 2004: 624). Poland's historical security perception has thus been shaped to a great extent by its geopolitical position between its more powerful German and Russian neighbours (Sanford 2003: 178-9). Sokoła (2005: 135) describes the situation as a battle for survival against Germany and Russia, which are considered 'eternal' enemies.

Grzeszak (2005) reflects these perceptions and interpretations concisely in a journalistic contribution included in our analysis:

> 'In Poland, the North European Gas Pipeline [Nord Stream] agreement [...] is considered to be an unfriendly political act. We are upset that Germans ignore our interests, and that the European Union tolerates Germany's egoistic attitude. We are also upset with the Russians, who instead of building a second branch of the Yamal pipeline through Poland have decided to construct a much more expensive sea route, bypassing our country. We suspect that the pipeline is a punishment for our support of the Orange Revolution in Ukraine as well as our refusal to construct "pieremychka" (a gas connector to transfer Russian gas through Poland, bypassing Ukraine)'.

With this perception, the Polish debate does not allow for a compromise. The Nord Stream pipeline is described as a threat to Poland's national security. Seen from this perceptive, the only solution is the termination of the project. At the same time, Poland must reduce its external dependency in order not to be vulnerable to blackmail.

5. The German debate about Nord Stream

The discussion in Germany has been more positive toward the Nord Stream pipeline which has often been presented as an alternative transport route that avoids transit countries and, therefore, increases Germany's energy security. Statements by the German government illustrate this:

> 'With the NEGP [Nord Stream Pipeline] a direct connection with Russian natural gas resources, which are the largest on a global scale and with additional transport capacities will be created. Thereby, gas supply security in Germany but also in the European Union will be secured. [...] [The pipeline] is a commercial project. The pipeline's planning, construction and financing lie solely in the hands of the companies involved: Gazprom, E.ON Ruhrgas and BASF. Concerning supply security, the government generally welcomes the

> commercial investment in supply infrastructure' (Answer of the German government to a parliamentary enquiry: Deutscher Bundestag 2006).

> 'According to [former German Chancellor Gerhard] Schröder, [Nord Stream's capacity] amounts to only a quarter of the additional demand needed in a few years. The limited capacity of the pipeline alone would prove that Nord Stream is not directed against any littoral states such as Poland or the Baltic States that are bypassed by the pipeline. "We need additional transport routes" Schröder said' (Spiegel Online: Wittrock 2008).

> '"The pipeline is a strategic European project", said Merkel' (Die Welt: Flückiger 2008).

Dissenting voices in the German debate point to the environmental risks involved in the pipeline's construction, the harm to relations with Poland and the Baltic States, which strongly oppose the pipeline and the increasing dependency on Russian gas deliveries.

In the German parliament, there was only a minor discussion about the Nord Stream pipeline (leading to a total of 31 documents relevant for our analysis). While the respective government coalitions (no matter of which parties they were composed) were mostly in favour of the pipeline, it was the Green party (in opposition since shortly after the pipeline contract was signed) which was most critical; representatives of the Green party cited first of all the environmental risks involved in the construction and the harm for Germany's relations with Poland and the Baltic States as arguments against a construction of the Nord Stream pipeline.

In German media reporting (in total 66 documents), the pipeline was criticised for being a political project meant to exert pressure on transit countries for Russian gas and to harm relations with Poland and the Baltic States. The pipeline would also increase Germany's dependence on Russian gas imports, while risking environmental damage to the Baltic Sea; Nord Stream would also be too expensive in comparison to alternative pipelines on land. The following quotes highlight key points raised in German media reporting:

> 'The Baltic Sea pipeline bypasses Kiev and Warsaw and runs across areas of ecological concern and ammunition dumps from the Second World War. It combines the West's hunger for energy with Russia's power politics. The current [Ukrainian gas] crisis stems from the same desires. Thus, Russian supplies and Europe's dependency can no longer be judged solely by technical and commercial criteria. The reliability of gas supplies – which the Soviet Union had achieved despite the Cold War – is gone' (Die Welt: Stürmer 2006).

> 'The project was controversial from the very beginning because its route crosses dumping grounds of mines and ammunition which were sunk in the Baltic Sea after the Second World War. Environmentalists are concerned about the nearly unspoiled spawning grounds of codfish, herring and other fish.

However, ecological concerns were brushed aside by economic and geostrategic arguments: natural gas is a scarce commodity! Russia needs a new pipeline bypassing the old conflict grounds – such as Ukraine – which in turn will increase the supply security in Western Europe!' (Die Zeit: Tatje 2009).

'The project has been highly controversial in the littoral states. The Baltic States and Poland were concerned about an expansion of the Russian sphere of influence. In Sweden, too, politicians warned that Moscow might use the pipeline as a pretext for increasing its military presence in the Baltic Sea. Environmental organizations criticise that requirements are still not strict enough. In Germany [...] two environmental organizations filed a lawsuit. WWF and Bund Naturschutz want to make sure that the Nord Stream consortium will be obligated to compensation measures if the pipeline causes any damages' (Süddeutsche Zeitung: Herrmann 2010).

Interestingly, several articles (five documents, four of them from Süddeutsche Zeitung) discuss the Nord Stream pipeline in the context of Polish energy security, not Germany's; thereby, they mirror the Polish opposition toward Nord Stream and present the Polish threat perception to the German public. The articles follow Poland's position that the Nord Stream pipeline would endanger the country's energy security because it would enable Russia to put pressure on Poland and other transit countries for Russian gas and even enable it to stop gas supplies without harming its consumers in the West.

However, in the German debate the Nord Stream pipeline is first of all treated as an industrial project which raises serious environmental concerns. The growing dependence on Russia as energy supplier is also an issue in the German debate. However, in Germany the issue becomes politicised mainly through a reflection of political concerns in Poland. As a result, any search for solutions points in the direction of high environmental standards and diplomatic efforts to address the concerns of Poland and other transit countries.

As a common theme, unlike in Poland, all critics of the Nord Stream pipeline in Germany urge for more cooperation in the field of energy within the European Union and warn of further unilateral decisions.

Table 2: Perceived threats or risks linked to the Nord Stream pipeline by source (number of references)

Nature of perceived threat/risk	Polish politicians (118)	Polish media (106)	German politicians (31)	German media (66)
Political	48	57	9	25
Economic	62	45	4	3
Environmental	40	29	10	15
Technical	42	13	1	0

6. EU plans for an 'Energy Union' – the Tusk proposal

It is Poland which has been trying for a long time to address concerns about energy security at the European level. Reacting to the Russian-Ukrainian gas conflict of 2005/06, the then Polish Prime Minister Kazimierz Marcinkiewicz proposed the creation of an Energy NATO based on an idea of Polish President Lech Kaczyński (Pawlicki 2006). The proposal gained prominence through a contribution in the Financial Times, where Marcinkiewicz (2006) wrote:

> 'In Europe, there is a widespread feeling that EU countries should act in solidarity: after all, the Union is a vehicle for deeper economic co-operation. [...] The problems of energy security were thus at the very heart of the European integration process. We should remember this heritage. [...] It is the right time, in my view, to suggest a common effort to face not only current but also future challenges. That is why I want to propose to our partners from the EU and the Nato alliance a treaty on energy security. It would be an expression of solidarity for all parties, uniting them in the face of any energy threat provoked by either a cut or a diminution of supply sources that may occur because of natural disasters, disruption of wide distribution and supply systems or political decisions by suppliers. [...] A European energy security treaty along these lines could become a real tool that would give us some badly needed certainty, as well as security in crisis situations. That is why it is essential that the treaty contains a clearly and firmly stated guarantee clause based on the "musketeer principle": "All for one – one for all".'

Although the proposal gained some attention, no steps were made to follow up on it. Roth (2011: 620-1) has convincingly explained this outcome with the nature of the Polish debate, arguing that there is 'a high degree of "misfit" between EEEP [European external energy policy] and Poland's policy priorities, which was particularly marked during the reign of the PiS party. Besides the structure of Poland's energy imports, this "misfit" is to a considerable extent rooted in the powerful influence of Poland's broader geopolitical objectives, which manifests itself in a deeply entrenched sense of strategic vulnerability vis-à-vis Russia and a high degree of "securitisation" in Polish energy discourse.' The contrasts between the Polish and German pipeline debates, which we have presented above, are a clear illustration of this 'misfit'.

Only when tensions with Russia seriously increased in the wake of the Ukraine crisis of 2014, did Poland again get a chance to promote the issue forcefully. The then Polish Prime Minister Donald Tusk (2014) claimed in a highly influential contribution – again in the Financial Times – that 'a united Europe can end Russia's energy stranglehold'. This time, however, the Polish call for a European 'Energy Union' was first of all framed in economic terms, not in geopolitical ones. The EU should coordinate the purchase of Russian gas in order to counter the supplier's monopoly power. Moreover, it should develop 'mechanisms guaranteeing solidarity among member states' in case of supply shortages and it should invest in energy infrastructure. According to Tusk this economic project would 'return the European project to its roots.' Further proposals refer to the use of coal and shale gas in order to reduce the dependence on energy imports and to closer cooperation with alternative energy exporters like the US and Australia.

The Tusk proposal was taken up by the European Commission which on 25 February 2015 put forward 'A Framework Strategy for a Resilient Energy Union with a Forward-Looking Climate Change Policy'. This success of the Tusk initiative can only be explained in the context of the conflict with Russia in the wave of the annexation of Crimea and the armed conflict in Eastern Ukraine. It was obviously helped by the promotion of Tusk to the presidency of the Council of Europe in December 2014. At the same time, it has been argued that 'the Commission was looking for an ambitious European initiative on which all member states could work together. [...] In relation to energy, European countries have a common goal of decarbonisation, and face common challenges in areas like security' (Keay/Buchan 2015: 2).

However, part of the success is also due to the fact that the Tusk proposal is much closer related to established EU concepts. While both Polish proposals try to address the Polish threat perception through European solidarity, Marcinkiewicz framed this solidarity as a security issue, linking it to NATO, to disasters and conflicts. Tusk, on the contrary, presents energy solidarity as a logical consequence of the EU's economic project, thus largely de-securitizing the issue and turning it into an ordinary policy issue to be addressed within the standard framework of the EU's energy policy.

As a result, the major focus of the Energy Union was shifted to climate change and the liberalization of internal energy markets, but the European Energy Security Strategy and the Gas Security of Supply Regulation were also incorporated. In this respect, the EU document addresses the concerns raised in the Polish debate about Nord Stream, explicitly linking energy security to solidarity, trust and the diversification of energy supplies, i.e. to a united European approach to ensure independence from Russian pressure. It also states that 'when the conditions are right, the EU will consider reframing the energy relationship with Russia based on a level playing field in terms of market opening, fair competition, environmental protection and safety, for the mutual benefit of both sides' (European Commission 2015a, 7). In this context, 'the Commission reiterates that so far, Ukraine has proven to be a reliable gas transit country and it is in the interest of all parties for Ukraine to remain an important transit route to Europe also in the future' (European Commission 2015b).

It seems that in its policy towards Russia the EU was following Tusk's assessment that 'a united Europe can end Russia's energy stranglehold'. After three gas crises between Russia and Ukraine in 2005/06, 2009 and 2014, the attitude towards Russia as a reliable energy supplier had eventually changed. The EU started to act more assertively towards Gazprom, first initiating an anti-monopoly investigation (European Commission 2015c; Kropatcheva 2015) and then preventing Russia's plans for the South Stream pipeline, which would have delivered gas from Russia through the Black Sea and the Balkans to Central Europe (Henderson 2015). However, this more assertive stance did not gain the support of all EU member states.

7. Conclusion

Based on the analysis of the domestic Polish debate and the EU's conception for an Energy Union, one can argue that the Ukraine crisis of 2014 probably in combination with the promotion of Donald Tusk from the Polish premiership to the presidency of the European Council provided a window of opportunity for the Polish threat perception to Europeanise, that is to inform the approach of the EU towards energy security. However, the policy of several EU member states, including Germany, did not really follow this approach.

In this context, it is telling that Gazprom's 2015 proposal to expand the Nord Stream pipeline creates a strong sense of déjà vu. When the South Stream project had been cancelled in reaction to the EU's more assertive approach and the Turkish Stream project (a pipeline beneath the Black Sea to Turkey) had lost momentum, Gazprom in September 2015 signed an agreement with European energy companies, among them Royal Dutch Shell as well as Germany's E.ON (now represented by Uniper) and Wintershall. The agreement foresees the construction of two additional lines called Nord Stream II which would double the annual capacity of the pipeline from 55 billion cubic metres to 110 billion cubic metres.

The German government claimed that the pipeline extension is an economic and not a political project. In its answer to an official inquiry by members of the parliamentary faction of the Green Party it stated in April 2016 that 'Gazprom's position on the European domestic market depends first of all on the competitiveness of Russian gas deliveries in competition with other suppliers'. Polish demands to build the pipeline on land across Polish territory where countered with the proposition that the Nord Stream consortium is free in its commercial decisions (Deutscher Bundestag 2016).

Tusk, on the other hand, claimed that the Nord Stream extension does not meet EU energy rules on supply diversification and would undermine

Ukraine's role as a gas transit state (Lewis 2015). At a meeting with German chancellor Angela Merkel in June 2016, the Polish Prime Minister Beata Szydło (PiS) explained that the Nord Stream extension is 'an investment that will lead to a division of Europe' (Nienaber/Carrel 2016). In reaction to Polish anti-trust proceedings, the companies involved in the Nord Stream II project decided in August 2016 against forming a joint venture to build the expansion pipeline (NewsBase 2016, 9). Gazprom's applications for permission to build the pipeline again caused political controversies in the Baltic Sea states concerned in early 2017. Doubts about the commercial viability of Nord Stream II related to EU competition rules as well as declining demand for Russian gas may still put an end to the extension project.

This episode demonstrates that perceptions of energy security within the EU are as contrary as ever, clearly dominated by national concerns. The overall balance of power seems to have shifted in the direction of the Polish perception, but the multiple crises related to gas imports from Russia have not led to an EU-wide consensus. Instead the EU is muddling through, supporting the Polish threat perception without blocking Nord Stream II. Respective debates are again conducted mainly in the national political arenas and not in Brussels. That means the next crisis around Russian gas exports will most likely challenge the EU's energy security concept again.

References

Bouzarovski, Stefan/Konieczny, Marcin (2010): Landscapes of paradox: Public discourses and policies in Poland's relationship with the Nord Stream pipeline. In: Geopolitics 15, 1: pp. 1-21.

Deutscher Bundestag (2006): Antwort der Bundesregierung auf die Kleine Anfrage der Abgeordneten Rainder Steenblock, Hans Josef Fell und der Fraktion BÜNDNIS 90/DIE GRÜNEN – Drucksache 16/292 – 'Auswirkungen der Ostseegaspipeline auf die Bundesrepublik Deutschland', Drucksache 16/344, 5 January.

Deutscher Bundestag (2016): Antwort der Bundesregierung: Mögliche Folgekosten durch die Erweiterung der Erdgas-Ostseepipeline Nord Stream 2, Drucksache 18/8047, 7 April.

European Commission (2015a): A framework strategy for a resilient Energy Union with a forward-looking climate change policy, 25 February.

European Commission (2015b): State of the Energy Union, 18 November 2015.

European Commission (2015c): Antitrust: Commission sends statement of objections to Gazprom for alleged abuse of dominance on Central and Eastern European gas supply markets, 22 April.

Flückiger, Paul (2008): Angst der Balten vor Moskau überschattet Merkels Besuch. In: Die Welt, 26 August.
Grzeszak, Adam (2005): Spokojnie, to tylko gazociąg. In: Polityka 37, 17 September.
Heinrich, Andreas (2007): Poland as a transit country for Russian natural gas: Potential for conflict. Koszalin: KICES (KICES Working Papers No. 9-10).
Heinrich, Andreas (2014): Introduction: Export pipelines in Eurasia. In: Heinrich, Andreas/Pleines, Heiko (eds) Export pipelines from the CIS region: Geopolitics, securitization, and political decision-making. Stuttgart: ibidem Publishers, pp. 1-73.
Henderson, James (2015): Russia's changing gas relationship with Europe. In: Russian Analytical Digest 163, pp. 2-6, available online at http://www.laender-analysen.de/russland/rad/pdf/RAD_163.pdf
Herrmann, Gunnar (2010): Ostsee-Pipeline genehmigt: Finnland macht Weg endgültig frei für Bau der Gas-Röhre. In: Süddeutsche Zeitung, 13 February.
Jagiełło, Jarosław (2008): Interpelacja nr 4634 do ministra spraw zagranicznych w sprawie budowy gazociągu północnego, in: Sejm Rzeczypospolitej Polskiej, Kadencja VI: Aneksu do Sprawozdania Stenograficznego z 21 posiedzenia Sejmu w dniach 2, 3, 4 i 5 września 2008 r [2.-5.9.2008], pp. 208-209
Keay, Malcolm/Buchan, David (2015): Europe's Energy Union: A problem of governance. Oxford Energy Comment, November 2015, available online at https://www.oxfordenergy.org/wpcms/wp-content/uploads/2016/02/Europes-Energy-Union-a-problem-of-governance.pdf
Kropatcheva, Elena (2015): EC's anti-trust inquiry into Gazprom's practices: Its significance and meaning for Gazprom's role in the EU. In: Russian Analytical Digest 174, pp. 9-12, available online at http://www.laender-analysen.de/russland/rad/pdf/Russian_Analytical_Digest_174.pdf
Kublik, Andrzej (2005): Rosja i Niemcy zbudują gazociąg bez Polski. In: Gazeta Wyborcza, 8 September.
Larsson, Robert L. (2007): Nord Stream, Sweden and Baltic Sea security. Stockholm: Swedish Defence Research Agency (FOI).
Lewis, Barbara (2015): EU's Tusk says Nord Stream pipeline does not meet EU energy rules, Reuters, 18 December.
Lidskog, Rolf/Elander, Ingemar (2012): Sweden and the Baltic Sea pipeline: Between ecology and economy. In: Marine Policy 36, 2: pp. 333-338.
Marcinkiewicz, Kazimierz (2006): Europe's energy musketeers must stand together, Financial Times, 9 February.
NewsBase (2016): Nord Stream 2 hits roadblock after Polish anti-trust ruling. In: FSU Oil & Gas Monitor, No. 32, 17 August 2016, p.9.
Nienaber, Michael/Carrel, Paul (2016): Polish PM says Warsaw concerned Nord Stream 2 will divide Europe, Reuters, 22 June.
Pawlicki, Jacek (2006): Polska wystąpi do Unii o energetyczne NATO. In: Gazeta Wyborcza, 25 January.

Roth, Mathias (2011): Poland as a policy entrepreneur in European External Energy Policy: Towards greater energy solidarity vis-à-vis Russia? In: Geopolitics, 16, 3: pp. 600-625.
Rzeczpospolita (2008): Gaz to dziś groźna broń. In: Rzeczpospolita, 23 July.
Sanford, Georg (2003): Overcoming the burden of history in Polish foreign policy. In: Journal of Communist Studies and Transition Politics, 19, 3: pp. 178-203.
Sokoła, Witold (2005): Historical experience as a factor shaping Polish security policy. In: The Polish Foreign Affairs Digest, 5, 2: pp. 133-155.
Stürmer, Michael (2006): Russisches Gas: Ein neuer politischer Mix. In: Die Welt, 6 January.
Szejnfeld, Adam Stanisław (2004): Interpelacja nr 6806 do prezesa Rady Ministrów w sprawie zwiększenia polskiego bezpieczeństwa w zakresie dostaw gazu dla ludności i gospodarki, 28 February.
Tatje, Claas (2009): Von Russland lösen. In: Die Zeit, 12 November.
Tusk, Donald (2014): A united Europe can end Russia's energy stranglehold, Financial Times, 21 April.
Wittrock, Philipp (2008): Energiekonferenz des Umweltministers: Schröder singt Jubelarien auf Russland. In: Spiegel Online, 25 September.
Zarycki, Tomasz (2004): Uses of Russia: The role of Russia in the modern Polish national identity. In: East European Politics and Societies, 18, 4: pp. 595-627.

Abbreviations

Title	Abbreviation
Civic Platform (Platforma Obywatelska)	PO
European external energy policy	EEEP
European Union	EU
Law and Justice Party (Prawo i Sprawiedliwość)	PiS
Nord Stream Pipeline (North European Gas Pipeline)	NEGP

13. Theorising European integration and Europeanisation through a gendered lens[1]

Gabriele Abels

1. Introduction

The remarkable process of European integration has been the subject of intense theorizing since its beginnings in the 1950s and especially since the 1990s. This theorizing evolved in several stages and has contributed to an ever-increasing number of theories, a set of taken-for-granted insights and mainstreaming efforts. Today a rich body of integration theories exists. The three *classical* theories of federalism, neo-functionalism and intergovernmentalism are still out there, especially the last two ones have been updated. Secondly, there is an ever-growing set of new or *modern* integration theories, often derived from the field of comparative politics that are middle-range theories and focus on specific aspects of European integration such as, for example, the different neo-institutionalisms, multi-level governance, or Europeanisation. In addition, meta-theoretical approaches such as social constructivism have had an impact on how European integration is conceptualized. Thirdly, there are a number of interdisciplinary approaches that take up insights from legal, economic or social integration such as Foucault inspired governmentality or civil society approaches, such as political economy or legal theories. Especially within the last group we find what Manners and Whitman (2016) have recently called "dissenting voices": voices that question the insights of mainstream theories. Thus, there is a rich toolbox full of theories that help us to understand and explain European integration. However, integration theory is still in a "search mode" – especially in times of crises when "an ever closer Union" is a contested issue and when the struggle among scholars is

1 This contribution strongly draws on Abels, G. and MacRae, H. (2016), Gendering European integration theory: Introduction, in Abels, G. and MacRae, H. (eds.), *Gendering European integration theory: engaging new dialogues*, Opladen: Barbara Budrich Publishers, pp. 9-37. I am grateful to Heather Mac Rae for allowing me to make extensive use of our co-authored chapter. For this reason I speak of "we" in this chapter.

over who dominates the political discourse. In this sense, Manners and Whitman emphasize that "both the EU and EU studies are in analytical and normative crisis" (2016: 5).

At the same time, a gender perspective on European integration is beginning to develop more systematically. This gender research started with a sectoral, policy-driven "add women and stir" approach in the early 1990s. It has subsequently evolved into a sub-field

> (…) that illustrates the importance of gender relations in the European integration process in a more complex setting and criticizes the gendered nature of the supranational polity as well as the gender-blindness of established integration theories (Abels 2012: 295; translation by the author).

This growing body of literature has helped to shed lights on otherwise hidden effects and drivers. It has illustrated how gender affects the integration process and how this process impacts upon gender regimes in the member states. It is remarkable (although perhaps not surprising) that the two strands – the "mainstream" and the gender strand in European integration studies – hardly ever cross paths. Galligan (2019: 174) argues that "it is quite remarkable that despite a flourishing scholarly debate on the subject, awareness of the gender perspective on these conceptual frameworks is absent from these theories". Until today, there is very little systematic dialogue between gender perspectives and the existing theories of European integration. We argue that this silence is problematic from both sides: Certainly, gender remains sidelined and marginalized in integration studies. Mainstream scholars in their search for a "reliable theory" have not turned to gender studies to enrich their findings about the nature of the integration process. Concurrently, gender scholars have not raised their voices in the "mainstream" theoretical debates, since, for the most part, their ambitions have been mostly policy- rather than theory-driven (see also the review of the debate in Galligan 2019). Furthermore, exclusionary mechanisms towards non-mainstream voices can be found in the leading journals in the field and gendered voices are certainly not the only marginalized voices in the theoretical debate. Thus gender voices are part of a polyphonic chorus of "dissident voices" (Manners and Whitman 2016: 4;) which need to engage with the mainstream.

What we intend to do in this chapter is to end this silence and to engage in a fruitful dialogue between the mainstream and the gender strand. Given the richness of the theoretical debate we cannot address the full range of integration theories, but we will illustrate the potential of a gendered lens by discussing examples taken from the set of classical, modern and recent integration theories. The contribution is organized as follows: First, we will outline what is meant by "gender" and "gendering" a theory. Secondly, we will introduce intergovernmentalism, multi-level governance, and Europeanization to illustrate how "gendering" these theories works and what difference it makes. Thirdly, we will draw some conclusions for the future of European integration theory.

2. What is gender and gendering?

In order to take gender as the point of departure, it is necessary to clarify the basic terms. The terms gender and gender studies are used to refer to a meta-theoretical concept that assumes gender to be a socially constructed category that profoundly shapes people's lives; it is not a natural-given fact. Men and women, masculinity and femininity, sexual identities are not biologically given essentials, but are constructed and given meaning through human interactions. This has repercussions for our object of study. In line with the majority of gender scholars in our discipline we assume, as Karen Celis and others claim, that "[p]olitics as a real-world phenomenon and political science as an academic discipline are gendered" (Celis et al. 2013: 1). Hawkesworth argues that

> (…) gender as an analytical category illuminates an area of inquiry, framing a set of questions for investigation, such as how power operates in the production of sex, gender, and sexuality within specific … national [and we may add: also supranational] contexts (2013: 47).

In our book (Abels and MacRae 2016) we speak of "gendering" to refer to the process of viewing a particular theory or set of assumptions through a gendered lens. In other words, "gendering" theories of integration allows illuminating the hidden biases and assumptions upon which many traditional categories of analysis are built, e.g. the state as a gender-neutral institution, actors as non-gendered beings, or the division between public and the private, between the international and the domestic arena, between the economic and the social sphere.

Annica Kronsell demands that "For gender to be taken seriously in integration studies, we need to engage directly with existing theories." (2012: 40) Given the contestedness of gender as a category and given the dynamic process of European integration and theory-building (the famous moving target problem), Kronsell's request is far more difficult and complex than it first appears. It is, in fact, as much an epistemological and an ontological challenge as it is a normative challenge.

Furthermore, the result of gendering European integration theory cannot be one "grand" gender theory of European integration, which explains everything. In fact, in the same way as there are multiple "mainstream" and "dissident" approaches to understanding integration, there is a multiplicity of gendered approaches. Understanding gender as a meta-theoretical category allows for this multiplicity. Yet, there are some shared assumptions, starting with the axiom of the construction of gender as a social category. In additions, gendered approaches emphasize the interlinkage between politics and economics, between public and the private, the role of power relations as gendered, and of historically contingent gender regimes.

3. Three strands of gendered integration theories

3.1 Intergovernmentalism: Gendering a dinosaur?

Intergovernmentalism is derived from the realist school in International Relations and it developed as a "grand theory" of European integration in the mid-1960s as a response to the failure of neo-functionalism to explain the so-called empty chair crisis. Intergovernmentalism is a rationalist and state-centric theory that claims that nation states are, in Hofmann's words, "obstinate" and not "obsolete". Cooperation among European nation states occurs only if it serves national interests. Moravcsik's updated version of Liberal Intergovernmentalism (developed in the late 1980s) upholds the state-centrism and the narrow view of what power is; yet, it adds a liberal perspective of preference formation at national level and the dominance of economic interests. Recently, there is a revival called "New Intergovernmentalism", which insists on the possibility of integration also in high politics areas and on the impact of mass politics upon domestic preference formation.

Previous attempts of gendering integration theories by Kronsell (2012) or by Abels (2012) were most sceptical about the potential of intergovernmentalism to understand the gendered nature and impact of European integration. They have criticized four major points: (1) the inherent state-centrism, (2) the view of the state as unitary actor, (3) the non-structural view of power, and (4) the definition of the national interest understood as the state's control over national resources and the emphasis on security issues.

Against this background Anna van der Vleuten (2016) asks if intergovernmentalism is a "dinosaur", despite its ability to survive until today. And, yet, she illustrates that adopting a gendered lens allows for a useful modification. The empirical starting point for van der Vleuten's observation is how it was possible that an all-male team of negotiators in 1957 decided to include the right to equal pay for equal work for women and men in the Treaty of Rome (the famous Art. 119), including a hard deadline for implementation of this binding stipulation. This case was hardly addressed and discussed in intergovernmentalist accounts of the early days of integration. In this sense, as van der Vleuten (2016: 89) argues "At least some of the limitations of intergovernmentalism seem to result from and mirror the gender-blindness of intergovernmentalists themselves".

For example, Liebert's work (cf. Liebert 1999) on the inclusion of anti-discrimination and gender mainstreaming in the 1996 Amsterdam Treaty demonstrates that gender issues can be part of a nation's key interests (in this case the Nordic States) in order to gain domestic support for European integration. Van der Vleuten illustrates that increasingly non-state actors begin to play in key role in negotiations over treaty changes in the 1990s, yet after Eastern enlargement in 2004 the situation changed again. Van der Vleuten emphasizes the existence of what she calls a "pincer effect", which puts national governments under pressure from two sides. She illustrates that intergovernmental negotiations are neither solely about security issues nor concerned with economic costs and benefits of integration only, but political and ideological costs are part of domestic preference formation – and gender equality does have a price attached to it. Along these lines van der Vleuten argues in favour of a "modified liberal intergovernmentalist tool box" (2016: 93). This modified tool box includes a more diverse set of assumptions concerning domestic preference formation as well as the role of domestic and European institutions. In addition, van der Vleuten argues that the relevance of these additional factors vis-à-vis the classical state-centric factors is contingent. She claims that

> (…) against the background of the financial crisis and the preceding era of deregulation and deliberalization, as well as hard distributional geopolitical conflicts involving the EU and Russia, the continuing relevance of state actors and the study thereof seems to confirm the usefulness of a (modified) intergovernmentalist approach. (Ibid.: 94)

Finally, Hofmann already drew attention to the quality of leadership as a factor in intergovernmental negotiations; this opens up opportunities for including female agency to strengthen the value of intergovernmentalism. The German Chancellor Merkel is a promising example.

To sum up, according to van der Vleuten, "The rationalist ontology and 'positivist' epistemology cannot be stretched to integrate a critical gender perspective to integration which would take social relations instead of the state as starting point" (ibid.), which is something that many EU gender scholars perceive as essential. However, in van der Vleuten's words, "intergovernmentalism can be applied in a gender-sensitive way to a far larger extent than intergovernmentalists and many feminist scholars would ever admit." (Ibid.: 94f.; see also the appraisal of a gendered approach to intergovernmentalism in Galligan 2019).

3.2 Multi-Level Governance: Tailoring a favourite coat

Let's turn now to a very different, but also most prominent theoretical approach: multi-level governance (in short: MLG). This approach has made a remarkable career since the early 1990s. According to Stephenson it has become "a favourite coat … in the European political science wardrobe" – a coat "worn so often that is has now become threadbare" (2013: 817). Abels (2016) demonstrates that this coat can be tailored to the needs of gender fashion.

MLG can be classified as "a leading example of the ascendance of meso-level theorizing in EU studies", as Pagoulatos and Tsoukalis (2012: 66) claim. The core question is not "why integrate", but *how* governance in the EU works on a day-to-day basis. Unlike intergovernmentalism MLG is a society-centric approach, which builds on pluralistic and partly also functionalist assumptions. MLG assumes that (1) there is a division of competences across (at least) three levels of governance, (2) this is accompanied by a loss of sovereignty and the monopolistic position of the central state in EU affairs, and (3) the levels of authority are interconnected rather than nested. The key ontological premise is that "(in) the MLG world view, national governments are far from omnipotent" (Pagoulatos and Tsoukalis 2012: 65); they have lost their decision-making monopoly in favor of more complex systems of shared policy-making. From an MLG perspective the process of EU policy- and decision-making is perceived as strongly sectoralized, segmented and fragmented.

There is a strong nexus between MLG and network governance. Networks are important for vertical and horizontal policy coordination. In these networks, non-governmental and social actors are organized and the network structures the capacity to reach "from the central EC-level to decentral sub-nationals levels in the member states". Therefore, Piattoni (2010) argues that the MLG approach is essentially about political mobilization at and across different levels. Simultaneously, the approach stresses the role of the European institutions vis-à-vis the national governments in the Council. The European Commission, in particular, holds a prominent position in these networks. In so doing MLG resembles neo-functionalism with its strong focus on supranational actors and their independent capacity to act (see MacRae 2016).

MLG has been widely criticized and we cannot go into the details here. Abels (2016) claims that it is especially this combination of networking and complex governance structures that makes MLG attractive for gender analysis. At the same time, this network governance approach needs to be gendered to fulfil the needs of gender fashion.

The first study explicitly employing the combined MLG/policy network approach with a gender lens was conducted by Charlotte Bretherton and Liz Sperling (1996). The authors start from the observation that, by and large, policy network analysis has investigated policy areas that traditionally exclude women and women's interests. They study UK women's networks and their relation to EU gender policies. They argue that the EU has evolved into a polity more sympathetic towards gender equality. Their main focus is on the access options to transnational policy networks and the reasons why some actors do not have access. According to them, inadequate resources and the nature of the EU policy process are the main factors restricting access to networks, especially for grassroots organizations. They criticize the classical policy network model for its inherent elitism, due to its tendency to make women's agency invisible and places women on the fringes by investigating only specific forms of politics and by employing narrow definitions of agency. In this way, the "gendered 'public-private' divide within the public policy arena" (Bretherton and Sperling 1996: 500) is replicated. Nevertheless, the authors argue that policy network analysis is "potentially inclusive, providing framework for analysis of the activities of, and interaction between, networks at different levels, from local communities to EU institutions" (ibid.: 489). They furthermore praise the focus on co-operative relationships and the political support for the creation of transnational networks by the EU institutions themselves. They call for the development of an inclusive model that is neither linear nor hierarchical, but that is "based upon concentric but interconnected circles" (ibid.: 502). Such a model would allow for the "understanding of the operations of women's networks and their potential for influencing policy agendas" (ibid.).

Kathrin Zippel's study on sexual harassment policy demonstrates how multi-level "boomerang effects", which were strategically used by transnational actor networks, put the issue of sexual harassment on the EU agenda (Zippel 2004). Also Birgit Locher's work on the EU's engagement in the fight against sex trafficking refers to transnational actor networks that provide specific opportunity structures for the diffusion of norms. Locher (2007) even expands the multi-level networks to the international level.

What makes MLG attractive for gender studies is, firstly, the dissolution of the boundary between domestic (i.e. national) and international (i.e. European) politics. Territorial boundaries are not taken as given, but it is an empirical question whether and in which way they become effective. Linkages between the (sub-)national and EU level are issue- and sectoral-specific and national level actors can even be circumvented. Overcoming the narrow conception of the international as the realm of the states is a great advantage; it leaves room for women's agency and for a re-conceptualization of sovereignty and statehood.

Secondly, the sectoral approach draws attention to the involvement of non-state actors such as feminist movements as well as of feminist experts on the one hand, and the role of different EU institutions on the other hand. Thirdly, mainstream network analysis neglects the power differences between actors based on their resources; they conceptualize actors as interdependent. Actors – especially organized actors such as interest groups – are not equal and their resources differ. In particular, the role of those actors that fail to even gain access to policy networks for a variety of reasons, even if they may have a vested interest in the policy under consideration, remains a blind spot. However, network governance also takes place in the famous shadow of hierarchy. This already hints at the fact that state actors still have a prominent role to play. Gender-sensitive governance studies are also interested in gendered hierarchies and power relations, which are often informal, yet structural. Studies illustrate that the degree of openness of policy networks varies and that some actors may serve as gate-keepers and control access points; the question is: how favourable are they to gender-oriented actors?

Fourthly, the MLG approach underlines the fragmented nature of authority. From a feminist perspective of power as domination, the dispersion of political and jurisdictional authority is often viewed as more favourable than a strong centralization. This entails some advantages; however, it also has some drawbacks in terms of efficiency, ambivalent power relations and the democratic question.

A fifth and final aspect concerns the expansion of the essentially three-level-model to also include the international dimension, which has often acted as a supportive level given the strong formal codification of gender equality in international law.

In sum, gender EU studies can clearly adopt and build on governance approaches, i.e. on the MLG theoretical approach and its strong linkage to network governance. This approach is more susceptible to the ontological and epistemological as well as to the empirical and normative perspectives and demands of gender studies on the EU. Yet, a one-to-one adoption of governance approaches is insufficient. They need to be adjusted to, specified and further elaborated to fit the needs of gender scholars.

3.3 Gendering Europeanisation in theory and practice

Europeanisation has become somewhat of a "catch-all" concept in EU studies. From a political science perspective, it is conceived to characterize a top down process according to which member states change as a result of European integration. Yet, this top down perspective is contested. A number of scholars perceive Europeanisation to be a "processes of social construction, contestation and collective action" (Liebert 2016: 148). A third reading sees down- and uploading, vertical and horizontal effects as interrelated. In gender studies all three conceptions are influential. According to Liebert, the

> (…) common aim can be summarised by the following key question: Assuming that gender equality is a constitutive norm for the EU, what are the mechanisms for, conditions of and challenges to incorporating it into domestic practices? In other words, what does it take to empower gender equality in the actual ways of 'doing Europe'? (Ibid.)

Liebert argues that it requires to develop a gender-sensitive framework in order to reconfigure the concept of Europeanisation. At the same time, Europeanisation research has changed. Against the background of the ongoing crises and the "internal backlash against Europeanisation" (ibid.: 151) it is, as Liebert claims, hard to sustain the Europeanization paradigm given the current process of disintegration.

The effects of the gender acquis on member states is, for instance, an important case for studying Europeanization and the changes over time. While much Europeanisation research focuses on convergence among the member states,

> (…) gender studies confirm the persistence of the variety of gender regimes in EU member states, where 'convergence' towards shared EU gender equality norms is not necessarily incompatible with cross- and subnational diversity (ibid.: 152).

Liebert emphasises that different mechanism such as environmental, cognitive, and interactional mechanisms are in place, which link "a chain of transitions from the macro-level to the micro-level and back to the macro-level" (ibid.).

Feminist accounts of Europeanisation link rationalist and constructivist perspectives. For example, studies on the compliance with the gender acquis provide evidence that there are "gendered patterns of Europeanisation" and that national gender regimes are very persistent. Women's agency at national level and multi-level action coordination (see also MLG), strategic policy (re-)framing, power structures in political discourse are among the important factors for successful Europeanisation.

The great asset of Liebert's contribution is that she proposes a gendered framework for studying Europeanisation. This framework

> (…) links the literature on 'social mechanisms' with social theory, to bring together institutional, behavioural and cognitive elements that account for Europeanisation in the domestic politics of gender equality (ibid.: 160f.).

In so doing, the dynamic "interplay between macro-structural and micro-discursive and cognitive processes' can be reconstructed" (ibid.: 161).

However, the ongoing crises in European integration challenges previous EU gender equality research. Besides the gender-blindness in the public debate over crises-related economic and social effects, the new and non-gendered governance architecture of the Economic and Monetary Union and the rise of popular Euroscepticism have an impact on gender equality and gender research. To analyse the crises and the challenges, Liebert suggests a gender-sensitive approach:

> Whereas the rule-based legal conception of EMU governance is blind to communicative, discursive and symbolic mechanisms and their impacts, a comprehensively gendered Europeanisation framework is more sensitive to the underlying dynamics leading to socially regressive impacts of the Euro-zone's crisis management. It can expose how gendered social identities are being re-articulated in the dominant narratives about the Euro-crisis (ibid.: 165; for a gendered analysis of the Brexit crisis see Guerrina et al. 2018, Guerrina and Masselot 2018).

Liebert concludes that "Europeanisation studies can benefit from gender approaches for conceptualisation, theory-building and methodology" (ibid.: 166). Gendered conceptualizations of Europeanisation "can contribute to our theoretical and methodological toolbox in a number of ways" (ibid.: 167), by bringing in the multi-level analysis, discursive and framing approaches, and external factor such as international law and its role in norm diffusion.

In the final analysis, Liebert's conceptualization of Europeanisation is also typical for the normative approach to be found in much gender EU studies and their linkage to a feminist agenda for change. Liebert argues that a differentiated understanding of Europeanisation will also support the political agenda for gender equality to be put in practice.

> In so far as this approach [narrative of Europeanisation focused on the value of gender equality] to the governance of gender equality differs from top-down bureaucratic and economic market-oriented modes, it will be innovative and labelled as a form of "participatory Europeanisation". Such reforms might bring the EU closer to its gendered constituencies … (ibid.: 169f.).

4. Conclusions

What can we learn from this? Some of the critique by gender scholars is, indeed, not unique. This is emphasized by Hans-Jürgen Bieling and Thomas Diez in their dialogue with gender approaches (Bieling and Diez 2016). They notice that

> The critique of state-centrism is an old one shared by a variety of approaches from functionalism to poststructuralism. Even liberal intergovernmentalism would agree that states are not unitary actors. By the same token, most analysts, apart from a small band of die-hard realists, share the view that the national

> interest is contested and needs to be problematized. And whole libraries have discussed the different 'faces of power' (ibid.: 290).

In this regard, gendered voices are becoming an essential part of the above-mentioned choir of dissident voice in integration theory. Nevertheless and irrespective "of how the common and divergent results of the gendering exercise are assessed and evaluated in detail, the contributions … show the need to gender existing integration theories …" (ibid.: 291). According to Bieling and Diez the contributions assembled in Abels and MacRae (2016)

> (…) have taken an important step from not only criticising other theories for being gender-blind but actually reformulating them to include gender inequality in a variety of ways. … They also urge theorists of European integration to problematize core categories of state and national interest, and be alert to power relations and their effects. In an era of crises, both analysts and practitioners of European integration would do well to heed these calls for gendering their perspectives." (Ibid.)

Yvonne Galligan agrees with this assessment and argues that

> Whichever lens or theory is used to examine integration, the case of gender is one that highlights a different set of dynamics with respect to group-institutional power interplays than is revealed in a gender-neutral analysis. (Galligan 2019: 193)

Hence, the need for intense discussions is obvious and we are only at the beginning of an exciting dialogue.

References

Abels, G. (2012), Feministische Perspektiven, in Bieling, H.-J. and Lerch, M. (eds.), *Theorien der europäischen Integration: Einführung,* 3rd revised edition, Wiesbaden: VS Verlag, pp. 295-318.

Abels, G. (2016), Multi-Level Governance: Tailoring a 'favourite coat' to the needs of 'gender fashion', in Abels, G. and MacRae, H. (eds.), *Gendering European integration theory: engaging new dialogues*, Opladen, Toronto: Barbara Budrich Publisher, pp. 99-121.

Bretherton, C. and Sperling, L. (1996), Women's networks and the European Union – towards an inclusive approach?, *Journal of Common Market Studies* 34 (4), pp. 487-508.

Bieling, H.-J. and Diez, T. (2016), Linking gender perspectives to integration theory: the need for dialogue, in Abels, G. and MacRae, H. (eds.), *Gendering European integration theory: engaging new Dialogues*, Opladen, Toronto: Barbara Budrich Publisher, pp. 279-292.

Celis, K., Kantola, J., Waylen, G., and Laurel Weldon, S. (2013), Gender and politics: a gendered world, a gendered discipline, in Waylen, G., Celis, K., Kantola, J., and Laurel Weldon, S. (eds.): *The Oxford handbook of gender and politics*, Oxford: Oxford University Press, pp. 1-26.

Galligan, Y. (2019), European integration and gender, in Wiener, A., Börzel, T.A. and Risse, T. (eds.), *European integration theory,* 3rd edition, Oxford: Oxford University Press, pp. 174-194.

Guerrina, R. et al. (2018), Does European Union studies have a gender problem? Experiences from researching Brexit, *International Feminist Journal of Politics* 20 (2), pp. 252-257.

Guerrina, R. and Masselot, A. (2018), Walking into the footprint of EU law: unpacking the gendered consequences of Brexit, *Social Policy & Society* 17 (2), pp. 319-330.

Hawkesworth, M. (2013), Sex, gender and sexuality: from naturalized presumptions to analytical categories', in Waylen, G., Celis, K., Kantola, J., and Laurel Weldon, S. (eds.): *The Oxford handbook of gender and politics*, Oxford: Oxford University Press, pp. 31-56.

Kronsell, A. (2012), Gendering theories of European integration, in Abels G. and Mushaben, J.M. (eds.): *Gendering the European Union. New approaches to old democratic deficits*, Basingstoke: Palgrave Macmillan, pp. 23-40.

Liebert, U. (1999), Gender Politics in the European Union: The Return of the Public, *European Societies* 1 (2), pp. 197-239.

Liebert, U. (2016): Gendering Europeanisation: making equality work in theory and practice, in Abels, G. and MacRae, H. (eds.), *Gendering European integration theory: engaging new dialogues*, Opladen, Toronto: Barbara Budrich Publisher, pp. 147-174.

Locher, B. (2007), *Trafficking in Women in the European Union: Norms, Advocacy-Networks and Policy-Change*, Wiesbaden: VS Verlag.

MacRae, H. (2016), Neofunctionalism: Spilling over to gender studies, in Abels, G. and MacRae, H. (eds.), *Gendering European integration theory: engaging new dialogues*, Opladen, Toronto: Barbara Budrich Publisher, pp. 57-76.

Manners, I. and Whitman, R. (2016), Another theory is possible: dissenting voices in theorising Europe, *Journal of Common Market Studies* 54 (1), pp. 3-18.

Pagoulatos, G. and Tsoukalis, L. (2012), Multilevel governance, in: Jones, E., Menon, A. and Weatherill, S. (eds.), *The Oxford handbook of the European Union*, Oxford: Oxford University Press, pp. 62-75.

Piattoni, S. (2010), *The theory of multi-level governance*, Oxford: Oxford University Press.

Stephenson, P. (2013), Twenty years of multi-level governance: 'Where does it come from? What is it? Where is it going', *Journal of European Public Policy* 20 (6), pp. 817-837.

van der Vleuten, A. (2016), Intergovernmentalism: gendering a dinosaur?, in Abels, G. and MacRae, H. (eds.), *Gendering European integration theory: engaging new dialogues*, Opladen, Toronto: Barbara Budrich Publisher, pp. 77-97.

Zippel, K. (2004), Transnational Advocacy Networks and Policy Cycles in the Euro-pean Union: The Case of Sexual Harrassment, *Social Politics* 11 (1), pp. 57-85.

III.
European Innovation and Development

14. The European Central Bank in the euro crisis: The case of the OMT program

Dennis Zagermann

1. Introduction[1]

The European Union has been the focal point of extensive economic and political turmoil since 2008. After the outbreak of the sub-prime crisis, the European Union (EU) has seen economic recession in all member states. The crisis, which was at first glance perceived as a crisis of the financial markets, quickly escalated into a widespread economic crisis, due to the interrelations between financial markets and other economic sectors. Some members of the Economic and Monetary Union (EMU) have seen the worst recession in their history since the Great Depression in the 1930s, which led to a short-lived return of neo-Keynesian economic policy (e.g. Schmidt 2014: 196). The stimulus packages, while being successful at stopping the crisis dynamic, led to massively increased sovereign debt – both nominally and in regards of Debt-to-GDP-ratios (Streeck 2013: 151-152). Banks, in return, demanded higher interest rates for bonds by countries with increased sovereign debts, budgetary problems, and high current account deficits. Thus, Eurozone members started to have difficulties to refinance their sovereign debt. A prominent case is the announcement of the Greek prime minister, in which he seeked financial assistance from the European Union. After his announcement, yield spreads on government bonds led to a situation in which state debt could become a potential trigger point for sovereign defaults in the European periphery (Scharpf 2013: 284) and thus potentially lead to an uncoordinated breakup of the Eurozone.

At the peak of the crisis in 2012, EU heads of states or governments appeared to be politically paralyzed. Despite several efforts in bringing down interest rates for long-term government bonds, interest rates remained on high levels. Talks about an end-date for the common currency where increasingly popular. Eventually, unsustainably high interest rates for government bonds were stopped by Mario Draghi's announcement of the Outright Monetary Transaction (OMT) program in August 2012. Despite not actually having been

1 I would like to thank Ulrike Liebert, Anne Jenichen, the participants of the CEuS conference in Bremen and the reviewer for their valuable comments.

in use so far, the announcement of OMT has potentially changed the European Central Bank's (ECB) role in EMU governance (De Grauwe/Ji 2015). Furthermore, the debate on Europeanisation vs. renationalisation of monetary policy has taken on again after the ECB became a more prominent actor during the euro crisis.

OMT and further activities of the ECB, such as its current quantitative easing programme, are not uncontroversial. Unlike origininaly set out, the ECB moved away from the ordo-liberal orthodoxy and, to some degree, became a neo-Keynesian "lender of last resort" (Schmidt 2013: 458). This is astonishing, as the ECB's personell were very much immersed in ordo-liberal discourse and policy programs (Schmidt 2014: 194). At the same time, bargains between France and Germany, as still the two most prominent engines of ideas for European integration (Brunnermeier et al. 2016), suggest that ordo-liberal frames of reference are still very stable (Crespy/Schmidt 2014: 1199; see also Schmidt 2014) and have been adopted, to a certain degree, by French political leaders (Crespy/Schmidt 2014: 1195).

The ECB, however, appears to be acting outside oft he predominant frames of reference. Thus, the case of OMT is thus a perfect example for European polycentric governance in action. Several strong publics have been arguing over its legal and politico-economic basis. This debate is based on very different views on central banks and their role in economic governance. While ECB is generally perceived as the most politically independent central bank, it is also said to have the most predetermined scope of actions due to its legal mandate[2]. At the same time, it has become a key policy maker in the European Union to resolve the crisis (Scharpf 2013: 282).

The article will explore these phenomena and will answer the central research question: *How is the current role of the ECB in European economic governance perceived in European strong publics?* In order to address this question, I first propose an analytical model for the ECB's role during the crisis which hypothesizes the ECB's role as a mediator between different strong publics (Eriksen 2004; Eriksen and Fossum 2002; see also Fraser 1990: 74-77) engaged in European governance and sovereign debt in financial markets. The central hypothesis here is that, while there are different demands to possible ECB action, it mainly serves as a mediator between conflicting political and economic interests. Secondly, I present the findings from a qualitative discourse analysis of the ECB's role and its OMT program based on official documents and media coverage. In the conclusion, I summarize findings.

---

2 With the Treaty of Lisbon, the ECB has obtained the status of a EU-Institution. Its legal mendate is constituted in the articles 282 to 284 in the Treaty of the Functioning of the European Union. Its statue is attached as Protocol (No 4) to the treaty (European Union 2012).

2. The ECB's role within the Euro Crisis

Drawing on Susan Strange's theory on structural power and market influences on state activity (Strange 1988, 1996, 1998), central insights into the functionality of general, segmented, and strong publics in European discourse (Eriksen and Fossum 2002; Eriksen 2004; see also Fraser 1990: 74-77), theories on the societal role of knowledge and non-knowledge within hyper-complex societies (Willke 2002, 2007; Strulik 2004; Luhmann 1995; Innerarity 2013), and theories of private authorites (Sinclair 1999, 2005, Strulik 2004; Cutler *et al.* 1999), the role of the ECB during the crisis and its unconventional policies can be hypothesized as that of a mediator between conflicting societial systems and strong publics. Furthermore, the ECB's mediating role has be to hypothezised as containing two distinct dimensions: the mediation on financial markets regarding sovereign debt as well as the mediation within the EU's polycentric strong public structure. The latter, as it is hypothesized here, is unlikely to find common grounds due to paradigmatic differences.

2.1 The politico-economic role of the ECB: mediation of financial markets

Rating agencies have become private authorities within the governance of financial markets (Sinclair 1999; 2005; Cutler *et al.* 1999). They are restructuring non-knowledge, which are blind spots in the knowledge structure of complex, knowledge-based societies, in a way that market participants are able to calculate risks instead of being overwhelmed by complexity (Innerarity 2013: 145; Strulik 2004: 16) and thus form one of the most important governance architecture of financial markets (Willke 2003: 211). Their ratings are acknowledged as the benchmark in managing credit risk and investments (Sinclair 2005) and thus carry out structural power (Strange 1988, 1996, 1998) by setting informal investment rules. This unrivaled position of authority was visible during the euro crisis a couple of times. European institutions tried to stop growing spreads on sovereign debt after downgrades by the agencies (Illing 2013: 47-115; Prager 2012).

The argument proposed here is that the ECB seizes the role of rating agencies with its OMT program: It made risk related to the ability of Eurozone members to meet their financial obligations calculable. After thc intervention, communication about the financial soundness of government bonds were framed in terms of calculable risks instead of predictions of catastrophes. Here, we can hypothesize a possible perception of the OMT announcement as a reduction of risk. Hence, the ECB produced trust, reduced complexity (Luhmann 2014[1968]) and thus led to a decrease of interest rates for sovereign debt. Thus, the new politico-economic role of ECB, as it developed throughout the euro crisis, can be hypothesized as being a mediator on financial markets regarding sovereign debt and, to a lesser degree, regarding socio-economic developments in the Eurozone.

2.2 The ECB within Europe's polycentric political structure

Political discourse and governance of the EU take place within a multi-level system in which a wide number of political actors are debating and deciding on EU governance in different politico-institutional contexts (Hix/Høyland 2011; Wonka/Lange 2014). They are overlapping as EU politics and institutions span over national political spheres of the member states. The European Union does contain general publics, as well as several strong and segmented publics (Eriksen and Fossum 2002; Eriksen 2004). Strong publics, here, have to be understood as "institutionalised deliberation close to the political system that is legally regulated" (Eriksen 2004: 10), e.g. Parliaments, Courts, etc. General publics are deliberation spaces in which everybody is free to participate and includes media such as newspapers (Eriksen 2004: 16). Segmented publics are specialised deliberative spaces, which evolve around policy issues (Eriksen 2004: 16).

Taking the different national and European strong publics into consideration, the way the EU decides on social objectives and legislative processes to achieve them within a continuing political process (Hix/Høyland 2011; Wonka/Lange 2014), as we have seen during the euro crisis, allows for a characterisation of European politics as being polycentric: "EU business is conducted in multiple settings on virtually every day of the year" (Hix/Høyland 2011: 14). European political discourse reflects a network of political communication in multiple national spaces (Liebert 2003 cit. from Liebert 2007: 246) with specific points where these networks come together, such as the EU summits during the crisis.

In this polycentric structure, the ECB is one of the institutions that can be thought of as a non-majoritarian supranational institution, which would be able to mediate different, conflicting political claims concerned with monetary policies and the future of the common currency in times of political standstill. Habermas (2013) has portrayed the standstill in the case of the euro crisis as a failure of elites. In such cases, where European governments cannot come to a consensus on how to get a crisis under control and in which dominant frames of reference are under pressure, the ECB can act to ease pressure temporarily. The ECB would thus be able to produce trust in the common currency with policy-makers from different European centres and allow the political system to take productive risks instead of being paralyzed by the complexity of policy-making in times of crises. The role of the ECB within Europe's political structure of multiple strong publics can thus be hypothesized as a mediator in times of political standstill between different strong publics.

Taking these insights into consideration, the following chapter will provide an empirical-analytical assessment of the ECB's hypothesized mediation role on financial markets and within the polycentric structure of European strong publics.

3. Perceptions of the ECB and its OMT program

To empirically measure perceptions of the role ECB's role and the role its OMT program took on during the crisis, I conducted a qualitative discourse analysis. While the ECB has a legal mandate and its action could be traced via economic statistics, its role during the euro crisis is highly debated and still up to bargain. It is debated in the general as well as different strong and segmented publics. Applying discourse analysis methodology, as developed by Liebert *et al.* in the ConstEPS project (Liebert 2007; see also Maatsch 2007; Packham 2007) allows me to analyse the claims and narratives on the definition, substance, functionality, and further implications of OMT as they have been posed by European and national institutions. Building on the ConstEPS research, I define political communication here as "communicative actions taking place in networks of information, of argumentative as well as symbolic exchanges" in and between political arenas concerned with the Euro, "as well as exchanges between political elites and the citizenry, where the news media play a central mediation role" (Liebert 2007: 238).

The analysis is based on data collected from different documents between July 2012 and June 2014. Documents have been selected from different contexts identified via the analytical model. The data incorporates European and national institutions, ECB representatives, the European Parliament's (EP) Economic and Monetary Affairs Committee (ECON) Monetary Dialogues, European Council summits, and the news media. For the time period, 298 documents were collected. Presented in the analysis here are twenty-two substantive documents. Their selection was based on peaks in media coverage, which were matched with key events in the euro crisis, in order to cover central moments in the discourse on OMT and include data from the general public (newspaper articles) as well as data from different strong publics.

The coding scheme includes four main categories: 1) definitional discourse, 2) evaluative discourse, 3) substantive discourse, 4) discourse on further strategies. The coding scheme was applied to whole passages in the data. Instead of looking for specific keywords, the general meaning articulated in the passage was considered for coding in order to extract key strands in argumentation.

Table 1: Coding scheme for qualitative data analysis

Definition	Evaluation	Substance	Strategies
• What is OMT? • What role does the ECB take?	• Approval • Rejection	• Functional Reasoning • Political Reasoning • Institutional Reasoning • Normative Reasoning • Causal Reasoning	• Monetary Disintegration • Deepening integration • Further austerity • New economic governance

Source: own compilation

3.1 Definitional discourse about the ECB

As it might be expected, the role taken by the ECB is heavily debated throughout the political discourse. While the topic of the ECB's role comes up regularly, there are two definitional argumentative strands that stand out. First, the ECB is portrayed as an organisation that effectively did work as a backstop facility to secure the Euro. Here, the argumentation focuses on the ECB merely supporting politically decided economic policy in giving structural reforms time to develop their positive effects (*European Central Bank* 2012, 2013a; 2013b; *Financial Times* 2012a, 2012b, 2013b, 2014) and thus resembles noe-Keynesian arguments to a certain degree. The second definitional discourse is negative. Here, the ECB is portrayed as an organisation that is effectively overstepping its institutional competences, is engaging in policy fields beyond its legal mandate and is linked to a debate on European technocracy (*Bundesbank* 2013; *German Constitutional Court* 2014; *Handelsblatt* 2012a, 2013b, 2014; *European Parliament* 2012, 2013). The arguments presented here resemble ordo-liberal reasoning on central banks to a certain degree.

The definitional discourse on the OMT program goes into the same direction. While OMT is debated considerably less than the ECB's role, it still is an important topic. Two characterisations stand out: The first is proposed by the ECB itself in different institutional contexts: OMT is portrayed as a backstop facility, which does not relief countries of the need to implement painful reforms (*European Parliament* 2012; *European Central Bank* 2012, 2013a,

2014). The second interpretation is that of OMT being a lender of last resort-program which resembles a step of the ECB out of its mandate, thus relieving member states of disciplinary effects on bond markets (*Handelsblatt* 2012a, 2012b, 2012c, 2013a, 2014; *Bundesbank* 2013, *German Constitutional Court* 2014).

3.2 Evaluative discourse regarding the ECB's OMT program

In the evaluative discourse, passages that approve of the ECB and its OMT program occur more often than rejections. Unsurprisingly, the analysis shows a lot of approving passages on ECB activities by the ECB itself in all institutional contexts (*European Parliament* 2012, 2013; *European Central Bank* 2012, 2013a, 2013b, 2014). Its approval is mostly matched with arguments concerning the necessity, effectiveness, and legality of the ECB's policy decisions. The Financial Times does not only approve of OMT (*Financial Times* 2012c, 2013a, 2013b), but would also approve of a more active central bank in general (*Financial Times* 2012a, 2013b, 2014).

Rejection of a more active role of the ECB was articulated by some Members of the European Parliament (MEPs) during the ECON Monetary Dialogue. The reasoning is twofold: First, MEPs questioned the accountability of the ECB to decide and implement policies with possible widespread consequences (*European Parliament* 2012). Secondly, MEPs voiced their concerns about stagflation for the Eurozone, which could be a downside of an expansionary monetary policy (*European Parliament* 2013).

This rejection discourse is resembled by the German Constitutional Court (GCC) hearing. First, Jens Weidmann, president of the German Bundesbank, is a prominent opponent of a more active European Central Bank. His rejection is grounded on a narrow interpretation of the legal mandate and his politico-economic positions on price stability (*Bundesbank* 2013). Secondly, Weidmann's rejection based on the ECB's legal mandate was picked up by the GCC in their rejection of ECB activities and its referral of the case to the European Court of Justice (ECJ) (*German Constitutional Court* 2014).

3.3 Substantive discourse for and against the ECB'S OMT program

When considering the substantive discourse, it should be mentioned that most arguments about the substance of the ECB's activity are based on functional and institutional arguments. While political reasoning also plays an important role, it does not match the frequency of other arguments. Normative and causal argumentation only play a minor role. Here, I will focus on functional, institutional, and political reasoning.

The ECB itself poses two functional arguments in different arenas of governance: First, the ECB argues for an ongoing transmission failure of traditional monetary policy, which makes more unorthodox measures necessary to ensure price stability (*European Parliament* 2012; *European Central Bank* 2012, 2013b). Secondly, the ECB argues that the failure of positive market reactions to ongoing reforms made it necessary for the ECB to support economic policy. It did so by producing trust and thus generating more time for reforms to work (*European Parliament* 2012; *European Central Bank* 2012, 2013a, 2013b). MEPs in the ECON Monetary Dialogue agreed with this to a large degree (*European Parliament* 2012, 2013). The ECB is not engaged here, yet the ECB does acknowledge its functional role in terms of a banking union (*European Council* 2012a, 2012b). The GCC picks up on both arguments by the ECB and dismisses both due to the ECB's legal mandate (*German Constitutional Court* 2014, *Bundesbank* 2013). News media portrays both positions: while the Financial Times is arguing in favour of the ECB's actions (*Financial Times* 2012a, 2013a, 2013b, 2014), the Handelsblatt focusses on functional risks (*Handelsblatt* 2013b, 2014), although they do admit that the OMT did have a calming effect on bond markets.

The debate on institutional reasoning is largely concerned with institutional boundaries of the ECB. The ECB itself is using a broader understanding of its institutional boundaries in the debate, arguing that at certain times it is necessary for the ECB to support economic policy set out by the member states with untraditional monetary policy (*European Parliament* 2012; *European Central Bank* 2012, 2013a; 2013b). A diametrically opposed position is proposed by Jens Weidmann and the GCC. They provide a narrow understanding of the institutional underpinning of ECB activities. Being active in more fields than price stability, they argue, would lead to a more fragile institutional framework of the common currency. Therefore, monetary policy should be strongly divided from economic policy (*Bundesbank* 2013; *German Constitutional Court* 2014; *European Central Bank* 2013b). News media resembles these different positions. While Financial Times does make a case for Weidmann's position (*Financial Times* 2013a), it does not argue against OMT on institutional grounds (*Financial Times* 2012c, 2013a, 2013b, 2014). Handelsblatt does not present a coherent position.

Political reasoning, the third important argumentative strand, and the issue of political accountability, is debated in almost all documents. MEPs regularly bring up the issue of the ECB being a non-majoritarian institution which is not directly accountable to European citizens. While the ECB is generally getting good feedback in the ECON Monetary Dialogue, MEPs also perceive the ECB as blurring the lines between monetary policy and other policy fields, producing uneasiness (*European Parliament* 2012, 2013). Jens Weidmann points out a different aspect: He argues that the ECB should not make politics for countries that appear unwilling to implement structural reforms (*Bundesbank* 2013). The GCC only refers to a possible lack of accountability of the ECB to European voters (*German Constitutional Court* 2014). The political reasoning discourse in the news media is best described as undecided. While the Handelsblatt is arguing for Weidmann's critique (*Handelsblatt* 2013a, 2013b), it also gives room to political reasoning in favour of OMT (*Handelsblatt* 2012a, 2012b). The Financial Times argues that the ECB is actively surging political support and thus portrays the ECB as a more politically accountable organisation (*Financial Times* 2012c).

3.4 Strategic discourses for/against deepening fiscal integration

The discourse on further strategies is mainly based on two strands: Deepening the fiscal integration and new forms of economic and monetary governance. While current austerity measures are also viewed as a strategy that should be followed, monetary disintegration is rarely brought up.

The primary discourse topic on further strategies is deepening fiscal integration. The key institutional debate on this topic is the banking union and the supervisory role the central bank is supposed to adopt. The ECB's argumentation for its new role is especially focused on the fact that supervisory roles and monetary policies are often combined in central banks. ECB representatives also argue that it would be a necessity to break the vicious circle between banks and sovereigns which was visible during the crisis (*European Parliament* 2012, 2013; *European Central Bank* 2012). The completion of EMU is further discussed by the European Council which argues for several institutional innovations and more integration to cope with the crisis (*European Council* 2012a, 2012b). MEPs are widely in favour of more fiscal integration. Yet, they are unsure about the supervisory role of the ECB in the banking union (*European Parliament* 2012, 2013). The news media points out two different perspectives on further fiscal integration. Handelsblatt is reluctant, it puts forward differing national interests and the potential loss of monetary stability as reasons against more integration (*Handelsblatt* 2012a, 2013a). Financial Times is only marginally concerned with further integration processes (*Financial Times* 2012a, 2012b, 2013a).

The topic of a new economic governance of the Eurozone appears a couple of times in the data. While the ECB is seeing good progress in budget consolidation, the economic consolidation still needs time. The ECB focusses on better possibilities for member states to gain access to credit. Yet, the argumentation is vague and the ECB constantly underlines that they could only support economic policy and not decide on it themselves (*European Parliament* 2012, 2013). MEPs are more direct. A point in case is the MEP George Cutaş (S&D, Romania) who asked Draghi if full employment should be an objective of monetary policy (*European Parliament* 2012). The European Council is highly engaged in the debate about new modes of economic governance. However, it is not proposing a more central role of the ECB in this regard (*European Council* 2012a, 2012b). In the news media, only the Financial Times is concerned with a new economic governance. It does take into consideration a lender of last resort-scenario (*Financial Times* 2012a) and does not reject the idea of quantitative easing (*Financial Times* 2012b) to secure states and start economic growth. Financial Times also approves of ECB interventions on financial markets via OMT to reduce uncertainty (*Financial Times* 2013a). The Handelsblatt does not engage in a debate about new economic governance.

Continuing the current austerity measures is brought up in different institutional contexts by different actors. The ECB argues for further austerity measures as far as the debate is concerned with the conditionality of their policy measures. OMT and other unconventional policy decisions, the ECB argues, will not relieve countries to engage in further structural reforms (*European Parliament* 2012, 2013; *European Central Bank* 2012). MEPs question to some degree, whether the policies proposed by the ECB will help to achieve further structural reforms, as they might take pressure off the countries in crisis (*European Parliament* 2012, 2013). The European Council also argues for further austerity measures and structural reforms in their conclusions (*European Council* 2012a, 2012b). The news media has different positions on austerity. On the one hand, Handelsblatt is effectively arguing for a continuing of austerity with a rationale of preventing further monetary transfers to countries in crisis (*Handelsblatt* 2012a, 2012b, 2012c, 2013a). Financial Times does only touch on the topic of austerity a couple of times. Austerity is held up as a necessary conditionality for ECB activity, but not as a purpose in itself (*Financial Times* 2012c, 2013b, 2014). Only Handelsblatt picks up monetary disintegration (*Handelsblatt* 2013b, 6).

4. Conclusion

The European Union has seen some of the most difficult years in its history. The euro crisis has not only put the irreversibility of the common currency in question. It also had an immense effect on the daily lives of European citizens, it produced economic recessions, and led to huge increases in unemployment and poverty. Rising interest rates on government bonds could have potentially led to an uncontrolled break-up of the monetary union. In the summer of 2012, when talks of an end of the euro were prominent, the European Central Bank stepped forward as a non-majoritarian supranational institution and claimed to do "whatever it takes" to secure the euro.

The article has asked how the new, more active role of the ECB in European economic governance during the crisis has been debated, despite being generally described as the central bank with the most predetermined scope of action (Scharpf 2013: 282). To answer this question, I proposed theoretical insights on the ECB's response to the euro crisis. The ECB, as argued here, acted as a mediator to overcome the political stalemate. Hence, the ECB's role has been hypothesized as offering mediation on financial markets as well as mediation between the different strong publics in the EU's polycentric political structure in times of economic and political standstill. For illustrating this argument, I conducted a discourse analysis of political and legal contentions about the ECB's OMT program. In the light of my results, the research question can be answered as follows: Perceptions on the ECB's more active role and its OMT are diverse and the debate is highly political, despite the politically independent role of the ECB. While there is a consensus that the crisis has triggered a more active role of the ECB, the analysis highlights the differences in its evaluation. The ECB itself approves of its actions and receives support by parts of the media as well as by MEPs. However, there is considerable rejection by parts of the media and other political institutions, especially the German Bundesbank. Actions taken by the ECB are either perceived as monetary support for political decisions taken by European governments or as a lender of last resort-scenario, which would exceed the ECB's legal mandate. While there is some consent on functional reasoning behind the actions taken by the ECB – their announcement of the OMT program did secure the institutional stability of the Eurozone -, institutionally and politically there is less approval. Here, the interpretation of the ECB's legal mandate is up for further debates. Because there is no consent on the ECB's new role, several further strategies are debated with little chance of a general agreement on further policies.

The data highlighted that the hypothesized mediation on financial markets is widely acknowledged in the discourse on OMT, although there is an ongoing dispute on its legitimacy. The data also showed that the ECB's action did allow for a political debate again, after the EU had been politically paralysed in 2012 when talks of an end date of the common currency emerged and interest rates for sovereign debt were unsustainably high. Here, the ECB's role of mediation within the EUs strong publics was visible. However, as the data also showed, the ECB's role as a mediator between different string publics has its limits. It was unable to mediate ongoing politico-economic disputes on which kind of economic policy is necessary to cope with the crisis. According to the data, the ECB cannot mediate between ordo-liberal and neo-Keynesian positions.

The discourse about the ECB and its OMT program, as I have highlighted, will most likely go on as the crisis has not ended and the ECB has remained an active participant in the crisis management. Whether the debate on its legal mandate will lead to further Europeanisation or a renationalisation of monetary policy is not decided yet, but remains a fascinating research topic. Therefore, further research should be conducted on the influence of the ECB on economic activity, its political accountability as a non-majoritarian supranational organisation, about the interconnectedness of ECB activities, and new governance instruments implemented during the crisis (e.g. Fiscal Compact, European Semester, etc.). More data and the debate on its current Quantitative Easing program should be incorporated in future research. Research should also be conducted on the effect the ECJ and further GCC rulings on the OMT program will have.

References

Brunnermeier, Markus K./James, Harold/Landau, Jean-Pierre (2016): The Euro and the Battle of Ideas. Princeton: Princeton University Press.

Bundesbank (2013): Eingangserklärung anlässlich der mündlichen Verhandlung im Hauptsacheverfahren ESM/EZB. June 11th, 2013. URL: https://www.bundesbank.de/Redaktion/DE/Kurzmeldungen/Stellungnahmen/2013_06_11_esm_ezb.html (March 10h 2017).

Crespy, Amandine/Schmidt Vivian A. (2014): The clash of Titans. France, Germany and the discursive double game of EMU reform. In: Journal of European Public Policy 21, 8, pp. 1085-1101.

Cutler, A. Claire/Haufler, Virginia/Porter, Toni (1999): Private Authority and International Affairs. In: Ibid. (eds.): Private Authority and International Affairs. New York: SUNY Press, pp. 3-28.

De Grauwe, Paul/Ji, Yuemei (2015): Correcting for the Eurzone Design Failures. The Role of the ECB. In: Journal of European Integration 37, 7, pp. 739-754.

Eriksen, Arik Oddvar/Fossum, John Erik (2002): Democracy through strong publics in the European Union? In: Journal of Common Market Studies 40, 3, pp. 401-424.

Eriksen, Arik Oddvar (2004): Conceptualizing European Public Spheres. General, Segmented and Strong Publics. In: ARENA Working Paper Series 3/04. URL: http://www.sv.uio.no/arena/english/research/publications/arena-working-papers/2001-2010/2004/wp04_3.pdf (July 17th 2017).

European Central Bank (2012): Eröffnungsrede im Deutschen Bundestag. Rede von Mario Draghi, Präsident der EZB, Erörterung der geldpolitischen Maßnahmen der EZB mit Mitgliedern des Deutschen Bundestags, Berlin, 24. Oktober 2012. URL: https://www.ecb.europa.eu/press/key/date/2012/html/sp121024.de.html (March 10th 2017).

European Central Bank (2013a): Responsible leadership in times of crisis. Address by Mario Draghi, President of the ECB, on the occasion of receiving the ESMT Leadership Award 2013, Berlin, 13 June 2013. URL: http://www.ecb.europa.eu/press/key/date/2013/html/sp130613.en.html (March 10th 2017).

European Central Bank (2013b): Einleitende Stellungnahme der EZB in dem Verfahren vor dem Bundesverfassungsgericht Jörg Asmussen, Mitglied des Direktoriums der EZB, Karlsruhe, 11. Juni 2013. URL: https://www.ecb.europa.eu/press/key/date/2013/html/sp130611.de.html (March 10th 2017).

European Central Bank (2014): The path to recovery and the ECB's role. Speech by Mario Draghi, President of the ECB, at the Symposium on Financial Stability and the Role of Central Banks organised by the Deutsche Bundesbank, Frankfurt am Main, 27 February 2014. URL: http://www.ecb.europa.eu/press/key/date/2014/html/sp140227.en.html (March 10th 2017).

European Council (2012a): Euro Area Summit Statement. June 29th 2012. URL: https://www.bankingsupervision.europa.eu/about/milestones/shared/pdf/2012-06-29_euro_area_summit_statement_en.pdf (March 10th 2017).

European Council (2012b): Europea Council 18/19 October Conclusions. URL: http://www.consilium.europa.eu/uedocs/cms_Data/docs/pressdata/en/ec/133004.pdf (March 10th 2017).

European Parliament (2012): Committee on Monetary Affairs. Monetary Dialogue – October 9th 2012. URL: https://polcms.secure.europarl.europa.eu/cmsdata/upload/7ad6390e-235f-4943-be4d-a4db9dbdb13a/Hearing_oct_2012_mixed.pdf (March 10th 2017).

European Parliament (2013): Committee on Economic and Monetary Affairs. Monetary Dialogue – July 8th 2013. https://polcms.secure.europarl.europa.eu/cmsdata/upload/5b3f7bd7-0e8a-49df-b3b9-72ac0244af5a/Hearing_july_en.pdf (March 10th 2017).

European Union (2012): Consolidated versions of the Treaty on European Union and the Treaty on the Functioning of the European Union in the Official Journal of the European Union, 2012/C326/1.

Financial Times (2012a): This will not be enough, Mr. Draghi. August 7th 2012. URL: https://www.ft.com/content/e3504ed0-dfcb-11e1-9bb7-00144feab49a (March 10th 2017).

Financial Times (2012b): Policy makers need to reduce uncertainty. August 20th 2012. URL: https://www.ft.com/content/3a646886-e79d-11e1-86bf-00144feab49a (March 10th 2017).

Financial Times (2012c): Draghi says he needs to explain plan. September 14th 2012. URL: https://www.ft.com/content/3e88a7e0-fe7e-11e1-a2e2-00144feab dc0 (March 10th 2017).

Financial Times (2013a): In defence of OMT and Draghi's ECB. June 10th 2013. URL: https://www.ft.com/content/7c10e8ee-d1d6-11e2-9336-00144feab7de (March 10th 2017).

Financial Times (2013b): Bundesbank in court clash with ECB over bond-buying plan. June 11th 2013. URL: https://www.ft.com/content/1ecb4826-d25f-11e2-aac2-00144feab7de (March 10th 2017).

Financial Times (2014): Karlsruhe fallout highlights the power of ECB. February 12th 2014. URL: https://www.ft.com/content/9b48ade6-93f5-11e3-a0e1-00144 feab7de (March 10th 2017).

Fraser, Nancy (1990): Rethinking the Public Sphere. A Contribution to the Critique of Actually Existing Democracy. In: Social Text 25/26, pp. 56-80.

German Constitutional Court (2014): Pressemitteilung Nr. 9/2014 vom 7. Februar 2014. URL: http://www.bverfg.de/pressemitteilungen/bvg14-009.html (March 10th 2017).

Habermas, Jürgen (2013): Ein Fall von Elitenversagen. In: DER SPIEGEL 32/ 2013, pp. 26-27.

Handelsblatt (2012a): Der EZB ist es verboten, Staaten zu finanzieren. July 25th 2012. URL: http://www.handelsblatt.com/politik/international/spanien-krise-der-ezb-ist-es-verboten-staaten-zu-finanzieren/6918922.html (March 10th 2017).

Handelsblatt (2012b): Euro-Krise. Die EZB als Allzweckwaffe. August 17th 2012. URL: http://www.handelsblatt.com/politik/deutschland/euro-krise-die-ezb-als-allzweckwaffe/7014768.html (March 10th 2017).

Handelsblatt (2012c): Draghi hat zu viel versprochen. September 5th 2012. URL: http://www.handelsblatt.com/meinung/kommentare/ezb-draghi-hat-zu-viel-versprochen/7096114.html (March 10th 2017).

Handelsblatt (2013a): Staatsanleihen. Gericht soll Bundesbank-Mithilfe an EZB-Politik stoppen. June 11th 2013 URL: http://www.handelsblatt.com/politik/deutschland/staatsanleihen-gericht-soll-bundesbank-mithilfe-an-ezb-politik-stoppen/8327966.html (March 10th 2017).

Handelsblatt (2013b): Wohl kein Votum gegen die EZB. Karlsruher Richter in der Europa-Falle. June 12th 2013. URL: http://www.handelsblatt.com/politik/deutschland/wohl-kein-votum-gegen-die-ezb-karlsruher-richter-in-der-europa-falle/8338136.html (March 10th 2017).

Handelsblatt (2014): „Das Euro-Abenteuer geht seinem Ende entgehen". February 10th 2014. URL: http://www.handelsblatt.com/meinung/gastbeitraege/gast beitrag-das-euro-abenteuer-geht-seinem-ende-entgegen/9457312.html (March 10th 2017).

Hix, Simon/Høyland, Bjørn (2011): The Political System of the European Union. 3rd. Edition. Houndsmills: Palgrave Macmillan.

Illing, Falk (2013): Die Euro-Krise. Analyse der Europäischen Strukturkrise. Wiesbaden: VS-Verlag.

Innerarity, Daniel (2013): Demokratie des Wissens. Plädoyer für eine lernfähige Gesellschaft. Bielefeld: transcript Verlag.
Liebert, Ulrike (2007): Introduction. Structuring political conflict about Europe: National media in transnational discourse analysis. In: Perspectives on European Politics and Society 8, 3, pp. 235-260.
Luhmann, Niklas (1995): Die Soziologie des Wissens. Probleme ihrer theoretischen Konstruktion. In: Ibid.: Gesellschaftsstruktur und Semantik. Studien zur Wissenssoziologie der modernen Gesellschaft 4. Frankfurt am Main: Suhrkamp, pp. 151-180.
Luhmann, Niklas (2014[1968]): Vertrauen. Ein Mechanismus zur Reduktion sozialer Komplexität. 5. Unveränderte Auflage. Stuttgart: UTB-Verlag.
Maatsch, Sönke (2007): The struggle to control meanings. The French debate on the European constitution in the mass media. In: Perspectives on European Politics and Society 8, 3, pp. 261-280.
Packham, Kathrin (2007): From the contentious constitution to the awkward other … social model. The constitutional debate in the British print media. In: Perspectives on European Politics and Society 8, 3, pp. 281-313.
Prager, Martin Harry (2012): Die aktuelle Finanz- und Wirtschaftskrise. Ursachen, institutionelle Konsequenzen und Bewertung. Eine theoretische und empirische Analyse anhand der Europäischen Union. Bayreuth: P.C.O. Verlag.
Scharpf, Fritz W. (2013): Die Euro-Rettung als Demokratieproblem. In: dms – der moderne staat – Zeitschrift für Public Policy, Recht und Management 6, 1, pp. 279-288.
Schmidt, Vivian A. (2013): Arguing about the Eurozone crisis. A discursive institutionalist analysis. In: Critical Policy Studies 7, 4, pp. 455-462.
Schmidt, Vivian A. (2014): Speaking to the Markets or to the People? A Discursive Institutionalist Analysis of the EU's Sovereign Debt Crisis. In: British Journal of Politics and International Relations 16, 1, pp. 199-209.
Sinclair, Timothy J. (1999): Bond-Rating Agencies and Coordination in the Global Political Economy. In: Cutler, A. Clair/Haufler, Virginia/Porter, Tony (eds.): Private Authority and International Affairs. New York: SUNY Press, pp. 153-168.
Sinclair, Timothy J: (2005): The New Masters of Capital. American Bond Rating Agencies and the Politics of Creditworthiness. New York: Cornell University Press.
Strange, Susan (1988): States and Markets. London: Pinter.
Strange, Susan (1996): Retreat of the State. The Diffusion of Power in the World Economy. Cambridge: Cambridge University Press.
Strange, Susan (1998): Mad Money. When Markets Outgrow Governments. Michigan: University of Michigan Press.
Streeck, Wolfgang (2013): The Politcs of Public Debt. Neoliberalism, Capitalist Development and the Restructuring of the State. In: German Economic Review 15, 1, pp. 143-165.
Strulik, Torsten (2004): Nichtwissen und Vertrauen in der Wissensökonomie. Frankfurt/New York: Campus.

Willke, Helmut (2002): Dystopia. Studien zur Krisis des Wissens der modernen Gesellschaften. Frankfurt am Main: Suhrkamp.
Willke, Helmut (2003): Heterotopia. Studien zur Krise der Ordnung moderner Gesellschaften. Frankfurt am Main: Suhrkamp.
Willke, Helmut (2007): Smart Governance. Governing the Global Knowledge Society. Frankfurt/New York: Campus.
Wonka, Arndt/Lange, Gesche (2014): Politische Entscheidungen im Mehrebenensystem der EU. In: Liebert, Ulrike/Wolff, Janna (eds.): Interdisziplinäre Europastudien. Wiesbaden: VS Springer, pp. 153-171.

Abbreviations

Title	**Abbreviaton**
German Constitutional Court	GCC
Economic and Monetary Affairs Committee	ECON
European Central Bank	ECB
European Court of Justice	ECJ
European Monetary Union	EMU
European Parliament	EP
European Union	EU
Member of the European Parliament	MEP
Outright Monetary Transaction	OMT

15. Global climate change governance from Paris to Montreal: Enabling factors for ambitious EU climate action

Tilmann Morata Liebert[1]

1. Introduction

To avert catastrophic climate change, ambitious climate action is required from all greenhouse gas emitting sectors. With this objective in mind, efforts are being pursued at many levels and by a multitude of actors. These range from grass-roots initiatives to municipalities, sub-national regions and States to the supranational level, such as the European Union (EU). At the global level, meetings under the United Nations Framework Convention on Climate Change – UNFCCC – serve as the multilateral forum to address climate change. Its most significant success so far has been the Paris Agreement at its 21st Conference of the Parties (COP21), in December 2015. Therein the international community agreed on ambitious objectives for the rest of this century and on a plan to achieve them, to which all countries committed to contribute.

Nevertheless, while the Paris Agreement's *objectives* apply to all anthropogenic greenhouse gas emissions, the scope of the agreement's *measures* to reduce emissions has two significant gaps: CO_2 emissions from international, transboundary aviation and shipping activity. This stems from the fact that a part of these emissions occurs above international waters and thus does not fall under the clear responsibility of individual States, unlike other sectors that exclusively emit on countries' territories. This is a concern as international aviation now already makes up 1.3 per cent of global CO_2 emissions and is projected to grow 300 to 500 per cent by 2050 compared to 2010 (ICAO 2013). The European Parliament has presented an analysis whereby such unchecked emissions growth by the international transport sectors would, by 2050, lead to a joint share of 25 per cent to 39 per cent of the worldwide CO_2 emissions permissible to stay on the path for achieving the below 2°C global warming objective (European Parliament 2015). Clearly the projected business as usual

1 The author is affiliated to the European Commission, Directorate General for Climate Action. All views expressed in this article are those of the author and do not necessarily reflect those held by the European Commission.

emissions increase would undermine the implementation of the Paris Agreement and make the achievement of its objectives practically impossible.[2]

To address this challenge, already the 1997 Kyoto Protocol to the UNFCCC called on industrialised countries to "pursue limitation or reduction of emissions of greenhouse gases [...] from aviation and marine bunker fuels, working through the International Civil Aviation Organisation [ICAO] and the International Maritime Organisation, respectively".[3] For aviation, the international community has agreed on a global market-based measure to address CO_2 emissions from international aviation at ICAO's 39th Assembly in 2016 in Montreal. The measure represents the first-ever agreement to regulate CO_2 emissions from a global economic sector.

The results from Paris and Montreal are not easily comparable due to their different natures. While the former, for instance, addresses all domestic emissions and has a long-term horizon the latter is for a specific economic sector and extends only to the medium-term. In terms of type of instrument under international law, the former is a multilateral agreement, while the latter is a resolution of an assembly of a UN body. Nevertheless, it is possible to compare the levels of ambition of the two agreements' goals. The ICAO agreement has been criticised for a lack of ambition as it does not call for emission reductions, but only their stabilisation. The Paris Agreement's emission reduction objectives, by contrast, are directly based on recommendations from climate science, i.e. to keep the global temperature rise to "well below" 2°C and to "pursue efforts" to limit the temperature increase to 1.5°C.

In both negotiations, the EU has been at the forefront of efforts to achieve ambitious agreements that translate into strong climate action. This paper compares the two negotiations based on a series of success factors that enabled the ambitious agreement in Paris. To what extent were these factors present in the Montreal process which led to an arguably less ambitious result? What conclusions can be drawn from this for future negotiations? The analysis is based on first-hand experience in the Montreal negotiations process and primary and secondary documents. However, no claim is made that the success factors have been exhaustively identified and analysed. Neither are the factors weighted or prioritised against one another, and their relevance should not be inferred from the order in which they are raised.

The comparative analysis concludes that the identified success factors for Paris were less present in Montreal. This contributes to explaining the arguably less ambitious climate action agreed in Montreal compared to Paris. The lesson learned, nevertheless, is that with the right circumstances found or fostered,

---

2 It is noteworthy that the mentioned projections and policies so far only take into account CO_2 emissions, whereas there are a range of further, non-CO_2, climate impacts from aviation that require climate action.

3 For the text of the Kyoto Protocol to the UNFCCC, see: https://unfccc.int/resource/docs/convkp/kpeng.html (last check 29.3.2019).

the EU can play a leading role in working towards an effective global climate change regime.

The chapter is structured as follows: Section 2 provides an overview of the respective agreements and their assessment by selected actors. Section 3 identifies and compares the success factors, based on which section 4 provides the conclusions.

2. The two agreements

2.1 Paris

To date, the Paris Agreement adopted at the COP21 climate conference in December 2015, is the culmination in international climate policy-making. Following years of negotiations, the agreement sets out a global action plan to limiting global warming to well below 2°C. It entered into force in November 2016 after the necessary number of ratifications had been reached in less than one year, an unusually short period for such an international process.

The agreement sets bold global objectives while letting countries specify their own "ambitious" contributions to achieve them.[4] This combined top-down and bottom-up approach was essential to reach consensus, where previous attempts, notably in 2009 at COP15 in Copenhagen, had failed.

The comprehensive agreement covers mitigation, transparency and global stocktaking of emissions, adaptation to climate change, loss and damage, the role of cities, regions and local authorities, and support to developing countries. Mitigation, i.e. by reductions of greenhouse gases in the atmosphere, includes the objective to keep temperatures "well below" 2°C above pre-industrial levels as well as to "pursu[e] efforts" to limit the temperature increase to 1.5°C. To get there, countries establish their "nationally determined contributions" setting out their climate actions and report, review and ratchet these up over time. Practically all countries have submitted their contributions, overcoming the traditional developed-developing countries divide.

The agreement is the first major multilateral deal of the 21st century and a strong signal to policy makers, investors and businesses to work towards the decarbonisation of the world economy. Nevertheless, the Paris Agreement's success ultimately depends on its effective implementation. The bottom-up approach to the top-down 2°C target still leads to a mismatch: Adding up the

4 For the text of the Paris Agreement, see: http://unfccc.int/files/essential_background/convention/application/pdf/english_paris_agreement.pdf.

contributions as they presently stand, were they to be fully implemented, this would result in about 3°C warming (UNEP 2018). In short, the Paris Agreement is not the definitive solution to climate change but a promising joint approach with objectives to tackle the problem which needs to be filled with operational substance and appropriate execution in countries around the world.

The European Commission described the agreement as historic, ambitious and balanced (European Commission 2015). NGOs have widely praised the Paris Agreement for its level of ambition and the clear signal it sends to policy and economic stakeholders, some large and usually critical civil society organisations calling it "historic" or a "turning point in history" (Climate Action Network International 2015).

2.2 Montreal

The 2016 ICAO Assembly in Montreal agreed on a global market-based measure for CO_2 emissions from international aviation. The so-called *Carbon Offsetting and Reduction Scheme for International Aviation*, or CORSIA in short, is planned to start running from 2021. Similar to the Paris Agreement, the agreement reached in Montreal followed years of lead time. It was in 1998 that ICAO started considering market-based measures for aviation emissions (European Federation for Transport and Environment 2010). The 2015 Paris Agreement created a favourable context which was more conducive to agreement in Montreal in 2016.

CORSIA's objective is to stabilise CO_2 emissions at 2020 levels by requiring airlines to compensate the growth of their emissions after 2020.[5] Its underlying logic is that in-sector emission reductions through operational or technological improvements or alternative fuels are outpaced by emissions growth of the sector for the time being. Airlines will thereby be required to offset emissions from routes included in the scheme by purchasing eligible emission units generated by projects that reduce emissions in other sectors – for instance renewable energy or energy efficiency. The scheme is route-based, whereby all airlines *should* be treated equally on the same routes, avoiding discrimination. The system is planned to be implemented with voluntary participation from 2021-2026 – so far 44 European and 35 other States have indicated participation, some pending confirmation. From 2027 to 2035[6] participation is to be universal save for those countries exempted from the scheme, namely States with small aviation activity and categorised by the United Nations as Least

5 ICAO Resolution on CORSIA (undated): https://www.icao.int/environmental-protection/Documents/Resolution_A39_3.pdf

6 Regarding the time after 2035 a decision is foreseen to be taken in 2032.

Developed Countries, Small Island Developing States, or Land-Locked Developing Countries. Despite these provisions, China has reserved its rights not to participate. In addition, a triennial review of the scheme is set out in the CORSIA agreement.

Similarly to the Paris Agreement, the work did not end with adoption of the CORSIA Resolution. Efforts are ongoing at ICAO in 2019, to define the necessary implementation rules and tools to make the scheme operational. These will then have to be developed and enforced at domestic level.

For the entire 2021-2035 period, and based on currently confirmed participation, the EU estimates that around 80 per cent of the emissions above 2020 levels will be offset, i.e. it predicts a 20 per cent shortfall compared to the 2020 emissions stabilisation target.[7] This is a consequence of the voluntary nature of participation until 2026 and the above-mentioned exemptions thereafter.

The European Commission pursued a robust and effective global scheme in line with the levels of ambition of the EU's climate policy and of the Paris Agreement (European Commission 2016). It deems the CORSIA a "positive first step forward to address international aviation emissions". It also points to the currently expected gap in stabilizing emissions at 2020 levels and to the review clause that the EU pushed hard for in the negotiations, which "should allow for continuous improvement, including in how the scheme contributes to the goals of the Paris Agreement".[8]

The European Parliament, in a resolution issued shortly before adoption of the CORSIA agreement, "expresse[d] its deep disappointment with the current proposal being discussed at the ICAO" (European Parliament 2016). Around a month after the ICAO Assembly, the chair of the Parliament's environment committee told a press conference that while he welcomed the agreement, the offsetting scheme "fell short of ambition".[9] On the side of civil society, the NGO coalition specializing on aviation has criticised the CORSIA for falling behind the Paris Agreement goals, too (International Coalition for Sustainable Aviation 2016).

Having described the respective results of the Paris and Montreal negotiations and concluded that a higher level of ambition is embodied in the former, the next section turns to examining the factors that could be responsible for this difference.

7 European Commission – DG Climate Action, Reducing emissions from aviation (website), undated, https://ec.europa.eu/clima/policies/transport/aviation_en.

8 European Commission – DG Climate Action, Reducing emissions from aviation (website), undated, https://ec.europa.eu/clima/policies/transport/aviation_en.

9 UNFCCC, European Commission and European Parliament video stream, 17 November 2016, http://unfccc.cloud.streamworld.de/webcast/european-comission-and-european-parliament.

3. Success factors – a comparative analysis

As a starting point in what follows, a set of characteristics of the negotiation processes are identified as relevant factors for the success of the European Union in the Paris negotiations (see Table 1). These factors are used as a yardstick to comparatively determine whether and to what extent they were present in the Montreal process. The identified differences in negotiation characteristics are not intended to exhaustively explain the different outcomes. They do, however, highlight some significant differences between the UNFCCC and ICAO negotiations that help explain the different levels of ambition of the agreements reached in Paris and Montreal.

Table 1 – Success factors in Paris negotiations compared to Montreal negotiations

Factor	Paris	Montreal
1. Issue under negotiation	Broad on climate change, climate action as opportunities and threats	Specific on aviation, climate action perceived as cost
2. Participating officials' expertise	Strong climate backgrounds	Mostly transport and less climate backgrounds
3. Private sector role	Diffused representation, both winners and losers, incl. interests in reduced emissions	Concentrated representation, jointly in favour of stabilizing emissions
4. EU formal status and role	Party to Convention (as are States); strong practical role	Observer status; thereby less strong leadership role
5. EU common position and coordination	Position-forming process more political; coordination among EU Member States	Position-forming process less political, also with ECAC; coordination among EU + ECAC Member States
6. Coalition building	Successful EU leadership of High Ambition Coalition	Little coalition-building dynamic

Source: own compilation

3.1 Issue under negotiation

While both negotiation processes dealt with climate change, the scope of what was being negotiated differed considerably. UNFCCC negotiations concern all anthropogenic greenhouse gas emissions; ICAO's only a specific subset thereof: CO_2 emissions from international aviation, which at present constitute 1.3 per cent of global CO_2 emissions. In addition, the UNFCCC's *measures* regard national emissions, while ICAO's trans-boundary emissions are not clearly attributed to one state or another.

The broad nature of the issue underlying the *UNFCCC* process allowed States to see it in a multitude of dimensions: Both in terms of threats to growth through traditional fossil-fuel-based economic development, as well as opportunities to meet emissions reduction targets by fostering what can be summarised as a green economy. Moreover, the solidarity-related negotiation strands covered issues as diverse as climate finance, technology transfer, capacity building, loss and damage and adaptation to climate change. These were critical to convince many developing countries that the outcome would be in their interest. Overall this was very much a package deal, in which no nation was fully satisfied but neither fully dissatisfied, and thus everybody willing to subscribe.

This broad multidimensionality did not exist in the *ICAO* negotiations which were specific to one economic sector, aviation, and, more specifically, its international operations. With technological and operational measures holding limited potential in the short to medium term and outpaced by the growth in aviation emissions, the consequences of the measure under negotiation were framed almost entirely as costs of compliance, rather than opportunities. Hence most States – while recognizing that a global measure on the issue was needed for the industry to keep growing – were primarily concerned with ensuring their own aviation industry would not be unduly burdened.

In summary, the specificity of the ICAO issue compared to the broad nature of the UNFCCC issue created fewer positive opportunities from ambitious action than under the latter stream.

3.2 Participating officials' expertise

The difference in respective issues also had implications for the expertise of officials involved in each negotiation.

Officials involved in *UNFCCC* negotiations are clearly climate-focused. COP21 having been preceded by more than two decades of climate talks, the UNFCCC process was by then long-standing and well established. Simultaneously, climate policy has been increasingly institutionalised at the international, regional and national levels, respective examples being the UNFCCC Secretariat, the European Commission's Directorate General for Climate Action, and a multitude of dedicated national "climate" or climate and environment ministries. Many developing countries cannot dedicate as much specific expertise due to resource limitations, but are supported by the UNFCCC to attend the COPs and preparatory meetings. Overall, the consequence for COP21 was that, while sectoral expertise and foreign relations ministry staff was present, the overarching climate change-specific perspective dominated the process. In the negotiations leading up to Paris – multiple meetings in each of the preceding years – saw participation of all parties to the UNFCCC through representatives from capitals, mostly climate change specialists.

In terms of background and expertise of officials involved in the *ICAO* negotiations, the default competence for ICAO issues in general lies with ministries of transport in virtually all States. Some countries complemented this for the climate-specific discussions with dedicated climate expertise from relevant ministries. Nevertheless, the majority of officials present in ICAO negotiations had a transport rather than a climate background. The negotiations leading up to the Montreal Assembly were conducted by a limited group of countries and through the 36-member ICAO Council, which were not climate policy specialists. Representatives from capitals, including climate experts, were involved only in the final months of the process leading up to the Assembly.

The differences in officials' expertise meant that those involved in the UNFCCC had inherently stronger expertise and awareness of climate issues, often with years of climate diplomacy experience, than those with transport dominated backgrounds in ICAO, albeit complemented with climate expertise. This overall difference in backgrounds could also likely have contributed to a lower level of climate ambition in Montreal compared to Paris.

3.3 Private sector role

The difference in the nature of core issues under negotiation (see Section 3.1. above) had direct consequences for the way the private sector engaged in both processes. In Paris, the broad-based character of the UNFCCC issue led to moderate and diffuse private sector representation. In comparison, in Montreal the specificity of the issue translated into a strong representation of a well-organised aviation industry.

Addressing economy-wide emissions of all countries, the *UNFCCC* negotiations attract interests from a wide range of private sector actors. In summary, these include both winners and losers of more ambitious climate policy, both holding explicit positions on the issue. At COP21 itself, as at other COPs, business was also highly visible, virtually always advocating or showcasing climate action. Among officially accredited "non-governmental observers", 275 currently fall into the "Business and Industry" constituency category.[10] These

10 UNFCCC, list of admitted NGOs, undated: https://unfccc.int/process/parties-non-party-stakeholders/non-party-stakeholders/admitted-ngos/list-of-admitted-ngos (last check 1.4.2019)..

represent very diverse interests including commerce, industry, fossil fuels, carbon market actors, energy efficiency and renewable energy. A further private sector category is the "Farmers" constituency. For many of these different organizations COP21 provided a platform to present or announce their work addressing climate change to other COP participants.[11] The *nationally determined contributions*-approach under the Paris Agreement means that countries commit at the international level but design their specific policies domestically, at which level they are a more promising target of private sector lobbying.

In the *ICAO* process, on the other hand, a measure was negotiated at the international level with concrete impact on specific private sector actors. Those that will be subject to obligations as a result of the agreement are airlines whose degree of organisation is very high. The International Air Transport Association (IATA) is the largest aviation industry trade association with 273 members that account for over 80 per cent of total passenger transport capacity. Advocacy and lobbying, explicitly on environmental issues, are among IATA's self-ascribed functions.[12] At the 39th Assembly, where the CORSIA measure was agreed, IATA was the private sector "observer" organization with the highest number of accredited participants.[13] In fact, ICAO and IATA share a long history of collaboration, since the 1940s.[14] Given the sectoral focus of ICAO it is not surprising that virtually all private sector organisations at its 39th Assembly represented the aviation industry. In addition, private sector carbon market actors are discovering ICAO. Although not at the Assembly itself, but at the various regional ICAO-organised Global Aviation Dialogues (GLADs) (ICAO 2015 and 2016) held in the run-up to it, some representatives from voluntary offset programmes were present, showing a new interest in the ICAO sphere. With the eventual demand for carbon offset credits from airlines needing to meet their CORSIA obligations, the hope and expectation arises from such programmes to become eligible and benefit by supplying credits.

The difference in private sector engagement in UNFCCC and ICAO was marked by diffuse interest representation in the former and concentration of specific interests in the latter, also due to the direct impact on companies by the ICAO measure and the indirect one through the Paris Agreement. In the

11 For all past 'Side Events' and 'Exhibits' see UNFCCC website archive: https://seors.unfccc.int/seors/reports/archive.html; for the private sector engagement at COP21, see: http://newsroom.unfccc.int/media/361572/flyer-private-sector.pdf.

12 IATA Members, undated: http://www.iata.org/about/members/Pages/index.aspx and IATA Airline Membership Benefits, undated: http://www.iata.org/about/members/Pages/benefits.aspx.

13 ICAO, 39th Session of the ICAO Assembly - List of Delegates, 6 October 2016, http://www.icao.int/Meetings/a39/Documents/List_Delegates/List_Del_9_1_en.pdf.

14 See e.g.: ICAO, The postal history of ICAO: IATA - International Air Transport Association, undated: http://www.icao.int/secretariat/PostalHistory/iata_international_air_transport_association.htm.

Montreal process, the private sector advocated a global offsetting system, practically with one voice, of the type ultimately agreed upon. The adopted measure's goal of stabilizing emissions at 2020 levels was the one originally adopted by IATA in 2009 (Carbon Neutral Growth 2020) (e.g. IATA 2009). In Paris, the outcome was the result of a process involving a wide range of stakeholders including more diverse private sector interests.

3.4 The EU's formal status and role

The EU has been at the forefront of international efforts towards global climate action in both the Paris and Montreal processes. However, the role the EU could play in them was also determined by differences in the EU institutions' formal status.

Regarding the *UNFCCC*, the EU – at the time still the European Economic Community – became a Party to the 1992 Framework Convention by ratifying it the year after. The Convention thereby allowed it to gain the same formal status as any of the other 196 (State) Parties. Since then, the EU has built a reputation as an international leader in climate policy (Oberthür/Groen 2017). In addition to the EU, which also includes European Parliament representation, each EU Member State is a Party to the Convention and represented at COPs. As a Party, the EU institutions have committed to the 1997 Kyoto Protocol and 2015 Paris Agreement objectives, and to implementation of measures through EU legislation to reach these objectives.

In *ICAO*, the EU holds observer status, just as accredited civil society organizations, such as IATA described above, do. The principal difference between ICAO member states and observers is that the latter are not allowed to vote or attend private meetings (ICAO 2004). For limited membership meetings they have to be invited to attend. At the ICAO Assembly, the EU was represented through a sizable delegation comprised of officials from the European Commission, Council, Parliament and European Aviation Safety Agency (EASA), in addition to EU Member States. EU institutions, moreover, closely collaborated with the European Civil Aviation Conference (ECAC) Secretariat, ECAC counting 44 member states.

In comparison, the EU's formal position is on par with that of States in the UNFCCC, which is not the case in ICAO. Thereby there is clear difference in the EU's formal status between the two processes, translating into a reduced leadership role it could play in ICAO.

3.5 EU common position and coordination

The formal status of the EU also relates to how it agrees upon common positions, and to its coordination mechanisms, which differ between the Paris and Montreal processes.

For the *UNFCCC*, the EU has developed formal processes for establishing negotiating positions for each COP on various technical and political levels up to Environment Council, including European Commission involvement.[15] Depending on the issue under consideration, debates frequently emerge. Preceding a COP, the Council of the EU will typically agree on a common position in the form of Council Conclusions; for COP21 these were an ambitious set of expectations (see Council of the European Union 2015). At the COPs themselves the current Council Presidency and the Commission will lead the EU delegation and the Presidency will chair the daily coordination meetings with Member States.

Similarly as in the UNFCCC process, EU positions for *ICAO* were agreed at technical and political levels. Prior to the ICAO Assembly, a coordinated common EU position on the global measure was agreed as a relatively un-politicized Council Decision (Council of the European Union 2016). At the ECAC level, the 44 ECAC member states agreed on a joint declaration prior to the Assembly in which they stated their intention to join the CORSIA from its start and "encourage[d] as many ICAO States as possible [...] to [also] join from the beginning of the scheme" (European Civil Aviation Conference 2016). At the Assembly itself, coordination meetings between these various European institutions and ECAC/EU Member States were held in different constellations throughout the process.

In summary, the process leading to agreement on a common EU position/mandate was more political for the UNFCCC COP than for the ICAO Assemblys, and the position under the former arguably more ambitious, calling for significant emission reductions. Coordination takes place in both contexts but regards a higher number of States and institutions in ICAO, in which it is conducted more informally. In the UNFCCC, it is more structured and formally led by the EU.

15 See e.g.: European Parliament, Legislative Train Schedule - Resilient Energy Union with a Climate Change Policy - 21st Conference of Parties - Paris Agreement, undated: http://www.europarl.europa.eu/legislative-train/theme-resilient-energy-union-with-a-climate-change-policy/file-cop-21-paris-agreement (last check 1.4.2019).

3.6 Coalition building

In any multilateral negotiation coalitions of like-minded States can play a powerful role in building momentum towards their desired negotiation outcome. In the Paris process, the EU was able to unleash a centripetal coalition-building dynamic based also on previously established alliances. For Montreal, while there were attempts to draw on alliances built in the UNFCCC context, 'structural' factors prevented the same coalition-forming dynamic.

Under the *UNFCCC*, the EU had learnt from the lack of agreement in Copenhagen in 2009 due to the "North-South" divide as well as from the limited participation of some developing countries in the Kyoto Protocol. The EU's strategy to build a broad coalition of developed and developing countries in favour of high ambition shaped the successful outcome of the Paris conference. Especially in the year leading up to COP21, the EU engaged in massive climate diplomacy through activities of the French COP Presidency, other Member States, the European External Action Service, and the European Commission, not least, through visits by the European Commissioner for Climate Action to a vast array of countries around the world (Oberthür/Groen 2017). This, as well as the EU's credible role of climate leadership, paid off in the decisive second week of the Paris conference, when it brought into action the "High Ambition Coalition" (HAC), starting with a joint statement by the EU and the group of 79 African, Caribbean, and Pacific (ACP) States. Throughout the week the HAC was then joined by more countries; first the United States of America, then Canada, Japan, Colombia, Chile, Mexico and Brazil. This dynamic culminated in an attention-grabbing walk-in of the coalition that set the ambition-bar high for the decisive conference session.

During the *ICAO* negotiations, efforts to build such a strong coalition were not as successful, despite targeted EU outreach on the issue through diplomatic channels, yet with fewer resources invested into this. The EU, the Republic of the Marshall Islands and Mexico called on the HAC for ambition in the CORSIA through a joint letter to the Coalition before the ICAO Assembly (High Ambition Coalition 2016). This failed, however, to lead to a dynamic comparable to the one in Paris. At least in part this was due to the different nature of the issue under negotiation. The responsibility of transport ministries for the ICAO dossier made it more difficult to draw on established climate coalition links. In addition, a structural impediment was that Small Island Developing States – natural allies under the UNFCCC and primarily behind the 1.5°C target – were exempted by default from CORSIA obligations and due to their remote geographic locations, most were not eager to volunteer to join the scheme from its start.

To sum up this final comparison, efforts at building a coalition for ambitious agreements were successful under the UNFCCC but did not develop a significant dynamic in the ICAO process.

4. Conclusions

Based on a non-exhaustive set of factors identified as having contributed to the EU's success at UNFCCC COP21 in Paris, this contribution has analysed to what extent these factors were present in the ICAO process towards the agreement on a global market-based measure. The characteristics under comparison range from the nature of the issues underlying the negotiations and the expertise of participating officials, to the role of the private sector, the formal status and practical role of the EU and its coordination at negotiations, and the ability to build ambitious coalitions. Summarising this comparative analysis, it shows that the identified enabling factors were not as present in the Montreal process which helps explain why its negotiation result is less ambitious in terms of the agreed climate action.

This leads to the conclusion that given the right circumstances, the EU can play a leading role in working towards effective global climate change governance, as proven by COP21. Based on this conclusion, the question to be tackled is to what extent the identified success factors can apply also to other multilateral negotiations. How can the factors be adapted, or further ones be developed, to serve other international policy areas where EU leadership is necessary or desirable? The analysis has shown that, under the right conditions – that can be found or fostered in the real world – the EU can act in unity, lead and deliver on complex issues to find solutions to global challenges.

References

Climate Action Network International (2015): Civil society responds as final Paris Climate Agreement released, 12 December 2015, http://www.climatenetwork.org/press-release/civil-society-responds-final-paris-climate-agreement-released.

Council of the European Union (2015): EU position for the UN climate change conference in Paris. Council conclusions, 18 September 2015 https://www.consilium.europa.eu/en/press/press-releases/2015/09/18/counclusions-un-climate-change-conference-paris-2015/(last check 1.4.2019).

Council of the European Union (2016): Council Decision on the position to be taken on behalf of the European Union with regard to the international instrument to be drawn up within the ICAO bodies and intended to lead to the implementation from 2020 of a single global market-based measure for international aviation emissions, 27 May 2016, partially available at: http://www.consilium.europa.eu/register/en/content/out/?&typ=ENTRY&i=ADV&DOC_ID=ST-8586-2016-INIT.

European Civil Aviation Conference (2016): Declaration of Directors General of Civil Aviation of EU Member States and the Other Member States of the European Civil Aviation Conference. Adhering to the Global Market-Based Measure (GMBM) Scheme from the Start ("Bratislava Declaration"), 3 September 2016, https://www.ecac-ceac.org/documents/10202/74122/2016-BRATISLAVA+DECLARATION.pdf.

European Commission (2015): Press release. Historic climate deal in Paris. EU leads global efforts, Paris, 12 December 2015, http://europa.eu/rapid/press-release_IP-15-6308_en.htm.

European Commission (2016): Fact Sheet – MEMO. 39th Assembly of the International Civil Aviation Organisation, 7 October 2016, http://europa.eu/rapid/press-release_MEMO-16-3332_en.htm.

European Federation for Transport and Environment (2010): Grounded. How ICAO failed to tackle aviation and climate change and what should happen now, 5 October 2010, https://www.transportenvironment.org/sites/te/files/media/2010_09_icao_grounded.pdf.

European Parliament (2015): Emission Reduction Targets for International Aviation and Shipping. Study for the ENVI Committee, November 2015, http://www.europarl.europa.eu/RegData/etudes/STUD/2015/569964/IPOL_STU(2015)569964_EN.pdf.

European Parliament (2016): Resolution of 6 October 2016 on the implementation of the Paris Agreement and the 2016 UN Climate Change Conference in Marrakesh, Morocco (COP22) (2016/2814(RSP)), 6 October 2016, http://www.europarl.europa.eu/sides/getDoc.do?pubRef=-//EP//TEXT+TA+P8-TA-2016-0383+0+DOC+XML+V0//EN.

High Ambition Coalition (2016): The 39th International Civil Aviation Organisation Assembly. Securing a Market-Based Measure to Achieve Carbon Neutral Growth from 2020. Letter supported by the European Union, the Republic of the Marshall Islands and Mexico as participants in the High Ambition Coalition, 16 September 2016, www.icao.int/environmental-protection/Documents/GMBM_Support/HAC_EU_RMI_MX_ICAO_Assembly_letter.pdf.

IATA (2009): Aviation and Climate Change. Pathway to carbon-neutral growth in 2020, July 2009, https://www.iata.org/whatwedo/environment/Documents/aviation-climatechange-pathway-to2020.pdf.

ICAO (2004): Standing Rules of Procedure of the Assembly of the International Civil Aviation Organization, Eighth edition, http://www.icao.int/publications/Documents/7600_cons_en.pdf.

ICAO (2013): Present and Future Trends in Aircraft Noise and Emissions, 18 July 2013, http://www.icao.int/Meetings/a38/Documents/WP/wp026_en.pdf.
ICAO (2015): 2015 Global Aviation Dialogues (GLADs), http://www.icao.int/Meetings/GLADs-2015.
ICAO (2016): 2016 Global Aviation Dialogues (GLADs), http://www.icao.int/Meetings/GLADs-2016.
International Coalition for Sustainable Aviation (2016): Global Aviation CO_2 Deal Adopted With Mixed Results, Just As Paris Agreement Takes Off, 6 October 2016, http://icsa-aviation.org/global-aviation-co2-deal-adopted-with-mixed-results-just-as-paris-agreement-takes-off/.
Oberthür, Sebastian/Groen, Lisanne (2017): The European Union and the Paris Agreement: leader, mediator, or bystander? WIREs Climate Change 8, 1, e445.
UNEP (2016): Gap report 2018, https://www.unenvironment.org/resources/emissions-gap-report-2018.

Abbreviations

Abbreviation	Term
ACP	African, Caribbean, and Pacific States
COP21	21st Conference of the Parties (under the UNFCCC)
CORSIA	Carbon Offsetting and Reduction Scheme for International Aviation
EASA	European Aviation Safety Agency
ECAC	European Civil Aviation Conference
EU	European Union
GLAD	Global Aviation Dialogue
HAC	High Ambition Coalition
IATA	International Air Transport Association
ICAO	International Civil Aviation Organisation
UNFCCC	United Nations Framework Convention on Climate Change

16. The European governance of economic and monetary crises – lessons for democratic legitimacy

Anders Hentschel

1. Introduction

Since the outbreak of the global financial crisis in 2008 the European integration project has been put to test in numerous ways. There was the banking crisis, subsequently a severe recession, next the sovereign debt and a social crisis – finally a refugee crisis. The frequency of emergency summits at the highest European level has increased clearly and decisions with far-reaching consequences have been made. During these years, the European Union's (EU) institutional setting has changed: there is a tightened socio-economic governance architecture, new institutions like the European Stability Mechanism (ESM) have been created and the European Central Bank (ECB) has gained an extended scope of action. However, the future of European integration is still shaped by uncertainty, which is mirrored in declining support of its citizens. Former euphoria has turned into EU fatigue, indifference or even refusal. While in the Eurobarometer survey[1] of spring 2008 50 per cent of EU citizens stated to trust the EU and 36 per cent said they tended not to trust the EU, in spring of 2016 merely 33 per cent stated that they trust the EU and 55 per cent said they did not. For the sake of fairness, it should not go unmentioned that EU citizens' trust in their national governments was even lower at both points in time. As a matter of fact, we can witness an unexpected resurrection of right-wing and populist parties across the continent. Considering this, the 'Brexit' referendum just seems like the tip of the iceberg.

But how are these developments connected to one another? And, are there structural reasons why citizens turn away from Europe? To find an answer to these questions, this chapter investigates recent institutional developments in the *Economic and Monetary Union (EMU)* from the perspective of democratic legitimacy. Its main argument is that the EMU's institutional changes Euro-

1 All Eurobarometer results can be accessed at: http://ec.europa.eu/COMMFrontOffice/publicopinion/index.cfm/General/index.

pean heads of state have initiated as response to the crises follow the constitutional path towards a technocratic inspired European confederation. This institutional choice undermines the EU's democratic legitimacy in governing this area and, moreover, it is inefficient in producing results that meet the demands of the citizens. Furthermore, this constellation allows nationalist and populist parties to exploit the situation.

In the following, I will first introduce Horeth's (1999) account of a legitimacy 'trilemma' in EU multi-level governance. Second, I will give an overview of institutional changes with regard to governing EMU that have been introduced in response to the financial, economic and sovereign debt crises. The focus of this analysis lies on the institutional developments related to the EU's emerging socio-economic governance architecture and the rescue of the eurozone. Third, I will use the account of the legitimacy 'trilemma' as analytical framework for assessing the consequences of the described institutional change for democratic legitimacy. Finally, I will conclude with considerations on how to overcome the current situation.

2. The legitimacy 'trilemma' in European multi-level governance

Following Horeth (1999), EU multi-level governance has basically three sources of legitimacy: democratic decision-making at the European level (input legitimacy), indirect democratic (input) legitimacy through the member states and domestic parliaments and output legitimacy, i.e. the effective tackling of political challenges. With regard to the future of European integration, each of these three sources of legitimacy is linked to one ideal type of constitutional choice: input legitimacy to a European federation, output legitimacy to a technocracy and indirect legitimacy to a European confederation. Horeth (1999: 257f.) argues further that these three sources of legitimacy reside in a "zero-sum game", what basically means: "strengthening the one weakens the others".

The main bearer of *input legitimacy* in multi-level governance is the European Parliament (EP) as it is the only EU institution that is subject to direct elections and thus may provide direct links with the citizen. Yet, although the EP's competences are ever expanding (see Liebert this volume), compared to its national correspondents its role in EU decision-making remains rather limited, and for governing EMU it is basically limited to consultation. Strengthening the EU's input legitimacy would require a complete democratisation of multi-level governance towards a *federal state*. In this constitutional choice, the EP's role in legislation and democratic control would need to be further strengthened and what is most important: the Commission, as government to-be, would be fully accountable to the EP channelling the will of the electorate. This arrangement would be complemented by the Council as a second parliamentary chamber representing the member states. However, this federal vision would undermine indirect legitimacy by domestic governments and parliaments. Strengthening of the EP and the Commission would require a weakening of the Council as a voice of the member states. Moreover, a European federal state could come at the expense of output legitimacy, as there is a general trade-off between, on the one hand, efficiency and effectiveness and, on the other hand, democratic decision-making and control. Decision-making in multi-level governance is already time-consuming and complicated and could become even more so.

Second, *democratic legitimacy arises indirectly* from the member states as 'masters of the treaties'. Domestic governments have negotiated European integration and the creation of European institutions, and national parliaments in all member states have approved this as legislators. Thus in a legal understanding, processes of multi-level governance rest on the consent of democratically elected domestic parliaments. Further, national governments acting via the Council in the European arena are accountable to their parliaments. According to advocates of a *European confederation* ('Staatenverbund'), member states should play a more important role in multi-level governance. Besides, from a communitarian understanding, the member states – unlike the EU – constitute communities which can provide a certain degree of social homogeneity and collective identity that is necessary for legitimising the political order (Horeth 1999: 261, Etzioni 2013). In a European confederation based on intergovernmental cooperation, national parliaments would be the main source of legitimacy. They would obtain a larger role in controlling EU decision-making, also in relation to national governments. Nevertheless, a stronger role of national parliaments in EU decision-making and control would go at the expense of both efficiency and problem-solving capacity in multi-level governance and input legitimacy of the supranational level through the EP.

Third, *output legitimacy* refers to the EU's ability to deal with societal problems. From a utilitarian perspective, the capacity of a political system to fulfil the citizens' expectations and to solve their problems is crucial for its legitimacy. In this understanding, multi-level governance is understood as "government for the people" whose legitimacy depends on the economic welfare it provides (Horeth 1999: 251; Scharpf 1999: 11). The constitutional choice to increase the EU's output legitimacy would be the move towards a *technocracy* or "regulatory state" (Majone 1996). Here, the EU should focus on such issues where it might reach higher efficiency in problem-solving than the member states can offer. The argument goes that independent specialised regulatory agencies, not accountable to parliaments, would be more efficient in satisfying the demands of the electorate than elected principals. Obviously, this approach would undermine the policy-making powers of parliaments at both the national and European level and therefore conflict with our Western understanding of liberal democracy. However, advocates of a regulatory state do not see an imperative necessity for democratic legitimation as long as issues that have a predominately redistributive character stay out of the game:

> "[…] the delegation of important policy-making powers to independent institutions is democratically justified only in the sphere of efficiency issues, where reliance on expertise and on a problem-solving style of decision-making is more important than reliance on direct political accountability. Where redistributive concerns prevail, legitimacy can be ensured only by majoritarian means" (Majone 1996: 296).

Nevertheless, in times of severe crises – when quick decisions are needed – the recourse to technocratic governance seems tempting in politics, and often it remains vague where the domains of "redistributive concerns" begin and where to draw the dividing line for technocratic governance.

3. Institutional change: Intergovernmentalism and EU technocracy after the crisis

The bankruptcy of the investment bank Lehman Brothers in 2008 and its aftermath have demonstrated EU stakeholders the consequences of a consummate monetary union, on the one hand, and an incomplete political union, on the other. After the beginning of the financial and economic crisis, it turned out that EU steering mechanisms had been incapable of formulating a common answer to the threat posed by financial markets to the internal market project. Member state by member state had sacrificed its budgetary discipline – initially for the rescue of domestic banking sectors, later for deficit spending to boost the economy. In this situation, the rules of the Stability and Growth Pact turned out to be inefficient in curbing rapidly increasing state borrowing; only in the years between 2008 and 2010 the sovereign debt ratio among EU member states increased from 62 to more than 80 per cent of GDP.[2] Also in the subsequent sovereign debt crisis the institutionalised steering mechanisms at European level were unable to formulate a joint response, so that essential parts of the 'euro rescue package' were predetermined by the two leading economies of the continent, Germany and France, on an intergovernmental basis. For some observers this was a "renaissance of intergovernmental bargaining" (Beichelt/Ondarza 2011: 18). In light of the crises, principles of the past, like

---

2 See eurostat (http://ec.europa.eu/eurostat).

the no-bail-out clause, were thrown overboard when nothing less than the single market's core, the future of the single currency, seemed to be at stake.

As a response to the financial, economic and sovereign debt crises, European heads of state and government agreed on the intensification of socio-economic governance via the *European Semester*, the new umbrella framework for policy coordination between the European and the domestic level in diverse fields, ranging from budgetary surveillance to welfare state modernisation (Hacker/Treeck 2010; Bekker/Klosse 2013, Zeitlin/Vanhercke 2014). With the adoption of the 'Six-pack'[3] and 'Two-pack'[4] legislation in 2012 and 2013 the coordination procedure gained its 'teeth' by strengthening enforcement and compliance in the member states. These acts encompassed a substantial tightening of the corrective arm of the Stability and Growth Pact and a new surveillance and enforcement mechanism, which aims at identifying and preventing macroeconomic imbalances affecting the proper functioning of the EU's economy – the *Macroeconomic Imbalance Procedure (MIP)*. These efforts were further underlined by the Euro Plus Pact, encompassing commitments of particular member states to take measures to increase economic convergence in the eurozone, and the Fiscal Compact, introducing stricter rules for sovereign debt reduction and prevention. In addition, eurozone members decided to institutionalise the procedures for state bailout and bank rescue by creating the *European Stability Mechanism (ESM)* in 2013 and bringing the *European banking union* (2014) on the way. What these institutional changes have in common is that they follow the path towards a distinct constitutional choice: a technocratic inspired European confederation.

With regard to the EU's *emerging socio-economic governance architecture*, there is a clear upgrading of the Commission's mandate. First of all, this encompasses the expansion of its surveillance and guidance capacity with regard to member states' structural reforms and budgetary decisions. Here, the Commission appears as a technocratic institution and 'guardian of the treaties' that both determines excessive deficits and excessive macroeconomic imbalances in the member states through an evidence-based analysis. It furthermore provides policy recommendations to the latter based on the knowledge of its sectoral experts. However, the final decision-making power in this institutional

3 The six legislative acts (Regulations 1173-1177/2011, Directive 2011/85/EU) encompassed a tightening of the Maastricht criteria for budgetary sovereign debt reduction, the revised majority principle for sanctioning non-complying states and the introduction of the MIP corresponding to the blueprint of the excessive deficit procedure.

4 The "Two pack" legislation (Regulations 472/2013 and 473/2013) underlines the efforts of the European level to shape national budgetary decisions. It foresees the obligation for Euro countries to submit their draft budgetary plans for the upcoming year to the Commission by mid-October. If there is a severe violation of the rules of the Stability and Growth Pact, the Commission may ask the respective member state to submit a revised draft budget.

setting remains with the member states. It is up to the Eurogroup and the Economic and Financial Affairs Council configuration (Ecofin) to amend or skip policy recommendations of the Commission and to suspend or enforce warnings and sanctions to a member state.

Subsequently, the *ESM* as the institutionalised 'lender of last resort' for bankrupt eurozone states was designed as an intergovernmental institution. The new organisation located in Luxembourg was established by a treaty under public international law among eurozone members, and thus outside the realm of European law. Although there are attempts to fully integrate the new institution into EU law at a later point in time, no further competences have been delegated to the supranational level. The ESM is de facto under control of the Eurogroup. Its highest decision-making body, the board of governors, is formed by the finance ministers of eurozone states and headed by the president of the Eurogroup. In contrast to the Council, votes in the ESM's board of governors are not weighted according to a countries' population but according to its capital share in the ESM. This arrangement makes Germany, France and Italy veto-holding powers in decisions on state bailouts which require 85 per cent of votes.

Last but not least, the institutionalised authority for supervising and rescuing system-relevant banks, the *banking union*, was basically initiated by the European Council. The European Commission's legislative proposals merely executed what the heads of state had decided before (Puetter 2015: 423). In the banking union, the ECB, in close cooperation with national authorities, takes the role of the leading supervisory body for system-relevant banks of the eurozone. The ECB's supervisory board consists alongside four ECB members of representatives of the national supervisory agencies. In contrast, the Commission's supervisory competences were not extended but transferred to the ECB. However, with regard to bank rescue, the banking union remains largely dependent on the intergovernmental ESM as sufficient own financial resources still have to be collected from the private financial industry; whereas the ESM has broadened its mandate in 2014 to support private banks directly, without needing member states as intermediary institutions for fiscal transfers.

For Puetter (2015) the driving force behind these institutional changes is an integration mode of *deliberative intergovernmentalism*. This approach is characterised by an intensification of intergovernmental policy coordination through deliberation and consensus finding, and a Commission that supports this development; while at the same time new institutional contexts are constituted instead of delegating new competences to the Commission.

4. Assessing the consequences for democratic legitimacy

The preceding analysis of EMU's main institutional changes due to the three-fold crisis has demonstrated how the latter follows the pathway towards a technocratic inspired European confederation. Following Horeth's (1999) account of the EU's legitimacy 'trilemma', one would expect that legitimacy of the EU's constitutional choice for the integration of EMU therefore relies mainly on indirect legitimacy through the member states and to some degree on output legitimacy, while neglecting input legitimacy via democratising multi-level governance. However, this diagnosis would come up too short as the new governance architecture neither resembles an ideal type European confederation nor a pure technocracy, but shows characteristics of both political systems. What follows in terms of legitimacy is that it also cannot take full advantage of the assumed benefits of either of the two systems.

4.1 Depoliticisation of political arenas at both levels

It is undeniable that the EP could not benefit from recent institutional changes in EMU. On the one hand, crucial legislative acts like the 'Six-pack' and the 'Two-pack' were adopted by the EP, on the other hand, the only EU institution that is directly elected by the citizens plays only a minor role in day-to-day EMU governance – one that is basically reduced to consultation. The frequency of consultation, however, has increased during recent years, and although the Commission's diplomatic efforts to strengthen the social dimension of EMU (European Commission 2013) can be interpreted as concession to the EP, it has to be stated that the EP does not play a role for decision-making in EMU. Or, to say it in Scharpf's words (2015: 39): "The EP has therefore consented to the *establishment* of a discretionary authority, but has no role in the *execution* of that authority".

Within an intergovernmental setting one should expect that domestic parliaments played a crucial role in controlling their governments and holding them accountable. Far-reaching decisions, like the ones on the creation of the ESM or on the several rescue packages for Greece, have to be adopted by domestic parliaments. However, even national parliaments become increasingly depoliticised as the subjects of their vote are basically negotiated and decided at the highest European level of governance and then merely passed to domestic parliamentarians for adoption. Domestic parliamentarians often have to decide on highly complex issues under immense time-pressure. The crucial point is: at this point in the decision-making chain, political choices have already been made via intergovernmental bargaining. What remains for national decision-making is rather a question of approval or refusal; which is in public opinion often further reduced to a question of being 'pro' or 'against' Europe (Scharf 2015: 20).

What is more, even with regard to decisions on subjects that are predominantly under national competence – like budgetary, fiscal and structural policy – there is only limited room for manoeuvre for domestic parliaments due to stricter EU macroeconomic governance and fiscal surveillance: "Although the eventual right to adopt the budget is preserved at the national level, governments' economic decisions are increasingly constrained and parliaments thus find themselves at the losing side of a reinforced two-level game" (Crum 2018: 269).

4.2 Limited capacity to act at the European level

Since democratic input legitimacy is underdeveloped in EMU multi-level governance, the EU is highly dependent on output legitimacy, i.e. the provision of economic welfare (Scharpf 2015: 38):

In its present form, the euro regime lacks input-oriented democratic legitimacy. Its claim to acceptance depends on the output-oriented and uncertain promise that the policies pursued by the ECB and imposed by the Commission will facilitate the economic recovery of the crisis countries in the foreseeable future, and that thereafter, they will prevent the generation of new macroeconomic imbalances among the members of the Monetary Union.

In the decade preceding the crises the continent was witnessing an economic upturn, especially in the southern and eastern periphery, that could compensate for lacking democratic legitimacy. Satisfying growth rates were mirrored in wage increases. Moreover, through low inflation and interest rates, the single currency had brought economic prosperity to many countries. Since the severe economic downturn of 2008 in contrast, this picture has turned into the opposite. The EU's economy has still not fully recovered from the great recession; high unemployment rates and moderate wage growth complement the picture. By now, the EU can no longer gain from output legitimacy. Instead, in times of austerity the understanding has developed in politics that European integration does not only bring benefits but also has costs.

However, the structural reasons for lacking output legitimacy in multi-level governance go beyond the economic cycle. At its core stands the division of competences between the European and the national level in EMU governance. While the member states have delegated their monetary instruments to counteract economic recession – e.g. through currency devaluation or inflation respectively deflation – to the supranational level, the remaining instruments like budgetary, fiscal and structural policy stay with the member states. Although coordination of the latter has been intensified by a tightened governance architecture of technocratic surveillance and policy guidance by the Commission, the final decision-making is subject to intergovernmental bargaining as legislative competences in these areas remain under control of the member states.

The consequences of this arrangement for output legitimacy are crucial. Although EMU governance has become more technocratic, its problem-solving capacity still remains limited, i.e. it cannot provide structural solutions to economic recession and high unemployment in Europe. At the same time, EMU governance heavily reigns into domestic domains that have a 'predominantly redistributive character', in order to tackle macroeconomic and budgetary issues that have a European dimension. Wages, taxation, pensions and social security systems appear as "adjustment variables for achieving the stability of monetary union" (Degryse/Pochet 2012: 216).

4.3 Lacking legitimacy and the turn away from Europe

Multi-level governance in EMU mainly relies on indirect legitimacy through the member states as there has not been a fully-fledged democratisation at the European level. And, in times of economic downturn it can benefit only to a limited degree from output legitimacy, due to its narrow problem-solving capacity. But as actions taken at the national level increasingly have a European wide dimension, there is a growing limitation of national governments' room for manoeuvre and we can witness a depoliticisation of domestic arenas.

Further, the complex institutional setting for governing EMU and its limited sources of legitimacy cause consequences for the political landscape in Europe: It structurally opens the electoral floor for nationalists and populists. By their nature, nationalist parties exploit the EU's democratic deficit for their struggle to return to the 'national container'. Populist parties promise the electorate 'easy' solutions to urgent societal problems. For both of them it is a simple task to make advantage of the current situation by blaming the EU or 'Brussels' for pressing issues like high unemployment, increasing poverty or the unequal distribution of wealth in Europe.

5. Overcoming current antagonisms

The constitutional choice towards a technocratic inspired confederation that European heads of state have been pursuing since 2008 might have helped the EU to 'muddle through' several emergency situations in the short term but does not offer a sustainable solution. Until now, the sovereign debt crisis has not been solved and the macroeconomic situation has not yet fully stabilised in large parts of Europe. The next economic shock or banking crisis could cause the house of Europe to collapse. In light of this, it seems necessary to ensure stability in EMU and therefore tackle issues with a European-wide dimension at the European level; but with regard to the negative social consequences of previous institutional changes it should happen in a more efficient and democratic way than "deliberative intergovernmentalism" (Puetter 2015) or "experimentalist governance" (Zeitlin 2016) have provided so far. In order to counteract nationalist and populist movements, pressing issues with a redistributive character can no longer be excluded from EMU politics. Why shouldn't there be a debate on the harmonisation of corporate income taxes or unemployment benefits? Because domestic governments fear they might lose some of their power? Why is there no debate about having an EU budget that is big enough to allow ensuring the EU target of improving living and working conditions for its citizens and providing adequate social protection all over Europe?

If we assume that the three sources of legitimacy in EU multi-level governance constitute a 'zero sum game', the only constitutional choice left for European integration would be the move forward by a 'coalition of the willing' towards a European federation. In order to overcome the current deadlock, this step would not only require a further democratisation of decision-making at the European level but also the transfer of further legislative competences to the EU. As the 'social dimension' of European integration is closely interwined with the proper functioning of EMU it seems likely that a federalist solution could provide better results for European citizens here than the status quo. Strengthening supranationalism in these areas could contribute to overcome the current state where self-serving national interest may block decisions intended for the common welfare of European citizens. However, the Europeanisation of social policy would require a fully fledged democratisation of the EU's polity to meet our understanding of Western liberal democracy.

The counter-argument to the federalist vision is usually a communitarian one: Europe is too diverse for a federal system. As there is no common language, no common cultural identity and no common media in the EU – i.e. no collective identity –, there cannot be common politics. Majoritarian democracy would never do justice to European diversity (Scharpf 1999: 7f.; Streeck 2013: 242f.). But does this still hold in the 21st century? And what could be the alternative, a European confederation or technocracy? Nevertheless, the institutional choice for a European federation requires a new narrative for the EU, one that has a more encouraging connotation for the constituency. Such a narrative would need to emphasise aspects of European integration that enjoy a more positive perception among its citizens instead of highlighting foremost utilitarian considerations like the common market. To say it with Etzioni (2013: 317): "[…] using text books in schools that contain the same chapter on the European narrative in all countries will do more for community building than starting and ending the school year on the same day".

References

Beichelt, Timm/Ondarza, Nicolai von (2011): Von der Schulden- zur Integrationskrise? Euro-Krisenmanagement und europäische Integrationsdynamik. In: Beichelt, Timm/Ondarza, Nicolai von/Verheugen, Günter (eds.): Die EU auf dem Weg zur Wirtschaftsregierung? Europäische Reaktionen auf die Finanz-, Wirtschafts-, und Schuldenkrise. Frankfurt (Oder): MES-Perspektiven 1/2011, pp. 15-21. http://www.kuwi.europa-uni.de/de/studium/master/es/MES-Publikationen/MES-Perspektiven/index.html. [Accessed April 2019].

Bekker, Sonja/Klosse, Saskia (2013): EU governance of economic and social policies: changes and challenges for Social Europe. In: European Journal of Social Law, 2013, 2, pp. 103-120.

Crum, Ben (2018): Parliamentary accountability in multilevel governance: what role for parliaments in post-crisis EU economic governance? In: Journal of European Public Policy 25, 2, pp. 268-286.

Degryse, Christophe/Pochet, Philippe (2012): The programmed Dismantling of the "European Social Model". In: Intereconomics 47, 4, pp. 212-217.

European Commission (2013): Strengthening the social dimension of the Economic and Monetary Union. Communication from the Commission, COM(2013) 690 final, Brussels.

Etzioni, Amitai (2013): The EU: The communitarian deficit. In: European Societies 15, 3, pp. 312-330.

Hacker, Björn/Treeck, Till van (2010): What influence for European governance? The reformed Stability and Growth Pact, the Europe 2020 Strategy and the »European Semester«. (International Policy Analysis). Berlin: Friedrich Ebert Stiftung. http://library.fes.de/pdf-files/id/ipa/07724.pdf. [Accessed April 2019].

Horeth, Marcus (1999): No way out for the beast? The unsolved legitimacy problem of European governance. In: Journal of European Public Policy 6, 2, pp. 249-268.

Majone, Giandomenico (1996): Regulating Europe. London and New York: Routledge.

Puetter, Uwe (2015): Deliberativer Intergouvernementalismus und institutioneller Wandel: die Europäische Union nach der Eurokrise. In: Politische Viertelljahresschrift 56, 3, pp. 406-529.
Scharpf, Fritz W. (1999): Governing in Europe. Effective and democratic? Oxford: Oxford University Press.
Scharpf, Fritz W. (2015): Political Legitimacy in a Non-Optimal Currency Area. In: Cramme, Olaf/Hobolt, Sara B. (eds.): Democratic Politics in a European Union under stress. Oxford: Oxford University Press, pp. 19-47.
Streeck, Wolfgang (2013): Gekaufte Zeit: Die vertagte Krise des demokratischen Kapitalismus. Berlin: Suhrkamp.
Zeitlin, Jonathan/Vanhercke, Bart (2014): Sozializing the European Semester? Economic Governance and Social Policy Coordination in Europe 2020. (SIEPS report No. 2014:7). Stockholm: Swedish Institute for European Policy Studies. http://hdl.handle.net/11245/1.442654. [Accessed April 2019].
Zeitlin, Jonathan (2016): EU experimentalist governance in times of crisis. In: West European Politics 39, 5, pp. 1073-1094.

Abbreviations

Title	**Abbreviation**
European Central Bank	ECB
Economic and Financial Affairs Council configuration	Ecofin
Economic and Monetary Union	EMU
European Parliament	EP
European Stability Mechanism	ESM
European Union	EU
Macroeconomic Imbalance Procedure	MIP

17. The European Parliament in hard times: potentials and practices of governing the euro crisis

Gesche Lange and Ulrike Liebert

1. Introduction

The Euro crisis has had direct impact on many ordinary citizens. However, the role of their directly elected supranational European parliamentary representatives in managing this crisis has hardly received much scholarly interest to date. Many accounts of how the European Economic and Monetary Union (EMU) has sought to restore "credible economic governance to the Eurozone" (Herzog and Hengstermann 2013) mention the strengthened role of the German Bundestag, yet leave the European Parliament conspicuously absent. A widespread view holds that the EU's responses to the financial and sovereign debt crisis have turned intergovernmental politics into a kind of "executive federalism" that leaves little room for national parliaments while marginalizing European representation altogether. Calls for "more power to the European Parliament" (EP) in European economic and monetary governance have met with cynical comments, depicting them as lip service to democratic legitimation with a clear subtext: "Let's democratize European institutions – so that we can legitimately impose the policies we consider economically necessary".[1] Yet, the positioning of the EP in the emerging new governance architecture for EMU should not be undervalued (Tuori & Tuori 2014). The present empirical analysis seeks to test Tuori & Tuori's claim and explain to what extent they are correct.

As a matter of fact, in the domain of EMU the formal powers and the legislative activities of the EP during the 2009-14 legislature have been numerous, extensive and multifaceted. They include, for example, the co-decision and consultation on the "Six-pack" (2011) introducing new measures for budget surveillance and enforcement of the correction of excessive macroeconomic

1 Quote from Fritz W. Scharpf „The Economics of European Democratic Legitimacy", talk delivered at European University Institute, Florence, October 11, 2012 (ppt, p. 2).

imbalances in the euro area, as well as on the "Two-pack" (2013) that has established budgetary surveillance of Member States in financial difficulties and common provisions for monitoring and assessing draft budgetary plans of the member states in the euro area. Moreover, the EP has drafted own-initiative reports, such as the so-called "Enquiry report on the role and operations of the Troika with regard to euro area programme countries" (2013). Thus, the EP can be considered a potential agency in Eurozone crisis management that offers possibilities for societal representation, executive scrutiny and co-legislative innovation. Yet, although an important co-legislative power in theory, in practice the EP's internal party political dynamic might frustrate any collective attempts to reshape the governance architecture of EMU in the public interest. A closer look at the EP's performance is needed, if we want to understand whether or not the euro has been saved at the cost of democracy (Crum 2013), that is in which ways democratic deficits can be expected to overshadow the future of European integration (cf. Schmitter 2013).

The aim of this chapter is to explore the practices and constraints of the EP's agency in the EMU reforms that have been adopted in response to the Eurozone crisis, hence during the most critical legislative term (2010 – 2014). To what extent has the EP been able to turn its relatively marginal role as a bystander in the Eurozone crisis into that of an agent shaping EMU reforms? This question is politically relevant for the debate on the future of Europe launched by the European Commission in 2017 (European Commission 2017). It is also theoretically important regarding a key controversy on European integration, the debate on the crisis and future of democracy in Europe (Brühlmeier and Mastronardi 2016; Forschungsjournal Soziale Bewegungen 2018). Our chapter makes two contributions: First, it offers an empirically grounded analysis of the influence of the EP in EMU reforms aimed at overcoming the euro-crisis. And, second, we develop the argument that the MEPs' successes and failures to influence legislative outcomes depend on four conditions that need to come together: formally, the co-decision procedure; in practice, intra-party cohesion, cross-party coalition building and external stakeholder involvement.

Our analysis proceeds in three steps: First, we give an empirical overview of the involvement of the EP in Eurozone reforms in response to the euro crisis, with a focus on the "six-pack" and the "two-pack" as relevant cases. Then, to explain the EP's successes and failures, we analyse the party politics of coalition-building in the EP. Finally, we draw a number of conclusions, arguing why the MEP's have been able to temper but not yet to settle the issues of democratic legitimation of EMU.

2. The impact of the EP on Eurozone reforms in the crisis: empirical findings

This section provides a survey of how the EP has performed in EMU governance reforms, in response to the financial and debt crisis in the Eurozone from 2010 – 2014. In particular, we assess the empowering - or disempowering - of the EP as citizens' directly elected representative agency vis-à-vis the other EU institutions (European Central Bank, European Council, European Commission, Eurogroup). The aim is to provide empirical evidence to support one or the other of these claims. To assess the activities of the EP in relation to the Euro-crisis during its last legislature 2009-2014, we scrutinize plenary debates, relevant committee reports, including those by the new Special Committee "Financial, Economic and Social Crisis", MEP amendments to Commission proposals and Council decisions. The following methodology is used: First, a combination of quantitative and qualitative, procedural and content analysis, to scrutinize both, the use of formal competences as well as the substantive influence of the EP. Second, the latter will be measured by the acceptance rate of amendments that the EP has introduced into the legislative processes. Here, we ask to what extent the EP succeeded in promoting its own influence and the influence of the national parliaments. Third, for this purpose, we compare the initial texts adopted by the EP before the 'trilogues' to the final legislative provision resulting from them. Fourth, we scrutinize voting patterns by using the Agreement Index (AI)[2]. Finally, fifth, we scrutinize all public hearings in the area of EMU reform to identify the relative proportions of different types of external actors that the EP invited for presenting their opinions/preferences in the two relevant committees, Economic and Monetary Affairs (ECON) and Financial, Economic and Social Crisis (CRIS).

Empirical findings

Among the activities of the EP in the domain of EMU during the 2009-14 legislature, here two of the most relevant legislative packages are selected, the so-called "six-pack" and the "two-pack". Both enhance the EU's supranational

2 The AI was invented by Hix, Noury and Roland to picture the cohesion of party groups, national parties and national delegations within the European Parliament. The Hix-Noury-Roland formula is Ai=(max(Y,N,A)-(0.5((Y+N+A)-max(Y,N,A))))/(Y+N+A), where Y = number of votes "FOR", N = number of votes "AGAINST", and A = number of "ABSTENTIONS".

powers to make significant incursions into national state and budgetary autonomy.[3] Our findings are structured by three questions, concerning the EP's formal competences, its legislative successes and failures, and its non-legislative activities of representation and enquiry.

First, given the EP's formal powers of co-decision, the respective legislative processes were exceptionally difficult. It took the EP more than a year to reach the necessary agreements on both, in many points amended legislative packages (Tuori and Tuori 2014). Four out of the six legislative processes in the "six-pack" and both regulations of the "two-pack" where adopted under the ordinary legislative procedure, formally known as co-decision procedure[4]. In this procedure the European Parliament is an equal legislator together with the Council of the European Union. The control of the public deficit, Regulation No 1177/2011 of the "six pack", has to be legislated with the consultation procedure based on article 126 par 14 al 2 TFEU. Here the Council legislates alone after it consulted the European Parliament. The last legislation of the "six pack" is legislated by a special procedure; here the Council shall decide on a proposal from the Commission and after consulting the European Parliament. Therefore 75% of the processes where decided under the co-decision procedure. This is an extraordinary high proportion compared to "ordinary" times and areas of legislation. The responsible (re) Committee has been in all cases the Committee for Economic and Monetary Affairs (ECON). Three more Committees were involved in the processes as well, Employment and Social Affairs (EMPL), Budgets (BUDG) and Legal Affairs (JURI). They presented their views as an opinion (op) on the proposal and recommended amendments. The rapporteurs of the different reports where from three different party groups: two from EPP and ALDE and one from S&D who was responsible for two reports. They were from four different Member states, two French, one Portuguese and one from the Netherlands (for responsibilities for legislation, see Table 1 below).

---

3 The **"six pack"** on the "Prevention and correction of macroeconomic imbalances" (Regulation 1176/2011, January 2012) consists of six legislative provisions aimed at establishing European rules against macro-economic imbalances that derive from exploding private debt, trade performance imbalances due to lasting import or export surpluses, by delegating powers of surveillance and sanctioning to the European Commission. Complementing these macro-economic rules, the **"two-pack"** (Regulations 472/2013 and 473/2013, June 2013) defines a new legal framework for "strengthening the economic and budgetary surveillance of member states in the euro area experiencing or threatened with serious difficulties with respect to their financial stability", hence defining rules for the reform measures to be adopted by crisis states.

4 This is based on article 121 TFEU.

Table 1: EP formal procedures in 'six-pack' and 'two-pack' decision-making

Titel of the legal act	procedure	Committee	Rapporteur	Adoption EC; E. i. f.
Regulation (EU) No 1173/2011 on the effective enforcement of budgetary surveillance in the euro area	Cod[*]	ECON (re) BUDG(op) EMPL(op) JURI(op)	S. Goulard ALDE, France	10.10 01.12
Regulation (EU) No 1174/2011 on enforcement measures to correct excessive macroeconomic imbalances in the euro area	Cod	ECON (re) BUDG(op) EMPL(op) JURI(op)	C. Haglund: ALDE, Finland	10.10 01.12
Regulation (EU) No 1175/2011 amending Council Regulation (EC) No 1466/97 on the strengthening of the surveillance of budgetary positions and the surveillance and coordination of economic policies	Cod	ECON (re) BUDG(op) EMPL(op) JURI(op)	C. Wortmann-Kool EPP, Netherlands	10.10 01.12
Regulation (EU) No 1176/2011 on the prevention and correction of macroeconomic imbalances	Cod	ECON (re) BUDG(op) EMPL(op) JURI(op)	E. Ferreira S&D, Portugal	10.10 01.12
Council Regulation (EU) No 1177/2011 amending Regulation (EC) No 1467/97 on speeding up and clarifying the implementation of the excessive deficit procedure	Con[**]			10.10 01.12
Council Directive 2011/85/EU of 8 November 2011 on requirements for budgetary frameworks of the Member States	non-leg[***]			10.10 01.12

Titel of the legal act	procedure	Committee	Rapporteur	Adoption EC; E. i. f.
Regulation (EU) No 472/2013 the strengthening of economic and budgetary surveillance of Member States in the euro area experiencing or threatened with serious difficulties with respect to their financial stability	Cod	ECON (re) BUDG(op) EMPL(op)	J.-P Gauzès EPP, France	11.11 06.13
Regulation (EU) No 473/2013 on common provisions for monitoring and assessing draft budgetary plans and ensuring the correction of excessive deficit of the Member States in the euro area	Cod	ECON (re) BUDG(op) EMPL(op)	E. Ferreira S&D, Portugal	11.11 06.13

* Cod stands for Ordinary legislative procedure (Art. 294 TFEU).

** Con stands for Consultation procedure (Art. 289 TFEU).

*** Art. 126 par 14 al 3 TFEU: Subject to the other provisions of this paragraph, the Council shall, on a proposal from the Commission and after consulting the European Parliament, lay down detailed rules and definitions for the application of the provisions of the said Protocol.

Source: own compilation

The second question aims at the successes and failures of the EP's activities in shaping these two legislative packages. We compare the pre-existing Troika programs with regard to euro area "programme countries" to the newly adopted EMU reforms. Regarding these latter, the EP succeeded in getting a number of significant innovations approved: First, budget cuts must protect state expenditures for education and health. Second, civil society obtains a right to be consulted about reform programs. Third, governments must report on the distributional effects of budget cuts in the population. Fourth, Member States must make clear the consequences of their fiscal adjustment plans regarding the EU 2020 goals such as education, combatting exclusion, research and development, climate protection etc. Fifth, both, the six- and two-pack provisions responded to criticisms for lack of democracy. For instance, they introduce provisions on economic dialogue between EU institutions, in particular the Parliament, the Council and the Commission. Moreover, the dialogue takes place in the competent EP committee which may invite the President of the Council and the Commission.

As we are interested in the influence of the European Parliament on shaping the EU's response to the Euro-crisis we only analyze those legislative processes where the European Parliament operated as an equal legislator. This is true for four out of six proceedings where the ordinary legislative procedure was used, four out of six proceedings from the "six pack" and both from the "two-pack" (see table 1, above). Following the ordinary legislative procedure, the main channel for the European Parliament to influence the final legal act is to table amendments to the draft proposal. To assess the EP's influence, the acceptance rate, namely the percentage of amendments of the European Parliament that were adopted in the final act, and the content of these amendments are of interest. The EP had a regular first reading in all six legislative processes under investigation before the Commission, the Parliament and the Council reached a compromise via the formal 'trilogue' meeting. Here they meet informally to reach a compromise and to shorten the procedure. After the 'trilogue' the European Parliament adopted in all six cases a new text, which reflected the compromise of the three legislators. Our analysis is based on a comparison of the first with the final version. Five points stand out:

(1) The acceptance rate of the amendments of the EP was high in the "six pack". 96% or more off all amendments where at least mainly accepted in all four processes. In the "two-pack" the Parliament could only get 76 and 53% of its amendments mainly accepted. Never the less this is still a quite high level, also compared with general average rates (see Table 2: Acceptance Rate of EP Amendments to Draft Legislative Proposals).

Table 2: Acceptance rate of EP amendments to draft legislative proposals

Regulation	Acceptance Rate[5]	EP social dialogue	National Parliaments
No 1173/2011	97% mainly accepted	No Dialogue	In the Recital by EP
No 1174/2011	97% mainly accepted	No Dialogue	In the Recital by EP
No 1175/2011	100% mainly accepted[6]	Economic Dialogue	By EP
No 1176/2011	96% mainly accepted	Economic Dialogue	In the Recital by EP
No 472/2013	76% mainly accepted	No Dialogue	Not mentioned
No 473/2013	53% mainly accepted	Economic Dialogue (rest mainly not adopted)	In Recitals and law text (accepted only in Recital)

Source: own compilation

(2) "Parliamentary self-empowerment": The European Parliament implemented the provision of obligatory information of itself in all six Regulations it could amend. Although it does not have the right to accept or veto any of the procedures based on the six-pack and the two-pack, it has to be informed.

(3) "Economic dialogue": The EP also invented the economic dialogue, where the competent committee of the European Parliament can invite the President of the Council, the Commission and, the President of the European Council or the President of the Eurogroup to discuss relevant topics. It also can offer the opportunity to the Member State which is the subject of a Council recommendation to participate in an exchange of views.

(4) Another interest pursued by the European Parliament has been the involvement of the national parliaments as early as possible. For example, Regulation No 1176/2011 includes the Recital 2a: "Strengthening economic governance should include a closer and more timely involvement of the European Parliament and the national parliaments."

(5) While the Commission neglected the social partners, the EP succeeded in including them within the European Semester, where "relevant stakeholders, in particular the social partners, will be involved within the framework of the Semester […]" (REF). The European Parliament could implement the mention of Article 9 TFEU in the Recitals of Regulation No 472/2013. Moreover, it managed to incorporate the text "the Union is to take into account requirements linked to the promotion of a high level of employment, the guarantee of adequate social protection, the fight against social exclusion, and a high level of education, training and protection of human health."

Our third question concerns non-legislative activities of enquiry and representation performed by the EP, such as hearings and reports. Its committees invited external or other European actors to public hearings aimed at collecting

5 Differentiation between the amendment and the final act whether it was totally accepted, mainly accepted, partially accepted or not accepted at all.

6 The final Regulation included a lot more changes, then the ones of the Parliament.

useful information from experts, stakeholders and civil society representatives (for an overview of EP activities, see Table 3 below).

Table 3: EP activities in EMU reforms

Activities	2009	2010	2011	2012
Plenary debates			Six pack	Two pack
Hearings	10.11. CRIS	28.01. CRIS 14.04. ECON 9.09. ECON 5.10. ECON	13.01. ECON 22.03. ECON 13.04. ECON 27.06. ECON 5.12. ECON	
Amendments		95 (six pack)	1435 (six pack)	540 (two pack)
Explanation of votes			Six pack	Two pack
Reports		05.10. CRIS mid-term report 10.05. Credit lost CRIS	15.06. CRIS final report	
others		22.04. Thematic Paper CRIS	14.03. Questions to National Parliaments CRIS	

Source: own compilation

Taking a closer look at the public hearings held by the two most relevant committees, ECON and CRIS, most of the speakers were private actors from the business sector. The second biggest group was constituted by officials either from EU or international institutions (see Table 4: External Actor Involvement in EP Hearings). Representatives from labor or civil society were not invited.

Summing these findings up, the EP has benefited in both cases – the 'six-pack' and the 'two-pack' from operating under the co-decision procedure. Thereby it co-operated at an equal footing with the Council in ordinary legislation. This provided the relevant parliamentary committees with decision-making powers. Moreover, the EP was capable of translating its potentials into legislative practice, hence it succeed in having a series of parliamentary amendments adopted by the final provisions. Hence, the EP has enhanced a range of institutional innovations in EMU governance, including the "economic dialogue" and improving its own position in the various procedures of European economic governance. However, apart from its 'Troika report', the EP did not live up to its potentials as a European public forum, where European citizens' general interests would have been negotiated vis-à-vis private economic interests, and where executive agencies in coping with the crisis would have been held to account in the light of the public. To explain these limitations we will take a closer look at the party politics within the EP.

Table 4: External actor involvement in EP proceedings

	Title	Committee	Scientists/Media	Pub. Nat.	Pub. EU/Int.	Private	Privatecs
1	The causes of the financial crisis and the consequences and challenges for the European Union	CRIS	2/1	1	2/0	1	1
2	The Social Impact of the Crisis	CRIS	2/0	2	0/1	1	1
3	Deposit Guarantee Schemes	ECON				4	1
4	Lessons from Greece	ECON			2/0	3	
5	State aid temporary rules	ECON		1	1/0	3	
6	Improving the economic governance and stability framework of the Union	ECON	1/0		2/1	1	
7	Global economic governance	ECON		1	0/1	2	
8	Strengthening Economic Governance in the EU	ECON	2/0	1			1
9	Opening the way for the Single Euro Payments Area for Consumers and Enterprises	ECON			1/0	3	1
10	Sovereign debt crisis in Europe	ECON		1	2/0		1
11	Credit Rating Agencies	ECON			1	3	1
12	EU Social Entrepreneurship Funds and EU Venture Capital Funds	ECON	1/0			1	2
13	Exchange of Views with the Troika on The Economic and Social Crisis in Greece	ECON EMPL			2/1		
14	Tackling the culture of market manipulation Global action post Libor/Euribor	ECON	0/1		CFTC EC IOSCO	3	1
15	Successes and Failures in Crisis Countries	ECON	4/0		2/0		
16	The prospects of establishing a debt redemption fund and introducing Eurobills	ECON	2/0		1	2	
			16	7	24	27	10

Source: own compilation

3. The party politics of the European Parliament in response to the euro-crisis

For explaining successes and limitations of EP legislative activities, the issue of party political coalitions and cleavage lines within the EP needs to be explored. Simon Hix has analyzed the voting behavior of the members of the European Parliament (MEPs) in legislation across a large range of policy domains. In his earlier work he found that "the main factors behind voting in the EP are the policy positions of national parties" (Hix 2002: 696). Later he specified his findings arguing that MEPs are more likely to vote along national party lines only if the electoral system within their country uses "closed-list proportional representation, small districts, or centralized candidate selection" (Hix 2004: 219-20). In view of building their intra-EP careers, however, MEP's are committed to the European party groups, which distribute positions and speaking time in debates within the European Parliament. Moreover, the 2014 European elections requiring European political parties to nominate "Spitzenkandidaten" for the European Commission presidency, have enhanced the need for European parties to strengthen their different programmatic profiles. This means that even under extraordinary conditions such as the financial, economic and social crisis we should expect that part of the MEP's will uphold their European partisan allegiances. More specifically, Hix found that "the main dimension of voting behavior both within and between the transnational political parties in the European Parliament is the classic left-right dimension of democratic politics." (Hix et al. 2006: 509).

From this research, a number of empirical questions arise concerning the party politics of the EP in response to the crises. One issue is whether the left-right pattern as the main dimension of EP legislative decision-making is still valid for Economic and Monetary policy reforms in the crisis. Alternatively, we might expect that the euro-crisis has blurred the traditional left right positioning of the party groups and that Eurosceptic and anti-EU voting patterns have become more salient. Another question is about the nature of the new kind of party political conflict that the euro crisis may have brought to the fore. In line with the theme "Europeanisation vs. renationalization" of this book, old and new kinds of coalitions among MEP's along national lines should be expected. If we put this prediction in Andrew Moravcsik's liberal intergovernmental terms, "the institutional structure of the EC [European Community] is acceptable to national governments only insofar" as it permits "them to attain goals otherwise unachievable", either by increasing "the efficiency of interest bargaining", or by strengthening "the autonomy of national political leaders vis-à-vis particular social groups within their domestic polity" (Moravcsik 1993: 507). Following these (old) assumptions, coalition formation within the

European Parliament will be shaped along national lines. For instance, the main conflict line shaping EP negotiations might divide MEP's from euro creditor states such as Germany, the Netherlands, Finland and the Baltic countries and those from debtor states, the so-called programme countries. Creditor interests would try to make sure they get their money back and gain control over the budgetary policy of the debtor states, while the latter would struggle for supranational redistributive policies to support their fiscal autonomy vis-à-vis financial markets. However, we might also expect a new pattern of conflict to emerge from the EP, that is the struggle between Europeanisation – aimed at strengthening European powers - on the one hand, and re-nationalisation – the return of EU competences to the member states, on the other. For instance, some MEP's might strive for the renationalization of monetary policy in opposition to others fighting to strengthen EP competences in EU economic and monetary policy-making.

In response to these questions, we scrutinise the roll calls in EP voting on the 'six-pack' and the 'two-pack' and summarise the findings in five points.

(1) The Average Agreement Index (AI, see above) of the roll calls shows that the MEPs manly vote along party group lines. An exception is Regulation No 1176/2011. Here the MEPs demonstrate more cohesion with the other MEPs of their home country (for EP voting patterns, see table 5). In the Regulation No 1173/2011, No 1174/2011 and No 1175/2011 a minimal winning coalition was formed. The other three regulations were the result of oversized coalitions of nearly all MEPs. In Regulation (EU) No 1176/2011, for example, the winning coalition was formed by 554 for, 90 against and 21 abstentions. Regulation (EU) No 1175/2011 on the other side received 356 votes for, 265 against and 35 abstentions[7].

Table 5: EP voting patterns I.

	Reg. No 1173/2011	**Reg. No 1174/2011**	**Reg. No 1175/2011**	**Reg. No 1176/2011**	**Reg. No 472/2013**	**Reg. No 473/2013**
Party Group Average AI	68.63	70.55	70.48	75.03	80.78	81.94
Member state Average AI	46.70	48.31	47.75	81.93	65.93	65.59
Winning coalition	EPP/ALDE	EPP/ALDE/Greens/EFA	EPP/ALDE	All states but UK/CR	EPP/S&D/ALDE/Greens/EFA	EPP/S&D/ALDE/Greens/EFA

Source: Votewatch.eu

(2) Taking a closer look at the winning coalitions of the "six pack"-votes, we notice that the minimal winning coalitions are either formed by the Christian

7 Based on data from votewatch.eu.

Democrats (EPP) and the Liberals (ALDE) or the Christian Democrats, the Liberals and the Greens (Greens). The "rebels" among the Liberals and the Christian Democrats always consisted of the same two Finish MEPs of the EPP group and two French and one Italian MEPs of the ALDE group, each in different constellations. All of them are part of different national parties. In the "two-pack" one can see quite high approval rates by the MEPs but on the other hand we found many more dissenters within the party groups, with the exception of the Greens (see Table 6).

Table 6: EP voting patterns II.

	Reg. No 1173/2011	**Reg. No 1174/2011**	**Reg. No 1175/2011**	**Reg. No 1176/2011**	**Reg. No 472/2013**	**Reg. No 473/2013**
Winning coalition	EPP/ALDE	EPP/ALDE/Greens	EPP/ALDE	EPP/ALDE/S&D/Greens	EPP/S&D/ALDE/Greens	EPP/S&D/ALDE/Greens
Rebels winning coalition	2 ALDE, 2 EPP	2 ALDE, 1 EPP	3 ALDE	1 ALDE, 2 EPP, 8 Greens	4 ALDE 5 EPP 5 Greens 53 S&D	5 ALDE, 8 EPP 7 Greens 6 S&D
Losing coalition	S&D/Greens/GUE-NGL	S&D/GUE-NGL	S&D/Greens/GUE-NGL	GUE-NGL	ECR/EFD/GUE-NGL	ECR/GUE-NGL

Source: own compilation

(3) The Social Democrats did not support three out of four legislative provisions of the "six pack". To justify their stance they argued that the "six pack" built on neoliberal ideas and austerity principles, only. They claimed investment policies and some went for Eurobonds. Monika Flašíková Beňová (Slovakian member of the group), for example, writes as part of the debate on 22. of June 2011 in Brussels concerning the six pack: "The proposals talk about tougher sanctions, about fines for the non-fulfilment of recommendations and about these being applied automatically […]" an later on "It is not just cuts and budgetary discipline that will bring a solution, but a policy of targeted development and support for the competitiveness of Europe's periphery." George Sabin Cutaş (Romanian member of the group) writes: "I think that the proposals in this package are not ambitious enough, as they are only geared towards austerity and curtailing citizens' social rights. There is no mention of elements which could underpin a European economic recovery, such as making investments in the key areas of infrastructure, education, research and innovation."

(4) For explaining his vote (28th of September 2011 Report of C. Wortmann-Kool) Roberto Gualtieri (Italian) gave a more concrete and nuanced response: "One cannot accept the reverse majority rule and tougher parameters

and sanctions without a golden rule to protect Member States' investments and without Eurobonds to fund European investments [...]." Sylvie Guillaume (French) explains in her writing her vote on the 28th of September 2011:

> I voted against the Goulard report [...]. Instead of guaranteeing policies for recovery that support consumption and investment for the future, this package is making the people pay for the crisis, by stifling growth and destroying jobs, and will consequently prevent any return to balanced budgets.

The social democrats were therefore mainly against three of the "six pack" Regulations, because they think they represent the wrong way to overcome the actual crises and to prevent any new one. They were in favor of investment policies together with some austerity. For them the legislation was neither inclusive nor balanced enough. Hence, the reason for voting against the legislations had nothing to do with the type of legislative procedure chosen and the lack of influence by the European Parliament.

To sum up this section we can say that no obvious new coalitions among MEP's along national conflicts of interest or indicating creditor – debtor or core-periphery cleavages have emerged. The main pattern of conflict within the parliamentary legislative processes remains structured by the classical left-right dimension that Simon Hix has identified for EP voting patterns in general. Hence, neither do we find that the most intense years of the financial and euro crisis (2010 - 2014) have *re-emphasized nor that they have altogether blurred the traditional left right positioning of the party groups as the main dimension of EP legislative decision-making.* Beyond the scope of the present research, future research on the 2014 – 9 legislative term will be needed to test the assumption that *the nationalist vs. supranational conflict has become more salient after 2014,* with a quarter of MEP's advocating renationalization, disintegration and exit from the EU, against whom the majority of MEP's have been defending piecemeal reforms or the status quo of European economic and political union.

4. Conclusion: Potentials and constraints of the European Parliament in governing EMU

Does the deepening of EMU necessarily mean less democracy? We have explored the European Parliament's responses to the Eurozone crisis claiming that the EP represents the major potential resource for democratic innovations and, hence, for a "credible governance" of EMU. Without doubt, the EU's need for legitimation has increased with the severity and the salience of the sacrifices its rescue programs and risk prevention regime have required from the citizens.

With our research, we further develop and contribute to Tuori and Tuori (2014) who, summarising their analysis of the political consequences of the Eurocrisis, have emphasized „the spillover effects which the crisis of the macroeconomic constitution has had in the field of the political constitution, especially with regard to democracy, legitimacy and accountability". In line with their research, we conceive of the changing division of competences between the European and national level as a „democracy issue". This derives from „the implications of the narrowing of the reach of national democratic legitimation, due to reductions in Member State sovereignty in fiscal and economic policy and the shrinking of national parliaments' budget autonomy". Moreover, this democracy issue reflects „the repercussions of resort to the intergovernmental way" and, finally, „the consequences of independent expert bodies, such as the ECB and the Commission, assuming features of a stakeholder or politician role" (Tuori and Tuori 2014).

For the present chapter, we argue that for coping with these new „democracy issues" of EMU the EP's legitimation potential is key. This rests on its capacities to enhance inclusiveness, to ensure accountability and to balance power monopolies in EMU governance. In particular, our research findings suggest that the strength of the EP's legitimation potential depends on its legislative performance in three respects: The EP can contribute to the democratic governance of EMU, depending on (1) the quality of its legislative output in terms of effective problem-solving that reflects the general interests of the Union citizens rather than those of private interests or the member states; (2) the quality of its procedures for transparency, information, deliberation and accountability; (3) the quality of its inputs in terms of representation and participation by stake-holders, that is those most affected by its policies.

In all these respects, the EP is a particularly complex, unique parliament, with weaknesses but also strengths in comparison to national legislatures. Most importantly, the very fact that the EP is on the way towards forming a European party government but that its majority is not (yet) responsible for supporting the EU executive vis-à-vis the parliamentary opposition provides individual MEP's and party groups with the freedom to perform a variety of parliamentary functions such as the scrutiny of the Commission, the Council, the ECB or other non-majoritarian agencies (Curtin 2014); or the communication and dialogue function with social and economic stakeholders in an emerging transnational sphere of European publics (Liebert 2007).

Appendix

European Parliament activities in the euro-crisis (2010 - 2014)

Title	Number Entry into force	Procedure Committees
Institutional Reforms		
Establishing a European Supervisory Authority (European Securities and Markets Authority), amending Decision No 716/2009/EC and repealing Commission Decision 2009/77/EC	Regulation (EU) No 1095/2010 (16.12.2010)	Cod ECON (re) BUDG (op) JURI (op) AFCO (op)
Conferring specific tasks on the European Central Bank concerning policies relating to the prudential supervision of credit institutions (Single Supervisory Mechanism)	Council regulation (EU) No 1024/2013 (3.11.2013; SSM one year later)	Con ECON (re) JURI (op) AFCO (op) LIBE (op)
REPORT with recommendations to the Commission on the European System of Financial Supervision (ESFS) Review	2013/2166	INL
DIRECTIVE establishing a framework for the recovery and resolution of credit institutions and investment firms and amending Council Directives 77/91/EEC and 82/891/EC, Directives 2001/24/EC, 2002/47/EC, 2004/25/EC, 2005/56/EC, 2007/36/EC and 2011/35/EC and Regulation (EU) No 1093/2010	In progress	Cod ECON (re) BUDG (op) IMCO (op) JURI (op)
Legislation		
On credit agreements for consumers relating to residential immovable property and amending Directives 2008/48/EC and 2013/36/EU and Regulation (EU) No 1093/2010	Directive 2014/17/EU 20.3.2014	Cod ECON (re) IMCO (op) JURI (op)
DIRECTIVE on markets in financial instruments repealing Directive 2004/39/EC of the European Parliament and of the Council (Recast)	Approval by Council 13.05.2014	Cod ECON (re) DEVE (op) ITRE (op) JURI (op)
REGULATION on markets in financial instruments and amending Regulation [EMIR] on OTC derivatives, central counterparties and trade repositories	Approval by Council 13.05.2014	Cod ECON (re) BUDG (op) DEVE (op)

Title	Number Entry into force	Procedure Committees
		ITRE (op) JURI (op)
Amending DIRECTIVE 2009/65/EC on the coordination of laws, regulations and administrative provisions relating to undertakings for collective investment in transferable securities (UCITS) as regards depositary functions, remuneration policies and sanctions	in progress	Cod ECON (re) JURI (op)
DIRECTIVE on the prevention of the use of the financial system for the purpose of money laundering and terrorist financing	in progress	Cod ECON (re) LIBE (re) DEVE (op) IMCO (op) JURI (op) PETI (op)
Amending REGULATION (EU) No 260/2012 as regards the migration to Union-wide credit transfers and direct debits	Regulation (EU) No 248/2014 21.3.2014	Cod ECON (re)
Amending REGULATION (EC) No 1060/2009 on credit rating agencies	Regulation (EU) No 462/2013 20.6.2013	Cod ECON (re) JURI (op)
REGULATION on key information documents for investment products	in progress	Cod ECON (re) IMCO (op) LIBE (op)
DIRECTIVE on insurance mediation (recast)	in progress	Cod ECON(re) IMCO (op) JURI (op)
Establishing a Union program to support specific activities in the field of financial reporting and auditing for the period of 2014-20 and repealing Decision No 716/2009/EC	Regulation (EU) No 258/2014 9.4.2014	Cod ECON (re) JURI (op)
DIRECTIVE On the comparability of fees related to payment accounts, payment account switching and access to payment accounts with basic features	still in Progress	Cod ECON (re) IMCO (op) JURI (op)
Amending DIRECTIVE 2009/138/EC (Solvency II) as regards the date for its transposition and the date of its application, and the date of repeal of certain Directives (Solvency I)	Directive 2013/58/EU 19.12.2013	Cod ECON (re)
On prudential requirements for credit institutions and investment firms and amending Regulation (EU) No 648/2012	Regulation (EU) No 575/2013 28.6.2013	Cod ECON (re) JURI (re)
On short selling and certain aspects of credit default swaps	Regulation (EU) No 236/2012	Cod ECON (re)

Title	Number Entry into force	Procedure Committees
		JURI (re)
REGULATION establishing uniform rules and a uniform procedure for the resolution of credit institutions and certain investment firms in the framework of a Single Resolution Mechanism and a Single Bank Resolution Fund and amending Regulation (EU) No 1093/2010 of the European Parliament and of the Council	in progress	Cod ECON (re) JURI (op) AFCO (op)
Amending DIRECTIVE 2003/41/EC on the activities and supervision of institutions for occupational retirement provision, Directive 2009/65/EC on the coordination of laws, regulations and administrative provisions relating to undertakings for collective investment in transferable securities (UCITS) and Directive 2011/61/EU on Alternative Investment Funds Managers in respect of over-reliance on credit ratings	Directive 2013/14/EU 20.6.2013	Cod ECON (re) JURI (re)
On OTC derivatives, central counterparties and trade repositories	Regulation (EU) No 648/2012 16.8.2012	Cod ECON (re) ITRE (op) JURI (op)
Implementing enhanced cooperation in the area of financial transaction tax (FTT)	in progress	Con ECON (re) BUDG(op)
On the effective enforcement of budgetary surveillance in the euro area (SIX PACK)	Regulation (EU) No 1173/2011 2.1.2012	Cod ECON (re) BUDG(op) EMPL(op) JURI(op)
amending COUNCIL REGULATION (EC) No 1466/97 on the strengthening of the surveillance of budgetary positions and the surveillance and coordination of economic policies (six pack)	Regulation (EU) No 1175/2011 2.1.2012	Cod ECON (re) BUDG(op) EMPL(op) JURI(op)
On enforcement measures to correct excessive macroeconomic imbalances in the euro area (SIX PACK)	Regulation (EU) No 1174/2011 2.1.2012	Cod ECON (re) BUDG(op) EMPL(op) JURI(op)
Prevention and correction of macroeconomic imbalances (SIX- PACK)	Regulation (EU) No 1176/2011 2.1.2012	Cod ECON (re) BUDG(op) EMPL(op) JURI(op)
Strengthening of economic and budgetary surveillance of Member States in the euro area experiencing or threatened with serious difficulties with respect to their financial stability (TWO-PACK)	Regulation (EU) No 472/2013 06.13	Cod ECON (re) BUDG(op)

Title	Number Entry into force	Procedure Committees
		EMPL(op)
Common provisions for monitoring and assessing draft budgetary plans and ensuring the correction of excessive deficit of the Member States in the euro area (TWO-PACK)	Regulation (EU) No 473/2013 06.13	Cod ECON (re) BUDG(op) EMPL(op)
REGULATION on European statistics repealing Regulation (EC, Euratom) No 1101/2008 of the EP and of the Council on the transmission of data subject to statistical confidentiality to the Statistical Office of the European Communities, Council Regulation (EC) No 322/97 on Community Statistics, and Council Decision 89/382/EEC, Euratom establishing a Committee on the Statistical Programmes of the European Communities	Regulation (EC) No 223/2009 (1.4.2009) Regulation (EU) No 1173/2011, Regulation (EU) No 1175/2011, Regulation (EU) No 473/2013	Cod ECON (re)
ENQUIRY REPORT on the role and operations of the Troika (ECB, Commission, IMF) with regard to euro area programme countries	Draft Report 17.12.2013	ECON (INL)

Procedures

Cod Ordinary legislation (ex-codecision)
Con Consultation
INL Own legislative initiative

Committees

AFCO Constitutional Affairs
BUDG Budgets
ECON Economic and Monetary Affairs
EMPL Employment and Social Affairs
DEVE Development
IMCO Internal Market and Consumer Protection
ITRE Industry, Research and Energy
JURI Legal Affairs
LIBE Civil Liberties, Justice and Home Affairs
PETI Petitions

Documents

European Commission (2012a) 'A Blueprint for a Deep and Genuine Economic and Monetary Union: Launching a European Debate – Communication from the Commission', 30 November 2012, COM(2012) 777 final/2, available at http://ec.europa.eu/commission_2010–2014/president/news/archives/2012/11/pdf/blueprint_en.pdf.

European Council (2012b) 'Towards a Genuine Economic and Monetary Union', 5 December 2012, available at www.consilium.europa.eu/uedocs/cms_data/docs/pressdata/en/ec/134069.pdf.

The so-called 'six-pack' was implemented in 2011 and consists of five EU regulations (Nos 1173/2011; 1174/2011; 1175/2011; 1176/2011; 1177/2011) and one EU directive (2011/85/EU).

The Treaty on Stability, Coordination and Governance (abbrev. 'fiscal compact') was signed on 12 March 2012 and came into force in 2013.

European Parliament and Council Regulation (EU) No. 472/2013 of 21 May 2013 on the strengthening of economic and budgetary surveillance of Member States in the euro area experiencing or threatened with serious difficulties with respect to their financial stability. 2013 OJ L140/1.

European Parliament and Council Regulation (EU) No. 473/2013 of 21 May 2013 on common provisions for monitoring and assessing draft budgetary plans and ensuring the correction of excessive deficit oft he Member States in the euro area (2013 OJ L140/11).

References

Brühlmeier, Daniel and Mastronardi, Philippe eds. (2016): Demokratie in der Krise. Analysen, Prozesse und Perspektiven. Chronos, Zürich.

Crum, Ben (2013): Saving the Euro at the Cost of Democracy? In: Journal of Common Market Studies. Vol. 51: 4.

Curtin, Deirdre (2014): Challenging Executive Dominance in European Democracy. In: The Modern Law Review. Vol. 77: 1.

Herzog, Bodo and Hengstermann, Katja (2013): Restoring Credible Economic Governance to the Eurozone. In: Economic Affairs. Vol. 33: 1.

Hix, Simon (2002): Parliamentary Behavior with Two Principles. Preferences, Parties, and Voting in the European Parliament. In: American Journal of Political Science. Vol. 46: 3.

Hix, Simon (2004): Electoral institutions and legislative behavior: explaining voting defection in the European Parliament. In: World Politics. Vol. 56: 2.

Hix, Simon, Abdul Noury and Gerard Roland (2006): Dimensions of Politics in the European Parliament. In: American Journal of Political Science. Vol. 50: 2.
Kopf, Christian (2011): Restoring financial stability in the euro area. CEPS Policy Brief, No. 237, 15 March.
Liebert, Ulrike (2007): The European Parliament and the Prospects for a European Sphere of Publics: A Question of Representation. In: Philip Schlesinger and John Erik Fossum eds.: The European Union and the Public Sphere: A Communicative Space in the Making? Routledge.
Moravcsik, Andrew (1993): Preferences and Power in the European Community: A Liberal Intergovernmentalist Approach. In: Journal of Common Market Studies. Vol. 31: 4.
Schmitter, Philippe C. (2015): Crisis and Transition, But Not Decline. In: Journal of Democracy. Vol. 26: Issue 1.
Tuori, Kaarlo, Klaus Tuori (2014): The Eurozone Crisis. A Constitutional Analysis. Cambridge University Press.

18. Intergroups as alternative venues to the European Parliament for civil society

Laura Landorff

1. Introduction

In times of continuing distrust in European Union (EU) institutions and increasing dissatisfaction of EU citizens with how (parliamentary) democracy works[1], demands for direct involvement of actors from civil society and experts in EU policy-making are becoming stronger (Kohler-Koch 2010). Already in 2001 the European Commission (EC), in its *White Paper on European Governance*[2], responded to the "decreasing popular support for the European integration project" by promoting a wider participation of civil society for the purpose of democratic and efficient governance (Kohler-Koch 2007: 255). In the follow-up a number of direct participatory policy tools, such as the European Citizen's Initiative (ECI), were launched[3]. The ECI, however, fell short of expectations. Designed to enable citizens and civil society organisations (CSOs) to initiate EU legislation, the ECI produced only modest results and has been criticised for "its lack of mandatory status" (Greenwood 2012: 332), and the complicated procedures of registering an ECI (Corbett et al. 2016, Garcia and Del Río Villar 2012).

In response to the Commission's efforts this contribution looks at the involvement of civil society in the European Parliament (EP). While the European Commission has always been eager to engage with European civil society, the EP's approach to organised civil society has been characterised by "a degree of ambiguity" (Greenwood 2007b: 184). On the one hand, the EP "enjoys direct democratic legitimacy based on elections" (Kohler-Koch 2010: 108). Unlike the Commission it does not depend on CSOs as its social constituency. On the other hand, the EP received in the past far less attention from interest groups and civil society than the Commission holding the sole right of

1 The European Commission Standard Eurobarometer in Spring 2016 reports that 48% of the respondents were "dissatisfied with the way of how democracy works in the EU". This constitutes the highest level since 2004 (European Commission 2016a: 122).
2 European Commission (2001).
3 Other participatory tools are the civil dialogue or the European Commission's online consultation system. For an overview, see Kohler-Koch and Finke, 2007.

policy initiation (Eising 2016). The EP's legislative empowerment over time, however, makes it today a key player within the EU institutional system, and thus an important partner for civil society. Consequently, this chapter analyses CSOs engagement in the Parliament. In particular, it focuses on EP Intergroups and thereby explores a phenomenon that thus far received only little attention in EP-civil society research.

Intergroups are informal cross-party, cross-committee groupings bringing together MEPs from different political groups, parliamentary committees and member states as well as representatives of civil society and other EU institutions in their meetings. The 7th EP (2009-2014) recorded 27 officially recognised Intergroups covering a wide range of topics from ageing to climate change, from traditional minorities to trade unions and animal welfare, and listing up to 126 MEPs as their members (European Parliament 2013).

The aim of this chapter is to explore Intergroups' potential to act as a participatory tool that contributes to democratic input legitimacy (pluralist interest representation and intermediation) by playing a central role in the way MEPs "interact with certain civil society organisations" (Mény 2009: 97, Liebert and Trenz 2011). Previous research on Intergroups as points of access for parliamentary lobby groups is so far inconclusive. Earlier studies on lobbyism in the EP have neglected this issue (Liebert 1995). Bouwen (2003: 7) argued that "the informal character and uncertain subsistence of many intergroups makes them attractive but unreliable arenas for [...] legislative lobbying" as opposed to parliamentary committees. Nedergaard and Jensen (2014: 11-12), by contrast, concluded that many Intergroups were affected by lobbyism, although to different degrees, ranging from "almost a fusion of interests" to Intergroups being of "very little interest for lobbyists".

Drawing on the often reported "numerical superiority" of business interests vis-à-vis other societal interests in EU policy-making and the suggestion that Intergroups "represent one of the main avenues for citizen interest groups lacking access to other institutional structures", Intergroups may raise the articulation and awareness of pluralist interests (Greenwood 2007b: 179, Greenwood 2011: 42). As a result, they may help to "redress inequalities" in terms of civil society representation in EU politics (Kohler-Koch 2011: 66-67). Anchored in the EP, Intergroups may constitute a participatory mechanism that complements models of representative democracy.

To explore EP Intergroups' potential to act as a participatory mechanism the chapter is divided into three parts: the *first* part provides a short introduction to Intergroups, including a classification of Intergroups in terms of social and functional representation. The *second* part focuses on the CSOs providing the secretariat for Intergroups in the 7th Parliament (2009-2014). By analysing who these organisations are, and what tasks they fulfil in Intergroups this part sheds light on Intergroups' potential to enhance pluralist interest representation and intermediation in EU policy-making. The *third* part offers a comparison between public hearings and Intergroups. Given that the EP provides with public hearings a formal forum to interact with civil society groups one wonders why MEPs perceive an additional need to interact with civil society in Intergroups. This chapter constitutes an analytical-empirical account of EP Intergroups. It draws on findings generated throughout extensive fieldwork in the EP during my PhD research, including 42 semi-structured interviews with MEPs, assistants, EP officials and representatives of CSOs and observational methods. For further insights, see Landorff (2019).

2. Intergroups in the European Parliament

Intergroups are not a new phenomenon in the EP. They have existed since the first direct elections of the Parliament in 1979. Amongst the first Intergroups were the Crocodile Club founded by Altiero Spinelli "together with other Federalist-minded MEPs" (European Commission 2014) in 1980 and the Kangaroo Group which started out as "an informal group of friends" (Kangaroo Group 2014) in 1979 around the British MEP Basil de Ferranti, who promoted the development of the Single Market (Corbett et al. 2011). Both Intergroups, or rather their spin-offs, have been active until today, such as the Spinelli Group that comprises of more than 110 MEPs as well as "EU experts, NGOs and think-tank representatives, politicians, academics" who advocate a "federalist approach in response to the numerous crises" the EU is facing (Spinelli Group 2016). Throughout the last seven parliamentary terms, the number and popularity of Intergroups among MEPs rose steadily, fostering an increasing formalisation and institutionalisation of Intergroups within the EP (Figure 1).

Intergroups vary substantially in their size, objectives, frequency of meetings, internal organisation and visibility. In the 7th EP, listed members of Intergroups ranged from 126 MEPs ('Climate Change, Biodiversity and Sustainable Development') to 12 MEPs ('Extreme Poverty and Human Rights') (European Parliament 2013). Moreover, 14 out of the 27 officially registered Intergroups met at least monthly or every other month, while the remaining met up to four times a year (Landorff 2019). In comparison, the transnational political groups in the EP meet during the monthly 'Group week' for two or three days, while parliamentary committee meetings take place at least twice a month for up to four successive half days during the committee weeks in Brussels (Corbett et al. 2011: 117). With regard to the internal organisation, Intergroups resemble existing official parliamentary structures, such as the parliamentary committees, as they consist of a 'Bureau' and 'Members'. The 'Bureau' steers the Intergroup and consists of chair(s) and vice-chairs. In addition, a little more than a third of the officially recognised Intergroups operated with an external organisation as their secretariat (e.g. 'Social Economy', 'Water' or 'Disability'). This aspect is discussed in more detail in the upcoming section. The remaining Intergroups were organised by the office of the MEP chairing the Intergroup (e.g. 'Urban', 'Baltic Europe' or 'Traditional Minorities, National Communities and Languages') (Landorff 2019).

Figure 1: EP Intergroups over Time: From the 2nd to the 8th EP (1984-2014)

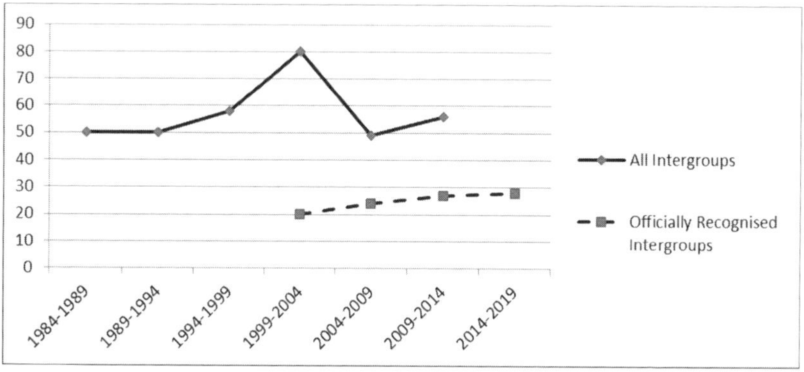

Source: Author's own figures based on Jacobs et al. (1992); Corbett et al. (2011); European Parliament (2002, 2003, 2005, 2016a).

Given the wide variation in Intergroup composition and themes, as well as the observation that "business interests are much better represented in Brussels than other societal interests" (Bouwen 2006: 277), the interesting question to explore is: What do these Intergroups and associated MEPs stand for and whose interests do they represent?

As *Table 1* shows, there are a number of Intergroups dedicated to social groups, such as minorities, older and young people. There are also a couple of Intergroups dealing with certain industries and sectors, such as the Intergroups on 'Wine, Fruits and Vegetables, Tradition and Quality Food/Viticulture' or 'Sky and Space'. There are a few Intergroups focusing on certain regions and a handful of Intergroups picking up on issues related to the common good, such as climate change ('Climate Change, Biodiversity and Sustainable Development'), human rights (e.g., 'Tibet' and 'Anti-Racism and Diversity') and culture ('Ways of Saint James/Caminos de Santiago'). Having this broad division, it does not mean that these categories are mutually exclusive. On the contrary, most issues dealt with by Intergroups on social groups relate also to human rights and the common good. Moreover, the 'Trade Union Coordination Group' may qualify as representing both a social group (workers) and certain sectors. In terms of representation this classification shows, however, that there are two broad groups among Intergroups: those dealing with general interests, including social and environmental interests or universal values (e.g. human rights), and those dealing with particular interests of certain industries, sectors and regions. These two groups appear broadly balanced among the entire population of officially recognised Intergroups. Bearing in mind that social and functional representation are viewed as critical for the legitimacy of democratic bodies, this insight constitutes an important finding with regard to Intergroups and their potential contribution to democratic governance (Marsh and Norris 1997, Norris and Franklin 1997).

Table 1 Social and Functional Representation through Intergroups

Social Representation	**Functional & Service Representation**
Social Groups	*Regions*
Ageing and Intergenerational Solidarity	Baltic Europe
Anti-Racism and Diversity	Mountains, Islands, Sparsely Populated Regions
Disability	Seas and Coastal Affairs
Extreme Poverty and Human Rights	Urban
Family, the Rights of the Child & Bioethics	Western Sahara
Lesbian, Gay, Bisexual, Transgender Rights	Tibet
Trade Union Coordination Group (Workers)	*Industries/Sectors*
Traditional National Minorities	Media
Youth Issues	New Media, Free Software and Open Information Society
Universal Values (Human Rights)	Public Services
Anti-Racism and Diversity	Sky and Space
Tibet	Small and Medium-sized Enterprise
Welfare and Conservation of Animals	Sustainable Hunting, Biodiversity, Countryside
Western Sahara	Social Economy
Climate	Trade Union Coordination Group
Climate Change, Biodiversity and Sustainable Development	Water
Culture	Wine, Fruits and Vegetables, Tradition and Quality Food/Viticulture
Ways of Saint James/Caminos de Santiago	
General Interests	Particular Interests

Source: Author's own compilation.

3. Intergroups and Civil Society Organisations

As outlined in *Table 2*, 11 out of the 27 Intergroups were supported by an external organisation that acted as the secretariat for the Intergroup.

Table 2: Intergroups and their Secretariats

Intergroup	Secretariat of the Intergroup	GIA, BIA, PO or TU[4]
Ageing and Intergenerational Solidarity	AGE Platform Europe	GIA (citizens' interests: social interests; human rights)
Climate Change, Biodiversity and Sustainable Develop-ment	European Bureau for Conservation and Development (EBCD) and International Union for Conservation of Nature (IUCN)	GIA (citizens' interests: environmental interests)
Disability	European Disability Forum (EDF)	GIA (citizens' interests: social interests; human rights)
Extreme Poverty and Human Rights	ATD[5] Fourth World	GIA (citizens' interests: social interests; human rights)
Seas and Coastal Areas	Conference of Peripheral Maritime Re-gions of Europe (CPMR)	PO (territorial interests)
Social Economy	Social Economy Europe	BIA (trade and business interests)
Sustainable Hunting, Biodiversity, Countryside Activities, and Forestry	European Federation of Associations for Hunting and Conservation (FACE) and European Landowners' Organisation (ELO)	PO/BIA (environmental interests, business interests)
Water	European Federation of National Associations of Water Services (EUREAU)	BIA (trade and business interests)
Welfare and Conservation of Animals	Eurogroup for Animals	GIA (citizens' interests: social interests, environmental interests)
Mountains, Islands and Sparsely Populated Regions	European Association of Elected Representatives from Mountain Regions (AEM)	-[6]
Anti-Racism and Diversity	European Network against Racism (ENAR)	GIA (citizens' interests: social interests, human rights)

Sources: individual websites of the Intergroups listed in Landorff (2019; European Net-work against Racism 2011); missing information on 'New Media, Free Software, Open

4 GIA – General Interest Association, BIA – Business Interest Association, PO - Profes-sional Organisation, TU – Trade Union (Kohler-Koch/Quittkat 2011: 27).

5 ATD – Agir Tous pour la Dignité, see European Commission (2016d).

6 Given that AEM is registered under the section of "Transnational associations and net-works of public regional or other sub-national authorities…" in the EC's Transparency Register it represents public actors. Hence, it does not qualify as CSO being defined as "voluntary, not-for-profit, organised at EU level and representing non-state actors" by Kohler-Koch/Quittkat (2011: 27).

Information Society', 'Family and the Rights of the Child & Bioethics', and 'Sky and Space' Intergroup.

What can we say about these organisations? What role do they play in Intergroups? Do they all qualify as civil society organisations as outlined in the EC's *White Paper on European Governance* comprising of Business Interest Associations (BIA), Trade Unions (TU), Professional Organisations (PO) as well as General Interest Associations (GIA) (European Commission 2001: 13)[7]? All of them are European associations, i.e. EU-level associations which have a seat in Brussels, Belgium. All but the European Association of Elected Representatives from Mountain Regions (AEM) are registered with the EU Transparency Register[8] under the section of NGOs, platforms and networks (European Commission 2016b). Exceptions are the European Federation of National Associations of Water Services (EUREAU) and Social Economy Europe (SEE). Both are listed as in-house lobbyists and trade/business/professional associations, or, more specifically, as trade and business associations (European Commission 2016g, 2016f). All but the European Bureau for Conservation and Development (EBCD) are registered as membership-based organisations (European Commission 2016e).

Employing the pluralist conception of civil society anchored in the EC's *White Paper*, stipulating 'representation' as the main function of civil society, the overview shows an almost balanced picture of GIAs on the one hand, and POs or BIAs on the other, providing secretarial support for the Intergroups (Kohler-Koch and Quittkat 2011: 23-24, European Commission 2001). There is, however, a slight predominance of GIAs pursuing either a public good or a universal value (Kohler-Koch and Quittkat 2011). Hence, the majority of these European associations represent citizens' interests, including environmental, social and consumer interests (Greenwood 2007a). Next to these GIAs, we see BIAs, such as the EUREAU, providing the secretariat for the Intergroup 'Water', as well as POs, such as the European Federation of Associations for Hunting and Conservation (FACE) and European Landowners' Organisation (ELO), providing the secretariat for the Intergroup 'Sustainable Hunting, Biodiversity, Countryside Activities, and Forestry'. While water is a public, common good, it is also a particular business that is represented by the EUREAU. Similarly, the FACE and ELO are not categorised as GIA despite their general interest in environmental sustainability, as they do represent particular professions and their particular interests (e.g. those of hunters and landowners).

7 General interest is associated with "the pursuit of a public good (such as social stability, environmental sustainability) or a universal value (such as human rights)" (Kohler-Koch/Quittkat 2011: 27).

8 The AEM got registered as "Organisations representing local, regional and municipal authorities, other public or mixed entities, etc." and more precisely as "Transnational associations and networks of public regional or other sub-national authorities" by November 24, 2016, see European Commission (2016c).

Consequently, in terms of representation, it is predominantly European associations representing citizens' interests and pursuing a common good (including social, environmental interests and human rights) that provide secretariats for Intergroups. In terms of access to other EU institutional structures, the EU Transparency Register also shows that, except for the European Network against Racism (ENAR), all identified GIAs do participate in other forms of civil society dialogue, such as expert groups of the European Commission (e.g. Eurogroup for Animals, AGE Platform Europe) or consultative committees (e.g. the ATD Fourth World, the EDF) (European Commission 2016b). These findings support the initial statement that Intergroups as a participatory mechanism may help to balance the numerical superiority of business interests by fostering predominantly the representation and involvement of societal interests in EU policy-making. However, focusing on the CSOs providing the secretariat for an Intergroup it is not necessarily citizen interest groups lacking access to other EU institutions, as suggested by Greenwood (2011)[9].

But what does it mean to provide the secretariat for an Intergroup? In the case of the Eurogroup for Animals that provides the secretariat for the Intergroup 'Welfare and Conservation of Animals', it is clear that the tasks are quite comprehensive, ranging from the organisation of Intergroup meetings and events (including the invitation of guests), to the set-up of the Intergroup agenda and the coordination of Intergroup actions (see Table 3). Hence, the Eurogroup for Animals has a substantial role in the organisation and management of the Intergroup.

The comparison with other Intergroups having an external secretariat (e.g. 'Climate Change, Biodiversity and Sustainable Development' and EBCD) reveals similar patterns and tasks (European Bureau for Conservation & Development 2012, 2014). However, my fieldwork suggests that, in terms of the Intergroup activities, the Eurogroup at date is one of the most active and organised secretariats. One reason for this may be that the Eurogroup for Animals has provided the secretariat for the Intergroup since its establishment in 1983, displaying long-term commitment and experience.

Beyond the organisation of meetings, the external organisations also provide Intergroups with logistics, visibility, such as a website and posters inside the EP premises announcing Intergroup meetings[10], as well as with contacts to guest speakers. Comparing those Intergroups run by external secretariats with

---

9 My fieldwork in the EP has also shown that Intergroup meetings are attended by a variety of CSOs, and thus citizen interest groups. Among these, there may be CSOs lacking access to other EU institutions. To substantiate this claim, a more systematic and comprehensive analysis of all civil society groups attending Intergroup meetings would be needed.

10 See e.g. Intergroups 'Welfare and Conservation of Animals', 'Climate Change, Biodiversity and Sustainable Development' and 'Water' observed during fieldwork in the EP in September and October 2012, March and May 2013 (Landorff 2019).

those organised by the office of an MEP (i.e. the Intergroup chair), the former have a higher visibility than the latter (Landorff 2019). Hence, being supported by an external organisation provides for more visibility.

Table 3 Tasks of Civil Society Organisations in Intergroups

Tasks of the Eurogroup for Animals
1. The organisation of the monthly Intergroup meetings in Strasbourg or of any other events.
2. The invitation of guest speakers for Intergroup meetings or for other events.
3. The setting of the Intergroup meeting agenda in accordance with the rules (*see* point 5).
4. The coordination of follow-up actions agreed during Intergroup meetings.
5. Assistance to the President with correspondence and any additional specific requests.
6. Preparation and distribution of Intergroup meeting agendas.
7. The regular update of the Intergroup website.

Source: Intergroup on Welfare and Conservation of Animals (2013: 4)

Given that the EP provides with public hearings an official format for MEPs and sectoral experts to enter into dialogue (Corbett et al. 2011), one wonders why parliamentarians perceive an additional need to interact with civil society in Intergroups. On the basis of interviews with civil society representatives attending Intergroup meetings and providing secretarial support, the following section provides a brief discussion of the advantages of Intergroups over public hearings[11].

4. Advantages of Intergroups over Public Hearings

Initially, public hearings were organised within the framework of parliamentary committees for the purpose of providing parliamentarians with the opportunity to seek expertise and to enter into dialogue with sectoral experts (Corbett et al. 2011). In total, 501 public hearings were organised during the 7th EP (European Parliament 2016b). The number of hearings organised by individual committees differs significantly. At best up to nine hearings per year were organised by a parliamentary committee (see the committee on Civil Liberties, Justice and Home Affairs [LIBE]) (European Parliament 2016b). At worst, only one hearing per year was organised (see the committee on Agriculture and Rural Development [AGRI]) (European Parliament 2016b). Interviewees

11 See interviews conducted with representatives of CSOs attending the Intergroups 'Welfare and Conservation of Animals', 'Trade Union', 'Climate Change, Biodiversity and Sustainable Development', 'Viticulture' and 'Extreme Poverty and Human Rights' (Landorff 2019).

pointed to two major advantages of Intergroups over public hearings which are presented in the following sections.

Easier, more exclusive and more frequent access

In the interviews, CSO representatives referred to an easier, more exclusive and more frequent access to MEPs across political groups and committees who share interests in relevant Intergroup topics[12]. Therefore, Intergroups represent *one* forum that gathers all interested stakeholders on a very specific subject of interest and, more importantly, connects these stakeholders with key legislative players, such as rapporteurs who present (draft) parliamentary reports during Intergroup meetings. By contrast, hearings are organised on a range of topics not necessarily covering the specific interests of the CSOs engaging in Intergroups[13].

In terms of Intergroups providing easier access to MEPs, interviewees argued that CSOs have to be invited to public hearings by the organising parliamentary committee[14]. By contrast, CSOs liaising with an Intergroup, such as the European Trade Union Confederation (ETUC) with the 'Trade Union Coordination Group'[15], or providing the secretariat for the Intergroup, such as the Eurogroup for Animals, have automatically a platform to speak, and thus have immediately access to MEPs through the Intergroup. Regarding the 'Trade Union Coordination Group', this access constitutes also a more exclusive access to MEPs by trade unions. As an interviewee argued, in the case that a parliamentary committee organises a hearing "on a topic […] the ETUC might be invited along with any other stakeholder"[16]. In the Intergroup, on the contrary, they "have a joint stake in relation […] with […] the chairs of the Intergroup"[17]. Consequently, it is only ETUC representatives and occasionally representatives of the ETUC's affiliates at the national and European level who attend Intergroup meetings. There are no other external guests. From this perspective, the Intergroup constitutes an exclusive participatory mechanism in terms of representing and including ETUC representatives only, and being restricted to MEPs. Looking again at the CSOs providing the secretariat for an Intergroup (e.g. the EBCD or Social Economy Europe) it shows that these

12 Interviews CSO 3, 5, 6.

13 Interviews CSO 2, 6.

14 Interviews CSO 2, 4, 5.

15 The secretariat of the Intergroup was provided by the Group of the European People's Party in the European Parliament (EPP-ED) and the Progressive Alliance of Socialists and Democrats (S&D) during the 7th EP (Landorff 2019).

16 Interview CSO 5.

17 Interview CSO 5.

CSOs regularly present at Intergroup meetings[18]. For instance, one part of the meetings of the Intergroup on 'Welfare and Conservation of Animals' is always reserved for a presentation by a representative of the Eurogroup for Animals, and thus provides them with a permanent and regular platform to speak[19]. They are, however, one speaker among others, one voice among other civil society actors in Intergroup meetings.

In addition, interviewees stated to gain more frequent access to MEPs through the Intergroup than through public hearings[20]. As previously addressed, the number of hearings organised by a parliamentary committee ranges from one to nine per year. By contrast, more than half of the officially recognised Intergroups conduct their meetings monthly or every other month. As a result, the Intergroup on 'Welfare and Conservation of Animals' organised 52 meetings in the 7th EP, the Intergroup on 'Traditional Minorities, National Communities and Languages' 53 meetings, and thus 53 opportunities for interested CSOs to interact with MEPs. While the AGRI committee organised only six hearings during the entire 7th EP, the Intergroup 'Wine, Fruits and Vegetables, Tradition and Quality Food/Viticulture', gathering interested MEPs as well as representatives of the wine industry, organised 21 meetings during the 7th term (from September 2009 to April 2014) (Landorff 2019). Hence, in doing so these Intergroups provide interested CSOs with more frequent opportunities to interact with MEPs on the premises of the EP than public hearings do.

More suited for dialogue

Besides an easier and more frequent access to MEPs, interviewees perceived Intergroup meetings as the better opportunity for dialogue with interested parliamentarians. Hearings were described as very formal, as being conducted under time pressure allowing invited CSOs to issue only short statements, and being constrained in terms of the meetings' agenda[21]. By contrast, the format of the Intergroup provides "more of an opportunity for a dialogue"[22] and in-depth discussion with MEPs that has an influence on parliamentary reports. Furthermore, interviewees observed that "the freedom of speech is not the same" in public hearings and in Intergroups[23]. This observation is attributed to

18 This insight is based on the analysis of a limited number of minutes available for the 11 Intergroups with an external secretariat in the 7th EP.
19 Interview CSO 1.
20 Interview CSO 6.
21 Interviews CSO 2, 5.
22 Interviews CSO 2, 5.
23 Interview CSO 3.

the fact that public hearings are official EP organs while Intergroups are described as informal gatherings[24]. Moreover, members of the Intergroup share an interest in the specific topic. These findings point to the deliberative aspect of Intergroups and constitute an important insight given that civil society's contribution to democratic governance is perceived, inter alia, in terms of better policy-making that is achieved "thanks to more extensive deliberation" (Kohler-Koch and Quittkat 2013: 174). Given these empirical insights, Intergroups have the potential to facilitate and nurture dialogue, political discussion and communication between MEPs and CSO representatives in the Parliament. As a result, they increase the awareness and articulation of pluralist interests as well as their involvement in EU policy formulation. This, however, does not mean that Intergroups are the only points of access to MEPs and the EP for CSOs. Interviewees confirmed that they are also invited to public hearings and that they attend hearings within EP committees[25]. In particular, the trade union representatives cultivate and maintain individual contacts to MEPs at their disposal and make use of these to initiate follow-up actions after they presented their position or heard the position of MEPs in Intergroup meetings[26]. In this context, Intergroups are perceived as complementary participatory mechanism to public hearings.

5. Conclusion

This contribution looked at the participation of civil society in EP Intergroups. Assuming civil society's positive contribution to EU democratic governance, this chapter explored Intergroups' potential to act as a participatory mechanism that fosters democratic input legitimacy (e.g. pluralist interest representation and intermediation). Focusing on the Intergroups of the 7th EP (2009-2014) and the CSOs providing secretarial support for these informal groupings, this contribution provides three major insights: *first*, Intergroups represent in equal parts social and functional/sectoral groups. This is of key importance with regard to the EP's democratic legitimacy. *Second*, in terms of their internal organisation Intergroups cooperate predominantly with General Interest Associations (GIAs) as their secretariats. As these GIAs represent citizens' interests, including human rights, social and environmental interests, Intergroups can be perceived as participatory mechanism that helps to balance the numerical su-

24 Interview CSO 3.
25 Interviews CSO 1, 2, 3.
26 Interview CSO 5.

periority of business interests represented in EU policy-making. *Third*, Intergroups provide those CSOs acting as the secretariat with a regular and permanent platform to speak in the EP. The comparison with public hearings has, however, shown that Intergroups do not constitute the only channel for these CSOs to the Parliament. As a result, Intergroups are perceived as a complementary tool providing easier and more frequent access to the EP, and being better suited for dialogue between MEPs and civil society. By providing CSOs that are in one way or another already involved in the EU's civil dialogue with an additional venue in the EP, Intergroups strengthen existing EU-civil society relations. In sum, this chapter finds that Intergroups do foster the involvement, representation and voice of societal interests in EU policy-making. Consequently, they make an important contribution to democratic input legitimacy, and constitute one participatory mechanism to counter the increasing trend of distrust and dissatisfaction among EU citizens in EU politics.

References

Bouwen, Pieter (2003): A Theoretical and Empirical Study of Corporate Lobbying in the European Parliament. In: European Integration Online Papers (EioP) 7 (http://eiop.or.at/eiop/texte/2003-011a.htm; access 20.04.2010].

Bouwen, Pieter (2006): Business interest representation and legitimate European governance. In: Smismans, Stijn (ed.): Civil Society and Legitimate European Governance. Cheltenham: Edward Elgar Publishing, pp. 277-296.

Corbett, Richard/Jacobs, Francis/Shackleton, Michael (2011): The European Parliament. London: John Harper Publishing.

Corbett, Richard/Jacobs, Francis/Neville, Darren (2016): The European Parliament. London: John Harper Publishing.

Eising, Rainer (2016): Interest Groups and the European Union. In: Cini, Michelle/Pérez-Solórzano Borragán, Nieves: European Union Politics. Oxford: Oxford University Press, pp. 179-194.

European Bureau for Conversation & Development (2012, 2014): EP Intergroup CCBSD. General Information (http://www.ebcd.org/en/EP_Intergroup_CCBSD/; access 08.03.2012, 13.06.2014).

European Commission (2001): European governance. A white paper. COM (2001) 428 Final – Official Journal C 287, 12 October 2001. Brussels.

European Commission (2014): Altiero Spinelli. An Unrelenting Federalist (http://europa.eu/about-eu/eu-history/founding-fathers/pdf/altiero_spinelli_en.pdf; access 03.06.2014).

European Commission (2016a): Standard Eurobarometer 85. Public Opinion in the European Union. Standard Eurobarometer 85 ed. Brussels: European Union.

European Commission (2016b): Transparency Register (http://ec.europa.eu/transparencyregister/public/homePage.do; access 10.01.2016).

European Commission (2016c): Transparency Register. Search the Register - Association Européenne des Élus de Montagne (http://ec.europa.eu/transparencyregister/public/consultation/displaylobbyist.do?id=124970724599-06; access 20.12.2016).

European Commission (2016d): Transparency Register. Search the Register - ATD Quart Monde (http://ec.europa.eu/transparencyregister/public/consultation/displaylobbyist.do?id=14200875377-44; access 20.12.2016).

European Commission (2016e): Transparency Register. Search the Register - European Bureau for Conservation and Development (http://ec.europa.eu/transparencyregister/public/consultation/displaylobbyist.do?id=704526524109-47; access 20.12.2016).

European Commission (2016f): Transparency Register. Search the Register - European Federation of National Associations of Water Services (http://ec.europa.eu/transparencyregister/public/consultation/displaylobbyist.do?id=39299129772-62; access 16.01.2016).

European Commission (2016g): Transparency Register. Search the Register - Social Economy Europe (http://ec.europa.eu/transparencyregister/public/consultation/displaylobbyist.do?id=078855521139-42; access 20.12.2016).

European Network against Racism (2011): Annual Report 2011 (http://cms.horus.be/files/99935/MediaArchive/publications/AnnualReport_LR%20final.pdf; access 31.03.2019).

European Parliament (2002): Activities. 12/A-2002 – Bulletin. Brussels: European Parliament Directorate for the Planning of Parliamentary Business.

European Parliament (2003): Activities: 03/A-2003 – Bulletin. Brussels: European Parliament Directorate for the Planning of Parliamentary Business.

European Parliament (2005): Activities. 08/A-2005 – Bulletin. Brussels: European Parliament Directorate for the Planning of Parliamentary Business.

European Parliament (2013): About Parliament. Organisation and Work - Intergroups (http://www.europarl.europa.eu./aboutparliament/en/00c9d93c87/Intergroups.html; access 24.01.2013).

European Parliament (2016a): About Parliament. Organisation and Rules - Intergroups (http://www.europarl.europa.eu/aboutparliament/en/20150201PVL 000 10/Organisation-and-rules; access 05.04.2016).

European Parliament (2016b): Committee. Archives - Hearings and Publications (http://www.europarl.europa.eu/parlArchives/comArch/comDocSearch/documentSearch.do; access 02.12.2016).

Garcia, Luis B./Del Río Villar, Susana (2012): The ECI as a Democratic Innovation: Analysing its Ability to Promote Inclusion, Empowerment and Responsiveness in European Civil Society. In: Perspectives on European Politics and Society 13, 3, pp. 312-324.

Greenwood, Justin (2007a): Interest Representation in the European Union. Basingstoke: Palgrave Macmillan.

Greenwood, Justin (2007b): Organized Civil Society and Input Legitimacy in the EU. In: DeBardeleben, Joan/Hurrelmann, Achim (eds.): Democratic Dilemmas of Multilevel Governance: Legitimacy, Representation and Accountability in the European Union. Basingstoke: Palgrave Macmillan, pp. 177-194.

Greenwood, Justin (2011): Interest Representation in the European Union. Basingstoke: Palgrave Macmillan.

Greenwood, Justin (2012): The European Citizens' Initiative and EU Civil Society Organisations. In: Perspectives on European Politics and Society 13, 3, pp. 325-336.

Intergroup on Welfare and Conversation of Animals (2013): Rules of Procedure (http://www.animalwelfareintergroup.eu/wp-content/uploads/2013/01/Rules-of-procedure-final-11-01-2013.pdf; access 31.05.2014).

Jacobs, Francis/Corbett, Richard/Shackleton, Michael (1992): The European Parliament. Harlow: Longman Current Affairs.

Kangaroo Group (2014): Who We Are. Origin (http://www.kangaroogroup.eu/E/032_origin_D.lasso; access 03.06.2014).

Kohler-Koch, Beate (2007): The Organization of Interests and Democracy in the European Union. In: Kohler-Koch, Beate/Rittberger, Berthold (eds.): Debating the Democratic Legitimacy of the European Union. Lanham et al.: Rowman & Littlefield Publishers, pp. 255-271.

Kohler-Koch, Beate (2010): Civil society and EU democracy. 'Astroturf' representation? In: Journal of European Public Policy 17, 1, pp. 100-116.

Kohler-Koch, Beate (2011): The Three Worlds of 'European Civil Society': What Role for Civil Society for What Kind of Europe? In: Liebert, Ulrike/Trenz, Hans-Jörg (eds.): The New Politics of European Civil Society. London: Routledge, pp. 57-72.

Kohler-Koch, Beate/Finke, Barbara (2007): The Institutional Shaping of EU-Society Relations. A Contribution to Democracy via Participation? In: Journal of Civil Society 3, 3, pp. 205-221.

Kohler-Koch, Beate/Quittkat, Christine (2011): What is 'civil society' and who represents it in the European Union? In: Liebert, Ulrike/Trenz, Hans-Jörg (eds.): The New Politics of European Civil Society. London: Routledge, pp. 19-39.

Kohler-Koch, Beate/Quittkat, Christine (2013): De-Mystification of Participatory Democracy: EU-Governance and Civil Society. Oxford: Oxford University Press.

Landorff, Laura (2019): Inside European Parliament Politics: Informality, Information and Intergroups. Cham: Palgrave Macmillan

Liebert, Ulrike (1995): Parliamentary Lobby Regimes. In: Döring, Herbert (ed.): Parliaments and Majority Rule in Western Europe. Frankfurt/Main: Campus, pp. 407-447.

Liebert, Ulrike/Trenz, Hans-Jörg (2011): The 'new politics of European civil society'. Conceptual, normative and empirical issues. In: Liebert, Ulrike/Trenz, Hans-Jörg (eds.): The New Politics of European Civil Society. 6 ed. London: Routledge, pp. 1-16.

Marsh, Michael/Norris, Pippa (1997): Political Representation in the European Parliament. In: European Journal of Political Research 32, pp. 153-164.
Mény, Yves (2009): Building Parliament. 50 Years of European Parliament History 1958-2008. Luxembourg: Office for Official Publications of the European Communities.
Nedergaard, Peter/Jensen, Mads D. (2014): The Anatomy of Intergroups. Network Governance in the Political Engine Room of the European Parliament. In: Policy Studies 35, 2, pp. 1-19.
Norris, Pippa/Franklin, Mark (1997): Social Representation. In: European Journal of Political Research 32, pp. 185-210.
Spinelli Group (2016): MEP Spinelli Group (http://www.spinelligroup.eu/mep-spinelli-group; access 10.01.2016).

19. What democracy for the European Political Union? Lessons for a European party system

Adriana Ciancio

1. Introduction

This chapter develops the argument that a genuine system of mature European parties is needed as a key for building a true Political Union, one that aims at overcoming the public distrust that has grown towards the EU and its institutions and among the peoples of Europe in times of crisis.

Actually, the aim of transforming the EU from an originally purely economic community into a full-blown political union is a long-lasting process. It started with the Maastricht Treaty and the introduction of the European citizenship and was deepened with the adoption of the Lisbon Treaty. Indeed, the EU is now shaped as a truly political union. Even if still in an embryonic form, its legal and institutional profile is sufficiently defined, although intentionally without any "federalist" reference (Weiler 2003: 511 ff.): It is provided with common institutions and related attributions and a defined balance of powers (legislative, executive and judicial), even if according to a scheme of collaboration rather than of separation; competences are assigned separately from those of the Member States; an original system of sources of law is established that is, moreover, destined to prevail over national ones. Even more upstream, European case law ensures uniformity in the interpretation of the law through preliminary ruling ex Art. 267 TEU, essential for the very process of, at least, judicial integration (Romboli 2014: 431 ff.). Above all, there is a Charter of Fundamental Rights that could be considered the 'core' of the current constitutional framework of the EU (De Vergottini 2009), especially after the Treaty of Lisbon came into force giving the Charter the same efficacy as the Treaty itself. Finally, Rule 2 of the same Treaty, which declares that the Union is based on some common principles (among others: democracy, human dignity, rule of law, equality, protection of human rights, pluralism, justice and solidarity), demonstrates that the EU is increasingly looking at itself as a Union of shared values rather than just a simple single market as it initially did (Caravita 2015: 15 ff.).

However, this process has not yet been completed due to the European peoples' trouble in understanding, let alone living fully their own status of European citizenship, alongside the traditional citizenships of their respective countries of origin. There is widespread scepticism towards the process of political integration as it is perceived by European citizens, that led in May 2014 to the most anti-European Parliament ever elected in history since 1979. This was due, in part, to the anti-European propaganda often pursued at the national level by political elites and counter-elites, at times also supported by the mass media (Magone, 2015: 33 ff.). This comes in addition to the recent increase in mutual distrust between citizens of countries that are still economically stable and those running large budget deficits, along with complaints from citizens of both (although for opposite reasons) about "technocratic" decision-making by "Brussels" (Ciancio 2014: 162 ff.; Murray/Longo 2015: 59 ff.).

Given these predicaments, one cannot but admit that it is possible to perceive a manifest lack of consent towards the project of ever closer political integration among the European peoples, a lack of consent that is in stark contrast with the existing "sophisticated" legal institutional system that defines the EU as a – however embryonic – political union.

2. Issues of democracy

The above-mentioned 'euroscepticism' is probably a result of the notorious, ever-lasting lack of democratic legitimacy of the Union in the new and different shapes it has taken after the entry into force of the Treaty of Lisbon (Manzella 2014: 5 ff.). Indeed, the Lisbon Treaty extended the European Parliament's legislative and political control powers (Fasone/Lupo 2012: 329 ff.), as well as the national parliamentary participation in European decision-making (Lupo 2014: 101 ff.) Despite these changes, European politics still lacks its own 'natural interface' between voters and institutions. This function should be provided by European parties that convey the political will of the electorate within the decision making bodies according to their respective particular views of the general interests of the Union. Conversely, the still-lingering issue is the profound "detachment" between European society and the Union's institutions (Grimm, 2014: 2).

A distance largely explained by what could be defined a mere "formal" representation of the EP (Ciancio 2016a: 8), due to suffrage's direct expression (Kelsen 1981: 124 ff.), but unsupported by a so-to-say "substantial" representation.

The argument I want to develop here is premised on my conviction that this issue of citizens' detachment from the EU will persist as long as people's incentives to participate in the vote and their identification with what this vote stands for in terms of legitimization will be managed by national parties and not be the prerogative of parties of a true European scope. Indeed, still the most recent elections for the European Parliament have been almost entirely entrusted to national parties. Actually, the anomaly therefore persists that voters are *European* citizens that are entitled to appoint a *European* institution, but that this appointment is mediated by parties of essentially *national* dimension acting as middlemen (Ciancio 2016b).

Furthermore, since MEPs are proposed and supported by national parties, it is difficult for them to exercise their mandate in line with the primary general interests of the Union. They are, therefore, driven to take charge of local political interests and in any case of State needs (Goulard/Monti 2012: 43 ff.). This notwithstanding the fact that the Treaty of Lisbon has changed their mandate, making them direct representatives of the Union citizens (Article 10.2 and 14.2 TEU) and not any more "representatives of the peoples of the States brought together in the Community", as previously laid down by the Treaty establishing the European Community (Article 189.1 TCE). Moreover, national parties often cannot resist the temptation to use the European Parliament campaigns as another opportunity to argue issues of strictly local interest and little relevant to the big issues that are currently affecting the Union's very existence as a whole (Offe 2015: 81 ff.).

Hence it is difficult for the citizens-electors to grasp the true supranational dimension of their vote. Elections are the main instrument of democratic participation, but the current functioning of European elections creates an unbridgeable gap between the electorate and the European Parliament, exacerbating the fact that Union citizens are still unable to fully take part in European political debates.

3. The role of European parties in political integration

The peculiar anomaly that the Union citizens' vote for their European representative assembly is mediated by national parties hampers the process of political integration in Europe considerably. This is because in the run-up to the European elections, the different political visions and interests concerning Europe itself, its policies, its role in the global context, its future, etc. are not fully presented to the electorate. Rather, election campaigns are played first and foremost in the national political arenas, leaving voters ignorant about the actual Union policies that would result from their votes. This state of play hinders the creation of a "European political awareness", as was hoped for by the Treaties, which ever since Maastricht have identified European parties as the privileged channels to express the political wills of Union citizens (Tsatsos 1995).

And yet, it does not seem possible today to refer to European political parties already as a true "system" (Niedermayer 1983; Hix 1993). This would entail a structured and stable party set-up with defined ideological and organizational identities and characteristics and a sufficient autonomy from national parties (Allegri 2013).

This statement is supported by considerations regarding the creation of European parties, which did not sprout from spontaneous phenomena of social aggregation around common ideas and political objectives; rather they formed as "extra-parliamentary projections" from political groups within the European Parliament, that is from reunions of representatives from different national parties with similar political profiles (Hix/Lord 1997: 77 ff.; Ciancio 2007: 153 ff.; Lelieveldt/Princen 2011: 151 ff.). This is to say that European parties are characterized by "internal" – *id est*, parliamentary – origins rather than representing "social outcomes", (Duverger 1954). Indeed, their creation has featured a "party-parliamentary group" dynamic that brings them close to the British historical experience (Tripaldi/Teklè 2001: 217 ff.) and that differs from the typical formation of most representative democratic systems on the European continent.

Actually, some progress has been made towards the consolidation of a true European-party system as shown by the elections of 2014, through the single nominations to the Commission presidency made by the political entities identified as the main European political families (Cartabia 2014). However, despite these efforts, the leading candidates remained largely unknown to the majority of Union citizens, and for many voters even the affiliation of the national parties to the European families was unclear.

This fact leads us to the main issue regarding the actual role that a genuinely European party-system is supposed to play for shaping the EU as a true political (no longer solely economic) community that is grounded on the principles of representative democracy, as laid down by Art. 10 TEU. This article – as it is well-known – stresses the role of the Parliament as the venue of citizens' direct representation (Art. 10 par.1 TEU), even if it also provides for the indirect (but however democratic) legitimacy of the Councils (European and of the EU, Art. 10 par. 2 TEU). Moreover, it states citizens' right to take part in the democratic life of the Union (Art. 10, par. 3), tasking European parties with the creation of political awareness and identifying them as the privileged channel to express citizens' will (Art. 10, par. 4).

And yet, these provisions and, more in general, the whole legal system established by the Lisbon Treaty still look insufficient to help the Union take roots in a deep sense of common political belonging, as easily ascertained among European citizens. This statement can be easily verified; it suffices to look at the genuine hostility that many EU citizens expose towards European integration, and moreover, their growing support for rising nationalism and populism in domestic elections. These facts lead to doubts that the mere force of legal provisions would be sufficient to make European citizens share that *idem sentire*, the feeling of a shared identity that arguably is a necessary condition for the establishment of any political community.

Therefore, we can assume that the consolidation of a structured system of European parties that have real bonds with society is a favourable condition for creating that sense of common identity among European citizens that is necessary for transposing national identities into a wider supranational context. Conversely, lacking any European-wide political associations that effectively function first and foremost as tools to foster and to receive citizens' political will and to represent it within the institutions, it will be difficult to identify alternative integration mechanisms capable of functioning despite the lack of natural cultural identifiers, e.g. a common language (Grimm 1996: 360 ff.), for promoting a general sense of belonging to the Union. Therefore, European Parties deserve being acknowledged as necessary mechanisms for political integration.

However, it should be mentioned that at present at the European level parties do not seem sufficiently involved in the setting of the political agenda (Hix 1995). National parties traditionally have been the main makers of economic and social planning at the national level. At the supranational level, by contrast, this essential political function appears to be lacking. On the one hand, big decisions are taken elsewhere – either solved case by case by judges or regulated differently by national systems. On the other hand, macroeconomic decisions in practice are left to the ECB, an independent and, therefore, apolitical agency by definition (Ciancio 2015a). Given these constraints, the would-be European parties cannot develop their capacity for political identification, mobilization and integration. Even appointments to the European Court of Justice and to the Commission seem to be entrusted to the strongest national party at the time within each Member State (Bardi-Pizzimenti 2013).

To sum up, European political parties should be expected to accomplish the essential task of what has been called "performances of political unity" (Ridola 2009: 6), aimed at further contributing to the creation of a European political awareness. More generally, European parties should learn to perform a task defined here as "political-cultural mediation" between institutions and citizens. This means that European parties would develop and use their genuine societal roots for identifying citizens' views, aggregating constituency interests and representing them in the European decision-making processes.

4. Towards a true European party system

In promoting European political unity, each European political party will be different regarding the emphasis on and specific mix of "partial" political ideas of Europe it endorses and around which it seeks to mobilise popular consent. At the same time, all European parties will be expected to support the idea of the EU as a true political Union more generally. They will be called to work for promoting the "effectiveness" of the European political project. This means they will exhibit *spontaneous and generalized adherence to the Union's legal system and its values*, beyond the effectiveness through judicial means that have represented an important channel for integration thus far (Ruggeri 2014: 473 ff.; 2016: ff ss.).

The provisions of the EP's Rules of procedure reinforce the attribution of these tasks to the European political parties (Chapter IV). These self-organizational rules refer to internal groups within the European Parliament as "political groups" that are differentiated from parliamentary "groupings" of members who join for only "technical" reasons, but lack any political affinity. Indeed, the EP's regulations have always required MEP's to share "political affinities" in order to constitute a "political group" (Baroncelli 2001: 14 ff.; 2014: 104 ff.), in addition to quantitative and transnational requirements (Art. 30 Reg.). Actually, according to the interpretations established by European case-law[1], only shared ideologies and program affinities, even if generic and not excessively strict, allow EP groups to transcend local political particularisms and, in addition to the exercise of more traditional parliamentary functions, to constitute privileged "venues" for carrying out significant political tasks (Ciancio 2008: 76 ff.). These party political European tasks consist in providing venues for representing and aggregating national political parties and, moreover, for creating supra-national parties capable of promoting European integration as required by the Treaties.

To that end, a roadmap for consolidating a genuine European system of mature political parties is paramount. This should focus on a revision of the "Statute and Funding of European Political Parties" aimed at setting up the conditions for a true unitary model of European parties that are independent from national parties' structures (and limits) but favourable of supranational political groups engaged with the elections for the European Parliament.

It is not necessary to retrace here in detail the events that led to the approval of the provisions regulating the financing of European parties (Grasso 2008: 623 ff.). It should suffice to highlight that the regulation born in 2003 with the

1 Court of First Instance, sez. III expanded session, 2-10-, joined cases T-222/99, T-327/99 e T-329/99, Martinez – De Gaulle – Front National- Bonino et al v. European Parliament, in Racc. giur., 2001, II-2823.

ambitious name "statute"[2] was a far cry from a true statutory scheme shared by all European political entities. Instead of featuring the typical content of party statutes, these provisions have initially pursued the more limited aim to define the requirements that supranational political associations must comply with in order to get the status of "European parties" and to become eligible for financing from the European budget (Martinelli 2004: 418; Grasso 2010: 620 ff.). The 2003 norms showed the subordination of the "European party" under the structures established by political parties within the national systems (Porras Ramírez 2016: 3). Notwithstanding this fact, it is possible to read the original regulation as a push towards institutionalizing supranational political groupings (Lippolis 2002: 959). This started the process of consolidating a system of European political parties independently from national political groupings (Fusacchia 2006: 88), achieved mainly through the prohibition to use funds provided to European parties for financing national ones (art. 7).

This purpose was further advanced through the first amendments to the European party statutes in 2007. The principle goal of the new rules on the activity and financing of European parties[3] (Ciancio 2009: 19 ff.) was to make European political parties "active players in choices of European politics, connected to all levels of society and open to the effective participation of citizens not only through European elections, but also in all other aspects of European political life"[4]. In view of these explicit aims, it is worth assessing the amendment allowing European parties to use EU contributions to finance activities connected with the campaigns for European elections (Art. 8, III co), an option that was prohibited before. Hence, it is easy to grasp the innovative meaning of the provision, which for the first time considers parties with a European scope as entities capable of autonomously engaging with the elections for the European Parliament, together with and in addition to national parties.

Also worth noting among the 2007 amendments is that "European political foundations"[5] are expected to work together with parties in order to accomplish their political tasks of carrying out training and information activities, such as "activities of observation, assessment and enrichment of the debate on European public policies and the European integration process", as well as promoting actions concerning "issues of European public policies", including semi-

2 Reg. EC No. 2004/2003, 4 November 2003, in OJ L 297, 15.11.2003, p. 1.

3 Reg. EC No.1524/2007, 18 December 2007, in OJ L 343, 27.12.2007, p. 5.

4 Point 2 of the Chapter on "The political contest", cit.

5 Art. 1 Reg. 1524/2007, amending art. 2 of the 2003 Regulation, adding point 4 which identifies as the political foundation at the European level "an entity or network of entities" with legal personality in one Member State, "affiliated with a political party at the European level, which through its activities, within the aims and fundamental values pursued by the European Union, underpins and complements the objectives of the political party at European level".

nars, training events and conferences with the purpose to "promote democracy" (Gagatek/Van Hecke 2011). It is significant that European political foundations are considered entitled to apply for financial contributions exclusively if they are associated with existing European parties, and by doing so contribute to strengthening the latters' political and so-to-say cultural mediation role.

Indeed, the norms regulating European party financing constitute an important step in the direction of providing the European political debate with an autonomous dimension, different from the local and national ones (Statham/Trenz 2013). Such a transformation may occur through the intervention of political groupings that are institutionalized at the supranational level, tasked to perform as the key actors of European elections and, more in general, required to live up to the mandate that the Treaties ascribed to them, i.e. articulating the voice of the European citizens, representing their political demands, enabling their effective participation and thus contributing to the consolidation of European democracy.

From this perspective, the most important changes appear to be the most recent amendments and newly drafted rules for the "Statute and Funding of European Parties" that were approved in 2014[6] and entered into force on January 1st 2017 (Allegri 2014; Savoia 2014: 10 ff.). The most significant amendment consists of the possibility for eligible political groupings to obtain, upon registration with the European Parliament, a European legal personality and a related common *status*. Through the acquisition of a single status based on Union law political parties are conferred independence from the national jurisdictions that have so far influenced their structure and defined their limits.[7] Thus, European parties are finally enabled to effectively deliver on the abovementioned tasks assigned them by the Treaties.

Indeed, only an electoral competition that is truly managed by supranational political parties will realistically achieve the objective of gathering citizens' consent on European issues, programs, policies and ideals, thereby shaping their "European awareness".

In any case, it was widely argued that even the most recent amendments will not fully accomplish these desired objectives without finally adopting a uniform electoral procedure, according to the first part of Art. 223.1 TFEU (Vigevani 2003: 175 ff.; Raspadori 2009: 121 ff.; Habermas 2014)[8]. This would allow electoral constituencies of supranational scope to present unitary lists of candidates committed to common political programs and centred on strictly European objectives and issues. Such an organization would foster public debate at a supranational level and truly structure parliamentary elections

6 Reg. Eu, Euratom No. 1141/2014, 22 October 2014, in OJ L 317, 04.11.2014, p. 1.

7 As ultimately stressed by futher amendments approved in 2018 in order to foster the transnational character of EU parties.

8 We refer to a not-new provision, preceded by a similar rule already stated in art. 190.4 TCE.

as "genuinely" European choices. It would also constitute a further step towards the ultimate goal of consolidating a real system of European parties that are sufficiently autonomous from national ones (Lippolis 2002: 956 ff.).

However, considering the actual developments, up until now the maximum achievement has been the 2002 reform of the 1976 European Electoral Act with the mere introduction of some common general principles, among which the main one concerns the adoption of the proportional method by all Member States (Pasquinucci 2014: 53 ff.). In 1998 the EP proposed to attribute a percentage of seats to a single electoral district made up by the whole Union's territory and based on the proportional method. Thc proposal was declined by the Council which preferred to have Member States adopt only a common electoral method in the procedure for the EP elections, thereby making the alternative (already laid down by the Maastricht Treaty and today by the last part of art. 223.1 TFUE) prevail that elections "according to principles common to all member states" will respect the diversity of the single national laws.

Indeed, in November 2015[9] the European Parliament decided to initiate once again the reform of its electoral procedure. Well ahead of the 2019 elections, its reforms aimed at "enhancing the democratic and transnational dimension of the European elections and the democratic legitimacy of the Union decision-making process, reinforcing the concept of citizenship of the Union and electoral equality, promoting the principle of representative democracy and the direct representation of Union citizens in the European Parliament (...), improving the functioning of the European Parliament and the governance of the Union, making the work of the European Parliament more legitimate and efficient, enhancing the effectiveness of the system for conducting European elections, fostering common ownership among citizens from all Member States, enhancing the balanced composition of the European Parliament, and providing for the greatest possible degree of electoral equality and participation for citizens of the Union" [10].

The EP Resolution demonstrates the will to enhance the connection that ought to exist between the electoral procedure for the European Parliament and the role of European political parties in managing the elections, with the aim to strengthen democratic development and political integration in the EU, without overlooking the new rules for choosing the President of the European Commission that is supposed to strictly depend on the results of thc elections since the Treaty of Lisbon entered into force (Curti Gialdino 2014; 2015).

In this direction, the drafters of the reform have stressed the need to show voters the true "political" meaning of their vote during the campaigns for EP elections, beyond the choice for a particular national party, by establishing a

9 EP's Resolution of November 11th 2015 on the Reform of the electoral law of the European Union [2015/2035 (INL)], in www.europarl.europa.eu.

10 Point 1of the EU Parliament Resolution of 11 November 2015 on the Reform of the 1976 Electoral Act.

link between the vote itself and its impact both on the size of a European political group inside the Parliament and, indirectly, on the nomination of the Commission President. Hence, it has been highlighted that the procedure for the selection of the leading candidates for this position should be an integral part of the election campaigns and constitute an important aspect of it, because the nomination provides a link between votes cast at national level and the European dimension and, moreover, enables European citizens to be informed about alternative political programs (Bonvicini/Tosato/Matarazzo 2009: 182 ff.).

Above all, given that European political parties are best placed to "contribute to forming European political awareness" (Art. 10.4 TEU), they should play a stronger role in the whole management of European elections and increase their visibility (Calossi 2015: 16). With this aim, it has been laid down to place their names and logos on the ballot papers and wherever possible on posters and other materials used in election campaigns, in conjunction with those of national parties affiliated with them. These rules intend to highlight the link between national parties and the big European political families. By making European elections more transparent and improving the democratic way in which they are conducted, citizens will be able to clearly connect their vote to the impact it has on the political influence of European political parties and their ability to form political groups inside the Parliament. For the same reasons, Member States' television channels and other media outlets should include in their coverage of the electoral campaigns references to the manifestoes of the respective European parties, if any, to which the national party is affiliated (Art.3e).

However, the most notable amendment to the 1976 Electoral Act is the rule of the approved 2015 Resolution establishing that "the Council decides by unanimity on a joint constituency in which lists are headed by each political family's candidates for the office of President of the Commission" (Art. 2a).

This is precisely the rule that would both greatly strengthen European democracy fostering the role of the European political parties in the elections and also contribute to "create a pan-European moment" (Ciancio 2015b), enhancing the common European character of the European elections. Indeed, this purpose would be further served by lists of candidates evenly led by the leaders of the big European political families who compete for the Presidency within a joint constituency.

In principle, the Council's finally approved 2015 Amendment of the 1976 EP's Electoral Act should have represented a fundamental step forward towards the development of a genuine system of European parties as a necessary propulsive factor in the European political integration process. In practice, however, the Council has so far postponed the decision, delaying a great opportunity.

Indeed, a true turning point towards the adoption of the so-called "political fundamental decision" could be reached only by fostering an *idem sentire (de "Europa")* (Morrone 2014: 95 ff.). Without it, it looks unlikely (and in any case pointless) to re-launch the constitutional process argued for to overcome the Lisbon "compromise" (Ciancio 2015c: 95 ff.) and all the limitations it has revealed for coping with the spread of the economic and social crisis and, more recently, with the big "external" challenges of immigration and international terrorism.

Above all, only by rooting a deep sense of belonging to the "European common home" it will be possible to cope with the widespread disaffection of European citizens regarding the prospects of a truly EU political union. How urgent it is to work towards the establishment among EU citizens of a sense of common belonging to the European Union after the "Brexit" referendum's outcome everyone can easily see.

References

Allegri, Maria R. (2013): I partiti politici a livello europeo fra autonomia politica e dipendenza dai partiti nazionali. In: federalismi.it, n. 22, pp.1-45.

Allegri, Maria R. (2014): Il nuovo regolamento sullo statuto e sul finanziamento dei partiti politici europei: una conclusione ad effetto ritardato. In: Osservatorio costituzionale, n.2, pp.1-9.

Bardi, Luciano/Pizzimenti, Eugenio (2013): Old Logics for New Games: The Appointment of the EU's High Representative for Foreign Affairs and security Policy. In: Contemporary Italian Politics, 5, n.1, pp. 55-70.

Baroncelli, Stefania (2001): I gruppi parlamentari nell'esperienza del Parlamento europeo. In: Merlini, Stefano ed.: Rappresentanza politica, gruppi parlamentari, partiti: il contesto europeo, I. Turin: Giappichelli Publisher, pp. 3- 54.

Baroncelli, Stefania (2014): Efficienza e deputati indipendenti nel Parlamento europeo. In: Ciancio, Adriana (ed.): Nuove strategie per lo sviluppo democratico e l'integrazione politica in Europa. Rome: Aracne Publisher, pp. 99-110.

Bonvicini, Gianni/Tosato, Gian L./Matarazzo, Raffaello (2009): I partiti politici europei e la candidatura del presidente della Commissione. In: Il diritto dell'Unione europea, n.1, pp. 179-189.

Calossi, Enrico (2015): Towards European Electoral and Party Systems. In: IAI Working Papers, n.47, pp. 1-20.

Caravita, Beniamino (2015): Quanta Europa c'è in Europa?. Turin: Giappichelli Publisher.

Cartabia, Marta (2014): Elezioni europee 2014: questa volta è diverso. In: Forum di Quaderni costituzionali. Rassegna, pp.1-6.

Ciancio, Adriana (2007): Partiti politici e gruppi parlamentari nell'ordinamento europeo. In: Politica del Diritto, n. 2, pp. 153-173.
Ciancio, Adriana (2008): I gruppi parlamentari. Studio intorno a una manifestazione del pluralismo politico. Milan: Giuffrè Publisher.
Ciancio, Adriana (2009): I partiti politici europei e il processo di democratizzazione dell'Unione. In: federalismi.it, n. 9, pp. 1-22.
Ciancio, Adriana (2014): How we might recover from the economic and social crisis through European integration deepening. In: Przeglad Prawa Konstytucyjnego, n.3, pp. 161-174.
Ciancio, Adriana (2015a): I nodi della *governance* europea: euro, politica fiscale, bilancio unico dell'Unione. Per una nuova legittimazione democratica della BCE. In: federalismi.it, n.16, pp. 1-27.
Ciancio, Adriana (2015b): A New Uniform Electoral Procedure to Re-Legitimate the Process of Political Integration in Europe. About The EU Parliament Resolution of 11 November 2015 on the Reform of the 1976 Electoral Act. In: federalismi.it, n. 23, pp.1-12.
Ciancio, Adriana (2015c): Con lo sguardo oltre Lisbona verso gli Stati Uniti d'Europa. In: Caravita, Beniamino ed.: Le elezioni del Parlamento europeo del 2014. Turin: Giappichelli Publisher, pp. 79-96.
Ciancio, Adriana (2016a): Democrazia e sovranazionalità: ripensare il Parlamento europeo. In: Riv. AIC, n.3, pp. 1-20.
Ciancio, Adriana (2016b): European Parties and the process of political integration in Europe. In: dirittifondamentali.it, n.2, pp. 1-22.
Curti Gialdino, Carlo (2014): Elezioni europee del 2014 e scelta del candidato alla presidenza della Commissione europea: i primi passi della procedura. In: federalismi.it, n.11, pp. 1-11.
Curti Gialdino, Carlo (2015): L'elezione di Jean-Claude Juncker a presidente della Commissione europea: profili giuridico-istituzionali. In: Caravita, Beniamino ed.: Le elezioni del Parlamento europeo del 2014. Turin: Giappichelli Publisher, pp. 29 – 74.
De Vergottini, Giuseppe (2009): Forma di governo dell'Unione europea. In: Treccani.it.
Duverger, Maurice (1954): Political Parties. Their Organization and Activity in the Modern State. New York: Wiley Publisher.
Fasone, Cristina/Lupo Nicola (2012): Il Parlamento europeo alla luce delle novità introdotte nel Trattato di Lisbona e nel suo regolamento interno. In: Studi sull'integrazione europea, n.2-3, pp. 329-358.
Fusacchia, Alessandro (2006): The party must go on! Il finanziamento pubblico dei partiti politici europei. In: Rivista Italiana di Scienza Politica, n.1, pp. 87-114.
Gagatek, Wojciech/Van Hecke, Steven (2011): Towards Policy-Seeking Europarties? The Development of European Political Foundations. In: EUI Working Papers RSCAS, n.58, pp. 1-16.
Goulard, Sylvie/Monti, Mario (2012): La democrazia in Europa. Guardare lontano. Milan: Rizzoli Publisher.

Grasso, Giorgio (2008): Partiti politici europei. In: Digesto Discipline Pubblicistiche, Agg. Turin: UTET Publisher, III, pp.609-637.
Grasso, Giorgio (2010): Democrazia interna e partiti politici a livello europeo: qualche termine di raffronto per l'Italia?. In: Politica del Diritto, n. 4, pp. 609-668.
Grimm, Dieter (1996): Una costituzione per l'Europa. In: Zagrebelsky, Gustavo/Portinaro, Pier P./Luther, Joerg eds.: Il futuro della Costituzione. Turin: Einaudi Publisher, pp. 339-367.
Grimm, Dieter (2014): La forza dell'UE sta in un'accorta autolimitazione. In: Nomos. Le attualità del diritto, n. 2, pp. 2-9.
Habermas, Jurgen (2014): La nuova Europa in quattro mosse. In: "La Repubblica", Feb. 7th.
Hix, Simon (1993): The Emerging EC Party System? The European Party Federations in the Intergovernmental Conferences. In: Politics, 13, n. 2, pp. 38-46.
Hix, Simon (1995): Parties at the European Level and the Legitimacy of EU Socio-Economic Policy. In: JCMS, 33, n.4, pp. 527-554.
Hix, Simon/Lord, Christopher (1997): Political Parties in the European Union. Basingstoke: Palgrave Macmillan Publisher.
Kelsen, Hans (1981): Essenza e valore della democrazia. In: La democrazia, with an Introduction by G. Gavazzi. Bologna: Il Mulino Publisher, pp. 37-144.
Lelieveldt, Herman/Princen, Sebastiaan (2011): The politics of the European Union. Cambridge: Cambridge University Press.
Lippolis, Vincenzo (2002): I partiti politici europei. In: Rassegna Parlamentare, n.4, pp. 941-959.
Lupo, Nicola (2014): I poteri europei dei parlamenti nazionali: questioni terminologiche, classificazioni e primi effetti. In: Manzella, Andrea/Lupo, Nicola (eds.): Il sistema parlamentare euro-nazionale. Turin: Giappichelli Publisher, pp. 101-131.
Magone, José M. (2015): Divided Europe? Euroscepticism in Central, Eastern and Southern Europe. In: Kyriakos, N. Demetriou (ed.): The European Union in Crisis. Explorations in Representation and Democratic Legitimacy, Cham: Springer Publisher, pp. 33-56.
Manzella, Andrea (2014): Verso un governo parlamentare euro-nazionale. In: Manzella, Andrea/Lupo, Nicola (eds.): Il sistema parlamentare euro-nazionale. Turin: Giappichelli Publisher, pp. 1-17.
Martinelli, Claudio (2004): Il finanziamento pubblico dei partiti europei. In: Quaderni Costituzionali, n.2, pp. 416-418.
Morrone, Andrea (2014): Crisi economica e diritti. Appunti per lo Stato costituzionale in Europa. In: Quaderni costituzionali, n.1, pp. 79-106.
Murray, Philomena/Longo, Michael (2015): The Crisi-Legitimacy Nexus in the European Union. In: Kyriakos, N. Demetriou (ed.): The European Union in Crisis. Exploration in Representation and Democratic Legitimacy, Cham: Springer Publisher, pp. 59-74.
Niedermayer, Oskar (1983): Europäische Parteien?, Frankfurt: Campus Press Publisher.

Offe, Claus (2015): Europe Entrapped. Cambridge: Polity Press Publisher.
Pasquinucci, Daniele (2014): La procedura uniforme per l'elezione del Parlamento europeo. In: Mascia, Marco ed.: Verso un sistema partitico europeo transnazionale. Bari: Cacucci Publisher, pp. 53-63.
Porras Ramírez, José M. (2016): La creciente consistencia de los partidos polìticos en la Unión europea. In: Italian Papers on Federalism, n.3, pp. 1-8.
Raspadori, Fabio (2009): Il *deficit* di rappresentatività del Parlamento europeo: limiti e soluzioni. In: Studi sull'integrazione europea, n.1, pp. 121-132.
Ridola, Paolo (2009): Il voto europeo del 6 e 7 giugno: la "sfera pubblica europea", l'integrazione multilivello e le sfide della complessità. In: federalismi.it, n. 12, pp. 1-6.
Romboli, Roberto (2014): Corte di giustizia e giudizi nazionali: il rinvio pregiudiziale come strumento di dialogo. In: Ciancio, Adriana (ed.): Nuove strategie per lo sviluppo democratico e l'integrazione politica in Europa. Rome: Aracne Publisher, pp. 431-471.
Ruggeri, Antonio (2014): L'integrazione europea attraverso i diritti e il "valore" della Costituzione. In: Ciancio, Adriana (ed.): Nuove strategie per lo sviluppo democratico e l'integrazione politica in Europa. Rome: Aracne Publisher, pp. 473-496.
Ruggeri, Antonio (2016): Costituzione, sovranità, diritti fondamentali, in cammino dallo Stato all'Unione europea e ritorno, ovverosia circolazione dei modelli costituzionali e adattamento dei relativi schemi teorici. In: federalismi.it, n. 11, pp 1-34.
Savoia G. (2014): Democrazia interna ai partiti in Italia e nell'Unione Europea: discipline a confronto. In: federalismi.it, n.6, pp.1-18.
Statham, Paul/Trenz, Hans J. (2013), The politicization of Europe. Contesting the Constitution in the Mass Media. London – New York: Routledge Publisher.
Tripaldi, Maria P.C./Teklè, Tzehainesh (2001): I partiti politici nell'ordinamento del Regno Unito. In: Merlini, Stefano ed.: Rappresentanza politica, gruppi parlamentari, partiti: il contesto europeo, I. Turin: Giappichelli Publisher, pp. 215-281.
Tsatsos, Konstantinos (1995): European Political Parties? Preliminary reflections on interpreting the Maastricht Treaty article on political parties (Article 138A of the EC Treaty). In: Human Rights Law Journal, XVI, n.1-3, pp.1-8.
Vigevani, Giulio E. (2003): Parlamento europeo: una nuova procedura elettorale uniforme. In: Quaderni *cost*ituzionali, n.1, pp. 175-177.
Weiler, Joseph H. H. (2003): La Costituzione dell'Europa. Bologna: Il Mulino Publisher.

Conclusion

20. Europe's unfinished journey: diverging narratives, innovative concepts, and political development

Ulrike Liebert

1. The European political project in the 21st century

After the fall of the Iron Curtain in 1989, ten East-Central and East European countries were eager to engage with the profound transformations necessary for membership in the European Union (EU), namely the Europeanisation of their post-socialist domestic economies, state institutions, and societies. In 2004/7, after the EU's most extensive enlargement ever, its 28 member states made up more than 500 million people with the largest single market in the world. Furthermore, as the prominent US social thinker Jeremy Rifkin noted, Europe became 'a giant laboratory for rethinking humanity's future': 'While the American Dream emphasizes unrestrained economic growth, personal wealth, and the pursuit of individual self-interest, the European Dream focuses more on sustainable development, quality of life, and the nurturing of community.' (Rifkin 2004). Ten years on, the winds for this unfinished European project have changed. In most new and old EU countries, protectionist forces striving for state control over national borders, people and the economy have gained leverage. The most intricate case in point for the dead end to which the new struggles against 'Europeanisation' in the name of 'neo-nationalism' can lead is the UK's attempt to divorce from the EU.[1] The post-world war II order seems to be dissolving while a new order has yet to crystallize. In these 'interim times', where will the 'unfinished adventure' of Europe go (Bauman 2004)?

In the wake of the decade of polycrises troubling the Europeans, the present cul-de-sac comes as no surprise. Given the global financial crisis of 2007/8, followed by years of economic recession and fiscal austerity, the social divisions in European societies have deepened, and EU-bashing has become the new norm within member states. Economic analysts tend to ignore Europe's

1 Following the outcome of a popular referendum in June 2016, the UK government led by PM Theresa May negotiated a 'withdrawal agreement' with the EU; this will only take effect, 2019 if approved by by the British parliament; alternatively, a 'Brexit' might occur without a deal.

fragmented public sphere. Yet, compared to other large currency areas, the euro area is split by widely diverging narratives about responsibilities for successes and failures of the member states vis-à-vis the EU in managing the financial market crises (Bruegel 2018). Arguably, the fragmentation of the European public sphere by national media systems further exacerbates the divisions between schools of economic thought and political ideologies regarding the role of markets, states and supranational institutions. Nonetheless, deeper social divisions and diverging narratives do not necessarily add up to a European project in decline. Contrary to the prophecies of an ill-fated EU, this chapter focuses on ideas for innovation and political development. Innovative concepts for a European political development capable of strengthening social cohesion and better coping with citizens' pressing challenges do indeed exist. The most important tasks include European Economic and Monetary Union, European Security and Defense Union, a European Migration Regime, a Union of Labour Markets, European Climate Protection and, as overarching tasks, defence of the rule of law and European democracy.

2. Diverging narratives: Europeanisation vs. neo-nationalism

The diversity of neo-nationalisms notwithstanding, one of their common denominator is to target Europeanisation as a common adversary. Their 'counter-revolution' aims to roll back European integration and to re-nationalise sovereignty, that is control over borders, citizenship, the economy and finances. If 'Brexit' epitomizes the divisions that the neo-nationalist challenge has triggered within the European Union, global Trumpism stands for the dismantling of the international order the European Union has helped to build during the second half of the 20th and that is becoming always more uncertain and fluid in the 21st century (Pollack 2017). Intellectual debates abound concerning how these backlashes could have happened and what they tell us regarding the European Union's future. It is an open question whether the Europeanisation of societies and state institutions is sufficiently resilient to withstand the pressures of neo-nationalism, or whether Europeanisation in itself has changed its meanings and lost legitimacy.

To discuss these questions, three clarifications are needed, regarding our notion of crisis for the present purpose, the discursive meanings of Europeanisation and neo-nationalism and their political implications for the future of the EU.

First, 'crisis' is taken here as another term for the lack of a stable equilibrium of rules and practices of interaction, resulting from conflict among dominant agents in favour of conserving the status quo and opposed agents seeking change (cf. Schmitter 2017). As a consequence, 'learning from crisis' means to take distance from political crisis-rhetoric and make use of knowledge from reflective political and social scientific research. For instance, the lessons Hauke Brunkhorst draws from the 'refugee crisis' suggest that "this is not a crisis of refugees but one of democracy and human rights" that requires the refoundation of the European Union (Brunkhorst 2016: 1ff.). More in general, "politics as a science" suggests to distinguish three dimensions of the politics of crisis, choice and change: whether relevant collective agents are either dissatisfied or satisfied with the current order; how given constellations of political conflict and power relations are changing; and the quality of politics (Schmitter 2016). A scientific approach to politics would depart from "perversions" of the social sciences, namely mainstream economics making "its usual prescriptions – always more markets, always less government" (Rodrik 2017). In an article on the role of the sciences in times of populism, the President of the German Science Community (DFG) takes issue with these paradoxical practices to provide expert knowledge for private power accumulation: "We claim that scientific knowledge is reliable and can be falsified by future knowledge. And we declare that knowledge is the primary driving force of economic prosperity, yet we consider ourselves non responsible for the injustices of capitalism" (Strohschneider 2017).

As a consequence, secondly, the discursive struggles between Europeanisation and neo-nationalism and their polarising rhetoric will need to be put in an analytical perspective. As a matter of fact, the divisive use of 'Europeanisation' versus 'neo-nationalism' is misleading as it misses the complexities of conflict about the European economic, social and political cultural order in any given historical constellation and feeds into further polarisation.

In the last quarter of the 20th century, 'Europeanisation' has been understood as a set of processes towards the convergence across different member states based on shared European norms and values. Yet, in the aftermath of the EU's failed Constitutional Treaty ratification in 2005 and, even more so, the financial crisis in the Eurozone and the migration challenge, Europeanisation has become more conflictive and ambivalent, especially in the European periphery (Worschech 2018). As the EU's norms and rules have become more politicised, the neutrality of this previously analytic term has given way to a normative template for enforcement, monitoring and surveillance, the effectiveness and legitimacy of which is highly contentious. Calls directed at EMU to learn from its mistakes have come from manifold sides, including from a Greek perspective, the IMF, the Financial Times, political scientists and policy analysts. In the Greek context, the euro crisis management has been widely criticised for privileging fiscal consolidation (austerity) and neglecting social solidarity for the sake of monetary stability and structural convergence (Sotiropoulos 2019). From the part of the IMF, its previous director took issue with the EU's, the IMF's and his own responsibility for fundamental flaws in designing the financial assistance programs for Greece. At the peak of the Greek Eurozone crisis in summer 2015 he asserted that "we need to think different, we need a change in the logic, we need a radically new direction to reframe the negotiations with Greece, (…) a radically new context of constructive cooperation rather than antagonistic conditionality".[2] Moreover, Financial Times columnist Martin Wolf, in his book "The Shifts and the Shocks: what we have learned and have still to learn" (Wolf 2014) critically noted the failures of the euro area leaders and crisis managers to take into account and correct the design flaws of Economic and Monetary Union. As a matter of fact, the three largest, founding euro-member states France, Germany and Italy reveal only a limited economic convergence, if compared by competitiveness, public finances, income development and labour market performance, and therefore put the stability of the EMU at risk (Tokarski 2018). For strengthening it, stricter conditionalities are no clear cut remedy. For instance, comparing the conditionalities used by the EU for the accession of candidate states on the one hand and for managing the Economic and Monetary Union on the other hand, Frank Schimmelfennig finds that positive conditionalities or incentives can be better reconciled with democracy than negative conditionalities or sanctions (Schimmelfennig 2015: 7f). As a consequence, the latter may have unwelcome consequences for the legitimacy of Europeanisation, not only in Southern Europe's fragile periphery but also in the new East and Central European member states. As Ivan Krastev puts it: "After 1989 the political philosophy of postcommunist Central and Eastern Europe could be summarised in a single imperative: Imitate the West!. This process had different names: democratisation, liberalisation, enlargement, convergence, integration, Europeanisation" (Krastev 2018). Krastev frames Europeanisation as forced imitation of the West by the East by asymmetric power relations between "we, the Europeans" versus "they, the people" (Krastev 2017). His narrative resonates with widespread popular feelings and discourses. But its tendency to polarise falls back into the logic of the Cold War: By portraying the EU as an enemy of the nation state, this account feeds into new East/West divisions (Assmann 2018: 172).

In turn, neo-nationalist narratives aim at reframing Europeanisation from a modernising notion to a contentious device for cultural globalisation. These have benefited from the EU's migration crisis of 2015, allegedly imposed by a dominant core ("the West") on the Southern and Eastern European periphery. Positioning themselves as an anti-dote against the pro-European establishment, new right-wing nationalist parties and movements within and beyond the EU

2 Strauss-Kahn, Dominique (2015): On learning from one's mistaktes. Retrieved online at: https://de.slideshare.net/DominiqueStraussKahn/150627-tweet-greece

are by no means restricted to the Eastern and East Central EU member states. Seventy years after the launch of European Economic Community, in the old as well as the new EU member states, Eurosceptic, illiberal, and even extremist political parties have gained enormous leverage on public opinion and on government EU policy (UK), have become significant parliamentary opposition forces (Netherlands, Germany, Finland), participate in government coalitions (Austria) or even control national governments (Hungary, Poland, Czech Republic, Italy). Catalyzing public anger at the migration movements of 2015, the neo-nationalist agenda also caters to the dissatisfaction of many citizens vis-à-vis the 'unjustifiable injustices' of the EU's crises management that has antagonised the national societies against each other, as Jürgen Habermas argues (Habermas 2014).

Further reinvigorated by the Trump presidency since 2017, right wing populism has spread within and across diverse national and regional contexts, from the US and Europe to Asia and Latin America. Cross-national varieties notwithstanding, global Trumpism launches a cultural backlash that appeals to "economic have-nots" (Inglehart/Norris 2016). Its "illiberal counter-revolution" (Zielonka 2018) aims at an anti-pluralist democracy (Crum 2019), and the spread of Euroscepticism (Schild 2019, Havlik 2019). Politically, populist neo-nationalist leaders apprize a majoritarian democracy devoid of liberal principles such as the rule of law and minority protection, culturally they promote a cultural back-lash, if not "conservative revolution" aimed at an anti-pluralistic, ethnically homogeneous society, while in the economic sphere they tend to privilege national protectionism. In their domestic politics, right-wing populists embrace ethno-nationalist identities with xenophobe, anti-Islamic, anti-Semitic and anti-feminist underpinnings. In the international sphere, they oppose multilateral international regimes, notably the fight against climate change, international human rights, international solidarity and European Human Rights (Guasti and Siroki 2019).

Finally, third, what do these on-going shifts and contradictory struggles of neo-nationalism against Europeanisation tell us about the future of European integration? Some policy-analysts have warned the EU might implode, for instance like the Soviet Union in 1991 (Krastev 2017). Arguably a symptom of the contemporary demise of the nation state (Dasgupta 2018), 'global Trumpism' is an outcome of and at the same time feeds into the crisis of liberalism (Zielonka 2018). Ultimately, it threatens to enforce 'ways how democracies die' (Levitsky/Ziblatt 2018). Against this international pessimistic vein, the EU's crises can also be analysed in the framework of transition, not decline (Schmitter 2012). For instance, intellectuals advise courageous innovative reforms, such as a "Europe first" strategy aimed at strengthening the EU's independence (Leggewie 2017), or encouraging citizens initiatives to raise up for "Europe now" on the short run, and for putting the political utopia of a "European Republik" in practice on the longer run (Guérot et al 2018; Guérot 2016).

To renew Europe as a political project, cultural theorist Aleida Assmann, in "Der europäische Traum", makes the case for a historical-cultural perspective on Europe. Drawing four lessons from Europeans' past failures she suggests to reconcile the presently divided European memories of the past as a precondition for building a shared European future (Assmann 2018). If we want to overcome East-West divisions, she argues, first of all we need to reconcile the Europeans' divided memories (id., 172ff). Criticising our present "asymmetric European remembrance", she insists that the competition between the official remembrance of Hitler's Holocaust and the lack of recognition of the sufferings that Stalin's Gulag has caused in Eastern populations have left scars that must be addressed (id.: 173). To tackle the deep seated social psychological roots of these new rifts in the European Union, Assmann calls for a dialogical European memory culture: "The East European states should not imitate the West but contribute to building a shared new Europe. This requires that Europe is not any more presented as a an enemy but acknowledged as a common project. For rescuing and developing this project, a consensus is needed about what this project is about" (id. 172).

Yet, even if we fully embrace Assmann's historical-cultural lessons for jointly building a future European order, Europeans will also have to come to terms with what Dani Rodrik calls the "political trilemma of globalisation": the alleged impossibility to reconcile the three goals of democracy, national self-determination and economic globalisation at the same time (Rodrik 2011). Rodrik's arguments challenge the conventional optimism about the stability of liberal democracy as well as pessimistic claims about its inevitable crisis and demise (cf. Brühlmeier/Mastronardi 2016). Academics still need to adjust long-held theories about democracy to the new internal and external challenges of the 21st century. For instance, recent social scientific research provides evidence that populist scepticism about constitutionalism and liberal protections for individuals is triggered by economic dislocation and democraphic change across the West (Galston 2018). Although the driving factors of popular dissatisfaction with political institutions and parties and democratic distress - spiralling income, wealth inequality and the increasing weight of money in politics – are more pronounced in the US, European political systems offer more incentives for anti-establishment parties (Brechenmacher 2018:17ff). Thus, Europeans have had to live with "anti-pluralist populism" for quite some time, for instance in Italy and the Netherlands (Crum 2019). Yascha Mounk has spotted a "technocratic dilemma" at the core of the "real threats" to liberal democracy's ability "to meet the public's twin demands of responsiveness and performance" (Mounk 2018: 98). Over the past decades, "the ability of liberal democracies around the world to translate popular views into public policy" has arguably declined. Mounk attributes this decay to two major developments: "Legislature have become less reflective of popular opinion because of the growing role of money in politics. At the same time they have also become less powerful because of the growing importance of bureaucratic agencies, central banks, judicial review, free trade and international organisations (id.). Generally speaking, the "populist challenge to liberal democracy" drives "a wedge between democracy and liberalism" that responds to a popular demand for strong leaders; but defining the people as homogeneous is incompatible with "the basis for a modern democracy, which stands or falls with the protection of pluralism" (Galston 2018:5).

Arguably, in the contemporary global constellation, the real existing liberal capitalist democracies display a series of internal contradictions that affect their prospects for survival in the 21st century (Liebert 2016; Schmitter 2015). To widen these chances, Europeans need to develop a political Union capable of choosing whether they want to further strengthen the agencies of liberal economic and financial globalisation at the expense of democracy – or, alternatively, renew their representative democratic institutions. Provided they prioritise the latter, democracy can go two ways: either back towards re-nationalising national democratic self-determination, or forward, towards a European democracy.

As to the first option, the Hungarian neo-nationalist leader Victor Orban has come up with the name "illiberal democracy", thereby positioning his Fidesz Party at the extreme right margin of the European People's Party (Platter 2019). This new term stands for an electoral, majoritarian democracy and ethno-nationalist ideology that reject progressive principles and practices established in the European Union in respect, for instance, of asylum rights, minority protection, gender equality and non-discrimination (Platter 2019). Very much following the model of "capitalism with Chinese characteristics", European neo-nationalists seek to build an "illiberal democracy" that hollows out democracy to strengthen the state capacities that are needed for implementing economic globalisation on the one hand, and for limiting social and cultural globalisation, on the other. They oppose Europeanisation as a way to detach economic globalisation from the EU's normative framework, from rule of law, fundamental rights and international human rights to liberal and pluralist democracy.

Recasting the second option, 'Europeanisation', in the framework of Rodrik's political trilemma, also this term can attain two different meanings. Europeanisation can either aim at a European constitutional order for the sake of economic globalisation, enhancing state capacities but undermining democratic qualities, such as representation and responsiveness regarding citizens' priorities and needs. Or, alternatively, Europeanisation can be used to expand representative democracy for governing the European monetary union and economy, for better managing global financial capitalism, for civilising the power of finance and for empowering social and ecological norms and common interests that transcend the member states. The field of "making gender equality work in theory and practice" is a telling test case for such competing meanings and expectations regarding Europeanisation (Liebert 2016).

In sum, both agendas of neo-nationalism and Europeanisation need to be scrutinized as to which hidden implications they carry regarding liberal, pluralistic democratic principles and practices in relation to economic and cultural globalisation. While neo-nationalists tend to be too short-sigthed, the politics of Europeanisation may be too far-sighted.[3] Populist nationalists refute looking beyond their own borders when propagating nationalist re-empowerment and conflict against European cooperation as a panacea to split up globalisation. To their mixed end of resisting cultural while empowering economic globalisation, they will eagerly sacrifice the European achievements of liberal and pluralist democracy and their peaceful transnational cooperation. Europeanisation, in turn, may go too far, subjecting European common interests to "Western" powers beyond the EU's control. Realistically speaking, not even Europe's most powerful nation states alone can come up with more sustainable solutions for governing the impacts of run-away globalisation on European societies than the EU.[4] The nuanced political and social scientific analyses of the EU crises and innovative conceptions suggest that this applies to a large range of policy domains where transnational interdependies exist. This is true especially for the crisis of human rights and illegal trafficking in the Mediterranean which only a combination of Community policies could ease: A European regime for legal immigration would supplement and develop the dysfunctional asymmetries of the present Common European Asylum System. While protecting the free movement of persons within the European internal market, the euro-area countries could reduce the problems of unemployment in some countries, and the lack of skilled workers in others by integrating national labour markets and helping migrants integrate in the European labour market. Moreover, a common European unemployment insurance scheme would contribute to building the European social pillar, enhance social cohesion in the euro area and the structural convergence of EU member states. From the euro-area crisis to the EU's human rights crisis – by populists so-called 'refugee-crisis' – the structural divergence among member states has increased, their cohesion is diminished, and, as a consequence, narratives diverge, and national interests grow more apart (Müller et al 2018). For building an antidote to the "great regression" (Geiselberger 2017) and the "counter-revolution" against liberal Europe (Zielonka 2018), the conclusion to this book wants to make the case

3 I owe this insight to former IMF president Dominque Strauss Kahn, see „To my German friends" (July 18th, 2015). Retrieved online http://de.slideshare.net/DominiqueStrauss-Kahn/150718-tweeteurope.

4 For more detail, see about the European governance of a common asylum policy (Zaun 2019), European monetary policy (Zagermann 2019), climate protection (Liebert Morata 2019); and European energy union (Heinrich and Pleines 2019), all included in this book.

for a kind of Europeanisation that is learning from past mistakes. Neither technocracy nor illiberal, anti-pluralist neo-nationalism are capable of reflecting and learning in the common interest. Only in a liberal, pluralist democratic framework European researchers and political leaders can conceive and advance devices of Europeanisation that will work for bridging Europe's divisions. To that aim, the renewal of Europe as a political Europe needs less misguiding ideas such as "TINA" and more deliberations about alternative narratives, their conditions and consequences (Liebert 2016; 2019). National fora for citizens' debates about Europe have flourished since 2017. But we also need a transnational format for publicly debating proposals for necessary and desirable reform, such as for a "sovereign, united, democratic Europe", one that "protects" the citizens (Macron 2017, Leonard 2017). Arguably, for protecting the citizens in Europe, liberal pluralist democracy must be reinvigorated. For putting new life into it, the European democracy must be upgraded (Liebert 2019).

As a matter of fact, the contemporary European Union is a far cry from an undemocratic regime as well as from a fully-fledged federal European democracy. Rather than by such binary frameworks, it is better described as a "system of differentiated integration" (Schimmelfennig et al 2014: 8-9): The Eurozone, Schengenland, or the Single Market have different boundaries and varying memberships; however, the EU has also developed an institutional core, namely the European Council, the European Commission, the European Parliament and the European Court of Justice; this centre "reaches across the EU's policy sectors with their variation in centralization and territorial scope", albeit "with to different degrees and with varying competences (id.). Many of the EU's current weaknesses are due to a lack of democratic legitimacy of the EU's institutional core for harmonising diverging member states policies in areas such as migration, fiscal or energy policy. In some critical cases, its shortcoming are due to a lack of willingness on the part of national leaders in the European Council to learn from past mistakes. This is true, for instance, for the EU's choice in the euro crisis "to save the Euro at the cost of democracy" (Crum 2013). The short-sightedness by European political leaders not to learn is predetermined by national election cycles. Sometimes it benefits EU-bashing and often a pro-European rhetoric without consequential political action. For getting the EU out of this impasse, Europeans need innovative ideas and conceptions aimed at renewing the European project of political unification.

3. Innovative ideas for renewing Europe as a political project

After 2016, the year of catastrophic setbacks to European integration, 2017 gave rise to new hopes. This optimistic trend benefited from a range of new political developments and innovative ideas. This political dynamics started with the seminal Brexit vote in June 2016. This came as a shock that indicated the first exit of a member state in the EU's 60 years of integration but, paradoxically, turned out as a catalyst for European and national political leaders and citizens to fight its divisive impacts. The EU designed the exit negotiations in such a way that it would not become a driving force for further disintegration. Moreover, from the Bratislava summit in September 2016 on and notably on the occasion of the EU-60 celebration in March 2017 in Rome, European leaders pledged to protect the EU's norms and values against internal and external challenges. Second, the rise of the citizen movement 'Pulse of Europe' since late 2016 provided a pro-European politics with a new considerable and lasting momentum. Third, Emmanuel Macron's election to the French Presidency in May 2017 signaled the success of the pro-European against the neo-nationalist camp. Fourth, European Commission President Jean Claude Juncker's afforded the EU with forward looking leadership by, structuring the European political reform debates by publishing a series of Commission White Papers, and developing his own realistic reform agenda and roadmap for the years to come until 2024 (Juncker 2017). Fifth, the confrontational politics of the newly elected US President, Donald Trump, provided the heads of EU states and governments with a renewed sense of purpose, including a commitment to new Community policies, such as the establishment of the Permanent Structured Cooperation (PESCO) by the Council in December 2017. Sixth, public support for the EU started to rise, and citizens, civil society and political parties engaged with new frameworks for European public debate, from public expert forums and structured citizens' dialogues to general public debates and even 'Citizens Conventions'.[5] Yet, seventh, the pro-European German 'grand coalition' government that formed belatedly only in Spring 2018, did not follow up on its promises for EU reforms until after the March 2018 Italian elections and the formation of an Eurosceptic coalition government in June.

Against this background of mobilisations for change as well as resistance and stalemate, a large variety of innovative ideas has been advanced, proposing to move the EU in fundamentally different directions. This contest of proposals for EU reform opened with the French President Macron's grand vision of a

5 See Eurobarometer 89, Spring 2018; Baden-Württemberg, Pressemitteilung no. 22/2018, 10 March 2018; and for pioneering democratic experiments in Ireland: Farrell 2014.

'core Europe' constituting a 'sovereign, united, democratic Europe' (Macron 2017)[6]. His radical reform proposal was softened by Commission President Jean-Claude Juncker's pragmatic and more inclusive reform approach aimed for an inclusive EU-27+ that would incorporate the euro area regime under the umbrella of the community method (Juncker 2017).[7] Neither Macron's nor Juncker's invitation to the 'Franco-German engine' to form a group of ambitious states for overhauling Europe by 2024 received any forceful acceptance by the German government. Both proposals have been fundamentally rejected by leading German economists, yet embraced by prominent German public intellectuals. On the critical side, Clemens Fuest, director of the Munich based Institute for economic research (ifo), and conomist Johannes Becker in a co-authored book 'Der Odysseus Komplex' (2017) position themselves squarely against Macron's aspirations for an empowered EU. They reject a democratically legitimated federal European economic government with a sizable budget due to fear of "moral hazard" they suspect from Germany's euro partners. Instead, Becker and Fuest favour a radically decentralised EMU. Here, euro members would enjoy a total fiscal autonomy that allows them even to fail. Instead of managing financial crises in the euro area by rescue programs for members in financial trouble, the euro area regime would provide member states with an insolvency regime (Becker/Fuest 2017). On the positive side and complementing Macron's vision, Claus Leggewie designs a 'Europe first' strategy to strengthen the EU's responsiveness, resistance and resilience vis-à-vis its internal and external enemies (Leggewie 2017). Radicalising Macron's quest for change even further, Ulrike Guérot's political utopia of a 'European Republic' conceives of the European regions as the basic entities that should replace the nation states by 2050 (Guérot 2016). Including also Jürgen Habermas and Sigmar Gabriel, German intellectual contributions to "rethinking Europe" clearly suggest that Macron's political ideas do resonate with public discourses in Germany (Liebert 2010; Macron/Habermas/Gabriel 2018). Yet, the "shadow of statism" remains characteristic of German debates on European integration (Müller 2010); this peculiarity explains why these ideas are not that well received by German mainstream economists.

Finally, the divergence of French-German political-economic positions has motivated transnational expert and advocacy groups to come up with constructive platforms. In 2018, a group of fourteen German and French economists

---

6 Macron's 'core Europe' is directed towards a compromise between stability oriented Germany and solidarity concerned France, yet disposed to leave those behind who are unwilling to give up national sovereignty, hence designed to alienate the new member states from East Central and Eastern Europe.

7 Allowing for different speeds, Juncker's method would reconcile three diverging camps, where one is most interested in a European stable order (Germany), others demand for transnational solidarity (France, Italy, Spain) while a third group is not yet ready to give up national sovereignty (East and Central Europe).

representing different disciplinary schools has delivered a joint proposal for reconciling the principle of risk sharing (advocated by the French) with market discipline (cherished by the Germans).[8] Also, a large group of European intellectuals has gone public with a "French-German manifesto" making the case that "economic freedoms in Europe threaten solidiarity", and that "The EU must be newly founded".[9] Moreover, from within and outside the European Parliament, a cross-party group of European federalists has published the "Manifesto for the Future of Europe: A Shared Destiny" (Spinelli Group 2018). Last but not least, a group of French intellectuals around the renowned economic historian Thomas Piketty has widely disseminated a "Manifesto for the democratization of Europe" on- and off-line in nine languages and collected more than 100.000 signatures in a few months.[10] This manifesto is supported by an elaborate "Draft Treaty on the Democratization of the Governane of the Euro Area".[11] The proposed reform aims at bringing the Eurozone's and EU's looming risks under control, from financial crises and social inequalities to illiberal neo-nationalism. It accepts that EMU will never become sustainable without tools that effectively stabilize and democratically legitimise the euro area, including a centralised European financial capacity. This Euro-Union budget should, on the one hand, be endowed with its own resources and thus be more independent of the member states' allocations. On the other hand, it should be strong enough to function as a stabilizing mechanism in times of crises. Last but not least, the future European economic government will be committed to principles of democratic representation via an assembly constituted by European and national members of parliaments. The executive, that is the future European Minister of Finance and Economic Affairs is supposed to be held accountable by the Euro-Parliament. The proposal that is supposed to "cure in the name of the European citizens the weaknesses of the EU and the euro area" has been submitted to critical examination by international scholars, experts and politicians (Hennette et al. 2019). Two contested issues stick out: the nature of the treaty bases that is international law and not Community law; and the establishment of a new interparliamentary body alongside the European Parliament. The first issue provides a (temporary) solution to the problem of treaty reform without unanimity. Under the euro crisis, adaptations of the

8 Bénassy-Quéré, A., M.K.Brunnermeier, H. Enderlein, E. Farhi, M. Fratzscher, C. Fuest, P.O.Gourinchas, P. Martin, J. Pisani-Ferry, H. Rey, I. Schnabel, N. Véron, B. Weder di Mauro, J. Zettelmeyer (2018): Reconciling risk sharing with market discipline: A constructive approach to euro area reform. CEPR Policy Insight No. 91.

9 See: "Die EU muss neu gegründet werden. Ökonomische Freiheiten bedrohen in Europa inzwischen alles, auch die Solidarität. Was kann man dagegen tun? Ein französisch-deutsches Manifest, In FAZ, 22. September 2018, p. 16.

10 This manifesto has been launched in November 2018, see: https://tdem.eu/en/manifesto/.

11 T-Dem can be retrieved online at: https://www.benoithamon2017.fr/wp-content/uploads/2017/03/traite-europe-EN.pdf

2009 Lisbon Treaty have been difficult if not impossible. European leaders made use of the simplified revision procedure, the so-called 'bridge clauses' (*passerelles*), and, in addition, adopted new international treaties that have remained largely under the radar of public politicisation. A price they had to pay was to drop a long list of reform proposals that would have required unanimous amendments to the Treaty.[12] The second bone of contention – the proposed Euro-parliament - responds to the fact that fiscal, economic and social policy competences are powers of the national legislatures which they cannot legitimately share in the framework of the euro-area without gaining political representation. However, for rethinking the representation of national members of parliament in the governance of the euro-area different models are possible, including a differentiated Euro-committee within the European Parliament composed of national representatives.

Beyond innovative reforms also procedures for putting them in practice are needed. To overcome the barriers against EU treaty reform, the European Convention would be the method to follow.[13] It is constituted by the representatives of the EU institutions, national governments and parliaments. Moreover, it is expected to go public and interact with civil society and the citizens, holding open and transparent dialogues with the representative associations and civil society which are open to the public. Thereby the Convention method contributes to the democratic legitimacy of EU reforms; moreover, it is a necessary prerequisite for creating a broad, inclusive social acceptance of the renewal of the European project. Therefore, a clearly defined mandate is pivotal for a successful European Convention. Arguably, the Convention method offers for the EU the best procedure developed so far to represent and reflect the needs and expectations of the citizen for EU reform. Yet, the Convention procedure carries risks, which is why EU elites have been reluctant to go back to it for nearly twenty years. Ratification procedures by the member states may fail, as the ratification referendums in France and the Netherlands in 2005 showed. The

---

12 The EU's list of unfinished reform projects includes the accountability of the President of the Eurogroup vis-à-vis the EU Parliament; the integration of the ESM and of the Fiscal Treaty into the EU Treaties and the strengthening the EP's control rights vis-à-vis the ESM; the introduction of EP co-decision-making powers under the European Semester; the fight against poverty through stronger provisions for social Europe; the formalisation of new EU projects in the framework of the EU Treaties; an up-grade of the information rights of national parliaments in order to better control the actions of their own governments in Brussels; and the protection of the fundamental values of the EU by providing it with stronger competences to intervene in the case of infringements on the part of member states.

13 The 2009 Treaty of Lisbon provides for the 'Ordinary Amendment Procedure' for future treaty reforms, under which a 'European Convention' is to be convened (EUV, Art. 48, 1-6). Article 48 of the TEU provides that the Governments of each member state, the European Parliament or the Commission submit to the Council draft amendments to the treaties aimed at extending or reducing the Union's responsibilities.

political capital of public support will be at risk if the member governments do not commit themselves to the results of the Convention process. Formally, the Convention shall examine the draft amendments and adopt, by consensus, a recommendation addressed to a conference of the representatives of the governments of the member states. However, the inter-governmental conference that follows the Convention should refrain from 'cherry picking' or even shredding the draft convention. This places high demands on the good-will and capacities of the elected members of the Convention.

In sum, the EU does neither fail nor successfully 'venture' towards its future, but performs as an adapting, failing, learning and innovating polity. Confronted with anti-pluralist populist political parties and governments, EU leaders, political actors and institutions can learn from past mistakes for coping with the present and shaping the future. In contrast to the boldness of innovative ideas, the step by step political developments of the European differentiated governance seem piecemeal, incremental and tiny in ambition and scope. Nevertheless, in a number of domains change is not only necessary but also achievable.

4. Conclusions

Ten years after the outbreak of the international financial crisis, the European Union has been muddling through a series of stress tests. Their many achievements notwithstanding, Europeans have still to find answers to a core question: Will the the EU's new divisions – its diverging narratives, its limited convergence – foster the disintegration of the EU or—contrarily—will the crises provide European leaders and citizens with a new momentum for developing new political forms of cooperation and integration, hence, renew Europe as a political project? The answers to this puzzle have varied, from the horrors of 2016, to the new hopes of 2017 and the search for compromise during 2018.

This chapter has explored the contradictory logics underlying the state of play between Europeanisation and neo-nationalism. It is impossible to predict where the European unfinished journey will be headed in the future. European societies are faced with ever more risks that ignore national borders; from terrorist assaults and cyber attacks to climate catastrophes and mass migration. These external disruptions and the EU's internal complexities challenge the beliefs in in the post-war European idea of an 'ever closer union'. Yet, the 'political development' of the EU does not necessarily require "more" or "stronger" European integration'. Instead, it is meant to refer to improving the quality of politics.[14] The quality of European politics will advance if power is exercised in ways that neither obstruct citizens' participating in the political game nor leave them to resort to individual or collective violence to resolve their disputes.[15] For instance, the quality of European political decision-making will progress if across all EU institutions lobby regulations increase their transparency and accountability. If democratic modes of governance embrace the needs and preferences of the discontented, and previously excluded social groups will develop political and social trust. If EU politics promotes common European goods, it will gain legitimacy for new forms of integration. If political development promotes new devices for constructive cooperation and replaces "antagonistic conditionalities" for Europeanisation, the 'finality' of the EU might move from that of an ever closer union to 'unity in diversity'. After all, renewing Europe as a political project means experimenting with innovative, flexible and inclusive modes of cooperation and integration.

My final conclusion is that the future of the European Union will very likely be troubled by outside disruptions as well as internally by limited structural convergence, conflicting national interests and identities and diverging narratives. In this constellation, the capabilities of the EU's actors, institutions and citizens' initiatives to learn from past mistakes are sources of hope. Arguably, as long as EU leaders and citizens embrace opportunities for improving the quality of politics and thereby renew the European project, their cooperation that has been a distinguishing feature of post-World War II and post-1989 European integration will further evolve.

References

Assmann, Aleida (2018): Der europäische Traum. Vier Lehren aus der Geschichte. München, C.H.Beck.

Bauman, Zygmunt (2004): Europe. An Unfinished Adventure. Polity.

Becker, Johannes, Clemens Fuest (2017): Der Odysseus Komplex. Ein pragmatischer Vorschlag zur Lösung der Eurokrise. München, Carl Hanser Verlag.

14 Drawing on Philippe Schmitter's realist approach to 'Politics as Science', 'politics' is conceived here as 'the exercise of power and resistance to it' (Schmitter 2016). These regulated exchanges, negotiations, deliberations and decision-making allow conflicts to be resolved pacifically and, thereby, preclude the resort to violence that would otherwise be needed to resolve the differences in resources and preferences that give rise to political activity in the first place" (Schmitter 2016).

15 See Schmitter 2016, fn 6.

Brechenmacher, Saskia (2018): Comparing Democratic Distress in the United States and Europe. Washington, Carnegie Endowment for International Peace, June 21.

Brühlmeier Daniel, Mastronardi Philippe eds. (2016): Demokratie in der Krise. Analysen, Prozesse und Perspektiven. Zürich, Chronos.

Brunkhorst, Hauke (2016): Neugründung der Union. Lehren aus der "Flüchtlinkgskrise", die keine der Flüchtlinge, sondern eine der Demokratie und Menschenrechte ist. In: Culture, Practice and European Policy 1, No. 1, pp. 1-13.

Crum, Ben (2019): Living with anti-pluralist populism in Europe: Insights from the Dutch 2017 elections. In: U. Liebert and A. Jenichen eds., Europeanisation and Renationalisation. Learning from Crisis for Innovation and Development. Budrich Publishers.

Id. (2013): Saving the Euro at the Cost of Democracy? In: JCMS Vol. 51: 4.

Dasgupta, Rana (2018): The demise of the nation state. In: The Guardian. April 8. Retrieved online at https://www.theguardian.com/news/2018/apr/05/demise-of-the-nation-state-rana-dasgupta

European Commission (2017): White Paper on the Future of Europe. Reflections and Scenarios for the EU27 by 2025. COM (2017)2025 of 1 March. Brussels.

Farrell David (2014): 'Stripped Down' or Reconfigured Democracy. In: West European Politics Vol. 37: 2.

Galston, William A. (2018): The Populist Challenge to Liberal Democracy.Yale University Press.

Id. (2018) The Populist Challenge to Liberal Democracy. In Journal of Democracy. Vol 29: 2.

Geiselberger, Heinrich eds. (2017): Die große Regression. Eine internationale Debatte über die geistige Situation der Zeit. Berlin, edition suhrkamp.

Guasti, Petra, and David Siroki (2019): European Human Rights between transnational order and domestic politics. In: U. Liebert and A. Jenichen eds., Europeanisation and Renationalisation. Learning from Crisis for Innovation and Development. Budrich Publishers.

Guerót, Ulrike (2016): Warum Europa eine Republik werden muss! Eine politische Utopie. Bonn, Dietz Verlag.

Guérot, Ulrike, Oskar Negt, Tom Kehrbaum, Emanuel Herold: Europa jetzt! Eine Ermutigung. Göttingen, Steidl.

Habermas, Jürgen (2014): Warum der Ausbau der Europäischen Union zu einer supranationalen Demokratie nötig und wie er möglich ist. In: Leviathan. Vol. 42: 4.

Havlik, Vratislav (2019): Europeanisation and renationalisation: The Czech Republic facing the euro-, economic and refugee crises. In: U. Liebert and A. Jenichen eds., Europeanisation and Renationalisation. Learning from Crisis for Innovation and Development. Budrich Publishers.

Hennette, Stéphanie, Thomas Piketty, Guillaume Sacriste, Antoine Vauchez (2019): How To Democratize Europe. Harvard University Press (forthcoming).

Inglehart, Ronald F., and Pippa Norris (2016): Trump, Brexit, and the rise of Populismus: Economic have-nots and cultural backlash. Paper presented at the APSA annual meeting, Philadelphia, Sep 2nd.

Juncker, Jean-Claude (2017): President Jean-Claude Juncker's State of the Union Address 2017. Brussel, 12 September. Online: http://europa.eu/rapid/press-release_SPEECH-17-3165_en.htm

Krastev, Ivan (2018): Europa, von Osten aus gesehen. In: DIE ZEIT Nr. 28, 5 July.

Id. (2017): After Europe. Philadelphia, University Pennsylvania Press.

Leggewie, Claus (2017): Europa zuerst! Eine Unabhängigkeitserklärung. Berlin, Ullstein.

Leonard, Mark (2017): L'Europe qui protège: Conceiving the next European Union. European Council on Foreign Relations, August.

Levitsky Steven, and Ziblatt Daniel (2018): How Democracies Die. Penguin Random House.

Liebert Morata, Tilmann (2019): Global climate change governance from Paris to Montreal: Enabling factors for ambitious EU climate action. In: U. Liebert and A. Jenichen eds., Europeanisation and Renationalisation. Learning from Crisis for Innovation and Development. Budrich Publishers.

Liebert, Ulrike (2019): Europa erneuern! Eine realistische Vision für das 21. Jahrhundert. Bielefeld, Transcript Verlag.

Id. (2017): How to Democratize Europe's Multi-level System. In: Journal of Social Democracy, NG-FH Quarterly No. 4.

Id. (2016): 'TINA' Revisited: Why Alternative Narratives of the Eurozone Crisis Matter. In: P. Iglesias-Rodriguez, A. Triandafyllidou, R. Gropas eds., After the Financial Crisis. Shifting legal, Economic and Political Paradigms. Palgrave.

Id. (2016): Hat die marktwirtschaftliche Dmeokratie im 21. Jahrhundert noch eine Chance? Die Europäische Wirtschaftsunion in der Finanzkrise. In: D. Brühlmeier/P. Mastronardi eds., Demokratie in der Krise. Analysen, Prozesse und Perspektiven. Zürich, Chronos.

Id. (2016): Gendering Europeanisation: Making Equality Work in Theory and Practice. In: G. Abels and H. MacRae eds., Gendering European Integration Theory. Engaging new Dialogues. Barbara Budrich Publishers.

Id. (2010): Contentious European Democracy: National Intellectuals in Transnational Debates. In Lacroix, Justine, Nicolaidis Kalypso eds., European Stories. Intellectual Debates on Europe in National Contexts. Oxford University Press.

Id., Josef Falke, Kathrin Packham, Daniel Allnoch eds. (2003): Verfassungsexperiment. Europa auf dem Weg zur transnationalen Demokratie? Münster, LIT Verlag.

Macron, Emmanuel, Jürgen Habermas, Sigmar Gabriel (2017): Rethinking Europe. A discussion. Berlin, Hertie School of Governance, 16 March. In: Blätter für deutsche und internationale Politik/Eurozine (20 April 2017), retrieved online at: https://www.eurozine.com/rethinking-europe/

Macron, Emmanuel (2017): Initiative for Europe. A sovereign, united, democratic Europe. Paris, Sep 26th.

Mounk, Yascha (2018): The Undemocratic Dilemma. In: Journal of Democracy. Vol 29: 2.

Müller, Henrik, Giuseppe Porcaro, Gerret von Nordheim (2018): Tales from a crisis: diverging narratives of the euro area. Bruegel Policy Contribution, Issue no. 03, Brussels, February.

Müller, Jan Werner (2010): In the Shadows of Statism: Pecularities of the German Debates on European Integration. In: Lacroix, Justine, Nicolaidis Kalypso eds., European Stories. Intellectual Debates on Europe in National Contexts. Oxford University Press.

Rifkin, Jeremy (2004): The European Dream. How Europe's Vision of the Future is Quietly Eclipsing the American Dream. New York, Penguin.

Rodrik, Dani (2011): The Globalization Paradox. Democracy and the Future of the World Economy, Norton, New York.

Id. (2017) Neoliberalism and its usual prescriptions – always more markets, always less government – are in fact a perversion of mainstream economics. In: The Guardian, Nov 14.

Schild, Joachim (2019): France's European politics in times of the 'polycrisis'. In: U. Liebert and A. Jenichen eds., Europeanisation and Renationalisation. Learning from Crisis for Innovation and Development. Budrich Publishers.

Schimmelfennig, Frank (2015): Konditionalität in der Wirtschafts- und Währungsunion. Was können wir von der EU-Beitrittskonditionalität lernen? In: Friedrich-Ebert-Stiftung, Internationale Politikanalyse.

Id., Dirk Leuffen, Berthold Rittberger (2014): The European Union as a System of Differentiated Integration. HIS Vienna, July 10.

Schmitter, Philippe C. (2015): Crisis and Transition, But Not Decline. In: Journal of Democracy Vol 26, Issue 1, pp. 32-44.

Id. (2012): European Disintegration? A Way Forward. In: Journal of Democracy. Vol 23: 4.

Id.: Politics as a Science (aka Politology). Book manuscript available at: https://www.eui.eu/DepartmentsAndCentres/PoliticalAndSocialSciences/People/Professors/Schmitter

Strohschneider, Peter (2017): Wissenschaft muss für die Demokratie streiten. In: Süddeutsche Zeitung, 24th January.

Spinelli Group: Manifesto for the Future of Europe: A Shared Destiny. Brussels 2018.

Tokarski, Pawel (2018): Deutschland, Frankreich und Italien im Euroraum. Ursprünge, Merkmale und Folgen der begrenzten Konvergenz. SWP Studie 25. Berlin, Stiftung Wissenschaft und Politik.

Wolf, Martin (2014): The Shifts and the Shocks: what we have learned – and have still to learn – from the financial crisis. Penguin Press.

Worschech, Susann (2018): The 'making' of Europe in the peripheries: Europeanization through conflicts and ambivalences. In: Culture, Practice & Europeanization. Vol. 3: 3.

Zagermann, Dennis (2019): The European Central Bank in the euro crisis: The case of the OMT program. In: U. Liebert and A. Jenichen eds., Europeanisation and

Renationalisation. Learning from Crisis for Innovation and Development. Budrich Publishers.
Zaun, Natascha (2019): EU decision-making in asylum policy: Lessons from the 'refugee crisis'. In: U. Liebert and A. Jenichen eds., Europeanisation and Renationalisation. Learning from Crisis for Innovation and Development. Budrich Publishers.
Zielonka, Jan (2018): Counter-Revolution. Liberal Europe in Retreat. Oxford University Press.

Authors' notes

Gabriele Abels is a Professor of Political Science and holds a Jean Monnet Chair for German and European Politics at the University of Tübingen (Germany). She graduated from the University of Essen (1999) and received her Habilitation from Bielefeld University (2006).
E-Mail: gabriele.abels@uni-tuebingen.de.
Website: https://uni-tuebingen.de/fakultaeten/wirtschafts-und-sozialwissen schaftliche-fakultaet/faecher/fachbereich-sozialwissenschaften/ifp/institut/lehrende/abels/team/gabriele-abels/

Adriana Ciancio is a Full Professor of Constitutional Law at the University of Catania (Italy), Department of Law, where she received her doctoral degree in 1992.
E-Mail: aciancio@lex.unict.it.
Website: http://www.lex.unict.it/docenti/adriana.ciancio

Ben Crum is a Professor of Political Science at the Vrije Universiteit Amsterdam (The Netherlands) and a member of the EU's H2020 funded RECONNECT research project: https://www.reconnect-europe.eu/. He received his PhD from the European University Institute (EUI), Florence, in 1997.
E-Mail: ben.crum@vu.nl.
Website: https://research.vu.nl/en/persons/ben-crum

Sezin Dereci is working as a project expert for the Third Sector Foundation of Turkey (TUSEV). She received her PhD at Bremen International Graduate School of Social Sciences (BIGSSS, Germany) in 2013.
E-Mail: sezin@tusev.org.tr
Website: https://www.linkedin.com/in/sezin-dereci-51455864

Petra R. Guasti is an interim Professor of Political Science at the Department of Political Science, Goethe University Frankfurt (Germany). She received her PhD Date from Charles University, Prague (Czech Republic) in 2007.
E-Mail: guasti@soz.uni-frankfurt.de
Website: http://www.fb03.uni-frankfurt.de/60977547/Dr__Petra_Guasti

Vratislav Havlík is an Assistant Professor at Masaryk University, Department of International Relations and European Studies, Brno (Czech Republic) where he also received his PhD (2013).
E-Mail: vhavlik@fss.muni.cz.
Website: www.mve.fss.muni.cz.

Andreas Heinrich, Dr., is a Senior Researcher at the Research Centre for East European Studies, University of Bremen (Germany). He received his doctoral degree in Political Science from the Free University Berlin (2003).
E-Mail: heinrich@uni-bremen.de.
Website: https://www.forschungsstelle.uni-bremen.de/en/3/20110606111622/20110620193911/Dr-_Andreas_Heinrich.html

Anders Hentschel received his M.A. in European Studies from the University of Frankfurt/Oder and is a Ph.D. Fellow at the Bremen International Graduate School of Social Sciences (Germany).
E-Mail: hentschel@bigsss.uni-bremen.de

Anne Jenichen is a Lecturer in Politics and International Relations in the field of equality and diversity, particularly gender and religion, at the Aston Centre for Europe (ACE), Aston University, Birmingham (UK). She received her PhD in Political Science from the University of Bremen in 2010.
E-Mail: a.jenichen@aston.ac.uk
Website: http://www.aston.ac.uk/lss/staff-directory/dr-anne-jenichen/

Laura Landorff is an Assistant Professor in European Studies at Aalborg University (Denmark). She received her PhD from Bremen International Graduate School for Social Sciences (BIGSSS, Germany) in 2016.
E-Mail: landorff@cgs.aau.dk
Website: http://personprofil.aau.dk/140229

Gesche Lange is a civil servant at the Office for Social Services of the Regional Government of Bremen and pursues a PhD in Political Science from the Bremen International Graduate School (Germany).
E-mail: gesche.lange@gmail.com
Website: https://www.linkedin.com/in/gesche-lange-a3ba9249/?originalSubdomain=de

Tilmann Morata Liebert, M.A. M.A., is a Policy Officer at the European Commission, DG Climate Action, International Carbon Markets, Aviation & Maritime Unit. He holds an M.A. in Law & Diplomacy from The Fletcher School, Tufts University (Boston, USA) and an M.A. in International Affairs & Governance from the University St. Gallen, HSG (Switzerland).

E-mail: tilmann.liebert@ec.europa.eu
Website: https://www.linkedin.com/in/tliebert/

Ulrike Liebert is Professor (em.) of Political Science and EU Politics at the University of Bremen (Germany) where she directed the Jean Monnet Centre for European Studies (2000 - 16). She received her PhD from the EUI in Florence (1983, Italy).
E-mail: liebert@uni-bremen.de
Website: http://ulrikeliebert.eu

Heiko Pleines, Prof Dr., is Head of the Department of Politics and Economics at the Research Centre for East European Studies and Professor of Comparative Politics, University of Bremen (Germany). He received his doctoral degree from the Free University Berlin (2002) and his Habilitation from Bremen University (2006).
E-Mail: pleines@uni-bremen.de
Website: https://www.forschungsstelle.uni-bremen.de/en/3/20110606111616/20110620171822/Head_of_the_Dept-_of_Politics_and_Economics_Vice_Director.html

Joachim Schild is a Professor of Political Science/Comparative Politics at Trier University (Germany). He received his PhD at the University of Stuttgart in 1999.
E-mail: schild@uni-trier.de
Website: https://www.uni-trier.de/index.php?id=67494

David S. Siroky is an Associate Professor of Political Science at Arizona State University (U.S.A.). He received his PhD from Duke University in 2009.
E-Mail: david.siroky@asu.edu
Website: davidsiroky.adu.edu

Dimitri A. Sotiropoulos is a Professor of Political Science at the Department of Political Science and Public Administration, National and Kapodistrian University of Athens (Greece). Currently he is a visiting scholar at Harvard University.
E-Mail: dsotirop@pspa.uoa.gr
Website:http://en.pspa.uoa.gr/academic-staff/section-of-political-science/dimitri-a-sotiropoulos.html

Stefan Wallaschek, M.A., is a PhD fellow expecting to graduate from Bremen International Graduate School of Social Sciences (BIGSSS) in 2019, and a research associate of the SOLDISK research project at the University of Hildesheim (Germany).

E-Mail: wallaschek@uni-hildesheim.de
Website: https://www.uni-hildesheim.de/no_cache/lsf/personen/person/?lsfid=6052&cHash=46e742e0e955a23d2a58841a815cfaae

Florian Wittmann is a PhD fellow expecting to graduate from Bremen International Graduate School of Social Sciences (BIGSSS) in 2019 (Germany).
E-Mail: wittmann@bigsss-bremen.de
Website: https://www.bigsss-bremen.de/people/phd-fellows/florian-wittmann

Natascha Zaun is an Assistant Professor at the European Institute at the London School of Economics and Political Science (LSE, UK). She received her PhD from Bremen International Graduate School of Social Sciences (Germany) in 2015.
E-mail: n.v.zaun@lse.ac.uk
Website: http://www.lse.ac.uk/european-institute/people/academic-staff/zaun-natascha

Dennis Zagermann, M.A., is a PhD candidate at the Department of Political Science, University of Bremen (Germany) and a fellow under the doctoral program of the Friedrich Ebert Foundation (FES).
E-mail: zagermann@uni-bremen.de
Website: https://www.researchgate.net/profile/Dennis_Zagermann

Index

administrative reform 143, 145ff., 149f.
ANO 2011 55, 60
Assmann, Aleida 299f.
asylum policy 14, 85, 127f., 135
aviation 213f., 216-221
Brexit 9f., 14, 17, 37, 114, 118, 229, 289, 296, 304
Bulgaria 134, 144ff., 149, 157, 160-164
CEAS 127f.
climate change 16, 44, 178, 213, 215f., 218-221, 225, 264, 266, 299
collective action 67, 128f., 190
conditionality 95ff., 99, 106, 143f., 147, 149f., 206, 298
core Europe 22, 304
Council of Europe 102, 114, 116, 122, 155, 158, 160, 163f., 178
counter-revolution 296, 299, 302
CRIS 243, 249f.
Czech parties 50, 53, 55f., 61
democracy, illiberal 301
democracy, liberal 39, 77, 232, 238, 300f.
democratic legitimacy 229ff., 235f., 263, 274, 280, 287, 303, 307
depoliticisation 235, 237
differentiated integration 303
discrimination 14f., 114-118, 120ff., 162f., 186, 216, 301
discursive construction of solidarity 81
discursive struggles 81, 297
diverging narratives 17, 295f., 308f.
domestic politics 13ff., 32, 155, 157, 160, 163, 191, 299
Dublin Convention 129ff.
ECB 16, 66, 198-208, 229, 234, 236, 255, 259, 283
ECHR 155-160, 163f.
ECJ 155f., 203, 208
ECON 201, 203ff., 243f., 249f., 256-259
ECtHR 132, 155-159, 161-164
election campaigns 27, 32, 281, 288
EMU 16, 25, 191, 197f., 205, 229f., 235-238, 241ff., 247, 249, 254f., 297f., 305f.
energy discourse 177
energy security 10, 15, 169-172, 174, 176-180
enlargement 95, 97, 99, 146, 187, 295, 298
ethnic minorities 113-121
EU energy policy 179
EU minority policy 115, 121
EU multi-level-governance 16, 230, 238
EU referendum 113, 118ff.
EU technocracy 232
euro crisis 13, 197-201, 207, 241f., 251, 254, 297, 303, 306
European awareness 286
European elections 9, 251, 281, 285-288
European federation 230, 238f.
European identity 14, 118

European memory culture 300
Europeanisation 10, 13ff., 17, 33, 49f., 52f., 55, 61f., 90, 95-98, 102, 127, 183, 190ff., 198, 208, 238, 251f., 295-299, 301ff., 308f.
Euroscepticism 28ff., 32ff., 39, 49f., 52, 59, 91, 191, 280, 299
fiscal austerity 295
fiscal consolidation 29, 297
fragmented public sphere 296
France 10f., 13f., 21ff., 25-33, 38, 41, 46, 119, 129f., 134, 198, 232, 234, 298, 307
Fuest, Clemens 305
gender studies 184f., 189ff.
gendering 184ff., 190, 192f.
Germany 13ff., 29, 38, 46, 81, 83f., 91, 127, 129ff., 134, 169-176, 179, 198, 232, 234, 252, 298f., 305
global warming 10, 213, 215
Greece 12-15, 52, 57f., 65ff., 69f., 74-77, 86, 130, 132, 134, 136f., 144, 235, 250, 298
human rights 15, 66, 115, 121, 138, 155-164, 266-270, 274, 279, 297, 299, 301f.
ICAO 214, 216-225
identity politics 43ff.
innovative ideas 9, 303f., 308
integration theory 183ff., 192
intergovernmentalism 183f., 186ff., 192, 232, 234, 238
intergroups 16, 263-275
international financial crisis 308
Ireland 13f., 81, 83f., 91
judgement 155, 157
Klaus, Václav 49f., 52ff.
Krastev, Ivan 298
learning from crisis 297
Leggewie, Claus 305
legislation 16, 75, 100, 116, 130, 143, 148f., 151, 158f., 222, 230, 233, 244, 249, 251, 254, 263
Macron, Emmanuel 13, 32, 34, 37, 304f.
media discourse 81f., 134
migration crisis 50, 59, 61f., 81ff., 85-91, 298
minority protection regime 114, 116, 122
monetary policy 16, 198, 203-206, 208, 251f.
neo-nationalism 10, 12-15, 17, 295ff., 299, 302, 306, 308
neo-nationalist narrative 298
Netherlands 10, 13, 37, 39ff., 43-46, 130, 144, 244, 252, 299f., 307
Nord Stream pipeline 14, 169-176, 178ff.
OMT program 197ff., 201-204, 207f.
Orban, Victor 301
Paris Agreement 16, 213-217, 221f.
party politics 22, 242, 249, 251
Piketty, Thomas 306
pluralism 38f., 46f., 279, 301
Poland 14, 38, 46, 89, 133, 143f., 146, 148, 169f., 172-177, 299
political claims analysis 84
political development 17, 295f., 304, 308f.
political economy 183
political integration 280f., 283, 287f.
political trilemma of globalisation 300
politicisation 21f., 33, 144, 148, 164, 306
populism 13, 14, 37ff., 43, 46, 49, 61, 134, 283, 297, 299f.

post-communist countries 145f.
power structures 83, 191
public hearings 105, 243, 248f., 265, 271-275
public opinion 22f., 25, 29, 33, 56f., 173, 236, 299
Pulse of Europe 304
racism 114, 117, 120, 122, 164
reform backsliding 150
refugees 12, 14f., 49, 60, 81, 83, 85-91, 99, 102, 127, 128f., 131-138, 158, 297
regulatory competition 129f., 136
re-nationalisation 10, 252
representation 76, 116f., 122, 218, 220ff., 241f., 244, 248, 251, 255, 264, 266f., 269f., 274f., 280, 282, 287, 301, 306f.
responsibility-sharing 132ff.
Rodrik, Dani 300f.
Russia 10, 15, 52, 156f., 159, 163f., 169f., 172-180, 187
Schengen Agreement 30, 89, 130
social protest 65f., 68, 70ff., 75, 77
Spinelli Group 265
TINA 303
UK 9, 13f., 21, 37, 39, 113-121, 129ff., 156, 159, 188, 252, 295, 299
UNFCCC 213f., 218-225
Wolf, Martin 86, 298
xenophobia 114, 120, 122